I'M NOT REALLY GUILTY

ANTON J.S. KEATING, ESQ.

ISBN: 0-692-64766-X
ISBN: 978-0-692-64766-0

Anton J.S. Keating
614 Colorado Avenue
Baltimore, MD 21210
antonkeating@mindspring.com
antonkeating@gmail.com

www.imnotreallyguilty.com

Cover and layout design: Andre Cawley (www.andrecawley.com)

Printed in the United States of America

ABOUT THIS BOOK

This is the true story of the brutal 1979 contract murder of Mary Ruth Myers, the 27-month long investigation of that murder, and the prosecution of the three co-conspirators. It led to the longest murder trial in the history of Maryland. Robert Myers, the victim's husband, had arranged the killing. The only plea offer was death in the gas chamber or by lethal injection.

Robert Myers' attorney, Anton J.S. Keating, had many personal and professional experiences with prisons, the death penalty and the justice system, making him uniquely qualified to defend him. As a boy in England, Keating's school had a prison in its backyard, where executions were performed routinely. As a lifelong competitive athlete, he appreciated the intense adversarial nature of a career in law. As a prosecutor in Maryland, he always attempted to ensure that a death sentence was never imposed. He succeeded in 69 out of 70 such cases.

As a defense attorney, he is credited with saving several people from the gas chamber, including Myers. In this case, however, Myers had actually confessed his guilt to Mr. Keating, so avoiding the death penalty was even more complicated. In recounting how he accomplished this, Keating not only outlines the history of the death penalty, but articulates some of the most poignant and powerful arguments against it.

Keating has been qualified as an expert in the prosecution and defense of capital cases. He has been sole counsel in over one hundred murder trials, and he has served as the foreman of a criminal jury. In this book, he shares his insights into the tactics, strategies, thought processes and the personalities of many of the participants in the Myers case and the criminal justice system in Maryland.

Myers had paid a respected Maryland criminal lawyer over $50,000 for legal representation during the two year investigation, but then that lawyer tried his hardest to push Myers into the gas chamber.

Finally, Keating himself was put on trial—as he had suspected he would be from the very beginning.

TABLE OF CONTENTS

About This Book..iii

Introduction 1

Cast of Characters...5

Part I...7

Chapter 1: "Maryland, My Maryland" 9

Chapter 2: Tina Needs a New Nest 16

Chapter 3: A Match Made in Hell—An Easy Seduction....................28

Chapter 4: The Murder...36

Chapter 5: The Wedding..50

Chapter 6: The Investigation Continues 60

Chapter 7: Bigamy in Bermuda 69

Chapter 8: Behind The Grand Jury Curtain 89

Chapter 9: The Arrests...102

Chapter 10: The Auction..107

Illustrations 112

Part II...125

Chapter 11: What's Past is Prologue..126

Chapter 12: The Novice Lawyer...154

Chapter 13: The Right to Counsel 172

Chapter 14: A Reasonable Doubt at a Reasonable Price................179

Chapter 15: Trademarks of a Defense Attorney.............................184

Chapter 16: Judges 191

Illustrations 205

Part III 217

Chapter 17: Myers and I Meet 219

Chapter 18: Removal To Garrett County..226

Chapter 19: A Lawyer's Ultimate Double-Cross 238

Chapter 20: Robert Myers Confesses to Me...................................250

Chapter 21: The Chadderton Trial...254

Chapter 22: Return to Carroll County for Trial 280

Chapter 23: Jury Selection 300

Chapter 24: The State's Case 309

Chapter 25: The Defense Case 344

Illustrations 373

Part IV 385

Chapter 26: The Sentencing 387

Chapter 27: The Testimony of Father Tobey 397

Chapter 28: A Plea for Life 408

Chapter 29: The Post Conviction Hearing—
Freedom from the Privilege 420

Epilogue 437

Afterword 458

Chronology 462

Acknowledgements & Websites 469

Bibliography 470

INTRODUCTION

"She's dead. Our job's done. She's dead. Shot nine times."
— Daniel Chadderton

At 5:20 a.m. on August 29, 1979, a phone call was placed to an apartment above the Electric Circus Club in Ocean City, Maryland. Staying at the apartment that night were Robert Lee Myers and Tina Marco, his new girlfriend whom he'd been dating for three weeks. The couple had been asleep after spending the day shopping and strolling on the boardwalk, and drinking and dancing in the evening.

Myers awoke and picked up the receiver on his side of the bed. Tina, barely awake, asked him who it was. In response, he held the receiver to her ear. "Hello?" A man's voice answered: "She's dead. Our job's done. She's dead. Shot nine times." Robert continued to speak quietly on the phone for a few more minutes, and then hung up.

Later that morning, employees of The Maryland Business Service, an accounting firm owned and operated by Robert Lee Myers, became concerned when their co-worker and Robert's wife, Mary Ruth Myers, did not arrive at work. Three employees drove to the Myers' residence at 4636 Turkey Foot Road, Westminster, Carroll County, Maryland. It was located on a twenty-one-acre expanse of land at the top of the hill in Silver Run Valley, a small affluent community of about one hundred families, eight miles northwest of the town of Westminster. It included a seven-acre vineyard and was half a mile from a new stable where some of the families housed their horses. Foals often scampered across the open fields in this peaceful, bucolic setting.

The house was a red brick, two-story dwelling, trimmed in painted white woodwork, with a brown cedar shingle roof, situated on a grass covered lot, partially surrounded by a cement driveway. The left portion of the residence consisted of a garage area large enough to store two vehicles. There was a sliding garage door on the extreme left side of the house. It had a basement level.

The employees found the front door open about eight inches and music playing loudly, so they entered the house and yelled out to Mrs. Myers. She never answered. They found her lying on her bed with a pillow over her face and a red spot on her chest. An autopsy completed the following afternoon revealed that Mary Ruth Myers had been shot nine times in the head and chest.

Although the bedroom looked ransacked with plants overturned, drawers open and a phone ripped from the wall, some jewelry and money in plain view had not been taken. Mary Ruth's white poodle was found penned in a hallway closet. A chess table in the poolroom had been knocked over and the gun cabinet in the den had been tampered with. The remaining rooms in the home appeared to have been untouched by the intruder.

The Maryland State Police Crime Lab Unit took photographs to preserve the scene as it had been found, before the victim's body was allowed to be removed. Numerous items were identified for further analysis by Maryland State Police chemists.

A .22 caliber Glenfield rifle, Model 25, was on the floor in the master bedroom and it contained one spent case in the chamber. A .22 caliber Astra handgun was also recovered from the bedroom. It contained eight cartridge cases and one unfired bullet. One flattened bullet was recovered from the floor below the headboard. Two other guns were found in the next room but they had not been used recently. One was a Colt Calibre 38, located in the second drawer of the dresser in the master bedroom, and the other was a shotgun located in plain view in the bedroom. Four other guns and several boxes of ammunition were in a cabinet in the den. Ballistics analysis showed that the Glenfield rifle and the Astra handgun had been the murder weapons.

Glass tubes were used to store hairs and fibers located on the blankets and sheets and pillowcases on the bed. Slides of these items were made. Head hairs were found on a hairbrush next to the victim's bed, on the blanket on the victim's bed, on an electric blanket on the bed, on a flat sheet under the victim and in the victim's right hand. They were not the victim's. Her fingernail clippings were preserved.

An overnight case belonging to the victim, containing $2,723 wrapped in a pink Kleenex, and a large red suitcase containing pornographic films and various sexual devices, such as vibrators and dildos was also found.

When the victim's body was discovered, Robert Myers could not be immediately located. He had last appeared in the Maryland Business Service office on August 16, 1979. It was later learned that he had been with Tina Marco. At the time of the murder they were three hours away, in a seaside resort in Ocean City, Maryland, where he owned a motel.

CAST OF CHARACTERS

Mary Ruth Myers
Murder Victim

Robert Lee Myers
Husband of Mary Ruth Myers

Tina Butcher Plessner Botteron Gillen Marco Myers
New wife

Daniel Lee Chadderton
Murderer

Sherrie Chadderton
Wife of Daniel Chadderton

Cpl. James M. Leete
Chief Investigator, MD State Police

Thomas E. Hickman, Esq.
State's Attorney of Carroll County, MD

Frank D. Coleman, Esq.
Assistant State's Attorney

Chief Judge Donald J. Gilmore Sr.
Circuit Court, Carroll County, MD

Chief Judge Fred A. Thayer, II
Circuit Court, Garrett County, MD

Associate Judge Luke K. Burns, Jr., *Circuit Court Judge, Carroll County, MD*

Alan H. Murrell, Esq.
Maryland State Public Defender

Phillip M. Sutley, Esq.
Robert & Tina Myers' original private attorney

Orrin J. Brown, III, Esq.
Daniel Chadderton's attorney

Anton J.S. Keating, Esq.
Robert Myers' assigned attorney

Father Meyer E. M.Tobey
Chaplain for Maryland Death Row inmates

Morris Lee Kaplan, Esq.
Robert Myers' post-conviction attorney

PART I

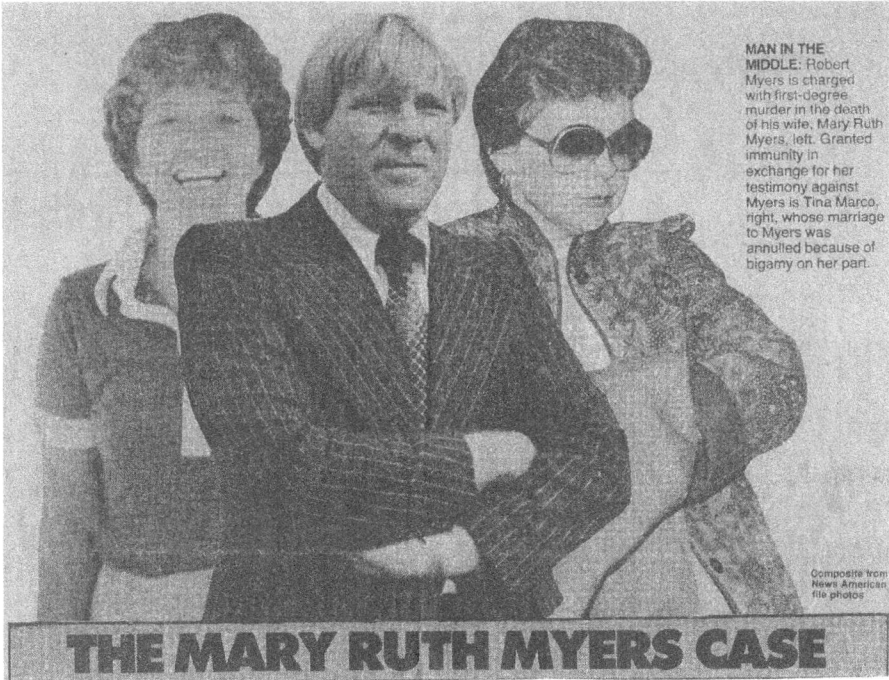

MAN IN THE MIDDLE: Robert Myers is charged with first-degree murder in the death of his wife, Mary Ruth Myers, left. Granted immunity in exchange for her testimony against Myers is Tina Marco, right, whose marriage to Myers was annulled because of bigamy on her part.

Composite from News American file photos

THE MARY RUTH MYERS CASE

State of Maryland

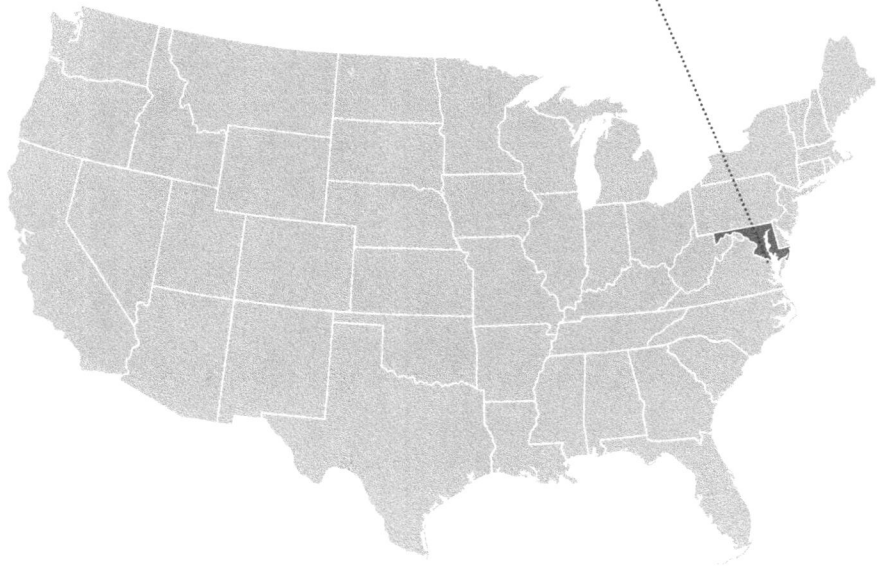

CHAPTER 1:
"MARYLAND, MY MARYLAND"

"For life and death, for woe and weal, Thy peerless chivalry reveal . . . "
— Maryland State Anthem

Maryland is "America in Miniature." Charles Mason and Jeremiah Dixon, experienced land surveyors, were employed by the Penns and the Calverts, the principal landowners in their respective regions, to establish the boundary line between Pennsylvania and Maryland. By 1767 the Mason-Dixon Line was drawn and soon became the dividing line between the North and the South. The distinct geographical regions stretching from the Atlantic Ocean in the East, present-day to West Virginia in the West, reflected a wide variety of historical, economic, ethnic, cultural, and political differences and concerns.

In Maryland there are twenty-four separate jurisdictions, each maintaining its own local government with its own District Court and Circuit Court. Most of the Courthouses were originally located in the center of the most populated town in each County, and was usually the setting for all local government. They were situated purposefully on a large "courthouse lawn" and played a critical role in the social and political life there.

Many English and Irish prisoners were deported to Maryland, to supply manual labor, and make room for others in England's desperately overcrowded prisons. Many of the 30,000 convicts who were transported to Maryland before the Revolutionary war, considered themselves fortunate not to be executed or shipped to Australia or the Caribbean, where disease, heat, and the brutality of life on the sugar plantations, resulted in a very limited life span.

Maryland Legislators brought Carroll County into existence in 1837, named in memory of Charles Carroll of Carrollton, a Maryland attorney and signer of the Declaration of Independence. The town of Westminster was selected as the County seat. One hundred and forty-two years later, it would become the location of a brutal crime that resulted in the longest murder trial in the history of Maryland.

*****

Robert Lee Myers was born on September 16, 1942. His father had a 4th-grade education and worked at a shoe factory before purchasing a grocery store in 1944. The store was attached to the house, on Route 97 in Carroll County, and Myers lived there until he was 20. Myers described him as "a very good man and he said his prayers every night." Agnes Jean Myers, Robert's mother, had a 6th-grade education, was very religious, and helped in the family grocery store. She read the Bible every night. Robert never heard them argue.

The Myers had four children, three sons and a daughter. Calvin, the oldest, was killed at 19 years of age serving in the Army in World War II. Sterling Myers was the next oldest, 16 years older than Robert. Elizabeth Null worked in a shoe factory in Westminster and was 11 years older than Bobby, who was born when his mother was 35.

Robert attended Westminster High School, where he played the tuba in the band and was on the varsity football and track teams. He graduated in June of 1960. Not only did he work in the family grocery store, but he also labored on farms in the community. He was never in trouble. He had never been arrested. He had been given one speeding citation and three parking tickets in his entire life.

Following his graduation, he enlisted in the military for six months of active duty in Fort Knox, Kentucky. While on active duty he was a clerical typist in the orderly room, as well as a Chaplain's assistant. He typed church bulletins, aided with the service, cleaning, and setting up meeting rooms. Myers then joined the US Army Reserve. He remained for six years. His father and mother sacrificed to help him graduate from Baltimore Business College in February 1961. He sang in the church choir at St. Mary's Lutheran Church and was a church usher for many years at Grace Lutheran Church.

He later went to the University of Baltimore, attending school both in the evening and in the summer. He took classes for six years and in 1970 received his B.S. degree in Accounting. He had worked during the day for A.C. Vander-bilt, the millionaire owner of Native Dancer. He then took a job with Black and Decker in their general accounting department, before moving to the Bendix Corporation where he worked until 1970. That year he purchased and managed Maryland Business Service, a general accounting firm. For the next 9 years he expanded it and, in addition, invested in real estate and other businesses. He was generous and kind-hearted, often consulting with needy elderly and disabled people about their taxes without charge. He joined the Westminster Lions Club to help raise funds for handicapped children. He began buying more apartments, houses, and land and did very well financially.

In 1963 at the age of 21, Bobby married Patricia Ann Bennett, whom he had met in business college. They had 3 children together: Shelly, Brian, and Robert. They were married for thirteen years and it was "all beautiful except for sex." He related that Pat's mother had taught her "it was dirty and wrong."

Myers then met Mary Ruth, a new client, in the mid-1970s in his accounting office and prepared her taxes. He instantly liked her, her short skirts and the fact that she actively pursued him. A short time later Bobby and Pat divorced, and Pat was given custody of the children and the five-bedroom home the couple owned.

*****

Mary Ruth was born on July 9, 1936 at home in Baltimore County, Maryland. She was described as exceptionally bright and energetic. She graduated first in her class at Hereford Senior High School in 1954. The photographs of her in the yearbook show her playing field hockey and dancing. Her photo caption read, "Dig that boogie beat. Here's the girl with the dancing feet!" Shortly after she graduated, she married Gilbert Herman, who was in the Air Force.

This first marriage, which lasted twelve years, produced four children: Dale, Dana, Kim, and Dwayne. After her divorce, though, she soon married another Air Force serviceman. It was a difficult relationship, and ended after six years.

To hear friends and family tell it, Mary Ruth loved life, lived to the fullest and enjoyed it all. She worshiped her family and her friends. She loved her home and country. She had a great sense of humor and could find the funny side in every situation. She had a beautiful smile and an engaging manner and seemed to be the center of attention in any group of people. Her energy was boundless in everything she did and, combined with her strict work ethic, helped her be successful at most everything she tried.

Even though she was an extrovert, she was a very private person. She never seemed to just relax unless she was at the beach, which was her favorite place to go. The rest of the time she was always on the go, keeping up with the latest fashion and events. If there was a new shop or restaurant opening, she wanted to be there and take her children.

*****

Mary Ruth and Robert Lee Myers were married in 1974; it was her third and his second. She was 38. Myers felt that Mary Ruth was domineering, materialistic, and selfish but he did believe she loved him. He resented the fact that although three of her children lived with them, he didn't think that they ever accepted him as a father. He felt that Mary Ruth was also opposed to his relationship with his own three children, and the issues surrounding their children had a disquieting effect on their relationship.

According to him, "Mary Ruth wouldn't let me buy anything for my kids, only for hers." When Myers learned that his ex-wife Pat's new husband was abusing his children, he wanted them to come live with him. Mary Ruth opposed this and on the few occasions when they did come, Mary Ruth herself was abusive to them. He claimed, perhaps in part because of this stress, she began taking "an awful lot of drugs." In addition to prescribed drugs, she was also taking "handfuls of pills."

Their sexual relationship began to deteriorate, although Mary Ruth continued to act in a sexually provocative but demeaning way toward him. Bobby began drinking on a regular basis and periodically frequented the "Block" in Baltimore. His daily drinking only began at the time of his marriage to Mary Ruth. He would work for four hours in the mornings, and around noon he would drive to the "Block." Mary Ruth never complained about his drinking and in return, he gave her anything materially that she demanded. To placate her, he bought the expensive home on Turkey Foot Road in February of 1979 that she had wanted, and he resentfully gave in to all of her wishes.

His heavy drinking began in 1978, starting with a few drinks with clients at lunch, then a drink or so at dinner, drinks during business entertaining, and then more drinks in the evening. He would also take a few "nerve pills," and would start the cycle all over again the next day. He felt that theirs was "basically a good marriage." This, despite the friction relating to his children by his first wife, and their different sexual needs.

He gave Mary Ruth and her children anything they needed during the short time they were married, but never felt he was appreciated by any of them. He bought Dana, her oldest daughter two cars, and helped her with expenses. One night she and her girlfriends hit a tree with her car, and he was distraught and rushed to the hospital to comfort her. He gave her jobs to help her pay her way through college and provided other financial support. He also helped Kimberly, giving her nice clothes and a down payment for a new car. He gave her a job working in the office, so she would have money for expenses. When the girls started to date, he was protective of them, often staying awake until they returned home safely. He tried to treat them as if he was their natural father, but he didn't feel they ever really accepted him as a father or as the man of the house. He attempted to justify this to himself by thinking that they were too old when he had married their mother.

He had little interaction with Dale, Mary Ruth's oldest son, since he was living on his own. However, Bobby helped him with wedding expenses. Myers liked and respected him a great deal.

Mary Ruth, by contrast, didn't even want him to give his own children presents for their birthdays and holidays. She constantly said she didn't want anything to do with those "Goddamn bastards."

An experienced businesswoman, Mary Ruth Myers was in charge of her husband's accounting firm and her business acumen was a key part of the firm's success. Their clients included a number of Carroll County's leading farmers, businessmen, doctors and lawyers.

The couple had lived in their lavish hilltop home since 1978. They had a sweeping uphill driveway and grand views of the rolling countryside and neighboring horse farms. Neighbors described them as workaholics and every morning they would see Mary Ruth, an elegant blonde, always neatly dressed, driving to work in her brand-new silver Lincoln Continental. She was usually followed shortly afterward by Robert Myers, in his matching brand-new silver Lincoln Continental, driving to their firm in downtown Westminster.

Robert Myers' three children remained with his ex-wife, but spent holidays and some evenings with Robert and Mary Ruth. Myers felt that Mary Ruth became abusive towards his children, verbally in his presence and physically when he wasn't around. Consequently, Pat then refused to send the children to their father's because of Mary Ruth, and Robert, quite distressed by the situation, began drinking very heavily.

By the spring of 1979 the couple's marriage problems had worsened irreparably. Robert had been telling friends for some time that he desperately wanted out of the marriage, but feared how much it would cost him to obtain a divorce. He had been drained financially by the divorce from Pat, and worried that divorcing Mary Ruth would be worse. He had begun drinking heavily in the afternoons—in taverns in Westminster, or visiting the seedy bars and hookers on downtown Baltimore's notorious Block.

He got through tax time, January through April, in 1979 only because he had a good staff and Mary Ruth had aggressively taken over the financial management of the business, as well as the home.

Mary Ruth had been worried about her safety. She was fearful that something might happen to her. She had given more than $8,200 to a friend to be delivered to her children in the event of her death. The money had been transferred in installments on several occasions, the last delivery coming two days before she was murdered.

The couple lived the comfortable middle-class dream of suburban America. They owned a thriving motel in Ocean City, MD, a trailer park in Pennsylvania, and a $140,000 boat. By the late summer of 1979, Robert had embarked on his last adulterous fling and the attractive wife who had encouraged him, and helped his business to grow had been brutally slain. At the time of the murder, the Myers' joint real estate assets exceeded $1.5 million. According to the victim's will, all of the property passed to Robert Myers.

It was no secret to Mary Ruth's children that her relationship with Bob was rapidly deteriorating. Dana, her oldest daughter had left to finish her final year at the University of Maryland. She started a conversation with her mother, telling her that she needed to leave and get a divorce. Mary Ruth was concerned that she wouldn't be able to afford the house, the motel, the boat, and the lifestyle. The idea of going through a third divorce was weighing heavily on her. Dana explained that the family didn't need the lifestyle that the relationship provided and that the two of them could get an apartment together and that it would even be fun. The last time Dana saw her mother, she said that she just wanted Mary Ruth to be happy and "you're not happy." As Dana was leaving for school, giving her mom lots of hugs and kisses, she prophetically said, "Don't let anything happen to you." Mary Ruth responded, "I won't."

CHAPTER 2:
TINA NEEDS A NEW NEST

"One of these days these boots are gonna walk all over you . . . "
— Lee Hazelwood

Ernestine ("Tina") Butcher was born on July 6, 1951 in Waynesboro, Virginia nestled in the foothills of the Blue Ridge Mountains. She had an older sister, Veronica. Her father was Ernest Butcher, a 30-year-old, soft-spoken man with little formal education. He worked as a pressman at the local newspaper, the Waynesboro News-Virginian. Ernest discovered early on that his 22-year-old wife, Tina's mother, Lana, was running around with other men.

When Tina was 3 years old, Lana Butcher left the house and didn't return. She and her friend met two guys in the service and left for North Carolina with them. When Ernest Butcher came home from work that final day, Teenie, Tina's childhood nickname, was in bed screaming and crying. She would not see her mother for another twenty-three years. After Earnest took custody of his two daughters, he sent them to live with two elderly women. On weekends, Tina and Veronica would visit him at his apartment.

Tina was shattered a year later when her father married Gay Kesterson, a 17-year-old bookkeeper at the Waynesboro newspaper. Tina could recall when her father used to bounce her on his knee, but when he married Gay, he never did that anymore. Gay knew that Tina resented her and anything she said. They moved across the country to California, where Tina spent the rest of her childhood.

At the age of nine, Tina said she was raped by a neighbor in Montclair, California. She claimed that throughout the rape he kept saying, 'I love you, I love you, and your parents never said that they love you. That's important." This led her to confuse kindness with love, and she spent almost two decades jumping from one unstable relationship to another. "If someone was kind to me, I thought it meant that he loved me," she said. "I felt the only thing I had to offer them was my body. I didn't know what love was. I confused it."

Tina contented herself with a fantasy world and dreamt that one day she would leave California, with its unhappy memories and go to Las Vegas and its lavish lifestyle. She began signing her homework papers with the name Sabrina, which is the name she wanted to take when she became a chorus girl in Las Vegas. From the age of six, she declared she was going to be a stripper. The adults around her shrugged it off thinking it was a joke. However, Tina was determined and this became a constant refrain. She constantly said she was going to be a dancer and change her name to "Sabrina," and that name would be famous and be up "in neon lights." Later, it would become the name of the daughter she had with Robert Myers.

Her low self-esteem created a great deal of turmoil for her and no amount of praise seemed to help. She was a small child with a shock of auburn hair and a spate of freckles across her nose. She learned at a very early age she could get attention by doing something wrong, and she felt that if she did something right she never got the attention she craved. She succeeded in getting a lot of attention, but it was ultimately negative.

Tina's behavior problems extended to school, too. Her guidance counselor said that she was a girl you just could not forget. At times she would get belligerent and talk back to teachers. She'd borrow things and wouldn't return them, and just would not conform to rules and regulations.

Her career as a criminal began at age 11, when she stole a set of clothes from a K-Mart. At age 12 she stole eighteen rings from a jewelry store near her school. A lot of the kids teased her because she had holes in her clothes and had often outgrown them. Consequently, she was miserable, an outcast, and used her poverty as an excuse for stealing. She felt like an ugly child with lots of freckles.

Things did not change when she enrolled in Montclair High School in 1963, where the guidance counselor felt that she had no social sense at all. She never gave any thought to the idea that her actions or behavior might cause harm to someone else. On several occasions when she was caught stealing, she was brought to the principal's office and while she could never explain why she stole anything, she would simply say, "I'm never going to do anything like that again and I've learned my lesson," and then she'd walk out the door and do it again.

She tried everything to make other kids in school like her, including one occasion where she took her stepmother's jewelry to school and gave it away. On a regular basis, she'd even use her intelligence to gain their favor by doing their homework for them.

She did have a way of charming people to make herself appear innocent. Her eyes were clear and pretty, and people looking into them wanted to believe anything she said. However, anybody that tried to get close to her was vulnerable to being taken advantage of. Anyone who did anything for her became an easy mark.

By 1966, when Tina was fourteen, her life was already marked by constant trouble with school officials and police. She stole books, lipsticks, purses, and money from other students, and was frequently caught shoplifting from neighborhood stores. When she got caught, she would bat her eyelashes and talk her way out of trouble. She had most people convinced after just a few minutes. But she was constantly stealing and running away from home.

Finally, Tina's father had had enough. On this day, when she got home from school, he gave her a spanking and told her to put her shoes on and say goodbye to Gay, because Tina wasn't coming back home. He then went out to the garage and returned with rope. He tied her hands behind her back and brought the rope down and tied her feet and threw her in the car. Ernest Butcher turned the radio up and never said a word the entire way to juvenile hall. He took her inside the front glass door and said to the receptionist there, "Here, you raise her!" and just turned and walked out the door. Weeping, Tina was untied and placed in a room. When she went over to the window she saw her father driving away. She shouted after him and begged him to come back. She promised she would never act out again, but he just kept going.

After spending several months in the San Bernardino Juvenile Home, she was placed with the California Police authority, in conjunction with a

Ventura-based agency that dealt with problem juveniles. Her father and step-mother no longer wanted her living at home. Her oldest sister Veronica and her husband, Tony Hamel, tried to adopt her. When they were turned down, Veronica asked her in-laws, Stanley and Mary Ellen Hamel, to help. A month before Tina's fifteenth birthday, in June of 1966, she went to live with the Hamels in their modest ranch house in Rialto, California. Soon, Tina was calling Mary Ellen "Mom" and they became very close. The Hamels felt that Tina's troubles were caused by the poor relationship she had with her father and stepmother, thinking she was starved for love.

After several months, however, a precocious Tina ran away to marry Bill Plessner, a 19-year-old that she had met at a drive-in movie theater earlier that year. His father bought her a dress and a pair of shoes, gave them $50, and Tina and Bill drove to Las Vegas that night and got married. Two weeks later, after living with Plessner and his parents in Rialto, Tina walked out. She'd been listening to the radio, was very bored, and decided to take a walk. She wore a green pantsuit, no shoes, no purse, carried $2 in cash. Tina said she'd intended to get a pack of cigarettes and then come back. She got lost and just kept going. Plessner, who was earning $45 a week at a carwash knew that she was upset about him not making enough money, and knew that she felt she could do better. He became convinced that she had married him just to get out from under the police youth authorities.

It was eighteen months before Plessner, or Tina's family and friends, heard from her again. On the day she showed up, Plessner had already divorced her. In the meantime, Tina had hitchhiked to Los Angeles. The day she arrived it was raining hard, and she was barefoot. She did not know anyone there and walked the streets for hours, before she finally found a doorway behind a restaurant to sleep. Several days later she noticed a sign outside the building saying, "Model wanted, cash daily." The firm doing the advertising, Pretty Girl International, hired Tina right away to do nude modeling.

Throughout 1967 and 1968, Tina traveled between Los Angeles and Las Vegas. Various men helped her out with her living expenses. She had one who paid her rent, one who bought her clothes, and one who bought her groceries. One of her new friends, whom she dated on and off through 1968, was Lee Hazelwood, the pop musician who wrote the song "These Boots are Made for Walking," made famous by Nancy Sinatra. They married in Mexico, although the ceremony was later declared invalid.

In 1968, at age 17, Tina had an affair with singer and actor Joseph Richard Dodd, Jr., and became pregnant, eventually giving birth to her first child, Bradley. Later that same year, Tina started dating Clarence "Skip" Botteron, a Los Angeles bail bondsman. In November 1970, Botteron divorced his wife and married Tina in a hasty Las Vegas ceremony.

Tina became pregnant a second time and gave birth to a daughter, Tracey Layne Botteron, on July 9, 1971. Tina listed her own name as Ernestine Layne Butcher (age 20). Clarence Irvin Botteron III was 36. Just at that time, Botteron's once flourishing business went bankrupt and Tina had to work waitress jobs to make ends meet. She worked 16 hours a day and he stayed home with the children. The couple moved to Las Vegas, hoping to make a living for themselves, but their relationship continued to deteriorate. Tina was wanted in Los Angeles for overdrawing their checking account, and Botteron told the Las Vegas authorities where they could find her. She was arrested, extradited to California, convicted on the charge, and spent the next six months in jail.

The judge then placed Tina on three years' probation, suspending the rest of the sentence and said, "You're a problem child. You have been that way for a long, long time. You're the only one that can help you. I think you will have to do something to correct your ways and see whether you can't find a proper course for yourself and your children." Her probation officer remembered Tina as "a high powered prostitute" in Las Vegas at the time. "She was very pretty, very mature, she really knew how to carry herself, and knew how to handle people. She was probably a sociopath. She was a manipulator, a very smooth operator, very intelligent, very smooth and very polished."

Following her release from jail, Tina began dating James "Jay" Gillen, a 37-year-old Las Vegas bartender she met while still married to Botteron. In November 1973 when she was 22, Tina married Gillen; his second marriage, and her third. Gillen felt as though he was the "fellow on the white charger who was going to rescue her" and described it as four years of a "hurt me, hurt me, love me, love me relationship." It was a roller coaster. Gillen felt that Tina was to blame for his many lows, and that the extreme changes in her mood made her swing from being kind and loving one moment to selfish and frantic the next. "It was her lifestyle to be up and down," he said. If there hadn't been a problem for a few weeks, she'd create one. It was Tina's belief that their relationship soured because of Gillen's excessive drinking.

Once, when Gillen had been on a week-long bender and was so drunk he could barely get in the back door. She said, "I'll be right back," and left him with the kids for three days. She used the incident as an excuse to spend the three days gambling, saying it was the way she would get back at Jay for drinking so much. She continued with that warped logic, sometimes even taking the grocery money and spending it at the blackjack tables.

Their marriage became a disaster. In 1976, she discovered Gillen was having an affair. She drove around town looking for him and then pulled her car into the driveway of a friend's home where Gillen had stayed during one of their many separations. She left the car in front of the garage, knocked on the door and rang the doorbell. There was no answer so she walked around to the bedroom where Jay slept and she could only see the television from the window. The window broke when she banged on it hard, and then she crawled inside the window and got to a light switch by the door. When she flipped it on she saw two bodies on the bed, with Jay standing and facing her. She started screaming and started throwing things on the bed, first a lamp, then clothing, and ashtrays, anything she could get her hands on. She yanked the television set, which was still on, out of the wall and threw it on top of them. She then ran out of the room down the hallway and as she ran she was still throwing things. Jay ran after her with his underwear down to his ankles screaming, "Nothing happened! Please listen to me!"

Tina ran to the car, got in and locked the door and Jay went to the front of the car and tried to lift up the hood. She put the car in drive and drove it through the garage door, and then backed up. He started to run toward the car, so she put it back in drive and ran through the side of the house. He ran naked to his car, a Lincoln Continental Mark Four, as if trying to protect it and Tina, like a bull seeing red, backed up and floored it and drove her car into the side of his. A year later, in 1977, Tina and Gillen were divorced.

After her marriage to Gillen was over, she had a longing to find the mother who had deserted her as a baby. Her reunion with her mother would be the first leg of a journey that ultimately would take her to Maryland. In November of 1977, with the help of her uncle, Carmen Butcher, Tina flew from Las Vegas to Jacksonville, Florida to see her mother. When Tina got off the plane her mother recognized her right away and they hugged and kissed and she kept repeating, "my baby, my baby." It was very emotional and comforting. It had been twenty-three years since they had seen each other.

Sadly, the good feelings were short lived, and within two weeks they were drinking heavily and having violent arguments. Tina's mother started calling her a whore. Less than a month after she had arrived in Florida, Tina called her uncle from a motel in Tallahassee saying that she had to leave. For the next three weeks she was allowed to share her uncle's three-bedroom house, living in a room with Brad, and Tracey sleeping in another room. Pretty soon those arrangements deteriorated as well, because Tina would work a day or two, and then lose her job. She was also running up hundreds of dollars of phone bills and had not been paying for any of them. In fact, she was not even earning enough to pay for any household bills.

Butcher signed a $500 note enabling her to buy a 1969 Plymouth Valiant for work. Tina promised to make the $45 monthly payments, but never did, and one Sunday she left her uncle's house with her children and the car and never returned. He ended up paying all but $45 on the car. She had made only one payment. He felt strongly that when you first meet her she seemed nice, but then she would "do a number on you, and overall she was bad news."

By January 1978 Tina was still living in Florida, but was haunted by her break up with Jay Gillen. She was drifting from one relationship to another. Luther Stewart, the 39-year old owner of Stewart's Seafood and Steak House in St. Augustine, was one of her boyfriends when she worked there for several weeks as a waitress. Stewart considered himself a playboy and knew that Tina was a good time girl who preferred rich men who would spend money on her. When he wouldn't, they went their separate ways.

Stewart accomplished this by introducing her to James E. Marco. He noticed one night that Marco left her a $100 tip, and that's all it took. James E. Marco was from Charlotte County, Georgia and lived in St. Augustine, Florida. He was a 47-year-old widower who was part owner of a nearby tavern, the Slipped Disk. He had been a plumber. After meeting Tina in June of 1978, he married her on August 2. Nine days later, she left.

James Marco thought she was fascinating and felt deeply sorry for the kids being dragged around home to home. He wanted to make a good life for them all, but their life together didn't get past the honeymoon. Marco later recalled that his nine-day marriage to Tina was a nightmare. After the brief ceremony they drove to Rhode Island, where they left Tina's children with her sister, and then drove on to Ellenville, New York to spend their honeymoon in a mountain condo. They stayed there all night. The place was stocked with food and liquor and they began drinking heavily. Tina claimed later that James Marco pulled a .45 Magnum on her and threatened her with it. He said she was the world's biggest liar and that after they had an argument, she retrieved her two children and they all drove back to St. Augustine Florida.

As soon as they arrived back home, she loaded her two children and their luggage into her trusty Valiant and headed north on Interstate 95. She drove all night arriving in Towson, on the outskirts of Baltimore, MD. At first she applied for a waitress job at a restaurant in Timonium, MD, but there were no job openings for her. A few days later Tina called her ex, Jay Gillen, in Las Vegas, and he provided the number of an old friend named Frank Watkins who lived in Maryland. Frank liked her and felt sorry for her two kids and became her new benefactor.

He gave her money, and also helped her find housing in the Westbury Apartments in Reisterstown, MD. He bought her a butterfly diamond engagement ring. She eventually found work as a cocktail waitress on the 6 p.m. to 2 a.m. shift at a restaurant in Finksburg, MD at Cal Bittner's. After work, she often went back to Reisterstown and shopped at the Pantry Pride grocery store across the street from her apartment building. There she met a tall, muscular man with blond hair who mopped the supermarket floors and stocked shelves. They had a brief intimate relationship and went on to form an even stronger and sinister relationship. That man was Daniel Lee Chadderton.

Chadderton would bring them groceries, and helped her when they moved. A few times her car broke down and he helped to fix it, and other times he helped her get transportation to and from work. She felt she had someone to talk to.

In October 1978, Tina lost her new job at Cal Bittner's, but she was resourceful and she found work at The Branding Iron restaurant next door. David Berquist, the owner, hired Tina as a waitress because she appeared very sweet, very quiet, and very demure. Within days, he knew he had made a mistake. He watched her flirting with the customers. It became pretty obvious to him that she was selling more than cocktails and meals.

The Baltimore County Police had also been involved with Tina shortly after her arrival in Maryland. On November 10, 1978, they responded to a complaint in the Westbury Apartment complex concerning her children fighting. The police had been to the Gillen apartment in reference to child neglect, and the Gillens had been served with an eviction notice, effective November 10, 1978. When the police arrived, Tracey and Brad were alone in the apartment. Brad advised the officer that his mother left them alone on Friday, Saturday, and Sunday nights from 5 p.m. until 11 p.m. while she worked at the Branding Iron restaurant.

The apartment was in disarray, with boxes of clothes and books sitting around on the floor. Tina told the police that she usually left the children with a babysitter. However, the sitter was ill. Tina could not recall the name of the sitter, nor whether or not the police had been to the apartment before, nor if her husband was coming to see the children.

A follow up investigation, on November 23, 1978 found that a green copy of the court order summons of eviction was taped on the apartment door. The apartment appeared to be empty. The Gillens had been evicted for non-payment of rent, and Tina contacted an old friend, Linda Williams, to see if they could live with her family "temporarily." Soon, Tina announced she had to go on a trip.

On November 28th, Mrs. Linda Williams telephoned the agency and reported the children as abandoned. Mrs. Williams said she and her husband had been caring for Tracey and Brad for approximately ten days. Tina had left town for personal reasons and had not contacted the Williamses at all. Mrs. Williams had an emergency phone number for Tina, but it did not help. The two children had been attending Reisterstown Elementary School. Mrs. Williams had been transporting them to and from school. She felt she could not continue to do this and wanted to enroll them in Sandymount Elementary School, the school closest to her in her district. Mr. Williams told Tina to leave with the children stating that she owed them money for all sort of bills. The Baltimore County Department of Social Services had referred their case to Carroll County. The agency became aware of the Gillen situation following a referral concerning the children being abandoned. The agency planned to seek temporary custody until their mother could be located. Tina returned to Carroll County and lived with the Williams family with her children until March of 1979, at which time she was forced to leave for the final time by the Williams family.

Tina and the children began staying with friends and in hotels for a few days at a time after they left the Williams' home. Then Tina and her children began staying with Steve Somers, their mother's new boyfriend, at Springfield Hospital Center where he worked.

The social services agency became increasingly concerned and placed the children in foster care. Tina agreed to come into the agency to discuss her situation, which she claimed was her only alternative until she found her own home for the children. She explained that she and Steve Somers had a wedding planned in May.

By the end of June 1979, Tina had not stabilized her situation. Tina was paying for lodging at Lee's Motel, and she had not married Mr. Somers. In July, Tina became hopeful of having her children returned before school began in the fall. She called to cancel an appointment for another interview, saying she had a family emergency in California. Tina also stated that she wanted physical custody of her children, and was returning to Las Vegas to reunite with her ex-husband.

Several appointments were made by the foster care worker for Tina to visit with the children and discuss her plans for returning them to her care. Tina did not show up for any of them.

Tina felt it was in the best interest of the children to go into voluntary foster care until she could re-establish herself in an apartment. She had been unable to stabilize her situation so that she could have her children returned to her. She worked evenings at Angelo's Restaurant. Plans had been made to begin weekend visits for the children, to ease them back into living with their mother. However, Tina cancelled the appointment.

On August 7, 1979, an emergency shelter case hearing was held and Social Services was granted continued custody. Tina lied and said she planned to return to Nevada. Social Services felt that Tina's past performance in Maryland warranted a final investigation into her desire and ability to take care of them. The children wanted to be reunited with their mother. Tina then promised she would stay in Maryland, and that she would be able to establish a permanent residence.

She stated she'd been unable to save enough money to find a place to live. She had to spend money on car repairs and lodging at Lee's Motel. The children had been in foster care since April and had visited with their mother only one time. Tina was getting desperate, and felt that she couldn't get ahead. At times, she felt totally isolated.

Master Robert J. Speaks, The Master for Juvenile Causes, for the Circuit Court for Carroll County, had threatened to terminate all of Tina's parental rights unless her situation changed in the near future.

Tina was working at John O's Restaurant in the Fairground Shopping Center, as well. After staying in Lee's Motel for several weeks, she moved to a boarding house. Protective services were to monitor Tina in establishing a plan for the return of her children to her custody. If she was unable to do so within the next several weeks, the social workers would need to petition that the children were in need of assistance, and find a permanent location for them. At that point, Tina's parental rights would be terminated.

The Carroll County Department of Social Services started actively trying to take her children away. In a letter dated August 13,1979, the husband of Melanie Haines, the social worker who had been investigating the case, took a personal interest in the matter. Director Lowell T. Haines requested a hearing two weeks before the murder of Mary Ruth Myers.

Tina requested assistance for dealing with Social Security and receiving survivor's benefits for Tracey due to the death of her father, James Botteron. Again, Tina did not keep the appointment. She notified the worker she would be out of town. Tina's appointment was for the 14th of August. On the phone, Tina said she would have to remain in Maryland to settle a civil suit she had filed against a former employer for assault. She hoped to receive a large cash settlement. She was depressed about her circumstances, yet claimed she did not apply for welfare benefits for the children because of "pride." She hoped to establish a permanent residence in Maryland if her luck changed.

CHAPTER 3:
A MATCH MADE IN HELL—
AN EASY SEDUCTION

"Come live with me and be my love . . . "
— Christopher Marlowe

On August 9, 1979, Robert and Tina first met when she waited on him at lunchtime at Angelo's restaurant in Westminster, MD. He had been flirting with her and teasing her and joking with her about the dilapidated condition of her old car, which was parked outside. She suggested playfully that he should buy her a better one. He agreed that he would.

Robert Myers showed up early the next day, August 10th, at the Dunkin Donuts where they had agreed to meet. Tina was already there. He waved wildly at her, parked his big white Lincoln and got into her rusty old car. He directed her to Park's Ford Used Car Dealership several blocks away, and purchased a 1977 Torino for her. It cost $2,700. They then went to get her children and Tina, Brad, and Tracey spent that day with him, driving to his trailer in Mount Holly, Pennsylvania. Several hours later she dropped him back at his car. She gave him a long goodbye kiss on his cheek and asked him to come and visit her at the restaurant.

He went there the next two days. He was clearly smitten, and she enjoyed the attention. A couple of days later, Myers called her from Ocean City and asked her to come and spend some time with him there, and said that she could stay there in his motel. She agreed. When she got off at two in the morning, she drove to Ocean City in the Torino. On the way she stopped at the Pantry Pride in Reisterstown to show her new car off to her friend, Daniel Lee Chadderton, who was working there on the night shift. She arrived in Ocean City early that Sunday morning and they spent the entire day Sunday together walking along the boardwalk and the beach.

She had a room at the North Winds Motel, and they returned there for their first lovemaking session. He was soon exhausted and left at about three in the morning. He crawled out the window to return to his apartment above the office in the motel.

An hour later, Tina was sleeping when she heard him outside her window again. After she let him in, he told her Mary Ruth had been in their apartment waiting and confronted him, asking where he had been. She had threatened to cut his nuts off if she caught him "running around." He showed her a stab-like wound in his stomach where Mary Ruth had stuck a knife when he got into their apartment. It was apparently just a warning since there was no blood. He stayed with Tina that night, and the following morning he snuck out the window, which was on the opposite side of where the office people would be able to see him.

Tina picked him up down the street and they spent that entire day together, sitting on the beach, shopping and drinking. That Monday evening, they dined in an expensive restaurant, several miles up the coast in Rehoboth, Delaware. Tina went back to Westminster to be at work the next day. Bob called her every day that next week when he came back to Westminster, and they met every morning for coffee.

That Friday, he came into her restaurant before the bar even opened and sat down at the bar. A short while later, around 7:00 p.m., Mary Ruth came in. She started arguing with Myers who got up and walked away. A few minutes later a bus boy came out and told Tina she was wanted in the kitchen. Tina walked into the kitchen and Bob grabbed her and said that he loved her that he would meet her when she got off work. Tina told him to get out because she didn't want Mary Ruth to walk back in and find them together. Bob left out the back door telling Tina to meet him at Sharkey's Cove Restaurant and Bar when she got off work.

Tina went back into the bar and served Mary Ruth for another hour. Mary Ruth sat there drinking wine and from time to time chatted idly with Tina. Charlotte Horton, a friend of Tina's and the owner of the Horton's Boarding House, where Tina was staying, was also sitting at the bar at the time when Mary Ruth came in. Charlotte went home after a short while, and soon Mary

Ruth also left. Tina called Charlotte and asked her to go to Sharkey's Cove, which was located a few blocks away, to find Bob and take him home so Tina could see him when she got off work.

Mary Ruth had followed Myers to Sharkey's Cove. Half an hour later, Charlotte called back and said that she had met Bob and had a meal with him but just as she was getting ready to leave, Mary Ruth pulled up. Charlotte told Bob where she lived and told Bob he should go there. As Tina and Charlotte were talking, there was a knock on the door.

Charlotte went to see who it was, returned to Tina on the phone, saying, "He's here." Bob walked in and he got on the phone and said "I'm here but I can't leave the car outside because she's going to be looking for me." Always in control, Tina said put Charlotte back on the phone, and Tina said "Would you see if you could put his car behind your house?" There was a hill there and she could hide it, and it wouldn't be visible from the street. Charlotte said, "No, I'll take it over to my son's house. He lives close by."

As soon as Tina hung up, she said to her boss, "It's a pretty slow night, could I close up? I want to go home," to which her boss responded that she could. Tina had one of the other girls close up the register and then Tina went straight to Charlotte's. When she got there, Bob was sitting on the couch. They talked for about two hours.

Tina asked him if he wanted to spend the night and cool off and then go home the next morning, but Bob said he was not going back home—he'd had enough. He said Mary Ruth was always threatening to throw him out, and that they were always fighting and he was just not going to go back anymore. He spent the night. The next morning, Charlotte came in and said, "Tina there is a black van outside." When Tina walked outside, it was her boss, Mr. Perry. He was upset and he said, "Tina, my wife left me and I'm going to close Angelo's down for a week, so you've got the week off."

Bob had been on the phone and he hung it up and then slammed it down. Bob said, "That bitch," and Tina asked him what was wrong. Bob said "Nothing, nothing." He then said, "Let's go for a ride, let's go check on the trailer."

Tina threw some clothes into the car, and they drove up to the trailer. Bob and Tina spent that day and the next day together. Tina told him he had started to smell terrible. He had the same clothes on for a few days. So they went to a nearby mall and he bought some jeans and shirts. They then embarked upon a road trip, which included stops in Mount Holly, Pennsylvania, Reisterstown, Maryland, Atlantic City and Wildwood, New Jersey, and finally Ocean City, Maryland.

While they were having dinner a few nights later in Mount Holly at the Deer Lodge, Bob said to Tina "You're from Vegas, do you know anybody that would kill her for me?" Tina thought he was kidding, and said, "No, I don't know anybody from Vegas that would kill her." She said, "Why don't you just get a divorce?" He replied "Because she would take everything." Tina continued to ask how much it would take just to divorce her. He said that he had lost everything from his first marriage, but he wasn't going to lose it again.

Bob asked, "Well, how long have you lived in Maryland?" Tina told him since August 1978. Bob asked, "Well, do you know anybody that would even rough her up?" Tina said, "I know one person." Tina then told Myers about her friend Dan. A boss had beaten her up, and Dan had offered to "do a number on him," offering to break the assailant's arms, legs, and burn his house down, "or whatever." Tina also told Bob that on her way to Ocean City, she had stopped in Reisterstown to show Dan her car and that Dan had said he would like to buy it from her.

The following night, they had dinner and then went dancing in Mechanicsburg, PA at the Cross Keys Inn. They were quite drunk and Bob asked her, "Are you going to call that friend of yours?" Tina still thought he was kidding and said, "Are you serious—do you really want me to?" Bob said yes, and Tina said, "Okay, I'll call him." Using a pay phone in the foyer, she called Chadderton, telling him that she had someone who wanted to meet him, and that he could possibly make some money. Bob had said he would pay anything, anything at all, just to get rid of Mary Ruth. Chadderton replied that Tina knew where he worked and to bring the person to the Pantry Pride.

The next day, August 23, 1979, Tina and Bob stopped in Reisterstown at the Dunkin' Donuts to have coffee there and Tina said, "I'll go call him from here." Tina called Dan and told him that she had Bob with her, and that Bob wanted to meet him so, "could he get away?" Dan said, "No, you should come to the store." So they drove to the Pantry Pride and they got out of the car and were sitting on a brick wall talking. Dan came out, introductions were made, and then Bob left to get some coffee and doughnuts for Dan. Dan and Tina stood there talking about Sherrie Chadderton (Dan's wife) and the kids, and Bob pulled up. Bob said he wanted to talk to Dan privately, and walked over to where Dan was standing. Tina got back into the Lincoln.

Ten minutes later, Bob came over to the car where Tina was seated and said, "Do you have any paper?" Tina said, "Yeah why?" He said, "Write down something for me." Tina said, "What?" and Bob replied, "4636 Turkey Foot Road." Tina just looked at him because at that time she didn't realize that was Bob's address. Tina wrote it down, though, and then Bob said, "Write the name Mary Ruth Myers. 43, 5'4" and 135 lbs, and blonde." Bob took the note and walked back over to Chadderton. Later on, Tina would claim that she really wasn't paying that much attention because she was listening to the radio.

Bob returned to the car and said to Tina, "You can come out and talk now." So Tina got out, but nothing unusual was mentioned when she walked back over. They started talking about Sherrie and the kids again. After a few minutes Bob said to Chadderton, "I'll get back to you in a couple of days," and said he had to go to Ocean City. Chadderton replied, "Don't forget I want half down and half when the job is finished."

Bob and Tina then drove on to the Myers' Northwinds Motel in Ocean City, driving directly there and arriving very late. Bob had left his keys in the trailer, so when they got to the motel he did not have a key to get into his apartment. Bob asked the maid to get him a key, and Tina and Bob were able to stay in the room right above the office. They were there just a couple of hours when Bob said, "Lay down and get some rest, because I have some business to take care of." When he returned a short while later, he had a paper sack with him and he said he was going to make a bank deposit. He then counted out $3,000 at that point and put it in his wallet.

Tina had a friend, Maria Poulos, who owned The Electric Circus Disco in Ocean City. Tina would sometimes stay with her, and had contacted her several days earlier, letting her know she had a new boyfriend whom she wanted to introduce to her. Tina asked if she could stay with Maria, whose residence was located above the Electric Circus Disco. When they arrived at Poulos' apartment, Bob asked Tina to prepare a bank deposit slip for the cash he had retrieved from the Northwinds Motel. He then asked Maria if he could lie down and relax.

Tina had bragged to her about the "wealthy" new boyfriend she had just met. He had a beautiful house on a hill that was worth about $250,000. Tina had told Maria a few days before that she was still in love with James Gillen, one of her former husbands who lived in Las Vegas. "If you're serious about this fellow why don't you play it straight with him, be honest with him," Poulos had said. Tina had no response.

Tina asked Maria if she would help her count out the cash to help make the bank deposit, and started pulling money out of a white paper sack. It was a mess, lying in stacks. It was dumped out on the table. Tina asked if she could freshen up and take a shower and when she returned, Robert was sitting there talking to Maria. The money was now organized and there was a total of $30,000.

When Tina returned, Robert told her that the bank deposit was now ready, and the couple drove to a bank in Ocean City. At the bank the couple ran into Robert's stepdaughter Kim Abbott, who was crying. She begged Robert to come home or to call her mother. Robert responded, "No, I'm not calling her."

That evening he and Tina drove to a Howard Johnson's restaurant on US Route 140 in Pikesville, Maryland to meet Chadderton to make the payment. When the couple entered the restaurant, Chadderton was sitting at the counter. The trio asked for a table, and then Tina excused herself to use the restroom so that the men could talk and "finalize the contract." When she came back several minutes later, they were finishing up, and Chadderton said that he expected the other half of the balance within a few days, and Robert replied that it was no problem.

The trio went out to the car and sat there for a few minutes before Robert pulled out the same white paper sack they had had earlier and counted out $3,000. He apologized that he did not have the whole $5,000, but said he couldn't take it out all at once and that they would be back in a couple of days. Chadderton said that was fine, took the money, and got out of the car. He explained he was on his way to work.

Robert and Tina then drove to Wildwood, New Jersey. They then went to Resorts International in Atlantic City, New Jersey. Tina took the opportunity to visit a friend of her former husband, Ted Knureck, who was working as a pit boss at the casino. They drank, danced, and gambled. Tina spent two hours at the blackjack table. They then drove on to Ocean City. It had been a long day, and Tina suggested that they go and say hello to Maria. When they did, Maria offered to let them stay there again.

On Sunday, August 26, 1979, the couple drove to the Pantry Pride Store. There was nobody in the parking lot when they got there except Dan, who was sitting in a car with a blonde female. It was Dan's wife Sherrie. Dan got out of his car and walked over to greet Robert and Tina forty yards away. They opened a rear door and he got in the backseat, and was handed a white paper sack. He counted out the $2,000 that was there and said he wanted the rest when the job was completed. As they were getting ready to leave, Robert said, "Make sure it looks like a robbery! I know where to reach you. Tina has given me your home number and your work number."

Robert and Tina drove to Ocean City and were going to stay at the motel, but when they got there, Mary Ruth's car was parked near their apartment. The couple laughed and returned to Maria's who invited them to stay again with her.

On Tuesday, August 28, 1979, Robert was having a beer, downstairs at the bar in the Electric Circus Discotheque, when the bartender handed him the phone. Robert had told Chadderton that they would be staying at his motel and where it was located. Tina soon joined him at the bar and Bob said to her, "Well, he blew it." Tina responded, "What do you mean he blew it?" "Well, he's in Ocean City. Not part of the plan," Bob said. "He was to 'take care of' Mary Ruth at the house, but he went to the motel and he was gonna get her there, but the maid wouldn't let him up the stairway." Tina said, "What are you talking about? Is he in town?" Robert said, "Yeah, just down the street." Robert added, "I told him to meet us at Granny's, which is right next door to where Maria's is."

Robert and Tina went back upstairs and met Maria. Tina and Maria had arranged to go on a shopping expedition. Robert explained to Maria, "We're just going over to Granny's for a cup of coffee to talk to some guy about a job, that's what that phone call was about." Robert added, "If you need us, we'll be over there."

Robert and Tina went to Granny's and saw Chadderton sitting at a table. He was playing with a knife in his hand and was speaking angrily, explaining, "I wanted to get her in Ocean City but I couldn't get near her at the motel."

About twenty minutes later, Maria walked in, and Chadderton put his head down so she couldn't see his face. Bob said to Maria, "This is the guy that wanted the job in my motel." Maria said, "Fine. Tina, are you ready to come?" As they exited the restaurant, Tina saw a brand-new, expensive looking motorcycle and said to Maria, "Well, that must be his new toy." Maria responded "Whose?" Tina replied, "That guy in there. He was telling us about his new bike." Maria and Tina went on their shopping excursion.

Robert and Chadderton remained for a few minutes, and then Chadderton left roaring away on the new toy. Two hours later when Tina returned to their apartment above the discotheque, she asked Robert "What did you tell him?" Robert said, "I told him just to go back home and then I would call him as soon as I knew Mary Ruth was gone."

A short while later Jerry Walsh, the manager of the motel, called Robert to tell him that Mary Ruth had just left, assuming Robert wanted to know because he was up to his usual philandering ways. At 7:00 p.m., Robert tried to call Chadderton, and when he returned he said to Tina, "I couldn't get a hold of him. Would you try?" Myers had talked to one of his stepchildren to confirm that Mary Ruth was going to the house on Turkey Foot Road, and would be home alone that night. Tina went out and called the Pantry Pride from a phone booth. She was left on hold and could not reach him. The guy who answered the phone laid the phone down and never came back after he put her on hold. Tina called back and was told the Chadderton wasn't there. So she called Chadderton's house and Sherrie answered.

At that time Tina had not yet met Sherrie, and she didn't know much about her except that she had just recovered from cancer. Tina said, "Hi, this is Tina, the one with the Torino. Is Dan home?" When Sherrie explained that he was not, Tina replied, "This is the number I'm at, would you please have him call me the minute he gets home?"

Later that night, Chadderton received the message from Sherrie and then called Tina. He then went straight to the Myers home on Turkey Foot Road.

CHAPTER 4:
THE MURDER

"If you believe in God you better start praying . . . "
— Daniel Chadderton

Chadderton parked about 50 yards away from the house, quietly walked up to it, and stood outside the garage. All the lights in the house were on when he got there and he could see Mary Ruth sitting on a couch in the living room, talking on the telephone. He grew impatient while she continued to talk for about twenty minutes. He watched her finally hang up the phone and turn all the lights off except in the bedroom, where he could see her moving around.

Chadderton went to the side door in the garage and broke in. He grabbed the small poodle, which had startled him, and locked the dog in a bathroom. He tiptoed into the living room where she had been seated. He sat down on the couch next to the pool table and lit a cigarette. He could hear Mary Ruth coming through the house, yelling, "Bobby is that you?" Chadderton just sat there and when Mary Ruth saw the light from the cigarette, she turned on the lights in the room. She was dressed in a négligée and nervously said, "You're not Bob? Who are you?" Chadderton responded, "I'm a friend. I'm a friend of Bob's. I'm waiting for him." Mary Ruth said, "Well, I don't expect him back." Chadderton got up and walked towards her and Mary Ruth repeated, "Who are you?" Chadderton said, "Just a friend. Are you all alone?" Mary Ruth replied, "Yes, I am."

Chadderton said awkwardly, "I would like to see your house, will you walk me through the house? Are you all alone?" Mary Ruth said again, "Yes, I am." Mary Ruth walked through the room and into the hallway and started to turn on the lights there, and in the other bedrooms, to make sure there was nobody there. Chadderton followed her and said, "I was hoping your daughter was here so we could have a party." Mary Ruth said, "She is in Ocean City."

They walked through the sitting room off the master bedroom. He had originally planned to use a knife, because he didn't own a gun, but when he saw the gun case off the sitting room, he grabbed her with one hand and held her, and with the other hand used the knife that he had brought to pry open the gun cabinet. He returned the knife to its sheath on his belt and told her to sit down on the couch in the room. He removed a rifle and a pistol and loaded the two guns. He then told her to go into the bedroom and lay down on the bed. Once they were in the bedroom, Mary Ruth said, "Why are you . . . why are you here?" Chadderton said, "Because your husband owes me money." Mary Ruth said, "How much money does he owe you?" Chadderton responded, "It doesn't matter, I'll get my money."

He then told her to get on the bed, and said, "If you believe in God, you better start praying." He then fired a shot from the rifle into her back, and she turned and looked at him and said, "My God, you're gonna kill me." Chadderton said, "That's right honey." He pulled the trigger again, but the rifle jammed, so he put it down and pulled the pistol from his waistband, and shot her eight times in her torso.

Chadderton threw a pillowcase on her and started to throw things around the room in order to make it look like a robbery. He moved through the house casually and randomly throwing items around. He pulled a green vase from the mantelpiece in the sitting room, smashing it on the ground. He did not leave the house immediately but slowly walked into the kitchen to get a soda from the refrigerator and skimmed through a TV Guide that was on the table. He pulled out another cigarette and lit it casually. He walked around pulling out drawers and scattering the contents on the floor, and overturned several houseplants. He then flipped on a radio in the corner, turning up the volume, then crushing out the cigarette, leaving it in the soil of one of the tall houseplants. After turning out the lights, he made his exit through the garage and went home. It was about 4 a.m.

When he arrived at his house in Hampden, Baltimore, about an hour later, Sherrie and his two children were asleep. He washed up and then about twenty minutes later, got on the telephone. He wanted to brag about his night's work.

In Ocean City, at about 5:20 a.m., Maria knocked on Bob and Tina's bedroom door and said, "Bob, telephone." The telephone was on Bob's side of the bed. Bob picked it up, and put the phone to Tina's ear so she could hear. "Our work is done. She was shot nine times. She's dead." Bob said, "Okay," and hung up.

That whole day Tina was a nervous wreck, but Bob seem relieved—even jovial. Bob made dinner arrangements with Maria for that night. Bob, Tina and Maria planned to go to a new restaurant in town that had just opened. Bob went out early and bought flowers for Maria and Tina, and later, Bob and Tina went shopping and took a long walk on the beach.

At about 7:30 p.m., Maria called upstairs and said that Bob had gotten a message from a gentleman by the name of Jerry Walsh, from the motel. It was urgent for him to return the call. Bob called and told Tina to pick up the extension and listen. Jerry said that Bob had better get down to the motel. Kim was on the phone, and said that his house had been broken into. When he got off the phone he said, feigning alarm, "Someone broke into the house! Call Charlotte and see if Charlotte heard anything on the news."

Tina always kept in close touch with Charlotte because she called her quite often to see if she had any messages. She called Charlotte, who asked, "Where are you?" Tina replied, "I'm in Ocean City." Charlotte responded, "Are you alone?" Tina said, "No, Bob is with me." Charlotte said, "Is he close to you?" Tina asked why, and Charlotte replied, "Because Mary Ruth shot herself. It's a rumor all over town."

Charlotte repeated that the news was all over town. finally Tina said, "Bob, pick up the phone." Bob acted very surprised. When he got off the phone, Maria had come upstairs and Bob said, "I've got to get down to the motel. Would you drive me down?" Maria agreed. Tina offered to drive him, but Bob said, "No, let Maria drive me down."

Bob said to Tina, "I'll call you in half an hour and let you know what's going on." When he didn't, Tina called the motel. Jerry told her, "Well, Tina, he's already gone back to Westminster with Kim."

Maria said, "Tina, why don't you just spend the night and go back tomorrow?" And Tina responded, "No, I think I should go back now." Tina didn't know the way to get back to Westminster, though, so she asked Maria for directions. Maria told her to just stay on Route 50, but Tina got lost and ended up in Washington, and got back to Westminster at about 2 a.m. Tina couldn't find Charlotte at first, but eventually did, and she asked her to go to the Dunkin Donuts shop to get some coffee in the afternoon. Tina then called Dan.

When Charlotte and Tina walked out of the doughnut shop, Corporal James M. Leete pulled up.

Cpl. Leete, a 16-year veteran of The Maryland State Police, arrived at the Myers' house a few minutes after 1:00 p.m. on that hot muggy August 29, 1979 day. He was experienced in homicide and sex crimes. His life soon became intertwined with the death of Mary Ruth Myers. Solving her murder became his focus for several years. The State Police Westminster Barracks had sent a young trooper to secure the scene initially, and Leete got there shortly afterwards. It was humid in the house, so hot the perspiration soaked through his shirt in a few minutes, and then through his trouser legs. Flies were buzzing around the woman's body. The rifle and a handgun used in the murder were in plain view in the bedroom. Leete sealed the house, and within hours he had obtained the necessary search warrants.

On the bed, next to the victim at the time the body was discovered, was an unloaded single-barrel shotgun. Beyond the bed on the carpeted floor, partially concealed by an upholstered chair with a skirt, was the nine-shot handgun prosecutors would later say Mr. Chadderton had used to fire eight bullets into the woman's upper chest and abdomen. The photographs also showed another gun lying on the carpet near the entrance to the long rectangular bedroom. It was the bolt-action rifle Mr. Chadderton was accused of using to shoot the victim once in the back.

A letter was found near Mary Ruth Myers' body. In it, she and her husband were referred to by nicknames—"Lizard" for Bob Myers and "Grasshopper" for Mary Ruth.

"Dear Lizard—Hope you are all right. I worried about you all night and got no sleep. I love you with all my heart. Love—Grasshopper."

Dr. Ann M. Dixon, Assistant Medical Examiner for the State of Maryland, performed the autopsy on Mary Ruth Myers. Mary Ruth was 43 years old, 5'4"

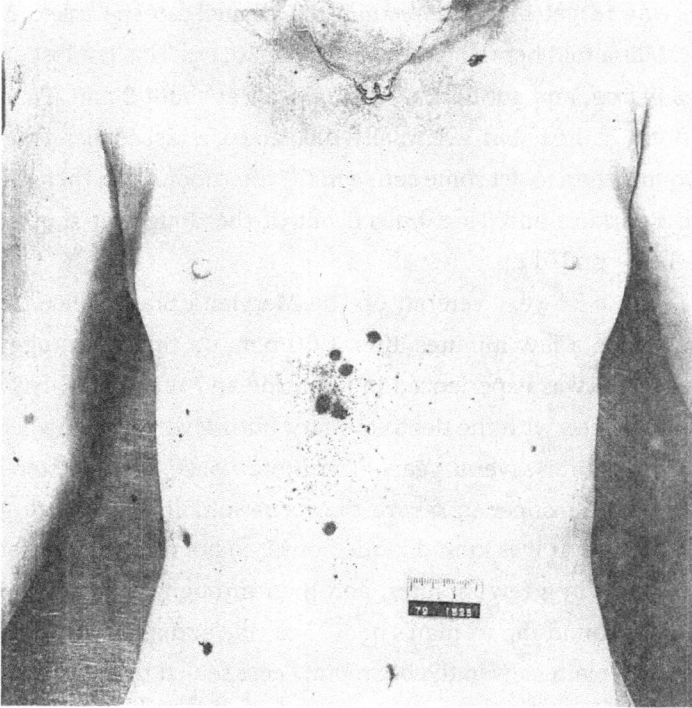

Autopsy photo of Mary Ruth Myers' gunshot wounds.

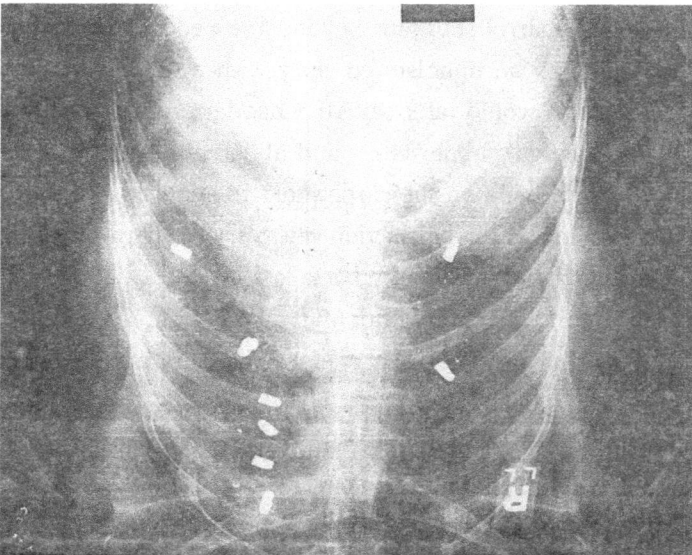

X-ray of Mrs. Myers' chest revealed bullets.

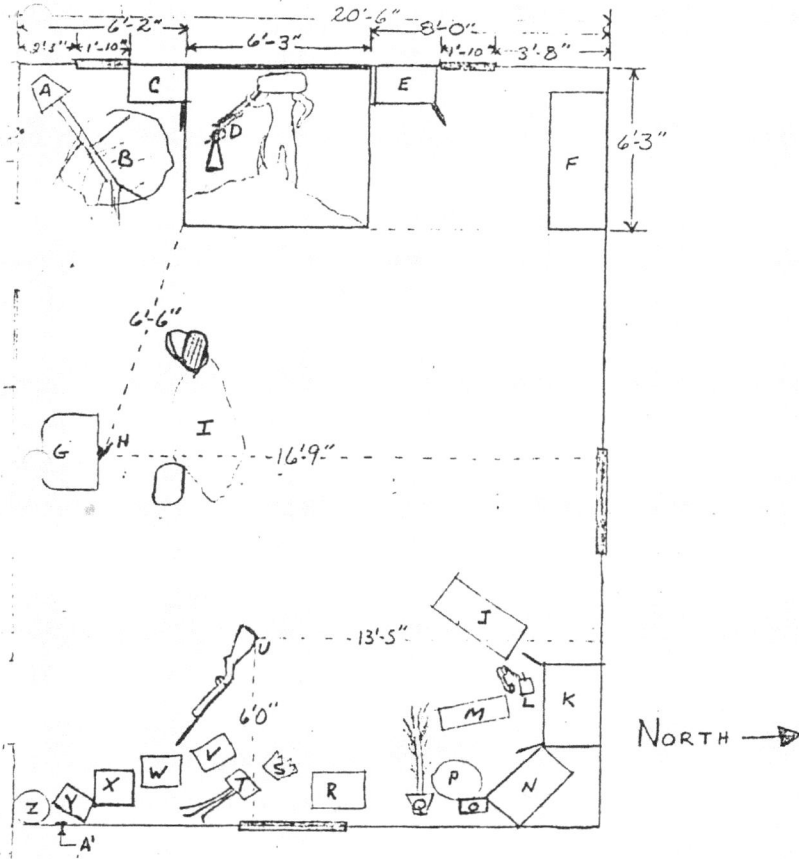

MASTER BE ROOM = 23'-4" X 20'-6

DRAWN BY: Cpl. J.M. Leete
MSP-1998

MARY RUTH MYERS
HOMICIDE
K-56-18718
8/29/79

NORTH ➡

Hand drawn diagram by Cpl. Leete indicating where
Mary Ruth Myers' body was found in her home.

and one hundred and twenty-five pounds. Her clothing consisted of a pale blue, frilly, bikini style two-piece night attire. Her hair was reddish-brown. She had a gold chain with a butterfly pendant around her neck and a ring containing clear stones on the ring finger of her left hand. Her toenails were painted bright purple.

Dr. Dixon determined that there were five entrance gunshot wounds and surrounding the shots was powder stippling. Five bullets were recovered from left to back. A bullet was recovered from her left chest. Two bullets were recovered from her right chest and abdomen. All these bullets had entered from the front. There was a perforating gunshot wound, the entrance was in her left back and had exited from her left upper chest. This bullet was not recovered from the body but had been found, flattened after it had exited her chest and struck a wall.

Mary Ruth's death was estimated to have occurred at 2:10 a.m. on August 29, 1979. Her body had been received at the Department of Postmortem Examiners at 7:15 p.m. on August 29, 1979, and the autopsy was performed the next morning, August 30, 1979 at 9:30 a.m. The stomach contained fragments of shredded cabbage, consistent with sauerkraut, and black olives. The body was then transported to the Pritts Funeral Home in Westminster.

A forensic chemist with the Maryland State Police testified that a light brown Caucasian head hair was found clutched in Mary Ruth Myers' right hand, and it did not match the hair of Mary Ruth or Robert Myers. Two white synthetic fibers also found in her right hand were not identifiable.

A team of State Police flooded the neighborhood in Carroll County and Westminster, MD. They talked to neighbors, friends, and acquaintances, and soon learned that Robert Myers had been seen with a woman named Tina in recent days. Westminster was a small town, and Tina had been a waitress in several local bars and restaurants. At the time, she was going by the name Ernestine Layne Gillen. Cpl. Leete contacted the State's Attorney so they could locate and interview her.

Cpl. Leete checked the telephone records from the house and the motel in Ocean City that the couple owned. He discovered several telephone calls that interested him. Over the next several hours he had troopers learn all they could about them. Soon, the names of Tina Marco and Daniel Chadderton were established as being "persons of interest."

Tina was picked up in a patrol car at a Dunkin' Donuts near her boarding house and taken to the Westminster barracks at 4 a.m. on August 30, 1979, a little over 24 hours after the murder. She was not treated as a suspect, but was simply told that she might have some information that would be of assistance to the police. She said she would be more than glad to help, and for two hours answered all the questions that Cpl. Leete and Trooper First Class Tom Hickman asked her.

She explained that she had been a waitress in Westminster for a few months and had met Robert Myers. One day she was waiting on him and he made a comment about her car, and said it was a safety hazard. She joked, "Well, why don't you buy me another one?" And he said, "I will." The following morning, Tina had her children Brad and Tracey with her, and Bob took them to a car dealership and he purchased a car for her.

She explained that this was on August 10, 1979. Right after he bought the car they all went to his trailer in Mountain Creek, Pennsylvania and spent the day. For the next week or so, they saw each other every day. He started to come in between 5 and 6 p.m., after work. He then invited her to go to Ocean City. She noticed he was drinking more and more because she was the server.

Tina told Cpl. Leete and TFC Hickman that on August 17, Myers took Tina and her children, and a friend of hers' grandson up to the trailer in Pennsylvania again and they went fishing. She returned to work at about 4 o'clock, and he came in as usual at about 5:30 p.m. At around 9 p.m., his wife Mary Ruth came into the bar and was very upset. Just when she walked in, Tina had been sitting down next to Robert. He was grabbing her by the arm, trying to pull her towards him, telling her that he loved her.

She looked up and saw his wife. Tina went to the other end of the bar and Mary Ruth sat next to Bob and they had a heated discussion. When Tina brought a glass of wine to Mary Ruth, she heard Mary Ruth say, "If you don't come home right now, you're not coming home at all." Mary Ruth stayed for about forty minutes. Tina, for most of that time, stayed in the kitchen. The bar was full of people. At one point, Robert walked back in the kitchen and grabbed on Tina's arm and said, "I love you." Tina responded, "How do you know? Get away from me!"

According to her statement, Tina told Robert, "Your wife is out at the bar and she's gonna come walking in here. I know she saw your hand on me, and I know she heard you tell me you loved me." Robert responded that he was going out to his car, and he left. Tina went out to serve the customers in the bar, and Mary Ruth, oddly enough, started talking to her as if they were long lost friends. Mary Ruth showed Tina some jewelry that Bob had bought her and started bragging about the motel they owned and telling Tina what an ass Bob had been at various times.

After about an hour Mary Ruth said, "I'm going to the back bar to check to see if my husband is still here." She returned a few minutes later and said Bob was gone. She then paid his bar tab, as well as her own, and left.

Tina told her boss that she was upset and that she wanted to leave. It was about midnight. Tina went back to the boarding house where she was staying and found that Robert was there. They spent the night there together. The next morning, which was a Saturday, the owner of Angelo's told Tina and said that he was closing the bar down that night and possibly for the rest of the next week. Tina went back inside the bedroom and told Bob that she was not working. Bob said, "Good, let's take a trip!" Tina grabbed some clothes, and they went to the trailer in Carlisle, Pennsylvania. They went out to eat later that night, and dancing. They stayed in Pennsylvania for a couple of days.

Cpl. Leete cleverly got Tina to commit to as much detail as possible, establishing what restaurants they were in at what times. Tina also cleverly answered all their questions, assuming that they would verify what she was saying and conclude she had no involvement with the murder.

She added that Myers had told her that he was supposed to meet Mary Ruth on Friday in the office. He had appointments in the office on that day, and that Mary Ruth was going to be there, and he was going to try and talk to her.

Tina knew there were phone records that could easily be discovered, so she explained that she got on the phone to her ex-husband in Las Vegas, where he owned a bar, to find out what was going on with him. Tina explained that Bob walked in carrying two bunches of flowers, one for Maria and one for her. Tina finished her conversation with her ex-husband.

She described that she then she took all her clothes off and got into bed with Bob and they had made love. An hour or so later, the phone rang and it was Maria who said that Jerry Walsh had called for Bob. He'd said it was an emergency and that he should contact the motel immediately. Tina relayed the information and when Bob called, Jerry Walsh explained to him that there had been some kind of break-in at his house. Kim Abbott, Mary Ruth's daughter, got on the line and said, "Where are you?" And Bob said, "I'm here in town, I will call you back."

Tina told Cpl. Leete that she then called Charlotte, who relayed the local rumors that Mary Ruth had shot herself. Tina asked Charlotte to repeat that information to Bob, and Bob got on the phone and Charlotte said, "It's all over town that your wife shot herself." Bob broke into a sweat. His hands were ice cold and he started to cry, and went in to put on a shirt. He stated that he thought it was best if Maria took him down to the motel. As he was leaving, he told Tina he loved her and that he would call her as soon as he knew what was happening. On the way over to the motel, he told Maria that his wife had cancer of the colon, which he had not mentioned to anyone before. He then said it was cancer of the bowel.

Hickman asked whether or not Myers had told her that Mary Ruth had ever threatened him. She said that, yes, the previous week when he had gone home, his wife was there and stuck a butcher knife in his back. Myers had shown her a red mark but it wasn't a cut. Mary Ruth said that if he ever stayed out that late again she would kill him, or if she ever caught him with another woman, she'd kill him. He said he had told her to put the knife down or he would make her eat it. Bob also said that Mary Ruth had threatened to cut his balls off on several occasions, and that she was a very violent person. She said that she thought he was afraid of her.

When questioned about whether or not Robert Myers wanted to marry her, Tina said that Robert Myers had asked her to marry, but said that if they did it would cost him an awful lot. However, he also added that he felt Tina would be worth it. Tina had discussed all this with her attorney, Alan Fox, about two weeks previously. Robert had said, "God, it's getting outrageous.

I can't breathe. She calls me at the office . . . she calls me names." Even when she was in Ocean City, she would call him and just fight with him.

Tina had said, "Why don't you go and see an attorney?" and Robert replied that he had discussed it with an attorney named Woody, and that he would try to make a cash settlement, which is what he did with his first wife. Hickman questioned, "Did you tell anyone that you are getting married?" Tina said, "Yes, I told Maria." It was dawn when the interview was concluded, and Tina was transported back to the boarding house.

Over the next several days the police investigators questioned people in Wildwood, New Jersey, Atlantic City, and Ocean City, and they investigated Myers' and Marco's travels in the days before the murder.

Eight days after his wife's murder on September 6, 1979, Robert Myers was met by Cpl. Leete outside of his office, and he brought up the possibility that Tina was involved. Myers said he didn't know if Tina could be or not, but that there had been a weird phone call to her former husband in Las Vegas. He said she asked him to leave the room, adding that the thirty-six minute phone call took place on the evening of August 28, from the Ocean City apartment where he and Tina were staying.

Tina, aside from the statement she had given to police the day after the murder, always refused to talk to Cpl. Leete. Robert Myers, on the other hand, talked freely about the case to Cpl. Leete until he was under indictment, despite admonitions from his attorney, Phil Sutley, that he and Tina say nothing. In these conversations, Myers always maintained his innocence. He told the officer that any further meetings with him would have to take place at Mr. Myers' business office, so that Tina wouldn't find out about them. Apparently, he complained, every time she found out he had talked to Cpl. Leete, she would withhold sex. Still, Myers continued to meet with Leete, always willing and congenial. While maintaining his innocence, on several occasions he joked that if he wanted to kill his wife, "he would have pushed her off his boat in Ocean City to the sharks."

Leete soon interviewed Judy Hoffman, a neighbor who saw Robert on the morning after the murder before the autopsy had been performed. Robert told Judy that Mary Ruth had been shot nine times. This was something which he should not have known at that stage, as it hadn't been revealed to the public.

The police were beginning to link the events to Daniel Lee Chadderton. They had checked phone records and his home number had come up. He was soon observed visiting the Turkey Foot Road home where Tina and Myers were living. The house had been put under constant observation on August 30th, shortly after the interview with Tina.

Tina was concerned about her police interview, particularly about Leete's questioning regarding the keys to the Myers' house on Turkey Foot Road. She didn't know where they were, and that made her nervous. When she got home from the interview, she asked Charlotte, "Do you feel like a drive?" Charlotte said, "You should get some sleep." Tina said, "I've got to find those keys." Tina knew the Bob had not given Dan a key.

Charlotte and Tina drove to the trailer and they found a bag, and the keys were lying next to it. Tina kept them, hoping to give them back to Bob the next time she saw him. Two days later, Charlotte and Tina drove by the Crowells' house and Bob came out for a few seconds. He then went back in quickly, though, and said, "I can't talk to you now."

On September 1, 1979, the day of Mary Ruth's funeral, Tina moved into the Myers' home on Turkey Foot Road. She took her two children there with her for a day visit. The blood was not yet dry on the carpet.

Robert Myers was hesitant about going to the viewing at the funeral home and the funeral, but Tina had lectured him that he had to go. His bad judgment made Tina nervous, and to determine whether or not he had visited the funeral home, she went there herself before the viewing. Robert was not there, so she left and then telephoned the home several times to see if Robert was there. The employees of the home became annoyed and told her not to call there anymore.

Robert threw down a few drinks to give him nerve. Clearly distraught, he met many friends and relatives at the funeral home and was considered by them to be an emotional wreck because he was incoherently weeping. At the funeral, Mary Ruth's teenage children refused to shake his hand or acknowledge him. After the funeral he returned to Mary Ruth's mother's house with friends and family and appeared to share their sorrow.

Several days later, Robert Myers, at Tina's suggestion, placed a bereavement and thank you notice in the local newspapers.

On the day of Mary Ruth's viewing, Tina had gone down to Angelo's to see if she could get her paycheck. Bob came in and was very upset. Tina was sitting at the bar. He spent the night with Tina at Charlotte's. The following day, Bob and Tina went up to the house on Turkey Foot Road. When they went in, the place was a shambles, and Bob asked if Tina had a camera and asked her to take pictures of it for him for insurance purposes. He also asked for her help cleaning it up. Tina got Charlotte to help, and then got Charlotte's son-in-law Brad, and his wife Marlene to come up and help her, too. Bob and Tina spent one night there before the house was cleaned.

The State and local police were still keeping the home under constant observation. They saw Tina there using her Polaroid camera to take photos. They also saw her cleaning the house.

The police had immediately talked to the employees at the motel in Ocean City and examined the telephone records there and at the residence. They discovered Chadderton's name and had determined his identity. A record check revealed that he was born on June 26, 1950 in West Virginia, fifteen miles from Garrett County. He lived at 1211 Walden Avenue in the Hampden neighborhood of Baltimore, with his wife Sherrie and two children. Sherrie was a little younger, born on November 16, 1954. They learned he worked at the Pantry Pride, Food Fair Inc. in the Reisterstown Shopping Center. He had worked as a janitor and shelf stacker for several years. Before that, he had served in the military for a short while before being discharged. He had a 7th-grade education.

Corporal Leete and another Maryland State Trooper went to see Chadderton on September 8, 1979, at the Pantry Pride. Before that meeting, they parked their car directly behind Chadderton's car, and when he came out of the grocery store they got out of their police vehicle. He looked at them and Leete asked him if he had a gun in his car, and he replied that he didn't. At that point, without any prompting, Chadderton went over and put his hands on the right front fender of the police car and assumed the frisk position.

Two weeks after Mary Ruth was shot to death, Tina and Robert arrived in Ocean City. Tina was wearing some of the victim's clothes and jewelry. They visited Maria Poulos. Noticing that Marco was wearing attractive new clothing and jewelry, Poulos remarked, "Gee, that's a pretty dress you're wearing." Tina said it was one of Mary Ruth's. Tina invited her to "come up to the house" in Westminster because "Mary Ruth had all kinds of dresses." Tina told Poulos there were many different kinds of dresses and some "still have the tags on them." Tina offered Maria all the size 12 dresses that once belonged to Mary Ruth, because "the 12s are really too big on me."

On another night Maria, Tina, and Robert went out to dinner. When Myers left them momentarily, Tina began showing off the new jewelry she was wearing. Then she opened up her purse and showed Maria even more jewelry. Several opal rings, a diamond ring with yellow and brown diamonds, another ring with diamonds, a sapphire and diamond ring and platinum diamond ring. Tina had two sapphire rings with diamonds, and an opal on her fingers. Maria said, "You're a lucky girl." Tina didn't tell her they were Mary Ruth's, and that she had just gotten them from the house. Tina did, however, ask Maria not to tell Myers about the jewelry in her purse. Later, when Myers returned to the table, Myers told Maria that a burglar might have killed his wife because some jewelry was missing. He then started describing things she had just seen in Tina's possession.

CHAPTER 5:
THE WEDDING

"Thank you God for the happiest day of my life . . . "
— Tina Gillen Marco

On September 9, 1979, a hearing was held on the merits of Tina's custody case. Her situation had changed drastically. She had gone to live with Robert Myers on Turkey Foot Road. At that hearing, Bob said that Tina could live in the house, that she had her own bedroom and the kids would have their own bedroom. Tina claimed she would soon start working for Maryland Business Services. Juvenile Court Master Speaks said he would not allow her to bring her children into that type of environment without marriage. Bob then offered to move out of the house, and Master Speaks said, laughing at that suggestion, "No, you could always drive up at night." It was agreed that there was adequate housing for the children as far as their physical needs being met on Turkey Foot Road. The case, however, was continued for forty-five days pending a home study of the situation.

When they left the hearing Tina was in tears. Tina immediately started suggesting to Bob that they should get married. She soon had him convinced. Bob said, "Okay, we will get married, we will get your kids back." He repeated, "We are going to get married!" Tina was still sobbing. They then talked to her attorney, Alan Fox, who advised them not to do it, and to hold off. Bob said, "I don't want her to lose her kids." The next day, Bob told Tina he didn't want to get married in Westminster, but that she should come up with three possible places and they would choose one of them. She started to look for a church.

Robert did not know that Tina was still married to James Marco. She feared that if they got married in the United States, there might be more likelihood that this could be discovered. She suspected that if they married in a foreign jurisdiction, her secret would be safe. She eliminated Mexico, since she had been married there before to Lee Hazelwood. She suggested Paris, Las Vegas and Bermuda, guessing expense and her previous experiences would eliminate the first two. She told Bob she did not want to be wasteful and wanted to make a brand new start.

They soon agreed that "The Pink Church," St. Andrew's Presbyterian Church in Bermuda, looked like a great place for the ceremony. Tina made all the arrangements. Now she had money available for a proper wedding. She wanted to be married by a minister. They visited several bridal shops in Maryland, and she tried on numerous gowns, finally settling for an expensive classic looking off-white dress.

A scheduling fee and security deposit were required, and it was promptly sent to guarantee the reservation at St. Andrew's. The church assigned its paid staff, including custodial and technical employees. Scheduling the wedding there included the use of the sanctuary, dressing areas, and restrooms.

An indispensable part of the wedding preparation and ceremony was the assistance of the wedding coordinator, who had special knowledge about the proper way to conduct wedding services. Tina was determined to get this wedding right and telephoned her constantly, sometimes three times a day.

She answered all of Tina's questions regarding the wedding procedures; she was used to new brides and their pre-marriage nerves. The coordinator helped complete the Wedding Information form, outlining the details of the service, assisted the minister at the rehearsal, arranged for the set-up of the church before the wedding, checked the sanctuary for the proper lighting, placement of flowers, and candles.

Tina coordinated the time of the wedding with the instrumentalists and the minister. She made plans with a photographer. She learned that posed pictures could be taken on the day of the wedding, immediately before or immediately after the ceremony. Tina requested in advance that the pastor be included in the photos.

A wedding service is an act of worship, and she was informed that the music was to be provided by the musicians at St. Andrew's Presbyterian Church. The couple received a sample recording of the wedding music, and then Tina contacted the music director at the church directly. They did not mind paying an additional fee for live instrumentalists. However, Tina insisted that she wanted a string quartet to play music that she had selected, including "I'm your Majestical Mystery Ride" and the classic "Jesu, Joy of Man's Desiring" by Bach. She also wanted the organist to play Mendelson's-Auf Flugeln des Gessanges (On the Wings of Songs). She demanded that Louis Armstrong singing "Wonderful World" be played through the sound system at the conclusion of the ceremony.

After several discussions with the wedding coordinator at the church, she got her way. An hour-long rehearsal took place the evening before the service. The wedding rings and some other jewelry had been purchased in Bermuda the day before.

Thirty minutes before the worship service began on the wedding day, the organist started the prelude and ten to fifteen minutes later, the pastor escorted Robert Myers to the waiting area in the church lounge. After another five minutes, the wedding coordinator escorted the bride and groom to the entrance area vestibule, and then the wedding coordinator gathered the ushers to begin the processional. Once it started, the two ushers extended the aisle runner. The Reverend Leslie G. Smith, the installed minister of The First Presbyterian Church, officiated at the wedding service. It was the 26th of September, 1979, just 28 days after Mary Ruth's murder.

Pastor Smith spoke loudly and clearly. He had his back to the altar and faced the couple:

"We gather in the presence of God to give thanks for the gift of marriage, to witness the joining together of Ernestine Layne Gillen and Robert Lee Myers, to surround them with our prayers, and I ask God's blessing upon them. So that they may be strengthened for their life together and nurtured in their love for God.

"God created us male and female and gave us marriage so that husband-and-wife may help and comfort each other living faithfully together in joy and in sorrow, in sickness and in health, throughout all their days.

"God gave us marriage for the full expression of the love between a man and a woman. In marriage a woman and a man belong to each other and with affection and tenderness freely give themselves to each other. God gave us marriage for the well being of human society for the ordering of family life and for the birth and nurture of children. In marriage husband-and-wife are called to a new way of life created and ordered and blessed by God. This way of life must not be entered into carelessly or from selfish motives but responsibly and prayerfully. We rejoice that marriage is given by God blessed by our Lord Jesus Christ and sustained by the Holy Spirit therefore that marriage be held in honor by all."

The wedding ceremony lasted exactly one hour. The new couple returned to their room in the luxury Boutique Hotel, The Royal Palms, in Hamilton, to cut the cake in celebration and change their clothes before going out on the town. Tina had ordered the large wedding cake adorned with a bride and groom the week before. For the next four days they enjoyed elegant dining at expensive restaurants, dancing, and live entertainment. They traveled to some tourist spots one day in a limousine with a driver, dressed in suit and hat, and on another day they hired a guide with a white horse and carriage.

On the official forms Tina gave her "full" name as Ernestine Layne Gillen, swore she was divorced, and that she was a restaurant owner. On the back of one of their wedding photos she carefully wrote, "Dear God, please bless this forthcoming marriage until death do us part. I love this man. Amen." On another she wrote, "Thank you God for the happiest day of my life . . ."

After a "honeymoon" that lasted four days, the couple flew back to Maryland, enjoying the celebratory champagne provided to them by the airlines and the toasts and good wishes of their fellow first class passengers.

The newly married couple wasted no time setting up house. Over the next several weeks, they purchased dining room sets of fine china and silverware. The Gorham Medici Sterling Silver Flatware Set that Tina purchased was fit for royalty. It cost $26,149.00. It consisted of a set of 12 place knives, forks, and spoons at an average of $200 each. Salad forks, butter spreaders, and beverage spoons at $180 each. The gravy ladles were $375 each, and the four pierced tablespoons were priced at $412 each.

A week later Tina purchased a ladies' platinum fashion ring. It contained 21 carats of aquamarine and .8 carats of diamonds, costing $8,000. On that day she purchased an 18-karat yellow gold gentlemen's wedding band for $2,800 for Robert. Later on other occasions, she purchased gold nugget neck chains, a diamond and ruby butterfly necklace, a pearl bracelet, a pair of matching pearl earrings, and several rings with diamonds, including a heart covered in diamonds, a diamond necklace with a chain, and a pair of matching earrings with diamonds. She also bought a rose gold watch, with earrings and a ring to match. She added a diamond watch-band and a diamond bracelet to her collection.

With her newly gained wealth, and no limits placed on her by Robert Myers, she took advantage of her new status. Soon she started to work at the Maryland Business Services office to the outrage of the other employees there who missed Mary Ruth. Two of them immediately quit.

Over the course of the next two years, Tina accumulated over 200 pairs of shoes, handbags, and elegant clothing. She acquired fur coats and hundreds of thousands of dollars of jewelry. Her new Mercedes-Benz had her own vanity plates, reading "Tina." She established her own bank account, and was now able to make unlimited phone calls across the United States.

She enjoyed designer fashion outfits accented by thousands of dollars worth of custom made jewelry, including her favorite, a pear shaped diamond worth $56,000. She routinely visited beauty salons for facials, manicures, pedicures, and hair styling. She spent two thousand dollars on baby clothes. No more Target or K-Mart for Tina.

She liked frequenting some of the restaurants where she had worked as a waitress as a patron, and inevitably was a generous tipper.

Tina occupied herself redecorating the house, installing a new bed, a heart-shaped jacuzzi, and mirrors on the walls and ceiling of the master bedroom. Expensive furnishings and art were purchased to keep her happy.

At the fashionable Mountz Jewelers in Carlisle, Pennsylvania, in March 1981, they bought an Aquamarine ring for $4,400. At the Manno Swartz Furriers on York Road in Towson, MD, on January 19, 1980, Tina saw a floor length Ranch Mink Coat with Black Fox collar, cuffs, and border that she just had to purchase for $10,000. The Ranch Mink Purse was a bargain at $500. She also bought a Natural White Fox cape for $2,000. Bobby gladly wrote the check.

On November 2, 1979, another court hearing was held. The children were continued in foster care with the establishment of overnight visitation for a readjustment period. Their return to their mother was scheduled for the second semester of the school year.

The day visits had gone extremely well and after an interview with the new "Mrs. Myers" on February 5, 1980, the social worker sent a letter to Master Speaks requesting that Brad and Tracey be returned to live with their mother and step-father, Robert Myers. The Myers had been able to establish a good relationship with the children, and Tracey and Brad looked forward to their weekly visits. The children had their own rooms in the new house and their physical needs had been more than adequately met. Both Bradley and Tracey had established good relationships with their mother and accepted Robert Myers as their "new father."

They often did things as a family, such as going out to dinner or the movies, or simply staying home and playing games. The Myers gave the kids chores to teach responsibility. Brad helped bring in wood, take out garbage, and keep his room clean. Tracey kept her room clean and helped with the dishes. The children accepted these chores and were proud to explain how they helped around the house. They were disciplined by reasoning and denying them privileges. The Department of Social Services had several conversations with Cpl. Leete, but since no charges or public accusations had been made against them, the Myers were deemed appropriate custodians, capable of providing proper care for the children.

Master Speaks accepted the recommendation and returned the children to their mother the next day, February 6, 1980. The case was then closed by Protective Services.

*****

The same day that Myers and Tina were getting married in Bermuda, Chadderton went to the Maryland State Police Barracks in Westminster. A State Attorney's summons had been served on him earlier at The Pantry Pride, where he worked, requesting telephone toll records, electric bills, and bank records. He had been told he did not need to bring the records himself, but Chadderton had insisted on personally bringing the documents to the State

Police Barracks immediately. Upon his arrival he was taken downstairs to the Criminal Investigation Section's office and was met by Cpl. Leete and Trooper Joseph Szyerbicki.

He was angry and complained that he didn't understand why they were asking him for records about the murder of a person he didn't even know. This statement was voluntary, and was not given in response to any question. Leete soon learned that the 1979 Honda motorcycle that he had parked outside had been purchased on August 25, 1979. A trooper had taken a photograph of it. Leete checked the title and then immediately showed it to a maid at the Myers' Ocean City Motel, who recognized and identified it. Chadderton had become a big problem for the Tina and Robert. Initially the two couples would socialize either at the Turkey Foot Road house or going out to dinner. But Myers and Chadderton began spending more and more time together.

Dan gestured that he felt the house was bugged because he kept acting like a big shot and saying that they should go outside. He wouldn't talk in the living room or in the bedroom, and made a big production of it, often pointing to the ceiling and calling Bob outside. They had all discussed about the phones being tapped because they could hear a clicking noise on the telephones.

Dan and Sherrie came up to the house on one occasion in January 1980, complaining because he had spent so much on lawyer's fees and he said he didn't expect to have to spend "his money" that "he had made" on attorney fees. His first attorney, Tom Ward, had charged him four thousand dollars for accompanying Chadderton to the police interview and the gun charge. Bob said, "Well, I'll help you out." Bob paid it in cash.

In addition to reimbursement for these legal fees. Robert continued to give Chadderton money. It was clear to Tina that Chadderton intended to milk Myers for as much as possible and prey on Myers' weakness. It wasn't long before she confronted Chadderton, letting him know that she was having none of it.

Tina said that it seemed like a weekly thing. Dan kept showing up, saying, "I need this, I need this, I need this." Bob and Tina argued. She asked Bob, "What the hell are you doing?" Bob replied, "Well I've got to help him." Meanwhile, Chadderton was asking for more and more money. Tina asked him, "When is it going to stop?" Bob replied, "You should stay out of it."

Bob and Tina had a big fight about the Lincoln when Bob came home one day and said he was selling the car to Dan. Tina knew that Dan was out of a job, and Bob and Tina had several fights about these constant handouts. Tina said to Bob, "You going to pay for his goddamn gas too?" She told Bob that Dan "can't even make payments on the car, let alone drive it." Bob said, "Oh no, he's going to get a job, he'll take care of the car. I'm going to get a note. A promissory note. He's gonna pay off the balance of the car and it's only gonna be $6,000." Tina replied, "Fine, I want it in writing." Bob ended up paying off the car because he gave Dan the money to pay it off.

A check had come in from the settlement from the lawsuit against his stepchildren to retrieve the money Mary Ruth had given them. Bob didn't tell her about it. Tina didn't learn about it until a month later, when Tom Stansfield slipped up and mentioned it when he was meeting with the couple discussing other financial matters. The case had been settled and the money was gone. When Tina got the items from the bank, the car was paid off and it matched the same date that he had gotten the money. Dan sold the car, though he told Tina the car was in Virginia.

Dan became very secretive about meeting Bob. He would call the house, or he would drive up and he and Bob would walk around on Turkey Foot Road, but they would not talk in the house because Dan knew that his welcome with Tina had been worn out. On three occasions, Tina was sociable with him when Sherry was along.

Tina estimated that Bob had paid Dan about $50,000. It was a weekly thing. She found many checks that Shelley had cashed. Bob would lie to Tina and said that the cash had been used to pay bills, but when Tina checked the receipts they did not match. Bob told Tina that he had told Shelley to go pick up supplies but the receipts and checks did not match.

Bob would make checks out to Shelley Myers, Bob and Mary Pat's 19-year-old daughter. Shelley worked at Bob's accounting office, and would cash the checks and return the cash to Bob. Dan would often show up at the office instead of coming to the house. Dan hung around the office an awful lot. All the women in the office would make remarks to Tina, "What's with this guy? He's always after you for something, Tina!"

Dan and Sherrie had driven to Las Vegas, and then Dan had gone to Texas. While there, Sherrie told Tina that she was afraid. She had talked to Cpl. Leete and was scared she was going to be dragged into the case. Sherrie said, "I just hope that Bob and Dan have their shit together." Sherrie told Tina that she was going to provide an alibi for Dan by saying that he had been home that night, when actually he had not been home with her.

Chadderton told Tina that if he killed her, she would never be found. During their arguments about Dan, Bob told Tina that she should just stay out of it and let him pay Chadderton a little money from time to time.

Dan threatened to kill Tina's kids several times after the murder. Her children at first were in foster homes, but Dan was up there on a couple of weekends when the kids were visiting at Turkey Foot Road. Dan would look at Tracey and rub her on the head, and look at Tina and say, "She sure is beautiful isn't she? You wouldn't want anything to happen to her would you?" And Tina would say, "No, I don't want anything to happen to her . . ."

Tina had a cedar closet made in the sitting room where the gun cabinet used to be, and surrounded herself with guns. When she and Bob fought, she would lock herself in that room, to which only she held the key, and just sit there. She'd also go there if she heard Bob on the phone with Dan. She was afraid Dan would come up there and do something to her. Tina spent many long hours in her closet, sometimes spending the time trying on Mary Ruth's clothes, writing letters and making telephone calls to friends.

On one occasion, Bob took Brad to the office and had asked Tina if she wanted to meet him for lunch. Tina called the office at about 10 a.m. and the girl who answered said that Bob was out, so Tracey and Tina got in the car drove to the office. Tina went to Christie's music shop and bought a couple of tapes, and as she was walking out, Bob walked in. When Tina kissed him she smelled alcohol on his breath and looked at her watch and said, "My God, it's only 10 a.m., Bob. Why are you drinking it 10 a.m.? I thought you were in here on business." Tina walked out with Tracey, and when she looked back, Brad was coming out of Frisco's Bar. Tina asked, "What's he doing in there? Bob said, "Nothing, just go on, I'll meet you back in the office."

Tina saw Bob go into the Frisco Bar, so she put Tracey in the car and then went into the pub to find Bob. He was sitting there with Dan and another guy, and they all had a bunch of empty beer glasses on the table. Brad ran to the men's room. Tina left and drove around back, and saw Dan's bike, as well as another motorbike and Bob's car.

Tina, furious, picked up Brad and drove the kids back to the house and told them to go pack a bag. Before they could leave, Bob was at the back door. He came in and was crying. He stopped. "What are you doing?," he asked. Tina said, "I'm leaving. I can't handle it anymore." Bob said, "You can't leave. You can't leave, please, don't leave," and Tina said, "I can't put up with this sneaking around you and Dan do all the time."

At that time, Tina heard motorcycles coming up the driveway and Bob said, "Well let's go for a drive and talk. We have got to talk." Dan pulled up outside the bedroom window, revving his big monster of a bike, and said, "Is she giving you a problem, Bob?" Tina turned around and said, "Just get off the property. Just get the hell out of here, I'm not up for you today." Dan yelled, "Is she giving you a problem? You want me to take care of her?" Bob said, "No. I want to talk it out."

Continuing his frightening behavior, Dan told Tina that he had threatened to kill Hickman and Leete. Bob and Dan were shooting pool in the house, and were talking about it. Dan said that he had followed Cpl. Leete on two occasions and that he was near where Bob lived. Dan told Tina on several occasions, "You'd better not testify about this. You'll never be able to, because they will never find you to testify."

Bob helped Dan by lending him money. Sometimes he would pay him back when his welfare check came in. He'd do some work around the house for Bob, and pick up odd jobs and delivery, and go to the bank and post office for Bob.

Dan couldn't find work, so Bob advanced him some money. Because of the newspaper articles and Cpl. Leete, it almost became hopeless here for him to find a job. Dan and Bob became close friends. They played cards, shot pool, and drank together. They even watched Bob's children together along with Brad and Tracey, and played with them and fed them, while Tina remained terrified.

CHAPTER 6:
THE INVESTIGATION CONTINUES

"Can you hear me coming?"
— Cpl. James M. Leete

Leete was obsessed with the case. It had taken over his life. The fact that Myers had married Tina and had set up house at Turkey Foot Road greatly offended his sense of decency. Wherever he could, he instigated, cajoled, and meddled, believing that if he continued to do so, sooner or later one of these suspects would slip up and give him an opening to pursue. He visited the Pantry Pride store several times, talking with employees and supervisors there. He visited Bob's accounting office. He would happen to "bump" into Myers and engage him in seemingly innocent conversation and encourage other officers to do the same thing.

On Tuesday, February 17, 1981, at 2:42 p.m., a white Lincoln belonging to Robert Myers was in front of Sharkey's Cove in Westminster. After checking the registration plate, it was discovered that the registration had been suspended. The police kept the car under observation. At 6:15 p.m., Chadderton was stopped while driving the vehicle by uniformed Maryland State Police Trooper Andrew Mays. While Trooper Mays was seated behind the driver's seat of the police car checking the status of Chadderton's operator's license, Cpl. Leete and Chadderton stood outside the car on the sidewalk.

Leete asked Chadderton if he had in fact met with Bob Myers in Ocean City, MD. Chadderton strongly denied ever meeting Robert Myers in Ocean City at all, but then added, "I think I did go there one time looking for Bob about buying Tina's Torino."

Trooper Mays found that there was an outstanding traffic warrant for Chadderton's arrest. He was then taken into custody. He was released on bail, but Leete persisted.

Leete let Chadderton know that he wanted to interview him, and instead of ignoring this request, Chadderton arrived with his lawyer, Tom Ward, at the police headquarters. He hoped by doing so he could make the investigation go away. The State's Attorney, Thomas Hickman, and another witness were present. The entire interview, including the careful advisement of rights was recorded. He answered the initial harmless questions, then Leete moved on to the more critical ones. He asked about the phone call Chadderton made at 5:20 a.m. on August 29, 1979 from his residence to Ernestine Layne Gillen. He asked Dan if he knew Tina Gillen. Did he know Robert Lee Myers? Did he know Mary Ruth Myers? Was Chadderton present when Mary Ruth Myers was killed? Leete then asked if Robert Lee Myers and Tina Gillen hired him to kill Mary Ruth Myers. Leete then asked Chadderton when the last time was he was out of the state.

Chadderton refused to answer each of these specific questions, citing the 5th Amendment. Leete concluded the interview, saying, "We know you were paid a sum of money by Robert Lee Myers and Tina Gillen for the murder of his wife, Mary Ruth Myers, and that you are still walking around free. We would arrest you now, but to do so would expose certain information that we have, that would hamper our attempts to gain further evidence against the other two principles in this case. You are free to leave."

Chadderton later complained that constant harassment by Corporal Leete and other investigators cost him his job, and that several months before his arrest his family was living on food stamps.

✶✶✶✶✶

The investigation into the murder took twenty-seven months. Valuable assistance was provided by members of the Criminal Investigation Section, under the supervision of Detective Sergeant Paul Utz, at the Westminster Barrack, and also by personnel of the Special Services Division of the Maryland State Police.

Mary Ruth's murder had occurred on the second day of employment for Assistant State's Attorney, Frank D. Coleman, and he was assigned to pursue the perpetrators from then until the final resolution of the last appeals seven years later. Coleman was from Finksburg, Maryland, and graduated from The Columbia Union College. During his years in law school, he worked for the U.S. General Accounting Office for seven years, analyzing government programs in an effort to eliminate fraud and waste.

On August 23, 1981, the Honorable Donald J. Gilmore, Chief Judge of the Circuit Court for Carroll County, Maryland, signed and issued an Ex Parte Order authorizing the interception and recording of telephonic wire communications over the telephone listed to Robert Lee Myers, at his office at 101 North Center Street, Westminster, Maryland.

The police immediately began tapping Chadderton's and Myers' phones in both his office and his house. They also received authority from Judge Gilmore to place a bug inside the residence on Turkey Foot Road. It's one thing to receive permission to install a listening device, but the implementation is often very difficult. In order to do so, stealth is critical so that the target subjects do not know that they are being "bugged."

To install the microphone in the living room of the home required a lot of patience, energy, and ingenuity. The small task force waited until Robert and Tina had left the premises, and then the officers broke into the house. Some kept watch, others monitored the phones at the Maryland Business Service office, and others followed Robert and Tina to make sure they would not return. The plan was to climb into the attic above the living room, deposit a microphone through a very small hole into the ceiling of the living room, and then leave. Unfortunately, one of the troopers slipped off the beam he was standing on and his foot and leg broke through the ceiling and was dangling there.

The troopers became hysterical, laughing at this strange sight. They called their supervisor, who was outside, and requested plaster and other materials so that they could repair the damage that they had done before Robert and Tina returned. If they did not patch up the hole, their activities would be discovered and their efforts thwarted. The State Police immediately acquired these materials and two hours later they had finished their temporary patchwork. Frantic plastering was completed to make the house presentable before the couple returned and could notice anything amiss.

There was no way that they could properly dry the patch and so the dark stain was visible. They panicked when they received notice that Robert and

Tina were on the way home and managed to exit the premises just in time.

When Tina entered the living room, she immediately noticed the wet repair work and went up to the attic to see what had caused it. The State Police had canceled their plans to leave a microphone there and so none was found. However, the only logical explanation for the wet repairs was an illegal intrusion. From that point on, Tina and Robert, and later Chadderton, would conduct any incriminating conversations outside the premises.

The State Police were determined to try again, and a month later the same team was assembled, and another surreptitious entry was made. This time it was at night, once the Myerses had gone out on the town. The three troopers, who went inside, saw a suspicious looking object glowing on a table in the living room near the door. They quietly moved forward, carefully hugging the wall and moving very slowly because they were convinced that Robert and Tina had set up an explosive device as a booby trap to hurt any unwanted visitors. After many minutes of slowly crawling forward into the room, they realized that what they thought would hurt them was just a fancy clock that had been glowing in the darkened room. Before they could begin to install their secret microphone, they were notified that the couple was on the way home, and so this effort, too, had to be aborted.

Eventually, bugs were successfully planted in their telephones. The secret recording of the conversations at the Myers' home and the office provided a candid picture of the everyday life and interaction between the co-conspirators, family members, and others.

Recording — Part of August 26, 1981 Phone Conversation:

Robert Lee Myers: Happy Anniversary.

Tina Myers: Yes. One year and 11 months, dear.

RLM: Isn't that nice?

TM: Um hum.

RLM: That's the way I feel.

TM: Yep.

RLM: All right honey, I love you. We'll do something special tonight for your anniversary, ok?

TM: Um hum.

*****

On September 4, 1981, Robert Myers' mother called him:

MOM: Bob, I just wonder, but that last article in the newspaper.

RLM: I'll get the last laugh.

MOM: Huh?

RLM: Before the year's out, I'll file a suit and then I can retire.

MOM: You'd do what?

RLM: I'll retire. I'll file suit before the year's out.

MOM: I can't understand what you're saying this morning.

RLM: You don't understand that?

MOM: No.

RLM: Matter of fact, I was thinking about getting a gun today and following the cop around myself.

MOM: Um.

RLM: I would be in the klink.

MOM: Oh.

RLM: (Laughing) I don't have to go tomorrow.

MOM: That's what I thought. The way that paper read this morning. I went out and got it. You know?

RLM: Really?

MOM: Tina don't have to go either?

RLM: Tina will have to go down there, Mom. I ran out of money. I worry for her. I'm just about done. Well, you don't have to worry about me Mommy.

MOM: Well, it does.

RLM: Tina was thinking about you today. We like you, you know?

MOM: Well.

RLM: Her mother is coming in from California, um, Friday.

MOM: How's the little girl?

RLM: The little girl? Oh, she's doing fine. She's pretty. You're a typical little Grandmother hen.

MOM: Uh huh.

RLM: You a little worry wart this morning?

MOM: Huh?

RLM: (Laughing) You worrying about your boy? (Laughing)

MOM: I hope to tell you, I'm about to.

RLM: You're about to?

MOM: You're my baby, yeah.

RLM: Well, Mommy maybe one of these days I'll just disappear.

MOM: So, when all this, you know, your Mother sees it, and they bring the papers over, and . . .

RLM: Well don't let that bother you Mom. You know better than that.

MOM: But this is a lovely picture this morning they got of you. And then, Ethel and them tells my sister what's in this paper about you.

RLM: Uh hum.

MOM: How can your Mother think?

RLM: (Laughing) Alright, Mommy…

MOM: OK . . . That's right. Okay hon.

RLM: (Laughing) Alright Mommy, I love you Mom.

MOM: Okay, hon.

RLM: I'll see you.

MOM: Okay.

RLM: (laughing) Bye bye.

On September 8, 1981, Robert Myers called Dan Chadderton:

Unidentified Female: Cal Bittner's. Can I help you?

Robert Lee Myers: Hey hon, let me speak to Daniel C. He's in there with a little blonde girl. Real big tall fella.

Daniel Chadderton: Hello.

RLM: Hey.

DC: What are you doing boy?

RLM: Christ, you're starting early again today.

DC: No, I'm eating a sandwich. I ran out of gas on the way down and had to walk about twenty miles.

RLM: Really?

DC: Yeah, did I.

RLM: Oh, uh huh. Well, meet me as soon as you can.

DC: Where?

RLM: Uh, at the Montour House. Well, I gotta get there as soon as possible cause you know Tina. The minute I call and tell her I'm comin' she expects me home.

DC: Did you tell her you were comin'?

RLM: Hell no. Not yet.

DC: OK.

RLM: I gotta call her though.

DC: Alright.

RLM: Cause if she calls here and I ain't here, I'll catch hell again.

DC: OK. Well call her. And tell her you're gonna stop with a client. And you'll be on your way home.

RLM: Yeah, I'll have a beer or two. Maybe I can try and talk her into letting me pick her up some food, see, and I got an excuse to be late.

DC: OK. Well then . . . Sherrie's gonna be with me.

RLM: That's fine. I don't care.

DC: It looks better. Right. What'd you do to my old woman, man? You kept her upstairs all night.

RLM: Not me.

DC: Yes, you did. Ain't it terrible?

RLM: That was Tina's doin'.

DC: You must have had a good time up there, fella.

RLM: You dumb shit.

DC: (laughing) Well, next time you can send them both down to me, you hear me?

RLM: All right.

DC: (laughing)

RLM: Shit. You got trouble handling just one of them.

DC: I heard that.

*****

On September 12, 1981, Tina Myers and a girlfriend, Mary Ellen, were recorded on the home phone:

Tina Myers: Yeah.

Mary Ellen: Yeah? Hello.

TM: Monday, we got a phone call from a newspaper reporter. He wanted to come out and interview us, or interview me, is what he said. So I asked him how he got my phone number and he told me he had talked to Phil earlier that day. Our lawyer.

ME: Uh hum.

TM: So I called Phil and I gave him hell for giving out my phone number, and he said before you start screaming, he said this guy is new on the paper and he wants to give you and Bob a chance. He said to talk to him. It can't hurt.

ME: Uh hum.

TM: So I did. We had him up at the house. He came up and he spent about two hours up here and he wrote an article of our side of this whole Goddamn thing. OK? We put Leete down so bad and the guy printed every word.

ME: Hmm.

TM: And made Phil, our lawyer, a quotation here and he says, "The attorney also said the blame for the Myers misery rests on Corporal Leete's shoulders. 'Corporal Leete is way out of bounds here,' said Mr. Sutley. He believes that Trooper Leete has wasted taxpayer money, traveling to eleven states and Bermuda to investigate the murder." OK. And then he quoted me saying, "If they, the State Police, spent as much time looking for the killers as they did looking at us they'd have solved the murder." (laughter) Anyway, we got our turn, we got our turn! They got our picture right on the front page of the paper. And I think that Leete probably called down to Bermuda and raised Holy Hell that I wasn't in jail.

ME: Probably.

*****

On September 14, 1981, Sherrie Chadderton called Robert Myers:

SC: Hello.

RLM: What's wrong? You and Danny have a fight again?

SC: Yeah.

RLM: Is that why he's coming up here?

SC: I don't know that. He told me you wanted him up there.

RLM: Yeah, well I wanted him up here to yak to him. I wanted him to know how . . . what Tina went through over there [in Bermuda.]

SC: Uh hum.

RLM: But I'm not going out drinkin or nothing. I don't go in no bar. I can't, Sherrie because if I do you know Leete's right on my ass and he's gonna run right back and tell Tina. Alright hon, well look I'll call you tomorrow when I'm downtown here where the phones ain't being tapped every word we're saying.

SC: Alright.

RLM: Alright, cause Leete tapes everything you're saying now and twists it all around.

SC: Yeah. I realize that the phones are [tapped] . . .

*****

On September 18, 1981, Sherrie Chadderton called Robert Myers.

RLM: Everything ok?

SC: Yeah, I guess.

RLM: Alrighty, well don't sound so down, girl.

SC: You know, I might need a little help.

RLM: Huh?

SC: I might . . . a little. I might need a little help, and I rather not talk to you on your phone. It's tapped.

RLM: You might need a little help?

SC: Yeah.

RLM: Alright, hon.

*****

CHAPTER 7:
BIGAMY IN BERMUDA

"Bigamy . . . the triumph of hope over experience"
— Oscar Wilde

Tina and Robert were beginning to feel the pressure. Convinced the police had been purposely making their lives unbearable, Robert eventually retained a lawyer, Philip Sutley, Esq., for advice. Myers did not know that Sutley would soon hurt him more than he would ever help him.

Tina Myers, Myers, and Chadderton had not been indicted and none of them were now cooperating. The State only had a weak circumstantial case. Consequently, Cpl. Leete was ecstatic when he learned that Tina had still been married to someone else when she had married Myers. He travelled to Florida to interview James Marco. He then decided to initiate a covert operation. The Maryland State Police entered into a secret agreement between the United States and Bermuda authorities to have Tina Marco Myers extradited to the island to stand trial on the bigamy charge.

When Carroll County officials informed Bermuda authorities about the alleged bigamy, Bermuda officials were not that interested and had to be convinced to prosecute her. They were told that Maryland would pay all expenses, including transporting James Marco to their court. Leete then contacted the State Department to coordinate Tina's extradition. The matter was then referred to the State Department's Office of International Affairs, which forwarded the case to the Baltimore Office of the United States Attorney.

Matters were complicated by the fact that Tina was now several months pregnant. Normally, persons sought for international extradition are not released on bail, but on June 22, 1981, Assistant U.S. Attorney Mark H. Kolman argued before United States Magistrate Paul M. Rosenberg that the advanced stage of Mrs. Myer's pregnancy constituted an extraordinary circumstance permitting bail. As a result, Tina Myers was not extradited to Bermuda until September 1981, several weeks after her daughter, Sabrina, had been born. The Myers' attorney, Phil Sutley, told the press that Corporal Leete was responsible for prodding the enforcement of what he called a rarely prosecuted bigamy charge and subsequent extradition.

On August 28, 1981 the State Police heard Tina telling a girlfriend that Bob tells Dan anything that she tells him. She then discussed writing a book about what's been happening to them. She said she didn't know what Bob was going to do when she had to go to Bermuda. She also discussed the fact that when Sherrie Chadderton had asked Bob for a small gun, Bob put the handgun in Dan's jacket without telling him. Later Dan was arrested for it even though he hadn't known the gun was there.

On August 29, 1981 the troopers heard her discussing the fact that there had been newspaper articles about her case in Bermuda.

Two days later, on August 31, 1981, they overheard Tina asking a reporter to come to the house so she could give him an interview.

She also was concerned that Bob was hyper and that all he did was talk about the case. It was something about which she repeatedly complained to Charlotte.

*****

Bermuda's Casemates Prison was built during the late 1830s by a large number of convicts brought in from England. They were, essentially, constructing a prison for themselves and their criminal descendants. The roof of the building had vaulted ceilings, and what was called a casemated roof. Its walls were 8 feet thick, made of bricks and concrete. It had been constructed to serve as a maximum-security prison and had been Bermuda's main prison for decades. In 1995 it was condemned, but for a few days in 1981, it was Tina's place of residence.

In September 1981, after Sabrina was born, Tina was flown to Bermuda under guard and placed in a damp cell at Casemates. A tough sandpaper voiced woman, who supposedly had been charged with running cocaine through the Caribbean, was Tina's cellmate.

That rough-voiced woman was Sergeant Diane Culp. She had been one of the first six women to join the Maryland State Police in 1974, and had taken on many dangerous undercover assignments. To many of her peers, she was one of the most colorful and creative people ever to wear a Maryland State Police badge. In her career she had acted like a biker chick in order to infiltrate the Pagan Motorcycle Gang, and as a sophisticate aboard a luxury sailboat to work cocaine smugglers. She was able to alter her personality to fit the mission. When not assuming another identity, she was described at times to be a know-it-all and crude.

When she joined the State Police, it was not easy breaking into the all male ranks. She refused, however, to have anything to do with any lawsuits filed for sexual harassment or discrimination. She had a tough childhood growing up in South Baltimore. Her work environment was not a friendly one. She had decided not to let the resentment from her male colleagues bother her, and was determined to handle it on her own. After a couple of months, the male police realized she was not making a statement as a feminist but that she really wanted to be a cop, and they realized when they saw her work that she never phoned in sick or complained. She earned their respect.

Sgt. Culp had been requested to help in the Myers murder investigation. In previous assignments, she had always stayed calm. She had been undercover, a hostage negotiator, a road trooper, and an investigator, but this mission in a dark smelly prison cell in Bermuda left her a little shaken. Her assignment was to get Tina to talk. She had been waiting in the cell for 2 days.

Tina was brought in, adorned in fur and jewelry, looking quite done up. Tina thought she was going to a hotel, but this place was far from luxurious. The cell was 10 x 10, with no windows, no toilet and no sink. There were two metal beds and a small sliding panel in the door for the guards to serve the prisoners hot dogs, bread, rice, and water. The guards there beat prisoners routinely for any minor infraction, such as talking back to them.

Sgt. Culp had been placed in the cell with no contact from the outside, and she had begun to worry—especially when she was taken to court for her supposed crime. Bermuda did not tolerate criminals. In court she watched as the judge gave a derelict five years, no parole, for sleeping on a park bench. Since the only people there who knew about her undercover role were the

Attorney General and the Chief of Police, when she was brought to court, she worried that they would really believe she was a foreigner charged with drug smuggling, and she did not quite know what was going to happen.

She started to think the State Police had forgotten about her, but the Attorney General happened to be in the courtroom. He helped her straighten things out with the Judge. Sgt. Diane Culp was ultimately not successful in obtaining any information, because Tina was too clever to talk about the homicide or her knowledge of it.

Cpl. Leete appeared at Casemates Prison along with State Trooper Edward Bailey a couple of days after Tina's arrival.. Ever tenacious and industrious, Leete thought perhaps if he fed Tina some lies about Bobby's activities with Tina's girlfriends back home, she might blurt out some incriminating facts. Again, Tina was too clever to be deceived so easily. Leete took his wasted effort in stride. He did not use the opportunity to enjoy Bermuda, even for a moment. He was totally focused on the investigation and he returned to Maryland immediately after conferring with the authorities there. Leete's visit did, though, have the effect of rattling Tina's nerves, as evidenced in this September 10th phone call between Robert and Tina.

Prison (Bermuda), September 10, 1982:

RECPST: Good evening, female prison.

RLM: Hello, this is Bobby over in Maryland. How are you doing?

RECPST: Fine, thank you.

RLM: That's good. Can I talk to my darling wife over there, Tina?

RECPST: Yes.

TM: Hello.

RLM: Hello. Hi love. How's my wife?

TM: Oh God. It's been hell.

RLM: I'm sure it is. Mentally draining, isn't it?

TM: Guess what . . .

RLM: What?

TM: I just had an hour-long meeting with Leete.

RLM: (Laughter)

TM: He's coming down with indictments.

RLM: On who?

TM: You.

RLM: Oh, good. Let him come. Let him come.

TM: Me? Anybody. He can . . .

RLM: Let him come. (Laughing) let him come. That's fine. He can indict anybody he wants to . . .

TM: Huh?

RLM: He can indict anybody he wants to. He can convict his mother if he tried.

TM: Well, when I told him where my mother was—he wanted to know who she was staying at the house with, because he was going to get, I think, Melaine Haines to pick them up. And I said my mother was there, and he said, "Oh, I want to talk to her." And I said, "She's not going to talk to you."

RLM: And . . . he won't talk to me either. I don't have to talk to him.

TM: That's exactly right. Well, they said something about what Maria said.

RLM: (Laughs) I never done nothing like that.

TM: He said, "Oh yeah, and Maria counted $30,840."

RLM: (Laughing Stops) Oh.

TM: He said you were dating my best friend.

RLM: Oh my god. Isn't that nice. Oh god. That's just nice. That's hell, ain't it?

TM: Well, it was you know. It wasn't much fun to sit there and listen to all of his crap.

RLM: But that's why he took you over there, cause I called Phil and he said the best thing you can do is just answer the questions, cause they're just going to—

TM: Exactly.

RLM: Because they're just going to keep you longer . . .

TM: And I told him, I said, "I know my husband would have nothing to do with anything like this and you can't tell me he would."

RLM: That's right.

TM: And he says, "Well you know your husband is slowly going broke?"

RLM: Huh?

TM: And I said, "Yea, paying all these god damn lawyer fees."

RLM: Uh huh. Did he like that?

TM: He said, "I'm not your enemy, I'm your friend." I said, "Don't tell me you're my friend!"

RLM: (Laughs)

TM: I said, "If you were my friend you wouldn't put me through all this mess."

RLM: Right.

TM: And he says, "Well, because of the article in the paper I'm going to hand down indictments." I said, "Well, be my guest."

RLM: Right, be my guest. Well, see how your mother and I are sitting here? We just want to tell you we love you and miss you, more than you'll ever know.

TM: Right. You make sure you tell my mother about, you know, what he might pull.

RLM: Yea, Leete—I told you. We knew this all along. We had it planned.

TM: Oh yea, I know. But, oh my God, I don't want her being brought into this.

RLM: Yea, well I'll let you tell her. So . . .

RLM: Darlin', I really love you.

TM: I wrote notes down while I was talking to him.

RLM: Good. Because the rougher he makes it on us, I think the more we can sue the state for . . .

TM: Well that, I think, is what he is worried about. He told me that you had met Dan at "John O's" and "Ted and Mary's," "Frisco Pub," "Sharkey's," "Cal Bittner's," "Herman Moffitt's," and "Seafarers."

RLM: (Laughing) Jesus cronies. Oh, God.

TM: Yea, you like that?

RLM: Yea, that's a good one. (Laughing) Oh God.

TM: You know this bigamy thing has got me . . .

RLM: Listen, the bigamy ain't got nothing to do with all he's doing . . .

TM: Oh, and by the way . . . Social Services is going to sue me.

RLM: Oh, they are? For what?

TM: When they had the children in care, and I had that jewelry, or the money from the jewelry that I had sold.

RLM: Yea?

TM: I said, "Well, I sold that later. I didn't even get that until later."

RLM: Uh huh.

TM: He said, "Well, I've got a deposition." I said, "I don't care what you've got."

RLM: Uh hum. Boy-o-boy, he don't give up, does he?

TM: No.

RLM: He's a real asshole.

TM: Yea.

RLM: You know that . . . Phil said that even in the State Police, they don't like him. So what, did you talk to him before you talked to Jeanne?

TM: Yeah, no.

RLM: No? Well, Jeanne told me you were sounding down then. Anyhow, we knew Leete was gonna, well, you knew he was gonna say all that, before he even told you. (Laughing) Oh God. Umm.

TM: How are the kids?

RLM: Oh, they are wonderful. They miss you. Our little Sabrina, she's throwing a regular tantrum tonight. I just had to put her in the crib and let her cry. She's stopped now. She probably cried herself to sleep. So now I can talk to you. You know what I mean?

TM: Yea.

RLM: But I'm managing.

TM: Are the kids and Brenda getting along?

RLM: Oh yea, Brenda and them are getting along fine. They're having a ball. Everything's going fine honey, except my wife isn't here.

TM: Yea, I know. You might have to talk mom into staying if, you know . . .

RLM: Yea, well, I'm not concerned and that's what he wants to do, let him do it. He don't have a damn thing more than what he had two years ago, except circumstantial bullshit to frame us.

TM: That's right.

RLM: So you know, if he wants to put innocent people in jail, he'll have to do it. It's that simple. You know?

TM: Yea.

RLM: So, I'm not concerned about it. God knows we had, you know, so I'm not worried about it. Okay?

TM: Well, I'm sure glad you called because after talking to him I was really down.

RLM: I knew you were. (laughter) Oh, I'm sure of that. That's what he's trying to do, to make you mentally drained.

TM: Yea.

RLM: If there is anything to know, you'll crack up. Thank God there isn't, or you would.

TM: Well, that's what I told him. He said he tried this business about you being used all your life. I said, "Don't patronize me."

RLM: Uh hum. Yea.

TM: I said, "Nobody's life is easy."

RLM: Uh huh . . . right . . . well, I'm going to call Phil now and put him aware.

TM: Uh hum. I don't have to talk to him. You tell mom the same. . .

RLM: Now, you know what he's gonna do to me now, he's going to come up here now and tell me you're over there going to bed with everybody and—

TM: Oh, sure.

RLM: And that you're over there drinking, and he's gonna pull the same shit with me. He's done it. He's done all this before.

TM: Yea.

RLM: But now he thinks that we are apart and can't see each other, and he can really get away with it.

TM: Uh hum.

RLM: (Laughs)

TM: And all your secret meetings with him . . .

RLM: Oh yea, you know about them every time. So, I'm not worried about it. (Laughs) And you know why I'm meeting a couple times? He gave me car payments.

TM: Yea?

RLM: That stuff, he knows why. Don't let that bother you sweetheart. I told him I'm with your best girlfriend.

TM: Well, yea?

RLM: You think I should tell her?

TM: Well, I hit her right in the mouth.

RLM: Right.

TM: I would, he said that he…that you and her had been seen together.

RLM: (Laughs) Well, you know that. We went up to the bank.

TM: Yea, well, that's, you know, he didn't use that. He didn't add that part. He just said, you know, your best friend, your husband's running around with. I said, "Don't give me that."

RLM: (Laughs)

TM: I said, "Who's seeing your wife?"

RLM: What did he say?

TM: He didn't answer.

RLM: Oh, I went down and got the corn for the garden. I'm bringing between eight and twelve dozen. Two grain bags full. Now if they want me to get them through customs, the guards are going to have to come and pick them up.

TM: Well, I'll ask them. When are you coming?

RLM: Well, truthfully, I want to see ya.

TM: I want to see you too. I'll have to talk to Mrs. Jacobs, but I'll see if one of them can meet you at the…(someone comes into room with Tina, interrupting).

RLM: Ask her if she'll make sure I'll have a place to stay if I come over there. That's cheap.

TM: What do you want? The guards to put you up? We could put you outside, maybe.

RLM: In a tent?

TM: Or maybe be arrested.

RLM: I don't care. I may as well join you.

TM: But you got the corn?

RLM: Yea.

TM: Ok. Well, they'll love that. She asked me about that silver queen.

RLM: Yea, that's what she got. Silver queen. Well, you wanna say hi to mommy?

TM: Yea.

RLM: Alright. Then come back to me and tell me goodnight.

TM: Yes.

RLM: You stinker. I really love you.

TM: I really love you too.

(Short conversation between Tina and her mother, then Robert takes the phone again . . .)

RLM: Hey sweetheart.

TM: Yea?

RLM: Guess what?

TM: What?

RLM: If I'm dating your best girlfriend, she just loaned me $300 for my airplane ticket. That's nice of her (laughs)

TM: Did she really?

RLM: Yea, she gave me $300 when she was up here today to pay my way over to see you. (Laughs) Maybe I'd throw that one back at Leete. (Laughs) Oh God. That guy's insane.

TM: That's the same friend the cop told me that you were having an affair with.

RLM: Yea. (Laughs)

TM: Now that doesn't make sense.

RLM: (Laughs) Oh my god. Um, well, he's trying all these silly games, honey. He probably lays awake trying to sleep, you know, and dreams them up.

TM: Yea.

RLM: You're worth being good a million years…

TM: And keep your hands off my girlfriends.

RLM: (Laughs) You're worth being good for a million years, right?

TM: Ok, give me a kiss.

RLM: I will (kiss sound).

TM: Bye.

RLM: Bye, Bye.

*****

On October 1, 1981, the Bermuda Attorney General, Saul Froomkin, argued that Robert and Ernestine Myers had married in an attempt to prevent official authorities from asking them to testify against each other in the murder proceedings, taking advantage of Maryland's spousal immunity law.

However, her attorney, Alan Dunch, had asked Bermuda Supreme Court Chief Justice James Atwood not to be influenced by what he had heard about the murder proceedings.

Tina had been released from prison, under house arrest, so she could care for her child and await trial on the bigamy charges. It was scheduled for November at the earliest. Her defense to the bigamy charge was to be simply that she thought Marco had obtained an annulment.

Bob was scared that something would happen to Tina in Bermuda, so he wanted to send Dan and Sherrie to protect her. At the last minute, Dan said he would not be able to go because he had to be back in court himself.

On Monday, September 21, 1981, Tina explained to her friend, Mary Ellen, that her children were going to other people's homes while Tina was in Bermuda, and that Tina had to sign in at the police station every day while she was staying with the family in Bermuda as a condition of her being released from prison.

While Tina was under House Arrest, she continued to talk to Robert by phone.

September 18, 1981 phone call to Tina in Bermuda:

TM: Hello

RLM: Tina?

TM: Yes

RLM: Where are you?

TM: What do you mean, where am I?

RLM: Oh, I got everything in order. I got your clothes. I took all three dresses, my suit, got 'em all back. Grocery store and all that.

TM: Oh.

RLM: I talked to Phil again tonight, private phone.

TM: Yea?

RLM: I'll talk to you when I see you.

TM: Ok.

RLM: And on that, everything's in place.

TM: Uh hum. What plans have you made for Brad and Tracey?

RLM: Well, none for sure, but I will tomorrow and I will know tonight.

TM: Did you talk to your brother?

RLM: Yea, he will take Tracey.

TM: Ok.

RLM: And Charlotte's going to take Brad. Jeanne or Dan, one or the other will take mom to the airport.

TM: Ok.

RLM: I mean, you're first in my life.

TM: Yes, dear.

RLM: And all I'm concerned about is getting you home and spending my life with you.

TM: Yes, dear.

RLM: You understand?

TM: Yes, dear.

RLM: I miss you so much tonight, you have no idea.

TM: Oh, yes I do. I miss you too. The baby's kept me up all day. Did you get diapers?

RLM: Yea, I bought more. I got everything. By the time you wake up tomorrow, I might be there.

*****

While Tina was in Bermuda, Bob was recorded on a couple of occasions talking to his own friends and associates.

October 8, 1981 phone call between Robert Myers and Dan Chadderton:

RLM: Where are you at? Are you in the area?

DC: No, you want me in the area?

RLM: Well, what I was gonna tell you is, if you're not, aren't you restricted to Maryland?

DC: No.

RLM: Well if you're not restricted to Maryland, maybe you and Sherrie might want to go over with me?

DC: Sounds good to me.

RLM: Aw Christ, Dan, I'm telling ya man. That common son of a bitch. I never hated no one, but this Leete's for the birds.

RLM: I'm gonna bullshit a little with ya. So ah, you know I've got a lot to tell you, but it's stuff I can't tell ya over the phone.

DC: I know.

RLM: It's about things that, what went on with her over there.

DC: Yea, I know. That's what I want to do . . .

RLM: If I can't be over there, I think you and your wife should be over there. I don't like her to be alone . . .

RLM: You're supposed to help your friends you know, and with anything. Hey, if you are a friend, do me a favor and see if you can lend me a little bit of money. Think you can?

DC: How much you need?

RLM: Well, see if you can borrow, if you can get $300 dollars for me.

DC: Uh hum.

RLM: Ok? Alright? Well try.

DC: Ok.

RLM: Well that will at least help me on an airplane ticket, if you can borrow $300 somewhere.

DC: Ok. . .

RLM: Well, see if you can help me, you know?

DC: Yea, where?

RLM: You wanna stop by the office?

DC: Yea.

RLM: There's no use in being sneaky.

DC: Right, oh, we haven't been.

RLM: I know, but . . .

DC: Why should we?

RLM: That's what I'm sayin'. But if you meet me anywhere other than the office then people will start, you know, saying I'm out drinking and all that shit again.

DC: Yea.

RLM: I'll see ya. But what everybody said, this Leete's just getting desperate. He's been spendin' money and vacationing for two years. And . . .

DC: Yea, he damn sure has.

RLM: (Laughing)

DC: He has one hell of a vacation. Doesn't he?

RLM: (Laughing) Yea, one permanent one. You know? Alright, I'll see you here at the office, Dan. Just come on up, cause I don't want to be seen in any bars or nothin' while she's in jail. You understand me?

DC: Yea, that's right.

*****

Bob was recorded talking to his friend, Ralph Stonesipher—making a very big deal about what awful conditions Tina was forced to endure in Bermuda.

October 14, 1981 phone call between Robert Myers and Ralph Stonesipher:

RLM: Hello.

Ralph Stonesipher: Morning Bob, how are you?

RLM: Oh pretty good. Now I got her out of jail again over there.

RS: I seen the paper . . . (inaudible)

RLM: It ain't right.

RS: Oh, I believe that.

RLM: If I, if I be guilty, I deserve everything I have coming, that's all I'm gonna tell ya.

RS: Uh hum.

RLM: But it's . . . this is not right. You have no idea what that girl's going through with over there.

RS: Well, you too.

RLM: Uh hum.

RS: You, as well as her. That there's a lot of respect against you, that's really something. When you going back again?

RLM: Probably going back soon as I get stuff taken care of here, Ralph.

RS: That's not my business.

RLM: Yes, it is. You're my friend, my God. Um, I'll tell you, I'll be going back as soon as possible cause it's not safe for her over there alone. I had a guard even tell me that in jail people disappear over there and, in other words, her life is in danger over there.

RS: Is that right?

RLM: Yeah. Them guards even told her she was safer in jail than out.

RS: Well, I'll be damned. Is things that bad over there?

RLM: Ralph, you don't know the half of it. Uh, what they done to her.

RS: Hum.

RLM: They had her in a, you know, I can tell you a little bit, but please don't repeat this because if this gets out and gets in the newspaper—

RS: Well, no.

RLM: She'll be killed.

RS: Don't worry about it.

RLM: Uh, they had her in a cell with wooden floors, with big roaches in it.

RS: Yeah?

RLM: And the ants were beating on the roaches. They have lizards crawling all over her at night. Her cot wouldn't even lay flat. They would jump on her and jump on the floor at night, those lizards, six and eight inches long. She went through hell over there, boy.

*****

Not everyone was sympathetic to Robert and Tina's plight. The few remaining employees in his office were angry and bewildered not knowing what to do. Some felt strongly that Myers was guilty, others not sure. One employee in particular, Diana Amspacher, was growing more and more outraged.

October 10, 1981 phone call from Diana Amspacher to Robert Myers:

Diane Amspacher: Hi Bob. I wanna talk to you about the checks that I talked to you about the other Friday. I don't know, I don't know if you want to talk over the phone or not? But I wanna talk to you about this before I see Cpl. Leete.

RLM: Well, it doesn't really matter. You can bring them over here if you want to.

DA: Well, I don't want to come to the office...You, you acted awful.

RLM: I don't care if these phones are tapped. I don't care.

DA: I don't either, because I, you know, I'm fed up. But I just want you to know when he talks to me all this stuff that I've talked to Shelly about . . .

RLM: Uh hum.

DA: And the things I've heard you and Dan talk about, and you and Henry, and he's gonna know it and I don't care cause I'm—

RLM: Well, I don't care either, cause there's nothing to hide.

DA: OK.

RLM: There's nothing to hide.

DA: OK.

RLM: I've never done nothing, or anything else, or anything that you can't tell him.

DA: Alright.

RLM: (laughing)

DA: You think so?

RLM: Yeah. I know so.

DA: OK.

RLM: There's nothing I didn't do.

DA: Alright.

RLM: And anything else. So . . .

DA: OK.

RLM: That's up to you as far as that part goes. Listen, has anybody, umm, is there any clients left, I should get, or anything?

DA: Aww . . . that's, that's gonna be your problem now, you know.

RLM: Uh huh. I was just wondering if anybody you know, anything I should go, you know, if there's anything special. I should go talk to or anything?

DA: Yeah. Will you tell me one thing?

RLM: What's that?

DA: Last year, all this crap you were feeding me all the time about Tina and I asked you . . .

RLM: What crap?

DA: All, all this shit you said, you know, how you, you didn't really get along with her and the way she treated you and all that kind of shit. I wanna know why you told me that if you left her she could tell the cops?

RLM: I never told you that Diane.

DA: BULLSHIT, Bob!

RLM: You're a liar. No, you're just making this up trying to hurt me.

DA: You think I am?

RLM: Yes, you are.

DA: You're a bunch of crap, Bob.

RLM: Yea? You're a liar, Diane—

DA: Who's the liar, Bob?

RLM: You are. You are.

DA: OK.

RLM: We'll see, cause you're a damn liar. I never told you no such thing.

DA: Bob . . .

RLM: I just don't want to talk to you, Diane. You're a damn troublemaker and you really shock me.

DA: Oh really?

RLM: Yeah.

DA: I . . .

RLM: I thought you had these checks for the bank over there and the bank wouldn't take them?

DA: I don't have the checks the bank wouldn't take. I wouldn't touch your stupid checks that the bank wouldn't take.

RLM: Oh, I thought that's where it was?

DA: No, no, no. Huh? Uhhh. You know what checks I'm talking about, and I know damn well they weren't for baby bottles.

RLM: What? The Hell they weren't.

DA: Yea. That's right. Because you don't remember the first story you told me. You don't remember the second or the third, and you don't remember anything right?

RLM: NO!

DA: Right. Right, Bob. Sure.

RLM: No, you're just a bunch of shit.

DA: Uh huh. And what about the other day when I was sitting there and I told you I didn't want to talk to Danny? You brought him in. You tell me you weren't scared that day?

RLM: I wasn't scared at all . . .

DA: Aww . . . no? Uh huh.

RLM: You don't know what you're talking about.

DA: Why did you tell me I was gonna hang ya?

RLM: Yeah, you were. You were just a damn plant in here. To find out all you could all along.

DA: Oh, really?

RLM: And now you're trying to twist everything all around.

DA: You think so?

RLM: I know it, Diane. I know it.

DA: You're a . . . Bob, you're crazy.

RLM: You're the one that's nuts. Just because you got your ass fired for goofin' off . . .

DA: I didn't get my ass fired for goofin' off.

RLM: Trying to make a whole damn month's work last, you know, you had a week's worth trying to drag it out to a month.

DA: Oh, really . . .

RLM: That's what you were doing to me.

DA: You're doing a good job here, but it isn't gonna work anymore.

RLM: Well, that's what you're doin'.

DA: Yea. And who's the Uncle that Dan got the money from to pay you back, Bob? Look . . . Look . . .

RLM: I don't know.

DA: I know, I mean I know this stuff . . .

RLM: I don't know which one it was.

DA: Yeah, sure.

RLM: He's supposed to have two or three of them.

DA: Oh yeah. I bet he does and I bet he really got you the money too. You're giving him the money . . .

. . .

RLM: You're just a liar, Diane.

DA: I'm a liar?

RLM: Yes, you are. You're a bunch of shit. Trying to make a big story out of this . . .

DA: Oh, really?

RLM: That's why you got your ass fired for goofin' off.

DA: Oh, sure I did.

RLM: Yes.

DA: And Nancy and Loretta got their asses fired for goofin' off?

RLM: No. They quit because you did.

DA: Oh, really?

RLM: Uh huh.

DA: You think so?

RLM: Yea.

DA: Uh huh. Did they tell you that?

RLM: No. Either that, or Leete harassed them.

DA: Did they tell you that?

RLM: No, but I'll ask them sometime when they get cooled down here and back here trying to find my way. It's nice for you to all walk out on me like that.

DA: You're damn right it was nice. Look at the shit you're putting us through.

RLM: All you through?

DA: Yea, yea. That's right.

RLM: Awww. No way.

DA: Uh huh. I want…why did you tell me I'm gonna hang you?

RLM: I never told you that at all.

DA: Aww . . . gee, Bob, that's you know . . .

RLM: Diane, you're a big fartin' liar, knock it off.

*****

CHAPTER 8:
BEHIND THE
GRAND JURY CURTAIN

"First of all, ladies and gentlemen . . .
I am here against the advice of my attorney . . ."
— Robert L. Myers

In response to a lawsuit that a newspaper had filed to obtain the autopsy report, State's Attorney Tom Hickman said the autopsy contained important clues he did not want revealed. Additionally, he announced that the State's Attorney's Office had charged Tina Myers with welfare fraud on October 1st, while she was waiting for her hearing in Bermuda.

On November 9, a special Carroll County Grand Jury was impaneled and began hearing testimony in the case. The 25 witnesses included Robert Myers' first wife, former employees at his accounting firm, and employees at the Ocean City motel he owned.

Myers and Chadderton were both summoned to the Grand Jury and testified on November 20, 1981. They had foolishly accepted the challenge. Apparently they had never heard the expression "Loose Lips Sink Ships," nor the biblical admonition from Proverbs 13: "He that keepeth shut his mouth, keepeth his life. But he that opens wide his lips shall have destruction."

Mr. Hickman could not believe his good fortune in their choosing to testify. Myers was chaotically guessing at the State's case, not in any way realizing that his audience had been listening to evidence for almost two weeks. Myers was taken first in the morning, and Chadderton was to testify in the afternoon.

Robert Myers was on the witness stand from 9:45 a.m. to 12:15 p.m. The prosecutors carefully explained his rights to him on the record. They emphasized that he did not have to testify, that nobody was forcing him to testify, and that he had not been promised anything in return for his testimony. They also established that he had retained a lawyer, Phil Sutley, and that he had discussed testifying with his lawyer. In short, the decision to testify was made knowingly and voluntarily.

All twenty-three grand jurors, the court reporter, and the two prosecutors stared at Myers because they could not believe that he was actually on the witness stand in front of them. Cleverly, the prosecutors started their examination by asking Myers if he wanted to make a statement, and after a few moments of awkward silence, Myers began in a rambling, sometimes incoherent, conversational tone while addressing this most attentive audience.

When asked his age, Myers said playfully, "39. I am not getting any older." Before he could be advised of his rights he stated, "First of all, ladies and gentlemen I'd like to make a statement. I am here against the advice of my attorney." The prosecutor interrupted, and Myers repeated, "Well I just wanted to make a statement, Mr. Hickman. I'm here against the advice—he told me to come in here and plead the fifth, but I have nothing to hide, and I'm going against his wish, and I'll answer any of your questions to prove my innocence."

Myers stated that his attorney's name was Phillip Sutley, and repeated, "Phil advised me he couldn't—he would be here late, but if I was going to go against his wish anyway, just to come on in. So, that's what I did." Myers explained that he discussed the situation with his attorney the previous evening. Myers stated that he had not consumed any alcohol, and that he was not on drugs. "Never. Never touched them, Frank," responding to Prosecutor Frank Coleman in this casual manner.

Myers started to ramble. "I'll stay here for a month, if it takes that, to clear your mind up. I'll answer anything you'll ask me. I want you to know that what this Trooper Leete has done, has harassed us for over the past two years. He's busted up our family, he has threatened us. But, the real point is, that wasn't the right way to go about something like that, because this Trooper told Tina that if she did not testify against me for killing my wife, he was going to prosecute her and turn her over to the Bermuda authorities. Now how can she testify against me killing my wife when I knew nothing about the crime? That's just one illustration. He's threatened her with a welfare charge. And that's the phoniest charge there ever was.

"And my wife did not know that I had $12,000, or if she did, she wouldn't have done some of the immoral things she's done. Let's see. Leete's been going around—he told different people he was going to frame me, no matter how long it took. There is word that the State's Attorney's Office was going to manufacture and fabricate evidence just for another stripe I imagine.

"Now, for example, I know that—I don't know how involved the girl [Tina] was with this—some of these crimes, but when Marco testified against her in Bermuda, she said she will testify against him, against the London Vault Job that was never solved, and there was seven men, and five of them are dead. And if this is going to be turned over to the FBI or somebody, and I got to do it myself, I will. He accused my daughter of having an affair with this guy Chadderton, and tells her she's lying. He put poor Charlotte Horton through the third degree. Saying that she's not telling the truth. And the truth is, there ain't nothing to know. And he'll try to put words in your mouth to answer anything he can. And it's all wrong. This Trooper is a very—and I'm sorry, he just don't belong on the force.

"Let's see. I mean, it's hard to remember two years, Tom." There was a long awkward pause, but everyone waited, knowing that Myers was incapable of keeping his mouth shut.

"This Maria, who was supposed to have been in Ocean City, was supposed to have been a friend of Tina's, well, I don't know why Tina did it to this day, but I had the money all in a briefcase and she went into Maria's and opened it up and showed her. Maria said there was $30,000 in there but there was only like $3,000 or $4,000. I don't know where she ever came up with that number. But I might have an idea; there might have been something in the background that might be gangster related, but I'm not sure of that because I haven't really cared about that kind of stuff.

"But, let's see. Trying to tell you all everything, it's hard." There were many long pauses in this rambling speech. "But, when I called her when the little baby girl [Sabrina, his daughter] was born, and I'm not gonna talk vulgar, but when I called from the hospital to tell Maria we had the little girl, Maria said, 'That's an expensive piece of ass, isn't it?' Just like that. And I'm sorry, ladies and gentlemen, but that's what she said. Let's see. I'm trying to tell you all the points. Also, I know for a fact, and I can prove it for a fact, and it will come out, that the prosecutor over in Bermuda, the State Department's been involved—Bermuda was also bribed. I was also blackmailed through this stuff from my first wife's husband.

"And, yes, like this Chadderton family that they think is involved with this thing. I did not know these people. I didn't meet Chadderton formally until this was all over about a month later. And, I think it's sad. Leete caused this man to lose his job, his two girls to starve. About the car that he supposed to have gotten from me—I sold the man the car because I couldn't afford to run a Lincoln no more, after Leete destroyed my business. Let's see. And you could probably go to Westminster Trust to find out how it was paid off and when it was paid off, but I did not do it, as the witness, if the people think it's payment for something or a service or something."

Myers really had no concept of the situation that he was in. These grand jurors had listened to over two-dozen witnesses over the previous two weeks, and had been guided by Tom Hickman and Frank Coleman. The Grand Jury is the province of the prosecutors, and over that length of time are easily controlled and guided by them. Inevitably the grand jurors come to like and respect the prosecutors. They are public servants and are attempting to bring out the truth and come to a just result. After a short while, a "team" atmosphere is developed because, unlike a trial, it is not an adversarial proceeding and there are no confrontations. The grand jurors and prosecutors usually are acting in harmony.

All Hickman had to do was prod Myers every now and again, and allow him to rant and complain about the way he had been treated. Over the course of the next two hours,

Myers proceeded to attack Tina, Chadderton, Cpl. Leete, other state troopers, individual witnesses. And eventually the prosecutors themselves. He even complained about the conduct of one of the "lady jurors."

His references to Tina were grossly inconsistent. He said "You know how barroom talk goes; it's cheap, but the state of mind I'm in today I wouldn't even wipe my hiney on a girl like Tina. There's nothing against all barmaids, but I wouldn't even have dated her in the state of mind I'm in right now." A short while later he said, "My lawyers did advise me against marrying Tina so soon. They told me I better think about it. A local businessman said 'Bob, it's a mistake to marry that girl.' And all that I can say is from the day I met her she was a perfect lady. Until that time I don't think she was worth a shit, putting it bluntly. But I don't think it was all her fault. She told her father, the way I understand what happened, she told her real father that her stepmother was going to bed, screwing the telephone man that was in there. The stepmother said, 'Well, either the kids go or I go,' and they threw the kids out. So there is no doubt about what Leete's dug up, it's all filth and dirt. A lot of it's true. But she's been a lady ever since, and I told her the last time I was over there in Bermuda seeing her, and she cried all night, I said, "I don't know if I'm going to marry you again on not," and I don't, because when I married her my mind was kind of messed up, I guess, or I wouldn't have taken off and missed a fishing tournament like I did."

After expressing his feelings about one topic, he would lose his train of thought and the prosecutors cleverly prompted him and urged him to take his time.

"Uh, shoot—let me think a little bit, Tom, let me think if there is anything else I can tell you all." Tom Hickman responded, "Yeah. We're in no hurry."

Myers expressed particular anger at Cpl. Leete: "He ain't gonna have nobody coming here and talk up for me because he wants an indictment. You will only hear the one side. For every one he brings in here to say bad, I'll bring you 100 to say good. But, I'm telling you, this Trooper Leete has been a real asshole through all this. I think Mr. Hickman's been pretty much of a gentleman through all this. I think Tom's trying to do his best job, but I also think that Tom's been like a mushroom. He's been bullshitted and kept in the dark. I don't believe Mr. Hickman is an unfair man. But Leete has had free vacations, and for two years he's traveled everywhere, he's bribed people, and he's let people off drug charges. Leete slammed his fist down on the desk near my daughter and said, 'Isn't it true you screwed Chadderton? Isn't it true?' My daughter wouldn't do that with the bum. She knows he's a bum, I told her he's a bum. But I feel sorry for the bastard, because he lost his job and stuff. And Leete follows poor Tom Hickman around like Mutt and Jeff. Everywhere that Tom goes, he's up Tom's hiney all the time, trying to tell them some more bullshit.

"Tom, man, I'm sorry, but boy this is hard on me. You understand?" At that point, Myers asked one of the grand jurors for a Kleenex. "Man . . . One of you ladies got a Kleenex around here? . . . But all this circumstantial bullshit, in two years' time they could have framed you, you, and you, and your brother, and anybody else they wanted to frame. And it took them two years because half the shit I forgot by now that they've done to me." After one of the jurors handed him a Kleenex, he said, "I thank you, ma'am. It's a damn wonder I haven't had a heart attack by now. Don't rush me yet, Tom. I'm trying to think if there is more."

Myers then continued, "But I think Leete is just trying to cover his ass, because between you and me, my attorney's got the Department of Justice involved; now we've got the State Department involved and they're on his ass heavy. And if you don't come up with an indictment, or somebody is freed, he'll get fired. But he don't care if I get the gas chamber, just to save him a damn job. And here I am, an innocent bystander, and I get hurt from all this damn bunch of bull."

Myers complained that there were many items, including guns, diamonds, and drugs missing from his house. He said, "They took my porno films. The State Police took my stag films out of my house. I guess it was 50 or 100 of them. And my wife used to have all of these sex gadgets. She would take these Quaaludes, and now I'm gonna defend her, because she had cancer of the colon. She was in a lot of pain, so that's why I really didn't want to bring a lot of this shit out. She would take these Quaaludes and be like a wirley-birley. I'd go home and she'd have all of her clothes off, and she'd be lying there with these vibrators playing with herself. Down in Ocean City, in the motel, she would take a Vaseline jar and be playing with herself and come in and stick her fingers in my face. I mean, come on, she was very vulgar. See what I mean? This goes against me circumstantially, but I'm trying to tell you everything.

"She pulled knives on me two or three times and she almost broke the skin. I just couldn't stand it no more—a woman like that. I just couldn't stand it. So I called the lawyer about three weeks before I took off so I could get a divorce.

"And if I was going to kill somebody when Captain Stu would take us out, I would just give her a little nudge and shove her overboard, you know what I mean? I mean, I don't kill anybody anyway; I'm a lover. We were out on our boat to go fishing and many a time there was a slippery seat right there if I wanted to do her, and the Captain would've never known. He wouldn't even have seen it. I could've done it easily.

"Let's see. And yes, ladies and gentlemen, I did say 'I wish the bitch was dead.' Yes, I did. And who wouldn't, to do the cruel things that she did to me! Ain't a man in here that wouldn't say that; they rub a stinking finger in your face and stuff. I couldn't take it. I must've told a hundred people that, but not really thinking it would happen for Christ's sake. She just needed help. She was in so much pain; she was on those drugs so heavy."

"I heard from Sherrie Chadderton, one of the people who may be accused in this thing, that Leete walked out of this Grand Jury with his arms around one of the ladies here in the Grand Jury. I think that's sick—the trooper investigating? I don't know which one of you that was, but you're all supposed to keep an honest opinion and listen to all the facts, not because somebody wants something to happen. I think it's wrong, and if it's true, if it's any one of you ladies that's guilty of that, it's because Leete wanted you to bring phony charges against me. And another thing about Leete, he farts in people's faces. He asks them if they want to hold his thing when he goes to the bathroom. And I can prove all these facts. And yes, I'm telling you the truth, and you all know it because nobody has the balls enough to say it, but I do now.

"One of the members of the ambulance crew told me that Mary Ruth was dressed in a sexy negligee. Why that, when she was alone? I don't think she would do it just to play with herself. Maybe you all can answer that question for me. I mean, I would like to know. I went to the funeral; I went to the graveyard and I stood beside her mother. Man, what a sad experience. I went down to the home. What really hurt me more than anything was that Mary Ruth's son, Dale, wouldn't even shake my hand. That hurt after all I've done for them doggone kids . . . paid for their weddings, and bought them cars and everything. That's real gratitude!"

"I do not want to tell you who Mary Ruth was having an affair with at this time, because I'm not sure whether she was too high on Quaaludes or not, but I would like to reserve the right to answer that at this time. If that would be a determining factor, then I will answer it. I was afraid Mary Ruth would have me on an adultery charge before I got a chance to get the paper signed. She wasn't having sex with me. She was using these artificial things. That doesn't say much for me, I guess, and this did upset me. That's why I left my first wife. I was married to her for thirteen years and only saw her in the nude just five times.

"My relationship with Dan became closer because Leete would put the fear of God into anybody who had contact with me. I helped the Chadderton's out by giving them $10 or $20 here and there. We bought them groceries. We fed them. Frank, I would help you out if you need help. I help anybody, do you understand? I mean, he's not the type of person I want to be associated with, let me tell you that, because he's a bum; he ain't working.

"I did not give Dan the thousand dollars so he could buy a motorcycle. But, Tom, I'm going to have to call you a liar to your face if you say I gave him more than that.

"Frank, I never said I hated her. I did maybe say I'd like to get rid of her and I may have said that if I wanted to, I could have her killed. But I never said that if I thought I could get away with it, I would kill her.

"I married Tina to save her kids. I didn't really give her a car but, yes, the Mercedes-Benz is in her name and has license plates 'T. Myers.' The car cost $37,000. From the day I met her, she's been good. But if I'm going to be harassed and have problems all my life, and have what she's done in the past haunt me and all this, then I will not remarry her. I did tell people that she cheated with Alan Fox but he even told me that himself. That's just one of them. Christ, I don't know how many men she went with that I found out about later. The state of mind I was in, Tom, at the time, the state of mind I was in, I may have done any damn thing at the time. When I took off with her I probably would have taken off with a snake. I was so hurt and stuff."

When a grand juror asked him a question about the missing money, Myers said, "I feel like you should be sitting over here beside these two gentlemen." Myers explained how embarrassing it was in the Court in Bermuda when Marco stood up and said "She's my wife!" Myers said, "Here I am sitting back in the courtroom saying, 'Well, I thought she was my wife.' That's a hell of a situation to be in too. It's embarrassing.

"At the time I married Tina, I didn't even know her last name. I was messed up in the head. If I gave up my fishing tournament I was supposed to fish in—I married her just strictly to save her children. It was sick. If Tina had anything to do with the murder of my wife, I hope she pays her dues. If she does, then sock it to her. If she did, then sock it to her!"

While discussing how unfair State Troopers could be, he complained they would give traffic tickets unnecessarily and unjustly. He said, "75% of them were committing adultery. In The Bible there are 10 Commandments, and they don't say murder is worse than adultery. It doesn't say that in there. And how these men can go out here and stop and give people tickets when they're out here cheating on their wives and stuff I'll never know. And that's what you ladies and gentlemen should investigate. Get these Troopers and punish them when they commit adultery and cheat and stuff. Throw them off the force."

Myers said, "I'll stay here for a month, if it takes that to clear your mind up." Myers concluded by saying, "If you all want me to come back, just let me know. I really mean that." When he left the room, Hickman and Coleman just looked at each other in amazement. The Grand Jurors broke out in many loud separate conversations. There was a lot of laughter and they waited for the prosecutors to say something to them, but Hickman simply smiled and said. "Be back at 2:00 p.m. and we'll see what Chadderton has to say."

Chadderton testified that afternoon. He explained that he used to work as a night crew clerk for the Pantry Pride but he had been unemployed for about two years. The prosecutors explained his rights not to testify and the right to consult with an attorney. They went through the rights that he was waiving by appearing there.

He said that the Pantry Pride was across from Franklin High School, and that he had worked the graveyard shift from about midnight to 8:30 a.m. He explained that he personally met Robert Myers for the first time at a birthday party at his house "to get to know the gentleman." He said that he had been invited along with his wife and his children to attend a birthday party for Mrs. Myers' children, and that it took place outside in July 1980.

He said that he first met Tina Myers when she used to stop in the store at night. He claimed they never dated. When asked if he had ever picked her up in a car, he responded, "Not to my knowledge . . . not to my . . . no . . . not to my knowledge." He said that the store was open 24 hours a day and that,

"If I recollect, I think she was tending bar or something to that effect, and she would come in off to work and stuff and, shop." He said that he had been to Bob Myers' house several times in the past year. When asked if he had ever visited Tina Myers at the house, he said, "Not to my recollection, no." When asked if he had ever talked to her while she was in the Dunkin' Donuts, he said he had. "I said hello. Every day, whatever you say to a lady." He repeated that he had never been intimate with her, and when asked by a grand juror if he had ever slept with her, he said no.

He explained that in August 1979, he inquired with Tina about purchasing a car, a Torino. At one point, Chadderton said, "I notice an ashtray here. Can I smoke?" Hickman responded sure. Chadderton was shown the receipt where he had purchased his new motorcycle on August 24, 1979, and he recognized it and indicated he'd paid a down payment of $1,000. He said he had saved that amount and that they were small bills, tens and "various ones." He indicated he has saved $2,200 over the past three years. He denied that he was behind on a lot of bills initially, but when pressed, he indicated that he did have bills.

When asked if he purchased a leather jacket on August 24, he said he had, and that after he bought the bike he also bought a new helmet. He said he owned a motorcycle when he had bought this one and that he sold it to his brother for $500, just before the bought this new motorcycle.

He admitted that his pay was being garnished by Sinai Hospital, and that he had paid Sinai off. He did not recall that after he had met with Tina and Robert on August 23, 1979, he went back into the store and said to his co-workers, "What do you think a human life is worth?" He did not recall asking them what they thought the mafia got for a contract killing.

He said that in the early morning hours of August 20, a Wednesday, he was at home. He said he knew that because he was a CB operator and ordinarily he would've been at work, except his wife had come out of the hospital on August 13 after surgery, and he had stayed home to mind the children. He told the jurors that the children were five and two. He claimed he had fudged the time card at the Pantry Pride store, indicating that he had worked, when in fact he was at home "waiting on her, giving her whatever she needed."

He admitted that he'd been to Ocean City on August 28. Tina had left him an Ocean City number to call and he did. He was supposed to call her to let her know about the car. He explained that it was necessary to "break in" the motorcycle because the engine was sluggish. He went to Ocean City to look for "Mrs.—for Tina," and went to the Ocean View Motel looking for Mr. Myers because he thought the Torino was in his name. However, he said, he had not personally met Mr. Myers at that point. When he got to the motel he asked many people if Mr. Myers was around and they said no. This was just before lunchtime, and he never saw either of them. When he returned in the early morning hours, he tried to call several times. He admitted that Tina Myers had called the Pantry Pride at 12:56 a.m. on the night of August 28, and had called again at 2:16 a.m. and said they talked for five minutes.

He testified that the next day he called her at 5:20 a.m. to inform her that there was no need for her to hold the car for him. When a grand juror asked, "At 5:20 in the morning?" Chadderton said, "Of course." The Grand Juror questioned this response and Chadderton responded, "Sure." Chadderton explained that he talks to a lot of people early in the morning, and when asked if he had only talked to Tina he said, "I'm not sure. I think I talked to Tina." Hickman asked, "Did you talk to Bob Myers?" Chadderton responded, "Not to my knowledge." Hickman showed him telephone records demonstrating that Tina had talked to him on August 28 at 12:56 a.m. for nine minutes, on August 28 at 2:16 a.m. for five minutes, and then on August 28 at 7:03 p.m. Chadderton said he did not know what the calls were about "other than the Torino."

Hickman asked why Chadderton had been unemployed for two years, and Chadderton responded, "You should know that, Mr. Hickman! Well it's kinda hard to get a good job when there's somebody always on your back—you fill out an application, somebody walks in behind you." Chadderton complained that the State Police had been on his back.

Chadderton admitted he had gone to Marshall, Texas. He maintained that he was looking for work. He said that he was working part-time for Bob Myers, and that while he was in Texas he checked out "a few computer systems through ITT." He wasn't sure who he talked to because he went to a lot of different places. He went to Houston and Marshall, and he was "looking into some computers for Bob Myers." He admitted he stayed in a couple of hotels down there.

He denied that he told anyone that he'd "break bones" for Bob Myers. Hickman asked, "Did you ever tell anybody you were a contract killer, Mr. Chadderton?" Chadderton responded, "Not to my knowledge, no." Hickman said, "Not your knowledge? Well, if you told someone that, you'd remember it wouldn't you?" Chadderton said, "Yes, I would."

When challenged again about the reason for going to Texas, he repeated while he was there he went to check and see how the prices and things were running on computers. When asked what kind of computer training he had, he said he can run any register, any type of register, and cash registers are all computerized. He said he didn't need computer training.

Chadderton admitted that he had purchased the 1977 Lincoln Continental from Robert Myers. He said he had paid $2,600 for it in October of 1980. He maintained that he had purchased it in cash. He said he got the money because "I gamble a lot." He said he didn't get the whole $2,600 in gambling. He'd gotten some for errands and said he got "pocket money" for being a "courier." When challenged, he said, "I picked up the paperwork and stuff, because I can't get a job. He's helped me out," referring to Myers. He said sometimes Myers pays him "gas money, and maybe $20 or $30 or something like that. But not too often—once in a while."

He said, "Sometimes I pick up paperwork and stuff and take them down to Baltimore." He gets paid $20 or $30 per run. But it was not every week. He maintained that he had to sell the car, and sold it for a little more than $2,000. Chadderton admitted that he had the title to Myers' car signed over to him. He maintained that he sold the car in Los Angeles, but that he still owed Bob about $1,500. The receipt indicated that Myers had sold the car for $6,500. When Chadderton was challenged, he said, "It's a possibility. I could still owe him $4,000 but whatever it is, I will work it out and pay him back."

He said that before he went to Texas, Myers had given him $300 in cash. While he was there he admitted he had called Myers and asked for him to send some money so he could come back. Western Union records showed he had received $400. Hickman asked again how much money had Bob Myers given him over the last two years, and the response was, "I don't know." Hickman said, "You got $800 on the Texas deal right?" Chadderton agreed, and Hickman responded, "You got $4,000 so far on the car?"

When shown the time records from the Pantry Pride that indicated that Chadderton had worked there on August 29, Chadderton acted confused and said he wasn't sure, but it was a possibility. He then again he said he was at home with his wife on August 29. He tried to claim that you can get over on the company when you put in an hour or two, but that he didn't recall, and that the company very rarely checked the timesheets. Again, Chadderton repeated, "I was home all that night. I got in from Ocean City—it was about six in the evening and I just lay down for a couple of hours. I would call work and tell them I'm taking the night off."

Chadderton was excused and he said, "Thank you, Mr. Hickman. Looking at the jurors, he said, "And, thank you."

During the testimony from Daniel Chadderton, Robert Myers returned and requested to appear before the Grand Jury again. He said he wanted to call a witness to prove to the jury that some information presented earlier was false and fabricated. The accused, however, may not present any evidence to a grand jury. The Grand Jury is peculiarly the province of the prosecutor, and only he presents evidence to it. The function of a grand jury is to hear evidence only on behalf of the prosecution and, if the necessary burden has been met by the state, return an indictment against the accused.

Since the prosecutors and jurors were tired and had what they needed, Myers' request to appear again was denied. So, Myers waited and then he left the courthouse with Daniel Chadderton.

A few days later, Myers left for Bermuda to be with Tina and their baby daughter, Sabrina Renee Myers. Chadderton had been named the child's god-father, in yet another massive error in judgment.

CHAPTER 9:
THE ARRESTS

"Why does Phil keep putting me off on trial?"
— Robert L. Myers

Myers had traveled to Bermuda to be with Tina and Sabrina for Thanksgiving. He had taken all the traditional trappings with him, including a large turkey. In his absence, the indictments were returned against Chadderton, Tina, and himself. When Phil Sutley telephoned his clients to inform them, they were not surprised. They said that they would voluntarily return to Maryland, and Sutley informed the State's Attorney.

Cpl. Leete and another State Trooper flew to Bermuda on November 25, 1981, in order to escort Robert Myers to Maryland. They met at the airport, but Myers was not formally arrested until their plane landed on Maryland soil at the Baltimore-Washington International Airport. When they emerged from the Eastern Airlines terminal, Myers had his gray overcoat draped over his hands, which were handcuffed in front of him. Myers was dressed in a dark blue three-piece suit, with a white shirt, and a striped tie. His blond hair looked disheveled, but his suit was immaculately pressed and he seemed in good spirits.

He laughed as he answered the reporters' questions, even appearing to make a joke: "What are you guys doing here?" he asked Cpl. Leete. Phil Sutley had been waiting at the airport with the reporters for two hours and had told them, "This case is the most complex of any of the more than 100 murder cases I have handled over the years." It was going to get more complex than he could imagine.

Myers had been interviewed by telephone by the Carroll County Evening Sun when he was in Bermuda, and had said, "I'll come back. I've got nothing to hide." Apparently unperturbed by the situation, he joked with his lawyer Phil Sutley, "Phil, did you call these guys? I told them I would come back and here I am." The reporters loved the fact that Myers was making comments because they were gearing up for what they knew would be a sensational case. There had already been a lot of press coverage and the next day, the public's prurient interest in the case would be further titillated by the media. One front page article declared "Businessman and Stripper/Lover Indicted In the Hit Murder of Wife."

Sutley said he expected his client to go before a Carroll County District Court Commissioner, and that later that day they would appear before a District Court Judge for a bail review hearing. He added that if bail was denied he would immediately seek an appeal in the County Circuit Court.

The next day the newspapers reported that "the Myers' attorney said he expects a lot of motions would be filed before this case comes to trial." Sutley added, "On behalf of Mr. Myers and his wife Tina, I want to tell you that they say they are innocent and I believe them. I intend to do everything possible to prove their innocence." He said that he was not surprised that the State was seeking the death penalty for Robert Myers and that he had prepared him for that possibility.

At the bail hearing, Cpl. Leete told the packed courtroom that Myers had warned him that he had taken out contracts to have both him and Carroll County State's Attorney Tom Hickman killed. Myers had told him during the flight from Bermuda that "I'm going to outlive you and Hickman. I have contracts out on both of you." Sutley asked Leete if his client seemed inebriated on the plane, and Leete responded yes, but he added he did not believe Myers' condition influenced his statement. "That's his normal pattern" of talking, the Corporal said.

Leete also told Judge Donald S. Smith that during his twenty-seven-month investigation of the murder, Robert Myers had been a primary suspect from the start, and that Myers had "demonstrated mental instability." Bail was denied, and Sutley filed an appeal to the Circuit Court.

Cpl. Leete, along with State Trooper Vicky Lutz, flew back to Bermuda a few days later to return Tina and her five-month-old daughter to Maryland.

Once the jet landed at BWI, Tina was formally arrested, placed in handcuffs and taken before the District Court in Westminster.

On December 1, 1981, the State's Attorney's office announced that while "no lawyer had yet entered an appearance on behalf of Mrs. Tina Myers, she was to be represented by "her husband's lawyer Philip Sutley" at the bail hearing which was scheduled for December 3, 1981.

At the bail hearing, Tina Myers laughed silently when Cpl. Leete testified that some witnesses and her husband had told him that she had shown a picture to them of her "Godfather," and that she had said she had organized crime connections in the city of Chicago and Las Vegas. Sutley could not resist asking Leete whether or not he had ever had a godfather. Leete admitted that he did at one time.

Bail was set at $750,000 and she was then taken to the Baltimore City Jail to await trial. Robert Myers was incarcerated in the Carroll County De-tention Center, a nice place by comparison. Tina Myers, 29, complained that the State Trooper had made their lives miserable and that the publicity had ruined Mr. Myers' accounting business. Tina added that she and Robert Myers had been treated as suspects from the beginning and Leete had begun ques-tioning her, and then Robert Myers, about his wife's death immediately after he had visited the funeral home. She added that Cpl. Leete said he would have the bigamy charge dropped if she would testify against her husband.

Phil Sutley told reporters he believed the investigation was misdirected. He said blame for the Myers' misery rested on Cpl. Leete's shoulders. Cpl. Leete "is way out of bounds here. The trooper has wasted taxpayer money traveling to eleven states and Bermuda to investigate the murder."

Mrs. Tina Myers told the reporters, "We got married so I could get my children. My two children from a previous marriage were in foster homes because I could not afford rent, make a living, or pay for babysitters on my bartending salary."

Daniel Chadderton was also arrested that week, and a bail hearing was conducted by Judge Luke Burns Jr., who set bail at $250,000. State's Attorney Thomas Hickman had argued for no bail, indicating that Chadderton had of-fered to kill another person "for several thousand dollars plus expenses earlier that year, for a Carroll County resident, interested in having a New Orleans resident murdered." While that contract had never been fulfilled, it showed, according to the prosecutor, how dangerous Chadderton was. Hickman also said that Chadderton had threatened several times to kill Cpl. Leete. Tom Ward, a Baltimore lawyer representing Chadderton, argued that his client was a devoted husband and father who would not flee and was not a danger to society. He claimed, in fact, that Chadderton was a hero because he had saved the life of an elderly woman in 1973. He explained that Chadderton had carried an elderly woman out of a burning building where she had been robbed and tied up. Because of him, the woman escaped certain death. "Are these the actions of a cold-blooded killer?" the lawyer asked. It helped a bit—he got bail.

While in their respective jails, Tina and Robert were still able to communicate. In a letter to Tina on December 9, 1981, Robert Myers wrote:

```
Hi Dearest,
I love you. Tell Phil to set up a phone call to me between
11:30 and 1:00. You call Phil's office and we can talk to
each other on that conference phone. Remember, Phil can hear
what we say. Why does Phil keep putting me off on trial? Do
you think we are having twins? If so, I get two "juniors"
right? If Phil wanted us to talk he could have arranged it
through his office on a conference call before this. I'll
continue to treat you like a queen, which you are.
Your husband, Bobby. XXOOXXOO
```

*****

On the 23rd of December, 1981, Sutley appeared on behalf of Robert Myers in open court to determine Myers' eligibility for representation by the Office of the Public Defender. Sutley explained to Myers that he would always be his lawyer, but that for public purposes—and to be able to use the resources of the Public Defender's Office—Sutley would represent only Tina publicly while Robert would be represented by a Public Defender. He informed Myers that even though there was no actual conflict between Myers and Tina, the court would not likely permit him to represent both. The judge would say that there was an appearance of a conflict and that it would not look good.

In order to show that Myers was impoverished and had no funds left to hire a private attorney, Sutley called Tom Stansfield Esq., Myers' business lawyer, as a witness to establish that Myers was bankrupt. The Court determined Myers was eligible to have a lawyer appointed to represent him. Once that was accomplished, Sutley and Stansfield convinced Myers to allow them to conduct an auction of all the personal items located in the house where Mary Ruth had been murdered.

The State's Attorney walked across the courtroom and handed Sutley a Notice of Intention to Seek Death, and Sutley said politely, "Thank you." When asked by Myers to see it, Sutley whispered, "I will show it to you later," and placed the death notice in his file. While nobody had been executed in Maryland for some time, there were ten people waiting on death row. Not the Christmas Myers was hoping for.

CHAPTER 10:
THE AUCTION

"Do I hear eight dollars for this box of Kleenex from the second bedroom?"
— Auctioneer

On January 2, 1982, more than a thousand people mobbed the hilltop estate to stroll through the house and gawk at the mirror accented master bedroom, and try to outbid their neighbors for furniture to cart home in the back of their pick-up trucks. Bargain hunters and thrill seekers alike packed the front yard of the Myers' home for the Saturday auction. A few shivering people sat around the living room inside to escape the wind. 500 had registered to bid on items, but more than 1,000 people turned out for a chance to look at the scene of the murder.

It started at 9:30 a.m., but avid auction fans began showing up before 8 a.m. Vehicles of every description were parked several layers deep on the yard outside the house. And those who were not there on time were forced to find parking a half-mile away. A line of parked cars and trucks snaked both sides of the long drive down the hill to Turkey Foot Road. From there, cars were parked on both sides of the rural lanes, heading in all directions. When people made it up the hill, they were treated to a breathtaking view. The brick house rests just above a vineyard overlooking Silver Run Valley. Far below, alternating patches of farmland and woodland roll in every direction in a picture postcard view. The auction was seen as a social event, with crowds touring the house.

Carroll County had never seen anything like the carnival that took place at the Myers' house in Silver Run Valley. While household auctions were a common social event in the rural county, the Myers' auction was different because the two owners were very much alive during the sale of these personal belongings. Robert Myers was ten miles away in his cell in the Carroll County Detention Centre in Westminster, and Tina Myers was thirty miles away in her cell in the Women's Detention Center in Baltimore.

With all the unusual circumstances, the public sale became much more than a routine auction. To the locals it was an event not to be missed. Of course, no one admitted they were there to get a look at the murder bedroom, or to buy a souvenir so they could say to their friends, "Yes, this used to belong to Bobby Myers." No one would admit that, but they said that's why everyone else was there.

The prices seemed to support the theory that many people saw souvenir value in the items. For example: a package deal consisting of a plastic dish rack, some disheveled straw flowers and a broken light fixture that looked like it was rescued from the trash was $37.50. A box of mismatched slightly soiled towels was bargain at $30. People got completely carried away and caught up in the bidding.

Mary Ruth had been discovered in the huge master bedroom. Furnished now with a new carpet, the room showed no signs of Mary Ruth Myers' violent death. It contained a motor-powered king-sized bed, which contorted to various positions, like a hospital bed. Where the 12-foot walls met the ceiling, mirrors were angled at 45 degrees to reflect the bed. Most of the wall at the head of the bed was covered with mirrors. The doors of the closets in the adjacent dressing room and the double doors leading from the bedroom were also adorned with mirrors.

Some people drank coffee while others sipped on cans of beer. Many admired the view from the house—rambling hills and pastures were visible in all directions.

In spirited bidding, the bed went for $750, and a set of reddish satin sheets and a comforter went for $83. Adjacent to the master bedroom, a large bath featured a red bidet and a large sunken bathtub with two gold spigots. The bath was equipped with gold Jacuzzi nozzles that rotated to direct streams of vibrating water where desired. Signs of love in the home abounded: a red plush chair with a heart-shaped valentine back, a picture of two children with the boy kissing a girl on the forehead, and a statue of a nude man and woman embracing, entitled, "The Kiss." Printed on two coffee mugs in gold letters was the phrase, "He who has the gold makes the rules."

In the bathroom next to the master bedroom, people posed for photos in the bright red sunken bathtub, with its gold tone fixtures, including submerged water jets. Outside, beyond the bathroom's sliding glass doors, one family was having a picnic lunch on the brick enclosed patio.

Meanwhile in the kitchen, the women from St. Mary's Lutheran Church dished out hot dogs, coffee and other drinks. Before noon they went through seventy-five pounds of hot dogs and countless gallons of coffee. Robert Myers had belonged to that church at one time. Around lunch time, hungry shoppers patiently waited up to half an hour in lines that wound through the house.

People crowded the rooms and talked about the murder while the auctioneers sold furniture, children's toys, stuffed animals, goblets, appliances and firearms.

In the formal dining room, some older women set up camp around a large table as they settled in for a talk. In the main living room, small children watched cartoons on television as their parents made themselves at home among the plush furnishings. A man in stained overalls plopped himself down in a delicate wingback chair and contentedly chewed on a fat cigar. One topic of discussion was a foot sized hole in the living room ceiling. Robert Myers had said in a previous interview that when he returned from vacation to his locked home, he found the hole. He believed investigators caused the damage.

A converted kerosene lamp brought $130; a covered bowl commanded $100. A four foot stuffed giraffe brought $17.50. Bidding continued on those and thousands of other items for the entire day. After most of the larger items were sold, including big-ticket pieces like a grandfather clock that sold for more than $1,400, the auction moved to the two-car garage, holding tables full of knickknacks among more substantial equipment. The auctioneers began throwing odds and ends into boxes for package deals as darkness made it increasingly difficult to spot bids. Some onlookers stared in disbelief as bidding escalated like a wild panic on some boxes full of unknown utensils. A box where only a rolling pin was revealed sold for more than $20. It seemed everyone wanted a souvenir and would pay inflated prices for ordinary household wares. "Do I hear 8 dollars for this box of Kleenex from the second bedroom?" Two local newspapers sent reporters and photographers. Almost everything was sold.

Finally, at 6 p.m., it was over. The huge lawn looked like a circus had been through. Paper cups and other trash were spread everywhere, but everyone seemed satisfied. Sutley and Stansfield, who had both been present all day, and the auctioneers were happy with the proceeds. At the auction, "checks were made out to Phil Sutley," the newspapers reported the next day. "Proceeds from the sale were to pay off debts and meet investigative and legal fees that Mr. Myers faced in defending himself against first degree murder charges."

The auctioneer's skilled manipulation of this crowd was energized by the "magic of murder." Although the house had been lived in for years, parts of it were still not finished. Contrasting with this disarray were nearly fifty rose bushes flourishing in the yard.

Approximately $30,000 was raised, however, there was never any accounting made to Myers. Stansfield brought that amount in cash, a week later, to Sutley's law office to be applied to his fee. No receipt was ever provided to Robert Myers.

Myers lived quite an extravagant lifestyle up until, and during his marriage to Tina. Now more than fifty creditors, including jewelry dealers, furriers, department stores, and banks were waiting to get their money. Within days of the auction, Myers' office furniture was being moved out of the large brick office building on North Center Street near the Carroll County Courthouse. The Turkey Foot Road house in Silver Run Valley sold for $205,000 a few months later. The proceeds went to Phil Sutley. The North Winds Motel was purchased for $425,000. The Rock Brook Trailer Park in Hampstead, which Mr. Myers also owned, was sold for $325,000. The boat Myers owned went to Sutley as further payment for his legal fees. The outstanding debts reflected both waste and sentiment. There were $25,000 worth of outstanding jewelry bills alone, including one for a 21-carat aquamarine ring, surrounded by full cut diamonds.

One group that attended the auction, however, was very unhappy and only there reluctantly. They were searching through the long halls and spacious rooms. They went to the auction to find personal belongings they were not allowed to take after the murder. They looked for pictures and other items that belonged to Mary Ruth. Mary Ruth's children were looking for photos and other items belonging to them and Mary Ruth..

Mary Ruth's four children filed a $3 million lawsuit against the three people charged with carrying out her murder. They had been considering it for almost two years but had waited so they wouldn't interfere with the criminal investigation. It claimed that Chadderton, Myers, and Marco caused "wrongful death" in total disregard for the rights and life of Mary Ruth Myers, and in utter disregard to the rights of the plaintiffs, who constituted all of the natural children of Mary Ruth—people who were entitled to and did enjoy her aid, assistance, and maternal care. By the time the case came to trial a few years later, there were no assets left.

Mary Ruth Myers (center), Tina Myers (right), Robert Myers (bottom),
Daniel Chadderton (left).

(Top) The murder scene at 4636 Turkey Foot Road, Silver Run Valley, Westminster, Carroll County, Maryland; (Bottom) The front door to 4636 Turkey Foot Road.

(Next page, clockwise) The Pantry Pride Store, Reisterstown, Maryland; A Thank You note Robert Myers placed in the local newspapers, September 4, 1979; The receipt for the cash down payment on the killer's new motorbike, purchased a few days before the murder.

ORDER SUBJECT TO PRESENT AND FUTURE GOVERNMENT REGULATIONS

MOTORCYCLE ORDER FORM

NATIONWIDE
1737 EAST JOPPA ROAD
BALTIMORE, MD. 21234
PHONE: (301) 668-5100

P R I D E

Come out ahead with Nationwide

DATE 8-24-79

PURCHASER'S NAME DANIEL LEE CHADDERTON   HONDA   Kawasaki

PURCHASER'S ADDRESS 1211 WELDON AVE BALTO MD   ZIP CODE 21-211

RESIDENCE PHONE 467-0038   BUSINESS PHONE

PLEASE ENTER MY ORDER FOR (1) New / Used   1979 HONDA CB750K
                                              YEAR MAKE MODEL

FRAME NO. RC01-2018151   TO BE DELIVERED ON OR ABOUT____ SALESMAN K.S

USED MOTORCYCLE TRADE IN INFORMATION			CASH DELIVERED PRICE OF MOTORCYCLE		
YEAR	MAKE		CASH DELIVERED PRICE OF MOTORCYCLE		
MODEL	SERIES		ACCESSORIES	$	
FRAME NO.			SAFETY BAR		
MILEAGE			LUGGAGE RACK		
BALANCE OWED TO	N/A		BACK REST K+G		
ACCOUNT NO.			COMBO RACK & REST		
ADDRESS			CUSTOM SEAT		
PAYOFF BALANCE $	GOOD TILL		HELMETS 1 BUCO		
GIVEN BY			EXTENDED WARRANTY		
	S.F.D. 2090				
USED CYCLE ALLOWANCE	$		VETTER FAIRING		
BALANCE OWED ON USED CYCLE	$				
EQUITY + OR –	$				
CASH WITH ORDER 14893	$	100000			
TOTAL CREDIT (Transfer to right column)		100000			

INSURANCE INFORMATION					
COMPANY NAME	PURITAN INS				
AGENT NAME	MANOR INS AGENCY		SUB-TOTAL	$ 3267 65	
BINDER NO	1195		LOCAL TAXES (If Any)	163 35	
EFFECTIVE DATE			TRANSFER & DOCUMENTARY FEE	15 00	
	D.O.B. 6-26-58		STATE LICENSE FEE	10 00	
DRIVER'S LICENSE NO	C-363 135 497 500		TOTAL OF ABOVE ITEMS	3456 00	
DATE OF BIRTH	55-765 524-878 1-16-59		TOTAL CREDIT (Transferred from Left Column)	1000 00	
DISPOSITION OF OLD CYCLE	B-261-76-298-070 1-26-33		BALANCE DUE 36 mon	$ 2456 00	

I have read the matter on the face hereof and agree to it as part of this order the same as if it were printed above my signature.
The least hereof compromises the entire agreement affecting this order and no other agreement or understanding of any nature
concerning same has been made or entered into. I hereby acknowledge receipt of a copy of this order.

THIS ORDER IS NOT BINDING UNTIL ACCEPTED BY DEALER

PURCHASER'S SIGNATURE X Daniel Lee Chadderton

St. Andrew's Presbyterian Church, "The Pink Church", outside and interior.
Pembroke, Bermuda.

(Left) Robert Myers and Tina Marco getting married in St. Andrew's on September 26, 1979; (Right) Tina Marco in her wedding gown, praying at the rehearsal, Bermuda, September 25, 1979.

(Left) Tina Marco praying on a bible, Bermuda, September 25, 1979; (Right) Tina Marco Myers, after the wedding, in her nightgown, Bermuda, September 26, 1979.

s. baltimore and somerset
ocean city, md. 21842
phone (301) 289-4171

lee graham's
jewelers

Insurance Appraisal

8|9|80
(Date)

Property of: _Mrs Tina Myers_   1-876-1996

P O Box 267

Westminster, Md 21157

To Whom It May Concern:

I have this date examined the below described item and appraise it at present estimated replacement value

$56,475.00

DESCRIPTION

One pear Shaped diamond as follows:
Cut - Pear shape - good symmetry
Color - fine white
Clarity - I,
Weight - 5.02ct @ $11,250.00 per carat or $56,475.00

Deft's Exh. #5
Date 4-22-82
No. 1734   Law
           Equity
           Crim'l. Trials

_____
LEE H. GRAHAM

(Above) The jewelers' appraisal for the wedding gift.

(Left) Tina Marco Myers wedding gift, a $56,000, 5-karat pear shaped diamond ring.

The Bermuda Parliament and Supreme Court Building, Hamilton, Bermuda.

Tina and Robert Myers, with baby Sabrina, and their Bermuda lawyer,
Alan Dunch.

Indicted Myers returns fro[m]

State Police Cpl. James M. Leete, left, escorts Robert Lee Myers, under indictment in the murder of his first wife, on flight from Berm

News article November 26, 1981. Robert Myers is returned to Maryland from Bermuda.

Murder suspect returns

State Police Cpl. James Leete and Tfc. Vicki   known as Tina Myers) through BWI terminal
Lutz, right, escort Brunel be Marco (also   after her arrival from Bermuda. Story on D 2.

By Joseph DiPaola—Evening Sun Staff

News article December 1, 1981. Tina Myers is returned to Maryland from Bermuda.

Bargain hunters and thrill seekers alike pack the front yard of the Robert Myers home for a Saturday auction, while a few shivering souls, below, take respite inside from the wind.

Magic of murder draws multitude to Myers auction

By Mark Parrent
Evening Sun Staff

Carroll Countians always have flocked to household auctions, but everyone agreed they never had seen anything like the carnival at the Myers place in Silver Run.

More than 1,000 people mobbed the hilltop rural estate Saturday to stroll through the house, gawk at the mirror-accented master bedroom and perhaps even outbid their neighbors for furniture to cart home in the back of their pick-ups.

Household auctions are a common social event in this rural county. They usually follow the death of someone with a big old house full of possessions gathered over a lifetime.

But the Myers auction was different. The two owners were very much alive during the sale of their personal belongings.

One, Robert Myers, spent the day 10 miles to the south in his cell in the county jail in Westminster. Ernestine Marco, the other owner, was in the

Women's Detention Center at the Baltimore City Jail.

Along with Baltimore resident Daniel Lee Chadderton, they are charged with first-degree murder in connection with the alleged contract killing of Myers' wife, Mary Ruth.

She was found shot to death in the master bedroom of the Silver Run home in 1979.

In the months after the killing, business dwindled at Myers' Westminster accounting firm. And, if anything, his expenses increased as his income disappeared.

Myers had married Marco shortly after his wife's death, but late last year Marco pleaded guilty to bigamy in Bermuda. Expenses related to that case helped push up debts to an unmanageable level.

And prospects of an expensive defense in the murder trial pushed Myers over the brink.

Through Westminster attorney Thomas Stansfield, Myers filed for a

[Continued, Page D4, Col. 1]

Evening Sun news article about the auction at Myer's house. January 4, 1982. The Magic of Murder.

Newspaper photograph of the thousand person crowd at the auction.

```
STATE OF MARYLAND            *      IN THE

                             *      C  .UIT COURT

        vs.                  *      FOR

                             *      CARROLL COUNTY

ROBERT LEE MYERS             *      NO. 6364 CRIMINALS

*   *   *   *   *   *   *   *   *   *   *   *   *   *   *   *   *
```

NOTICE OF INTENTION TO SEEK
SENTENCE OF DEATH

New comes Thomas E. Hickman, State's Attorney for Carroll County, and Frank D. Coleman, Assistant State's Attorney for Carroll County, and in accordance with Article 27, Section 412 of the Annotated Code of Maryland, hereby notify ROBERT LEE MYERS, the Defendant herein, that the State of Maryland, intends to seek a sentence of death at the trial of the case herein.

ROBERT LEE MYERS, the Defendant herein, is further notified that the State intends to rely on the aggravating circumstances as defined in Article 27, Section 413 (d) (7) of the Annotated Code of Maryland, to wit: The Defendant engaged or employed another person to commit the murder and the murder was committed pursuant to an agreement or contract for remuneration or the promise of remuneration.

THOMAS E. HICKMAN
State's Attorney for Carroll County

FRANK D. COLEMAN
Assistant State's Attorney for
Carroll County

CERTIFICATION

I HEREBY CERTIFY that on the 23RD day of December, 1981, a copy of the aforegoing Notice of Intention to Seek Sentence of Death was personally served on ROBERT LEE MYERS, the Defendant herein.

Notice of Intention To Seek Death.

The Maryland Gas Chamber.

PHILLIP M. SUTLEY
ATTORNEY AT LAW
1217-20 FIDELITY BUILDING
CHARLES & LEXINGTON STS.
BALTIMORE, MARYLAND 21201

(301) 727-2040

January 15, 1980

Thomas L. Hickman, Esquire
State's Attorney for Carroll County
Carroll County Office Building
Box 530
Westminster, Maryland 21157

Dear Mr. Hickman:

This is to advise that I have been retained by Robert Myers in connection with any possible charges which may be placed against him in Carroll County. I have been informed that he is the subject of some inquiry concerning the homicide of his former wife which occurred August 29, 1979 at the premises known as 4636 Turkeyfoot Road in the Silver Run area of Carroll County.

If there are any further developments or additional or clarifying information is needed, I would appreciate being contacted personally as opposed to Mr. Myers being contacted.

Very truly yours,

Phillip M. Sutley

PMS/lml
CC: Mr. Robert Myers

Retainer Letter, Phillip M. Sutley, January 15, 1980

PART II

CHAPTER 11:
WHAT'S PAST IS PROLOGUE

"A fighter is never happy unless he is fighting . . ."
— Anonymous

My early introduction to conflict, fighting and competition later awakened an interest in our adversarial system of justice. I had been methodically trained to enjoy the stimulation, excitement, and satisfaction that comes with trying your best, even when the stakes were inconsequential. In a courtroom, the result was paramount to the people whose lives might be changed permanently or even ended.

My mother, Margaret "Peg" Shevlin, was born 35 miles north of Dublin in 1920. She was one of six children. Her father, Patrick Shevlin, was mustard-gassed in the trenches in 1917 and lingered in bad health until 1925 when he died, leaving his family destitute. They lived in a small dirt floor cottage with no running water, which was supplied either from the rain barrels around the house or from a pump one third of a mile down the road. There were no luxuries, and as soon as they were able, all the children went to work. My mother left school at the age of 14 to work on the local farms. Soon males were circling and "fishing with their lines." My grandmother urged her to leave and seek a productive life elsewhere.

She had only ever been to Dublin on a handful of occasions, because it was a long bicycle ride, but she set her sights on London. At 17, she packed a suitcase. A neighbor took her to Dun Laoghaire, the port, in a pony and trap. She took a boat across the Irish Sea to Holyhead, in Wales. There she found the train that took her to Euston Station in London. She knew no one, but was undaunted and unintimidated, soon locating a room above a pub where she could work.

At 5'1" with her petite figure, flaming red hair, emerald green eyes and vivacious personality she was soon very popular and started to generate a lot of male customers and welcomed their generous tips. She had two tough older brothers who had taught her how to physically strike without hesitation anyone that laid a hand on her. It soon became a joke there, and she was respected because while she would flirt she was always in control.

A couple of years later, my father dropped by to see the sexy girl he had heard about. They were enthralled with each other and married shortly thereafter. By then it was wartime London, bombing had been persistent and the local population had learned that a "tomorrow" was not guaranteed.

We had a narrow escape during the second Battle of Britain, after which she took us back to neutral Ireland, but she loved the excitement in London and could not wait to return. Return we did. She immediately made daycare arrangements for us babies and went to work as a saleslady, first in Woolworth's and then when she realized that there was more money in selling women's clothing and that big commissions could be made, she switched to the "vanity" business. She spent the next 50 years persuading customers that they should purchase items that she selected for them.

She was reluctant to leave the high fashion "couture" in the West End of London, where she was making a significant income, but agreed that the future would be brighter in North America. She loved her work and for over 25 years after they moved to Florida, she sold a lot of clothes to a select clientele on Worth Avenue in Palm Beach, Florida.

She was inspired to participate in amateur theater productions after she had watched my brother's great success. She loved the limelight and would often appear as the MC in fashion shows. She had great verbal skills and used them to great advantage using various accents. She could often be heard on radio doing voice overs. We all enjoyed the fact that she was "Rose Auto-Parts," persuading the locals to buy them as she suggested.

She soon became an extra in several movies and was willing to wait for hours on the set, with many others, so that she could get a moment in them. Even if she felt the movie was "garbage" she would persist in trying to get a part. "Porky's" and "Porky's Revenge" were good examples. We thought it was amusing that she appeared as a legal secretary in an episode of "Rumpole of The Bailey" that was being filmed in Miami. She loved the actors and actresses who participated and enjoyed the excitement of "the set."

In 1980, when she appeared in "Caddy Shack" starring Bill Murray, several of us went to a local theater in Baltimore. Her ninety seconds of fame required her to pretend she had been hit in the head with a golf club. When she came on the big screen the rest of the viewing audience could not understand why we had applauded so vigorously.

*****

Daniel Keating, my paternal great grandfather, was a constable in The Royal Irish Constabulary at age 25, in his native Kerry. At 6'4", he was a giant among his fellow Irishmen. After three years on the force he was drummed out for drinking (too much.) He emigrated to London and took whatever manual labor he could get. However, he was articulate and un-intimidated by authority or the law. He learned to defend the rights of other poor immigrants in court and even made a few shillings doing so. His success encouraged him to obtain some old law books and by the early 1900s had made a reputation as a "poor man's lawyer." He had a large family, five boys, who were all big, and the two girls who grew to nearly six feet.

His eldest son Charles E. Keating, my grandfather, joined the London Metropolitan Police Force in his early twenties and he was stationed in the East End of London. He was 6'3" and strong and enjoyed the tough streetwise lifestyle that came with the job. He was domineering and aggressive. In 1914 he was drafted, and after he had served in the trenches in France and Belgium, he returned to the police force at Scotland Yard, and then New Scotland Yard, where he spent most of his time as clerk of the court, with the rank of sergeant.

He had fathered 4 children. My father was the eldest and had few good memories about him from childhood. One stuck out: an outing to a track meet in Battersea Park where Sgt. Keating won the Metropolitan Police Championship in the shot. He deserted his 3 sons and daughter and lived with someone else. Because he knew how to work the "justice" system he made sure that he did not have to pay more than 1 pound a week for their support. They often went hungry. His wife, Minnie Douglas Keating was a very mild mannered unassuming person, however she refused to give him a divorce. She sometimes gambled a few shillings at "the dogs" and was often lucky enough to provide food for her family.

Her economic condition improved greatly by the late 1940s as my parents started to prosper and provide for her. Her luck ran out when she was 60, in 1949, when she was struck and killed, by a "hit and run driver" who was never apprehended. The next week, Sgt. Keating married his paramour. Minnie's children refused to have anything to do with him. I only met him once.

While my father was first attracted to my mother because of her pretty face and slender figure, he was amazed by her tough, resourceful, kind and cheerful disposition. She was fully determined to overcome the seemingly perpetual problems and obstacles which were always presenting themselves. She never gave up, and her good sense of humor and attitude seemed to be in total keeping with the times, which required courage, resiliency and initiative. "T'was not her beauty that alone won him."

By the end of 1942, she had rented an apartment on the third floor of 14 Petworth St., Battersea. It was located a few hundred yards from Battersea Park near The Thames. Battersea Power Station loomed nearby upriver and because it had been a prime target for the nightly raids of the Luftwaffe, during the first Battle of Britain, there were plenty of vacant third floor apartments available. "Peg" was a fatalist, busy planning a home, buying furniture on the "never, never," the term used for installment purchases—the only way poor people could afford expensive items. 400,000 children were removed from London to avoid the German bombardment. My mother was nonchalant . . . que sera, sera! Much depended on the attitude of the primary care giver, most often the mother. If she was casual about it all, the children would be as well. If she freaked so would they. "Mother's gonna put all of her fears into you."

Were I able, I might have chosen a different time and place to be born. London had been battered for three years by the German bombing. My brother was 22 months old and my 23-year-old nine-months-pregnant mother had no help or telephone. She refused to take shelter in the sweltering subway stations, and was living in a small apartment, at the top of three flights of rickety stairs. My father could only visit occasionally from the army camp where he was stationed.

At around 10 p.m. on Monday, August 30, 1943, an air raid alert screamed its warning. My mother had other concerns and, leaving Charles alone, walked five blocks across Battersea Bridge Road through darkened streets to get the midwife. It was closing time and the inebriated clientele were leaving the local public house so she was greeted with their wolf whistles. After much effort, she found her flat and they both returned to 14 Petworth Street. Within a few minutes I "Entered My Appearance." The midwife cleaned up and left. My mother was grateful that for the next few days there were no air raids and she could get some intermittent rest and still nurture her two babies.

In late 1943, Hitler again ordered the mass bombing of southern England. The Luftwaffe sent 500 aircraft to carry out this order. On January 21, 1944 "The Little Blitz" or "Baby Blitz" continued as these planes attacked London. These raids continued for another three months, when fewer than 90 bombers remained. The V1 and V 2 rockets were used in their place.

I was a "Citizen of London." "Good Night and Good Luck," as Edward R. Murrow used to say in his nightly broadcasts. There was a life-and-death heroism everywhere. It was expected.

My mother heard about a ground floor flat two houses further down the block that had been vacated. It would be so much easier to handle the babies and would provide a more comforting feeling of safety. However, when she looked the place over, it had dismal, dull wallpaper and decor that would have needed much work, so she decided against it.

A month later at the end of February, a blockbuster bomb demolished about 100 houses on three surrounding streets. 14 Petworth St. was next in line. It was left standing. The ground floor flat they had been considering renting had completely disappeared. The people who experienced the bombing, the helplessness, the blackout, and the haunting cries and screams for help during those terrible frightening times never forgot the experience.

At about 9 o'clock at night, Peg, as usual had ignored the sirens, the bombing, and the anti-aircraft shelling. This time, though, it was close—and despite calls from the lady on the ground floor to bring the babies downstairs, Peg stayed above. She was sitting, writing a letter, when the bomb was dropped. The blast sent a heavy cut glass jug and dishes flying across the room, missing her head by fractions of an inch. Everywhere lights blacked out, there was a short silence then screams and then muffled cries.

Peg gathered her two babies in the darkness, but before she tried to descend, the Home Guard Sentry called out to not use the stairs because they were dangerous and to stay put until further instructions. A short time later, a fireman was in the window on a ladder. He took us babies down first, and then Peg was jackknifed over his shoulder in the fireman's lift. My father was given compassionate leave and raced home. It was a terrible shock to see the bombing scene. The stairs up to the flat were piled with soot and brick dust. In my cot was a section of concrete and plaster from the roof above it caving in. The wall alongside the cot was impregnated with glass caused by the blast which had caved in the window. Peg had not put me in my crib that night. We never dwelled on our close call in later years, we just accepted we had been most fortunate, that life was precious and everything from then on was an extra for all of us.

We were homeless, so Peg then took us to her mother's home in Drogheda, County Louth, where we stayed until the end of the war.

*****

Growing up in post-World War II Battersea, England, much of our lives revolved around athletic competition: boxing, track, swimming and soccer. My older brother, Charles and I enjoyed the camaraderie and energy in the local boxing club, and it seemed natural that our father should be shadowboxing with lead weights taped into his fists. We saw he was well-liked and treated with a certain deference.

My father started boxing when he was ten years old. By 1945, he had become the European British Army Heavyweight Champion. His aspirations to represent England in Tokyo at the 1940 Olympics were thwarted by world events. By 1948, he had been boxing for twenty years. At six feet six inches and 220 pounds, he was a formidable opponent and loved to fight. Years earlier, he had become friends with Anton Christoforidis, who was born and lived in

Greece, and had won the World Light Heavyweight Championship in 1941. He had successfully defended it that year in Baltimore. He lost the title to Gus Lesnevich several months later. My father greatly admired Anton's fighting skills and tenacity. He also liked the name Anton.

He traveled to Ireland in May 1947, where he knocked out Sam Edgar from Belfast in the All-Ireland Heavyweight Championship, in Tolka Park, Dublin. In April 1948, he fought Vic Rotherham in the Royal Albert Hall. He knocked down this 6'5" 240-pound opponent twice, and then knocked him out—all in the first round. Later in 1948, my father was offered the opportunity to box on the undercard of the Freddie Mills vs. Gus Lesnevich, World Light Heavyweight Championship at the Royal Albert Hall in June of that year.

My father faced a moment of truth when he realized that he could not work as an engineer during the day and also pursue his boxing aspirations at the same time. He was reaching a level in both activities that he had to choose between them, because he could not be successful in either unless he was totally focused. He was persuaded by my mother instead to retire from the ring and pursue his career as an engineer.

My older brother Charles and I grew up boxing as toddlers in The Cauis Boxing Club in London, where my father trained. It was one of the best clubs in the British Isles. It was located in Battersea, the poor working class neighborhood where we were born and lived. The club had produced many national champions at every weight, and a few had participated in the Olympics. After a fight, (but only if he'd won!) our father would often hoist us over his head in the ring. The facilities at "The Den" (as it was known) were very run down, but we were regaled with the stories of the champions who had trained there and we took pride in their toughness, their heroics and their desire to prevail, regardless of their lack of education, job skills or low-class accents.

My brother and I had a personal interest in a lot of the people who congregated there at the club. We had watched them progress over the years. We had both "sparred" with Don Cockell—who would later become The British Heavyweight Champion!—at The Den and he had been very playful with us.

In 1954, Donald Cockell boxed Rocky Marciano for The Heavyweight Championship of the World. The fight took place in San Francisco, and because of the eight-hour time difference, we were put in bed early so we could be awakened at fight time. My father, brother and I were glued to the radio broadcast. Our hero, Don Cockell, lasted nine rounds until he was totally overwhelmed. He put up a great show while absorbing Marciano's relentless punches. Marciano had hit him so hard with thundering right and left hooks that Cockell was vomiting as he sat on his stool between rounds. Marciano was surprised that he would keep rising again to take more punishment. He absorbed hundreds of Marciano's hardest blows. One national English news-paper reported, "This was the kind of extra courage which makes you proud to belong to the human race and to have been sired by the same breed as the boy who grew up in the back streets of Battersea." Even though he only won a single round he was considered a national hero.

My mother had come to detest the fight game, not so much for its brutality, but because of the crude and less refined people that the activity seemed to attract. My mother was not pleased when we returned home using the cockney slang we had heard and she was constantly correcting out speech, so that our potential in the larger class-conscious society would not be limited. She wished to influence "her men" to aspire to great heights in different venues. My parents were starting to have their own battles over the preoccupation with boxing and while my mother felt strongly that it might be a healthy developmental tool, it should not be an end in itself. She agreed that we should learn how to fight, always be ready to fight and that we should aspire to be the best at it, but she wanted to protect us from the "fight culture."

Boxing teaches you that you can get hurt unless you pay attention, focus and react quickly and boldly. One moment of negligence can result in swift punishment. Everyone's equal in a boxing ring, and the only thing that's guar-anteed when you step through those ropes is that you will find out who you are. Everyone has a plan until he gets hit in the mouth. Failure is a much bet-ter teacher than success. You must constantly believe before you can achieve.

I learned at a very early age to be brave, and that even if I wasn't I should pretend to be because no one could tell the difference. A fighter is never hap-py unless he is fighting. The whole world seems to slow down a little bit after you have experienced a fight. The adrenaline that comes from fear or from stalking someone across the ring while being stalked by that someone is exhilarating. The very real immediate currency is a lot of pain and humiliation, but the world seems alive.

The "Sweet Science of Bruising" teaches the participants and spectators a great deal. Fighting is not simply about winning or losing. No one "plays" boxing. You can play soccer, rugby, football, hockey, or lacrosse, but you do not "play" boxing. Hitting makes you feel alive, as does being hit. You soon discover that you are not always going to win, but you also come to understand that you will never really lose if you fight as hard as you can.

Seizing opportunities when they presented themselves was often the topic of lessons imparted in the ring and around our family table. Jumping at the chances life offers and daring to be great was ingrained in my brother and me. We were both trained to be aggressive and to take physical punishment without a lot of whining. It gave us both a big advantage in life.

*****

At 10 years of age I had been fortunate to win a scholarship to The Emanuel School, which, thanks to the interest of Queen Elizabeth the First, had been erected in Westminster in 1603. When it became necessary to expand, The School moved to Battersea in South London, on the edge of Wandsworth Goal. The 12-acre property was bounded by railroad tracks and a high wall with imposing gates which isolated it from the surrounding area.

As a boy, my father had seen the upper crust members of society send their children there. The school uniform was distinct and well known, and could only be purchased at Harrod's in the West End. He was proud one of his sons might get in. However, he also knew that it was a Protestant school which would not admit Roman Catholics. My parents were pragmatic about religion. They sent my brother and me off to a local Roman Catholic Church on nearby Trott Street, every Sunday, while they stayed home and worshiped each other. So my parents explained that, during the interview at The School with The Headmaster, if asked my religion, I was to say "Church of England." The Headmaster did inquire of me directly and I responded "Church of England, Sir!" He followed up with, "What Church do you go to?" I blurted out "Trott

Street." He replied "I don't believe I've heard of that one." They had coached me well enough and they then successfully diverted the line of questioning.

I was admitted to The School, and there were only half a dozen non-Protestants there. We thought nothing about the fact that they had to wait outside the chapel if they didn't want to come in. The administration was callous about their feelings and so were we.

Emanuel School was proud of its history, and insisted that the school's beginnings and development should be studied by all pupils. The Dacre Family had been rich and powerful when Henry VIII saw an opportunity to take all its property. Thomas, the heir, in 1541, along with some servants got into a brawl with the neighbors' servants, one of whom was fatally wounded. If a plea of not guilty had been pursued, Lord Dacre would have been acquitted of murder, receiving at worst, a fine or imprisonment. He was told it would be better to withdraw his not-guilty plea and throw himself on the mercy of Henry VIII.

Bad advice. He was executed at Tyburn at age 24. His young son was barred from the heritage of his ancestors because of "corruption of blood." He did, however, become "a royal ward," and was eventually allowed to use the family name.

The Dacre family had been befriended by an able lawyer, Sir Richard Sackville, who later became The Treasurer of the Exchequer. He had wide business experience, and was so successful that his nickname was "Fill-Sack." He helped get Lord Dacre's material possessions restored to him.

The Sackvilles were well-known in their own right. Sir Richard's mother was Margaret Boleyn, the aunt of the unfortunate Anne Boleyn. Anne's daughter would become Elizabeth I. The Dacres were inspired to leave, in their wills, provisions to help deal with the problem of poverty to supplement the official experiments in welfare relief. At their death, property was left to establish a religious house for the poor "along Protestant lines." A school was added a short time later. Boys could enter at age 7 and remain until 19—or even longer with the approval of the Headmaster. The core philosophy was still to be based on the ideal of a religious house and getting the boys to behave well by getting them to enjoy and appreciate their Chapel. The founders wanted to make religion a masculine, practical and very real thing. The daily service was conducted there, accompanied by the choir under the direction of the Organist and the Music Master.

The school kept discipline through the use of corporal punishment. Any individual Form Master or school prefect could "slipper" or cane an unruly student at any time. Detentions, up to three hours on Saturday mornings were also imposed. The miscreant could take two strokes for each hour if he preferred, instead. The most serious offenses brought more formality. Six sturdy bamboo canes with metal tips were displayed in a glass cabinet in the Second Master's office. Since two Masters were involved with these beatings, one to administer and one to witness, they would select their instrument in front of the wayward boy and march him to the Master's Bathroom where the punishment would be administered. They always looked severe in their black gowns and mortar boards.

Detailed records of these canings were kept. The "cause" and "penalty" were docketed, much like criminal court. Offenses included "deliberately throwing ink on the wall," "cutting work," "disobedience," "persistently talking in class," "continual lateness," "throwing stones and causing injury," "missing a detention on Saturday morning," and "cutting and forging."

A gang of us liked to go to local stores and shoplift. Some stolen items were found by a parent, and the school was notified. Our Form Master read out our names and ordered us to meet The Headmaster at the end of the day. We had never met The Headmaster in his chambers, except for "The Interview," so we knew we were in trouble. I was called in first, and he said, "Keating, I understand you have been stealing!" I, of course, denied the accusation, but when he ordered me to empty my pockets, and the evidence of my thievery (a magnet, a yo-yo and a water pistol) was placed on his desk, he frowned at me and said, "We are probably going to expel you. We will contact your parents and make a decision shortly." He refused to listen to my begging him not to contact my home. All the other boys immediately admitted their guilt, and some suggested that I had influenced their conduct.

The letter had already been sent and the next day, Saturday morning, my father shared it with me. He explained he was going to beat me and then take me to school on Monday morning. I was to go to my room and let him know when I wanted the punishment. Of course I had not volunteered before

Sunday evening, and so he beat me severely, breaking a bamboo stick over my backside. The next morning, he dragged me to The School and we waited to see The Headmaster. My father explained that I had been severely punished and respectfully requested that I not be expelled. "The Head" agreed but said I would have to be further beaten by them to make sure the student body understood that such conduct would not be tolerated.

A couple of hours later, during the morning recess, I was led by The Headmaster and The Second Master down two corridors, past scores of gaping boys, to the punishment place. I was informed that since my father had already punished me I would only receive two strokes. They really hurt. I burst into tears. However, my status among the boys was elevated a little bit when they saw the different patterns of welts and bruises on me in the shower after rugby practice. My father's left-handed approach contrasted with the other stripes. "The Punishment Book" recorded the event. Instead of branding me as a lying thief, the cause was listed as "untruthfulness; leading others astray." Perhaps I was being told that I had the prerequisite traits to be a good criminal defense attorney.

*****

There are fifteen members on a rugby team. At that time no substitutions were permitted, so if someone got hurt, there was no option but to play with fewer. Consequently, only fifteen boys were chosen when many more wanted to participate. Each week, the coach would sit with the respective age group captains, and together select the fifteen who could play that week. This was not a popularity contest. The school decided I should be captain of the Under-13 team, and then, the Under-14 team. Perhaps I would now use my leadership skills in a positive manner. It sometimes required leaving close friends off the team.

There were many places around The School that were supposedly "out of bounds." Across the playing fields that contained four full-sized rugby pitches and a cricket pitch, far from the prying eyes of the Masters and Prefects, stood an abandoned Cricket Pavilion where boys would sometimes enjoy an illicit cigarette. There was, however, another attraction that intrigued all of us.

If you climbed the surrounding wall you could see Wandsworth Goal located a short distance away. This was always the source of fascinating stories and gossip among the boys.

People were executed there routinely, and on each occasion a black flag would be raised over the prison. The British newspapers covered news about crime in great detail, and since there was never a long delay between apprehension and sentencing, the public interest was maintained. Until just a few decades before, murder had required a mandatory sentence of death, which often took place less than a year after the crime.

In the days when the great steam locomotives had not all been replaced by electric trains, most schoolboys were "train spotters," recording the famous trains that they had seen. So too with these executions. Many boys could recite the names of some of the notorious murderers who had been hung there. Traditionally, anyone caught attempting to satisfy their morbid curiosity in this restricted place would be caned severely, which of course only added to the allure of the activity.

We knew all about Albert Pierrepoint, The Public Executioner, who along with his father and uncle had become Britain's Chief Executioners during the previous 60 years. To us he was very much like the Masters who would take us, at the designated time, to the Second Master's bathroom to be flogged. The executioner's work just seemed to be a logical extension. Pierrepoint executed 600 people throughout the country, and we knew the names of many of the prisons where he performed this gruesome task. A supposedly accurate count was carved into the wood on the inside of the disused Cricket Pavilion. It showed that the "black flag" had been raised on over 45 occasions, 30 of which had occurred in the previous 10 years. Although Pierrepoint executed six people at Wandsworth during the years I attended the school, I never got to see the "black flag." Eventually as the abolitionist movement against the death penalty gained a large public presence, official policy was changed and the flag no longer was raised, because demonstrators often turned into an angry mob, frustrated that another "legalized lynching" had been performed in their name. Throughout the 1940s and 1950s, executions, the cat o' nine tails and other forms of corporal punishment were becoming obsolete.

When the British public learned, however, that Albert Pierrepoint had personally executed over 200 German war criminals, he became a very popular and well-known person. For many years, he had kept his occupation a secret and explained his frequent travels to his friends as being required by the company that employed him. Once the newspapers published his photograph, though, he became a cult hero—a role that he soon came to enjoy, because people warmed to his unassuming personality. He had a beautiful voice and enjoyed singing in public houses, where his version of "Danny Boy" would hush the most boisterous crowds. It was intriguing to us choir boys that someone blessed with such a melodic voice could so easily terminate the life of some stranger, who had personally done him no harm, in return for a small fee, expenses, prestige and power. His job made him an enigma and the center of attention. He was automatically respected, if not revered, because he cleverly disguised the intoxicating emotion he felt. He had fulfilled his life's ambition. When he was 11 years old he had written a long essay proclaiming, "When I leave school I should like to be the Official Executioner."

Some Masters effectively used the "black flag" and our close proximity to this place of execution to initiate debates and heighten interest in crime, the law, prisons and the death penalty. Most did not seem to be overly sympathetic or outraged, and there was no great outpouring of emotion on behalf of the condemned or the victims who had been murdered.

There were exceptions: some executions were recalled triumphantly. One such execution was that of William Joyce. He had joined the German propaganda machine and spent the war years urging the shell shocked population to surrender and submit to the inevitable German victory. As the propaganda minister for the British Union of Fascists, William Joyce—nicknamed "Lord Haw Haw"—had made many radio broadcasts from the safety of Hamburg and Bremen intended to demoralize the British population during World War II. He was despised and ridiculed by the shell-shocked working classes who mocked him for his sneering, nasal, phony upper class accent. "This is Jairmany calling . . . This is Jairmany calling." He was executed and then buried in Wandsworth Prison for Treason. These were compelling stories for us 700 boys just next door.

And what healthy English schoolboy would not be intrigued by John George Haigh, the "Acid Bath Murderer", who disposed of his victim's bodies by dissolving them in acid? Haigh had become frustrated with the intense police interrogation, and explained that since his victims no longer existed they had no case. "I've destroyed her with acid and you can't prove a murder without a body." Murder like every other crime can only be proved if there is independent evidence of the "corpus delecti" or the elements of the crime. However, the authorities had discovered one victim's gallstones and false teeth and that was enough to corroborate his confession that he had dissolved his victims in an acid bath. We callously chanted "Poor Mrs. Haig is dead and gone, her face you'll see no more—for what she thought was $H2O$ was $H2SO4$!" He had been executed there in 1949, but because he'd been a serial killer his fame lived on.

My interest in prisons and trials however had been awakened long before that in my home. My father had been sentenced to a year of hard labor in the 400-year-old H.M.P. Shepton Mallet. He had tried to dictate to the British Army the terms of his service, and when he did not get his way, he deserted. He was assigned a young inexperienced lawyer to represent him at his court-martial, so he soon decided to present his own case. The fact that he had aided the war effort when he was "on the run" by working in a war related industry helped him to mitigate his offense. The presiding judge complemented him on the way he had handled his case, and then imposed the one-year sentence. My father used to joke that it was like telling a fighter who had been badly beaten that he had "the best footwork."

The inmates in the prison, which had been condemned in the 1920s and then at times brought back to use, discussed the many executions that had been performed there over the years. My father expressed his contempt for the hangman and others like him, and explained that it was really the ultimate act of cowardice to inflict any corporal punishment on someone who was helpless and could not fight back.

Long before I became a lawyer it seemed prisons and executions were just a normal part of life, like athletics or cricket or boxing. Hell, even bombing seemed normal if you had lived through it. My family believed that there was enough arbitrary death in the world—if life was truly valued that would mean never intentionally trying to end it—especially not as a punishment, simply because that somehow made you feel better.

My father published a book about his exploits in the ring, the army and prison, entitled "The Soldier Who Wasn't." In it he described the bread and water diets, and the brutality in the prison. We, of course, had heard all these details long before around the kitchen table. The four of us were a close knit family, who spent most of our recreational time together.

After the United States entered World War II, in a very short time many American troops were based in Britain. They needed to be able to isolate and imprison those who committed military or domestic crimes, and arrangements were made for this to take place at the dreaded H.M.P. Shepton Mallet. The prison was soon placed entirely at the disposal of the American military, which immediately set about building a new and substantial execution house. It was made of red bricks and attached to the side of the main gray stone accommodation block; this incongruous extension was purposefully constructed as a reminder to all of its deadly purpose. A total of 19 Americans were hanged there before the American forces vacated it in 1945.

The court-martials and execution arrangements came under the jurisdiction of the Americans; however, the actual "drop" was the responsibility of the officially appointed British hangman. It had been the American practice to require that the soldier who was about to die stand on the trap door while his record, offense and the sentence of the court martial was read to him—a process which could take up to six minutes. It was only then that the sentence was carried out.

Pierrepoint had the official reading done the night before, so it would take him less than a minute to put the noose around his victim's neck, stand back and spring the trap door. He took pride in the ones who died quickly.

Pierrepoint insisted that the Americans' drinking and partying, which habitually took place before and after every execution, be prohibited as unseemly. He saw no need to release the pent-up emotions caused by the execution of their fellow Americans. He had a more stoic and detached approach, which he had developed over many years.

The American authorities were able to keep most of the terrible conditions at this "American Jail" secret for the most part; however, it was described as a "hellhole," a "blot on the Army and the conscience of the country" and a "terror jail." A book written by E.M. Nathanson entitled "The Dirty Dozen," later made into a movie, involved the release of 12 American servicemen who were housed there. All were sentenced to death or extensive prison sentences, and were offered the opportunity for release from "The Mallet," provided they participate in a dangerous military operation. In actual fact, the unofficial unit within the 101st Airborne Division was known as the "Filthy Thirteen." They parachuted into France on D-Day to take a bridge over the Douve River, where almost all of them were killed.

*****

Everybody seems to admire and respect a good fighter. Consequently, professional boxers and their art form have always been popular and attractive to politicians, film stars and others. Jack Solomons, the leading fight promoter in the United Kingdom, had begun to nurture and promote my father's boxing career. As the leading matchmaker, he monopolized the schedule of fights at The Royal Albert Hall and elsewhere. Not only did he enjoy the wealth that came with charging people to watch others fight, but he also liked the people who gravitated towards the enterprise.

Solomons established his headquarters in the West End of London on Great Windmill Street near the Theater District. His dingy office was on the second floor of a busy gymnasium. Many young men would train there. It was crowded and hot and damp almost any time of the day or night. Some contenders would be sparring and shadowboxing, while all around the ring, dozens more would be punching a light bag or a heavy bag or skipping rope or performing a variety of exercises, seeking to harden muscle, get fighting fit, maybe give or get a hiding. There weren't many unbeatable champions at any one time, so this gym was filled with angry and frustrated ambition. Solomons promoted contests all over the British Isles, on the Continent and in the United States.

He encouraged the talent of the British ring at all the different weights, and because of his magnetic personality, literary acumen, and his powers as a great showman, he encouraged and entertained many famous figures who were invited to stop by. My father enjoyed the cross-section of people who could be found there every day, and he would often take my brother and me there while he trained, and enjoyed incidentally showing off our developing boxing skills. Sometimes Charles and I would be put into the ring to spar. We had boxed together countless times and never lost our tempers or got out of control. We did not try to hurt each other or make each other look bad. We enjoyed ourselves there because our father was a well-respected and promising heavyweight. He trained us to be well mannered and polite as well as knowledgeable little boxers. We liked seeing the celebrities who frequented the place.

When Albert Pierrepoint would travel to Wandsworth or another London prison to perform an execution, he would visit Jack Solomons' Gym. He would be cordially greeted by the proprietor and given a respectful distance by the other people there. Although he was physically small and unimposing, the fact that he was a coldblooded killer got everyone's attention. He did make a big impression on my brother and me on the two occasions that we actually saw him at the club. He looked out of place and uncomfortable in his business suit, and did not engage anyone else apart from Solomons in conversation. My father pointed him out but didn't say much about him. His disdain, however, was obvious to us. After the executioner left, the atmosphere lightened as jokes were made about neck sizes and how the hangman had supposedly gazed longingly at all the ropes surrounding the ring.

I had already learned of his strong feelings in this regard. On one occasion I was beating up on another six-year-old, who was the same size as me, in the center ring in the Caius Boxing Club, and my father jumped in the ring and stopped the fight. My opponent had his hands down and was sobbing. I, of course, felt like I had won the World Heavyweight Championship. I thought that this was what I had been trained to do and was laughing happily at my success. I was about to turn around to return to my corner to receive my well deserved praise, but my father was already in the ring, grabbing me and with his angry face thrust into mine, shouted that you never acted that way to somebody else's pain or loss.

My father immediately arranged for me to fight a much older and bigger kid. I knew I was doomed. He whispered instructions to my opponent and left the two of us in the middle of the ring and commanded, "Box!" I had no chance at all, and this kid stood over me and immediately proceeded to repeatedly punch me in the face, even though after the first few blows I had already started to cry. A short while later, my father was back in the ring to stop the massacre and he sent me back to my corner with, "How does that feel? How does that feel?" It was an emphatic, if brutal, life lesson.

On another occasion around the same time, I was scheduled to box another boy who was more skilled and a little older, bigger, and stronger. My father, acting as my "second" in my corner, gave me prefight instructions. He told me that I could not beat this opponent, but I should not worry about that. "What I want you do is every time he punches you, I want you to try to hit him back twice!" I did my best to follow this advice and although I lost the bout, I was not knocked out, or hurt and at the end of it, he and my brother were full of praise for my spirited effort. I was starting to learn that you never really lose if you try as hard as you can.

*****

In 1953, my father took us to demonstrate against the execution of Derek Bentley, who at age 19, was hung in Wandsworth Goal that year. Bentley and his 16-year-old friend Christopher Craig had been seen on the roof of a warehouse attempting to break in. The police climbed up and arrested Bentley. Craig yelled at the police "Come on, you brave coppers, think of your wives." Bentley had yelled, "Let him have it Chris!"—at which point Craig fired his pistol and fatally shot one of the constables. Bentley's barrister argued that his client had meant for Craig to let him have the weapon and give himself up. The jury was not impressed. Because Bentley was over 18, he was given the death sentence, and Craig, 16, was sent to a juvenile detention center until he was 21. Even though the jury had recommended mercy for Bentley, The Lord Chief Justice refused. 200 members of Parliament and thousands of others—including the murdered officer's widow—demonstrated and petitioned for clemency. He was executed anyway. Bentley received a posthumous pardon 40 years later.

My mother had moved from her native Ireland to London as a young woman. She and her family were patriotic and instilled in us a great love for poetry, song and story—in the typical Irish tradition. We were enriched by our family holidays there, spending lots of time with her brothers and our cousins, who hated the English and the occupation of their country. We were regaled with rebel stories and mirth. Anyone who stood up against The Crown was admired, even if they had only been common criminals. They often repeated the Australian bandit Ned Kelly's last words before his execution "Oh well, such is life!" They sang "The Wild Colonial Boy" and "Kevin Barry" and insisted on our being able to do so as well.

The Republic of Ireland did not often sanction executions to control the population's behavior. Very few Irishmen would even attempt to become a public executioner, so Albert Pierrepoint would make the trip by boat from Holyhead across the Irish Sea to Dublin. He had attempted to train an Irish hangman, but the few drunks who volunteered were not suitable, so he assumed the role himself. The Irish were irate that here was another Englishman ready to spill their blood.

Pierrepoint had bragged, "I love hanging Irishmen. They always go quietly, and without trouble. They're Christian men, and they believe they are going to a better place."

Uncle Paddy Shevlin took Charles and me to Mountjoy Prison in Dublin to protest against the execution of Michael Manning, who had been convicted of murder. It was a memorable Easter Holiday for us as we joined the loud and angry crowd yelling "No More Black Cap! No More Black Cap! No More Black Cap!" The sentencing judge there as in England, was required to put on a black cap before pronouncing the death sentence. This was to be the last execution in Ireland.

Uncle Paddy educated us about Brendan Behan, who had been an inmate in Mountjoy Prison. He was serving 14 years for shooting at the gardai (the police,) and a warden had encouraged his literary talent. The result was "The Experiences of a Borstal Boy." In 1956 he created "The Quare Fellow" which was based on the hanging of Bernard Kirwan. Kirwan had killed his brother in a fight. The entire play takes place in Mountjoy Prison and focuses on the impact of Albert Pierrepoint's upcoming visit. The song "The Old Triangle" referring to the implement which controlled all movement in Mountjoy became famous because of its use in the play. Behan understood the cruelty and absurdity of prison life and wrote about it in "Confessions of an Irish Rebel."

*****

We left England in 1957 and moved to Niagara Falls Ontario, Canada. By the time our house and furnishings had been sold and the airplane tickets had been purchased, our small family of four had less than a $1000. My father was a very good petroleum engineer and had already obtained a good-paying job there. My mother immediately began selling "fashions" in local boutiques and soon developed a large clientele, fascinated by her engaging personality and her "accents." The fact that she knew some Yiddish was a big help in the "rag trade." She made a good commission on every sale.

Charles and I were quite different. He was 2 years older. He was supremely confident about his ability to speak in public, while I was quite self-conscious and nervous as a teenager about "public speaking," like most people are. He had no interest in academics and the adjustment to life in Canada was more diffi-cult for him. He was expelled in the 10th grade for setting off 50 firecrackers in a bathroom. He never went back to school, and to the absolute dismay of my parents, he announced he was "going to be an actor!"

My brother and I had initially worked in a local hotel as busboys. Money was always scarce, but after a year, they started to prosper. My parents purchased a small new house in a local subdivision. One summer, two friends and I hitchhiked a hundred miles to the tobacco fields in Simcoe, Ontario. We lived and worked with the migrant laborers there and "primed" tobacco. We stripped the fleshy, tar-laden leaves from the bottom up and then placed them in a long wagon, a "boat." Every day, except Sundays, for 10 weeks, we were in the fields from 7 a.m. to 6 p.m. We then spent another hour stacking the tobacco in the kilns, ready to be cured. Our backs were often sore and our hands and arms were coated with black resin. The bunk house and setting was memorialized in a play: "Tillsonburg, Tillsonburg, my back still aches when I hear that word." I got back to high school two weeks late for the 12th Grade, very happy to be there. The migrant workers moved on to pick apples. The experience was invaluable. I studied a little more than I usually did, inspired to try to ensure I would avoid their hard life.

Charles had taught himself to play the guitar and soon I was accompanying him to "coffeehouses" in Buffalo, New York, an hour's drive from our house. I did not participate, nor was I invited to. He joined some local amateur theaters, and got a few small parts. My ever supportive parents and I traveled to watch him deliver his precious few lines in very minor roles. He would have to elbow his way in, and soon did. His talent was obvious to all and he received an offer to join The Cleveland Playhouse, at age 19, along with a small allowance. Over the years, as his career advanced, we were some of his most ardent fans. We cheered him on at The Provincetown Playhouse, The Charles Playhouse, and The Roundabout. He became well known and soon was employed at The Guthrie Theatre in Minneapolis, Minnesota. Among many other roles, we saw him play 'Mark Anthony' in Shakespeare's Julius Caesar and 'Caliban' in The Tempest. There was usually an audience of 2,000, making a full house, six shows a week.

He soon moved back to England and appeared at The Chichester Festival and then became "a player" at The Royal Shakespeare Company in Stratford for many years. He was also in demand for film and television roles appearing in *Awakenings, Miami Vice, Crown Court, Brideshead Revisited, The Body Guard,* and *Deuce Bigalow: European Vacation.*

He appeared in a television movie in 1984 entitled "A Talent For Murder", starring Sir Laurence Olivier who was then in his mid-70s and attempting to build an estate for his family. He knew that he was terminally ill. Charles complained to Olivier, who Charles had always idolized, that the movie was very mediocre. Sir Lawrence, responded "What's the matter son, never been in the crapper before?" Charles was silenced.

Soon the fame and financial rewards associated with American soap operas beckoned. For over 10 years Charles played villains in "All My Children" and "Another World." He was nominated for an Emmy as "Best Actor in a Daytime Soap Opera" for several years, and finally won it in 1996. He was also nominated for a Tony and had his image displayed in Sardi's in Manhattan. He had certainly fulfilled his promise.

*****

Having participated in many individual sporting competitions, I learned at an early age that even if you tried as hard as you can, there were people who try just as hard, but seemed to have more aptitude or talent. This was true of my intellectual pursuits, as well.

My father had taught me to play chess at age 6, and for many years during the evenings we would play together. He was pleased when I finally was able to beat him five years later. I joined the chess team at Emanuel expecting to easily compete there. These kids, however, were brainy and gifted. Some of them even knew Greek and Latin already, and were often good musicians. They easily defeated me, no matter how much effort I expended.

In England I was the wicket-keeper on the cricket team; the goalie on the soccer team; I swam, boxed and competed in track and rugby. I enjoyed both the individual and the team effort involved. In Canada I had more success, playing linebacker and fullback on the school football team. I scored several touchdowns, for one of which, as the newspapers reported, I had "galloped" 59 yards for the score. I was also the top track and field athlete in the school and had some limited success in Ontario regional meets. High jump, shot put, javelin and hop, step and jump did not come easy for me but I tried very hard, trained very hard and there was limited competition.

In my senior year of high school in Canada, I decided to test myself at chess again. The football players thought it was odd that I wanted to play for the school chess team, and the chess competitors there were amused to have the fullback engage them in mental combat. I did not do that well, but I tried hard.

While I trained to be a good athlete and had been inspired to seek to be the very best, I learned at first in a ring, then in the pool, then on various athletic fields that there were lots of "wannabes" like me. Even though Olympic competition had always been the goal, it became clear that the champions there were not simply normal people who overcame their biological limits through sheer force of will and excessive training. The nature/nurture discussion usually concluded that the so-called 10,000-hour rule (called the magic number of greatness,) stressing the necessity of obsessive and rigorous practice, was starting to be reconsidered.

In short, "The Sports Gene" is far more complicated. Some characteristics which were assumed to be entirely voluntary, like an individual's willingness to obsess and train, also have important genetic components. Similarly, as with musicians for example, it was concluded that solitary practice was the most important dimension of the training, and that it was much more taxing than activities such as group practices or playing for fun. Talent and effort alone was often not enough.

When I was 19, we moved to the United States. I attended Boston University beginning in 1962. I knew I could not compete successfully on the college level in Track and Field or Football. My father used to take us to see the Oxford vs. Cambridge boat race on the Thames every year. Even though it was an elitist sport, he appreciated the stamina and strength it took to row the 4-½-mile course. Sometimes as many as a million people would line the Embankment, cheering for either light or dark blue. I walked over to the Boston University boathouse, and decided I wanted to start rowing in their 8-oared shells. I was in good shape, and I did well. I was named captain of the Freshman, and then the Varsity crew, and for four years we enjoyed competing against Harvard, Yale, Navy and the best crews in the country. It is a sport where there are no individual stars or glory. We were a team, and we all won or lost together.

My last slim chance at the highest level of competition came in 1964. In the spring, it was determined that two oarsmen from each of 20 major colleges would be selected to attend an Olympic camp. An eight would be selected from them to compete against California, Harvard, Yale and the Vesper Boat Club in the Olympic Trials to be held in July 1964 at the Orchard Beach lagoon course. It was certainly a long shot, but I passed the first test by being selected as one of the two from Boston University. The coach casually mentioned proof of "citizenship" and my heart sank. I was a "foreign student" and I could not become a U.S. citizen until 1968 at the earliest. If I wanted to go to Tokyo, or any other Olympic Games, I would have to buy a ticket like almost everybody else.

Several years later I decided if that was the only way I could go, I would gladly purchase plane tickets and event tickets for my father and myself for the 1976 Olympics in Montréal. I did just that and we had a wonderful time cheering the best athletes in the world. I had planned the trip for over a year, and we followed a tight schedule—rushing between The Olympic Village and The Olympic Stadium like schoolboys, cheering on gold medal winning boxers Teofilo Stevenson, the Spinks brothers, and Sugar Ray Leonard. We then rushed to see Bruce Jenner, Mac Wilkins, John Walker, Dwight Stones, and others medal at the track. Then onto the soccer venue.

*****

The United States won the gold medal in the eight-oared crew, 2000-meter event in every Olympics from 1920 to 1960. They were always the best in the world. In 1952 Navy had won in Helsinki, Finland and in 1956 Yale successfully defended the title in Melbourne, Australia.

In 1965 our Boston University Varsity crew was a determined group, and we had some success during the season. At the Eastern Sprints Regatta, the 15 eights from the top universities on the East Coast battled it out on Lake Quinsigamond in Worcester, Massachusetts. The two winners of the three heats in the morning would race against each other in the afternoon final. We eliminated Yale and Dartmouth, finishing behind Harvard in our heat. We were ecstatic to be in the final.

We battled Navy stroke for stroke down the entire course. We were right next to them and could hear their labored grunts as they could hear ours. They beat us by two feet after 1¼ miles. Even though we had placed sixth overall, it had been the best finish in Boston University history. Our ragtag group of "oars" were well pleased at the result, and felt all the work for the previous nine months had been worthwhile. It was an unlikely result since half the members of the eight were "walk-ons"—athletes like me who had only started rowing when they got to college. We pushed each other every day in practice . . . I led the exercises. For years I had done as many push-ups as I could before I went to bed every night, at my father's suggestion. I could do 85, nipples to the ground. All of my crewmates were in great shape, though, and most would leave me far behind when we ran our 2 miles, down to the Mass. Avenue Bridge, along the Charles River, every day after practice. I rowed for the 4 years that I attended

Boston University and was proud that I never missed a race.

My father was present to see the results of his guidance and nurturing that day. All of us envied the Harvard crew which had won The Sprints' title. The tradition of stripping the racing shirts off our backs and handing them to our opposite number, on the dock after losing a race still prevailed. It provided a personal moment between the vanquished and the victor. (It's certainly a good thing that this tradition was not followed in court.) Each member of The Harvard Crew at the Eastern Sprints that day had 14 sweaty shirts draped over their arms.) When women's rowing became an NCAA sport they did not carry on the tradition.) Shirts be damned . . . we had dreamed big and then followed through. The "Dare to be Great" business had paid off again.

In my senior year I decided I would play soccer as well as continuing to row. I had played in England and then in Canada in a league composed of foreigners like myself. I hadn't played in years and my limited skills had eroded, but I made up for it with effort and the Boston University team that year was weak. I played right half for a few games until the goalie got injured. They needed a volunteer to replace him. I had been the goalie on my school team at aged 10 and loved the green sweater that I was given to wear. My first few games went well. The Boston University News reported that "Senior Anton Keating was impressive in his first appearance in the Terrier goal." However, my luck and confidence soon ran out . . . my limited skills were rusty and I made some basic mistakes in the next several games. I started to second guess myself. In a televised game I let in 3 simple shots . . . I was dragging the team down and at half-time told the coach to replace me. I did not mind losing and looking foolish, as long as I had tried my best, but I had lost my nerve and almost anyone could have done better. The coach agreed and my soccer career came to a dismal end. We lost 6 to 0.

*****

I had not been a good student in college and I did not do well on the law boards, so I was rejected or put on the waiting list of several law schools. I flew down to the University of Maryland Law School after pleading for an interview, and met with the Vice Dean Hall to persuade him to admit me. "What did you want to tell me?" He liked my response and that I was making $1.60/ hour flat time, 70 hours a week—sweaty labor, moving furniture. It had cost fifty dollars to fly from Boston. Each way. Also a few of my wife's relatives who lived there made some calls . . . who knows? I was accepted.

When I first arrived in Baltimore in 1966 to attend the law school, I was employed for a few months by a detective agency. I knew that F. Lee Bailey had been a private investigator in law school and I wanted to emulate him. However, my assignment was to patrol a supermarket looking for and arresting shoplifters. I was supposed to be under cover, a difficult task at best for a white guy in an all-black neighborhood. I was offered a gun to protect myself, but refused it. Instead, I was handed a "blackjack." It was useful on two occasions. I soon realized I was in way over my head . . . I had to make a few arrests and then take the cases to the local district court. Since on weekends there were no prosecutors there, I had to present the case to the judge myself.

After a few months, I got a better job as a dispatcher for a local trucking company. I soon established a new routine. I would arrive home from law school at about 4:00 p.m., take a 2-hour nap, and then travel to the trucking company. As the dispatcher, I would receive telephone requests for oil delivery, and then instruct one of a dozen oil trucks to go to various destinations around Baltimore. At first it was very difficult, since I did not know the area at all. I sent trucks all over the place rather than have them make deliveries near each other. During the winter it was quite hectic. It was a good job, though, because when things calmed down and the weather was good, I could study. I worked 5 nights a week, always getting home before midnight and sleeping well.

I was working as an intern in the Office of the State's Attorney in April 1968 when Martin Luther King was assassinated. Because of the resulting unrest, anyone traveling without authority after the National Guard had occupied the city was subject to immediate arrest. I was given a pass to travel between the various police districts and the courthouse in Baltimore. Soldiers in jeeps and personnel carriers roamed the city struggling to bring order to the streets that were either deserted or mobbed. Smoke from burning buildings hung over the city and broken glass decorated sidewalks and streets.

Every available space in the jails and lockups was filled with snipers, arsonists, looters, and curfew violators, many of whom were innocent people who had been caught up in the anger and the rebellion. Many of them had just been traveling home from work when they were arrested en masse. Every seat in every courtroom in the Clarence Mitchell courthouse was occupied by defendants. Uniformed soldiers lined the walls of every courtroom and all the hallways. One young guard had accidentally discharged his rifle and the noise echoed throughout the building, as if to underscore the seriousness of the situation.

After the Civic Center had been filled to capacity, buses were used to keep several thousand detainees occupied while they were driven endlessly around the Beltway until space could be made for them to be presented to a judge. The courthouse "family" labored for several days and nights to process the cases of these individuals. The half-dozen law students there were needed to help. We each presented hundreds of cases to exhausted judges, attempting to help dispense justice fairly, even while those enforcing martial law tried to control the streets. The entire experience, perhaps, underscored the descriptions of this courthouse. It opened in 1900. It was called either "This Noble Pile" or "This Bastion of Racism." It could not be both.

I went to law school so that I could be a trial attorney because trials seem to afford an opportunity for contests and competition and the excitement of conflict. I had been methodically trained to enjoy the stimulation involved. By the end of college, I knew that my athletic days had come to a rapid end, but I did not want to eliminate the "thrill of victory and the agony of defeat" from my life. It had been such an important part of it for a couple of decades.

I had not won all the ribbons and medals or trophies that I wanted, but I viewed courtrooms much like boxing rings. The rewards were far more significant than could be provided by any athletic endeavor, and certainly more critical than any bloody lip or bruised ego that I had ever experienced. Freedom, life, or death were now at stake.

CHAPTER 12:
THE NOVICE LAWYER

"All the law is not in a book . . . "
— Arthur Miller

A lawyer's reputation, or at least the public perception of a lawyer's ability, is usually determined initially by what the lawyer does in the courtroom. It is in a court where that public perception is formed from newspaper, radio, television, or observer's accounts. The courtroom provides a public arena where his skills, competitiveness, tenacity, and desire to win can be displayed. Ironically, the greatest monetary awards go to those lawyers who stay out of court, retiring from active trial practice and becoming legal advisers rather than a trial advocate. The greatest financial rewards go to lawyers who specialize in legal corporate work, or to those who represent and involve themselves with great financial interests.

The courtroom is consequently the terrain for young lawyers who have the energy, desire, and ambition to prove themselves, and who want to establish a reputation in the legal community and in society at large. In the United States any lawyer who is admitted to practice may appear in court as a trial lawyer. The classification as barristers and solicitors does not exist as it does England, and as a consequence every lawyer is considered qualified to try cases. Thus, the quality of advocacy does not share the same uniformity.

Where the trial attorney is highly trained and qualified, the burden on the trial judge is simplified and the trial can be greatly expedited, because through painful experience, seasoned trial lawyers have learned to avoid unimportant questions and unnecessarily lengthy cross examination. They are more likely to refrain from unnecessary interruptions caused by objecting to relevant evidence and making protracted comments and arguments.

Many new admittees to the Bar would like to become qualified trial attorneys in all types of litigation, however the choices for such experience are
limited. If he associates himself with a busy law firm, joins the staff of a large
company or large industry or obtains office space in association with other
lawyers, he won't have many opportunities for significant litigation experience.
Thus many new lawyers seek employment in a prosecutor's office or a Public
Defender's office.

I wanted to start as a prosecutor to get trial experience immediately (there
was no Public Defender at the time.) Until the 1930s, the States Attorney's
Office, the City Solicitor's office and the Police Headquarters were all located in
the main courthouse which had been built on an entire city block in downtown
Baltimore. It opened in 1900. The historic Battle Monument commemorating
the successful stand against a British invasion in the War of 1812 was a few
yards away, and many important historical events had occurred nearby.

I had always loved the majesty of the white marble benches, highlighted
by the dark mahogany chairs and tables in many of the courtrooms. I had
watched many important cases being tried there, when I was a law student.
However, the courthouse soon became too crowded and some criminal courts
were added on the top floors of the "Annex"—a 10 story building located
half a block away. It was totally inadequate, dingy and had no air-conditioning.
The converted office building had never been erected with criminals and trials
in mind. In 1971, Joseph C. Howard, presiding in his ninth floor courtroom,
sentenced a 26-year-old prisoner to a 15-year term of imprisonment. Stunned
by the sentence, the defendant walked straight over to a window that had
no bars on it, broke it with his head and jumped to his death. I arrived a few
minutes later to find the distraught judge, chain-smoking and pacing back and
forth in his small chambers.

Three months later a 14-year-old girl jumped from a fourth floor window,
after being sentenced to a three-day observation period at a juvenile detention
center. She also died. After a third (unsuccessful) attempt by a defendant to
jump out of a courtroom in the annex, bars were put on the windows making
the courtroom seem even smaller. It was certainly a reminder to all the court
personnel that their roles not only had a permanent impact on people's lives

but in some situations the impact was sudden and unexpected.

I prosecuted many serious cases in the tiny courtrooms on the top floor of the "Annex" every day, for over a year. The presiding judges were either Joe Howard, the first African-American to be elected a judge there, and Shirley Jones, the first female ever to preside there.

In 1962, Governor Millard Tawes had appointed Shirley B. Jones as an associate judge of the Supreme Bench for Baltimore City, making her the first woman in the state to be a Circuit Court judge. She was 34. In 1965, Gov. Tawes appointed her, temporarily, to sit on the Court of Appeals so she could participate in the Schowgurow case, which he knew would be a landmark decision.

A Buddhist named Lidscha Schowgurow, an immigrant from Yugoslavia of Mongolian descent had murdered his estranged wife by shooting her in the heart and in the head. He had then shot himself making sure, however, that his wound was superficial. When he was arrested he filed an affidavit in which he stated that he'd been raised in the Buddhist faith and had continuously been an adherent of that faith; that the spiritual leader of the Buddhist faith is the Dhali Lama, and that the Buddhist religion does not teach a belief in the existence of God or a Supreme Being.

His conscientious defense attorney argued that the section of the Maryland Declaration of Rights that required public officers to declare their belief in God was unconstitutional, and that since the Grand Jurors that had indicted him had been required to assert their belief in a Supreme Being, that he had been denied due process of law. Buddhists, ethical culturists, Taoists, atheists and agnostics had historically been excluded from serving on a jury.

The judge did not agree. He proclaimed pompously, "God is not unconstitutional in the court in which I preside." A jury was quickly impaneled, and without much hesitation convicted Schowgurow of first-degree murder.

Shirley Jones ruled along with the rest of The Court of Appeals, while reversing Schowgurow's conviction, that anyone in the State whose case had not become final could have their convictions reversed. Several hundred cases had to be retried, creating a huge backlog in high-volume jurisdictions. Schowgurow's case was sent to Oakland, Garrett County for trial, but two of the jurors refused to impose death, so another mistrial was declared. By the time a third trial could be scheduled, the defendant's confession could not be introduced: in 1966 the Supreme Court had changed the law, with its Miranda decision. This Buddhist with a gun was allowed to plead guilty to second-degree murder and received the then-maximum sentence of 18 years. Because of the case, the maximum for second-degree murder was increased by the legislature to 30 years.

Shirley Jones was a delight and had to carefully negotiate her position as the only female among 22 white male and three black male associate judges. There was a lot of dissension and hatred on the bench. Segregation had only ended a few years earlier. As a young prosecutor, I was assigned to run one of the African-American judge's courtrooms and became very close to him. Joseph C. Howard had won his judgeship in a bitterly contested election. He had been the first African-American Big Ten football player and an active community organizer when he got out of the Marines. He had been a chief prosecutor.

Judge Howard often fought with some of the white racist judges on The Supreme Bench. One day he returned from a "bench meeting" particularly upset. He had an arch enemy on the bench named Judge William O'Donnell who was also big, strong and aggressive. He had been an All-American lacrosse player in college, served in the Navy and had been in charge of the State's Attorney's Office. He was an overt racist. What made him more dangerous was that he was brilliant, handsome and had a lovely smile. He saw no need to keep his virulent, antiquated views to himself.

On this day, Joe expressed his concern to me that he had said some things he should not have said at the meeting as the 26 judges, including Judge Shirley Jones, sat around a long conference table in their robes. O'Donnell would often work in devious ways, to bring about what he wanted. Judge Joseph Howard had confronted him with "Hey, O'Donnell! Why don't you pull your pants down? You fight like a girl! Let's see if you've got a pussy down there!" He then explained, that he had then looked up and said, "Oops . . . excuse me Shirley." She simply smiled. Silly boys. She happened to agree with Joe.

In 1978, President Carter appointed them both to the United States District Court for the District of Maryland, located in Baltimore. She was the first female and he was the first African-American to ever be appointed there.

Towards the end of my work with the State's Attorney, I tried a case involving Mrs. Delia O'Grady. In 1900 she had left County Galway, Ireland and moved to Baltimore. She enjoyed a full life there and by 1972, at the age of 86 she had 13 great-grandchildren. She was one of a few elderly white people who had not deserted the changing neighborhood. She had been burglarized several times, but stubbornly refused to leave.

It was rumored that the victim was wealthy, since a year earlier her mentally challenged niece sat on the steps giving money to passersby. On January 13, 1972, Tyrone Simmons, 17 and Lena Bryant, 21 both African-American, followed her back into her house after she had taken out the trash. They tied her hands and feet, threw an apron over her face and tortured her by spraying lighter fluid on her arms and legs, to learn where she kept "The money." They threatened to burn her house down if she did not reveal where the money was kept.

In fact, Delia O'Grady was on a small pension. The man raped her and moments later she heard them leave and then smelled smoke. She fainted and did not regain consciousness until she arrived at the hospital. Her assailants had started a fire in the pantry and it caused extensive damage to the house.

Mrs. O'Grady had only $90 stashed in a secret drawer in her dining room table. However, she kept a few other precious items there as well, which she was not going to risk losing. Her second son, Capt. Eugene P. O'Grady was the only Maryland Chaplain killed during World War II. She had been so proud when he joined the priesthood and had been devastated when he died. She only had one photograph of him, in his vestments, and she kept it safely hidden for safety. She wasn't concerned about the money, but would sooner die than risk losing her son's photo. Mrs. O'Grady died three weeks later.

It so happened that she was also the mother of John O'Grady, a Juvenile Court Master who had heard cases for 30 years in the downtown Courthouse. Tyrone Simmons had coincidently been sentenced to probation by him a year earlier. Master O'Grady stoically made the arrangements for his devout mother's funeral at St. Martin's Church in West Baltimore near her home. Many judges, prosecutors, other lawyers and members of the courthouse family attended.

Simmons and Bryant were arrested within a week, after eyewitnesses identified them as leaving the premises, and Simmons then gave an oral statement admitting his guilt.

Many people were screaming for the death penalty, but I was assigned to prosecute the case. It was understood that I would not seek death. I left my office on the second floor of the courthouse and walked down one flight to the chambers of Master O'Grady. I had never met him and spent an hour commiserating with him about the torture, rape and murder of his mother. It was very difficult, and he seemed unnaturally detached as he told me he was confident I would do my best to bring about a fair result.

The 3½-week jury trial before Judge Joe Howard ended in a mistrial. The jury deliberated for 11½ hours, but failed to agree upon a verdict. Some key eyewitnesses had changed their testimony and Simmons made a very sympathetic witness, who cleverly survived my cross examination. I was stunned to learn that the jury stood 11 to 1 for acquittal. I received a five-page letter from the white forelady explaining that the deliberations of the mostly African-American members kept coming back to race.

Many people urged me to dismiss the case. I refused and a second jury trial was conducted in October in 1972, Judge Marshall A. Levine presided. Simmons had entered an insanity plea and had been examined extensively at Clifton T. Perkins State Hospital. The psychiatrists there noted he was attempting to fake a psychosis and was much smarter than his tests had showed.

Armed with this new information, the second three-week trial came down to the cross-examination again. Simmons had forgotten what he told the medical staff. He had said, for example he couldn't recognize the American flag, that there were 10 months in a year and a number of other things he thought would help him look simple-minded. It would be easier to attack him this time. It was easy, at least I thought. "I'll bet you don't know how many months there are in a year do you?" "You do?" "How many are there?" "12 you say?". "How long have you been knowing that?" "All my life"

After a 12-day trial, this second jury deliberated for six hours and then announced they were unable to agree upon a verdict. They were divided 7 to 5 in favor of acquitting Simmons.

I had already announced my resignation from the States Attorney's Office, so I would not be available for a third trial, but I urged the Trial Division to prosecute the case again. Simmons had admitted his guilt to the psychiatrist's at Clifton T. Perkins Hospital. There was no precedent for using such an admission, but in a third trial, with nothing to lose I suggested that Simmons be asked if he ever told anyone else, apart from the police, that he had committed the crime. If he denied he had then perhaps the examining psychiatrist could be called as a State's rebuttal witness. J. Carroll Holzer, The Head of the Trial Division, decided to handle the case himself. I was gratified because he was a very sound, clever and capable prosecutor.

Judge William O'Donnell presided over the third trial, and allowed the psychiatrist to testify. After lengthy deliberations the jury could not reach a unanimous verdict. They were 10 to 2 for guilty. One of those who voted to acquit noted that Mrs. O'Grady was 86 while "the defendant had his whole life ahead of him." Another lesson, "that all the law is not in a book."

A month later the case against Simmons was dismissed and he was freed. Bryant (his accomplice) had not been put on trial because when the eyewitnesses recanted, the case against her evaporated. A short time later she was found shoplifting and the charges were treated as grand larceny. The judge knew who she was and sentenced her to five years.

My maternal white-haired grandmother, Minnie Shevlin Maguire, was at the time 84 and lived in Tullyallen, County Louth, Ireland. I tried not to let that interfere with my judgment, but I wonder if I succeeded. I certainly tried hard.

*****

In 1972, I attended The National College of District Attorneys in Houston, Texas, along with 120 other experienced prosecutors from around the United States. Many of the prosecutors there wore golden nooses or handcuffs as tie clips or lapel decorations, and the general philosophy there equated the ultimate penalty of death as some type of home-run, touchdown, or gold medal. It was a difficult month for me and I did not want to be associated with most of these people. I was astounded when we were instructed in discussions on jury selection to seek "the most biased and prosecution prone jury that could be assembled." The Dallas County Prosecutor's Office distributed a printed instruction manual warning that "any member of a minority group was to be eliminated wherever possible."

Prosecutors were advised: "Do Not take Jews, Negroes, Dagoes, Mexicans, or a member of any minority race on a jury, no matter how rich or well-educated." Another handbook stated: "You are not looking for a fair juror, but rather a strong, biased, and sometimes hypocritical individual who believes that defendants are different from them in kind, rather than in degrees; you are not looking for any member of a minority group which has been subjected to oppression—they almost always empathize with the accused. The best prosecution juror was a bigot. Gays, Native Americans, Hispanics, blacks or anyone who might fall into an oppressed minority category for any reason should be excused, if possible."

In 1986, Supreme Court Justice Thurgood Marshall pointed out, in *Batson v. Kentucky* that "the misuse of peremptory challenges to exclude black jurors had become both common and flagrant." In theory, there cannot be an appropriate race-based challenge to a juror; however, enforcement of this rule is very difficult because the prosecutor only has to state a believable, neutral reason for rejecting a minority member from the jury.

There were very few minority prosecutors in attendance at the National College of District Attorneys, and no consideration was given to their feelings. I was stunned to be confronted with such overt racism. At the Huntsville, Texas prison complex, which contained over 10,000 inmates, all of the field workers in the hundred-degree heat were black. When I confronted the Commissioner Corrections of Texas, who was leading our tour there and bragging about the excellent conditions for Texas prisoners, I questioned whether the fact that all the whites were inside and the blacks were outside was just a coincidence. He explained that it was "Just a coincidence!" And the overwhelming majority of the hundred and 20 prosecutors erupted in applause at his response to my perceived arrogance and rudeness. There were few of us, out of the 120, who were outraged, but the overwhelming majority of prosecutors there sincerely believed we were too sensitive and lacked an appropriate sense of humor.

I had always been fascinated with records, and at a very young age I had received a Guiness Book of World Records as a birthday gift. I always felt that it would be a great honor and distinction to get a record that would be included there. Since a major focus in my family was athletics, I naturally thought in terms of some sports activity. At the National College of District Attorneys, however, many would brag about the number of death penalties that had been secured by individual prosecutors. These "accomplishments" finally resulted in the inclusion in the Guinness Book of Records in a category entitled "The Deadliest Prosecutor." In the 1979 Edition, this "honor" was claimed by Joe Freeman Britt, a District Attorney in North Carolina who had obtained twenty-three death penalty verdicts in a 28-month period. He bragged that he personally had put thirteen defendants on death row by mid-1976. This category of accomplishments was eliminated from consideration after 1986 because it tended to encourage prosecutors to seek death—not the healthiest or most commendable achievement.

My experience in Houston, Texas and my disgust with some of the judges that I had appeared in front of had persuaded me to apply my talents and energy as a defense attorney. In January 1973, I resigned my position to fight from the other side of the trial table. I joined the Public Defender's Office. Soon I was fighting my old officemates. There were many serious cases to be tried. Just as many and just as serious as I wanted.

After I resigned, and before I began as a P.D., I cashed my pension and traveled to London with my wife. My brother Charles was appearing in a new television show "Crown Court" which appeared on ITV in the United Kingdom, in the afternoons. The show took place entirely in a court room and the scripts were taken from real cases. My brother took the part of a barrister, complete with wig and gown. The public was invited to apply to become a juror and the verdicts were not predetermined. There were only the BBC and this one, new, commercial station, ITV, available for viewers throughout the British Isles. That guaranteed an audience of many millions.

The show had created a great deal of excitement because the audience knew that the jurors had been selected at random and were free to decide the cases based upon testimony that the viewing audience had seen. It was one of the first afternoon television shows and so it was very popular. Each episode lasted for 90 minutes, shown in segments over a three consecutive day timeframe. An exact replica of one of the courtrooms of the Old Bailey (the principle courthouse in London) had been constructed in a television studio in Manchester.

The "barristers" argued their respective sides earnestly and everyone got caught up in this "reality" television. Consequently, the actors were quite serious about winning and convincing a jury to decide with them. Weeks ahead of time, scripts had been provided to the cast, and then they had assembled for two days on the set to rehearse.

Camera positions were carefully considered and on the third day the lucky viewers who had been selected at random from the viewing audience met for their instructions and then were placed in the jury box to watch the trial as it was being filmed. The jurors, at the conclusion of the closing arguments then retired to the "jury room" and discuss the case.

I had planned to resign on a Friday so that we could fly to England a couple of days later, in time to travel up to Manchester and watch the dress rehearsal. My brother arranged for me to be on the jury. I decided I could not miss this opportunity to travel there to be one of the people to decide the case. I was scheduled to prosecute a first-degree murder case during my last week as a prosecutor. The defendant Malcolm 5X Johnson had approached an individual sitting in an automobile and had fired six shots at him because that person had stolen drugs from Johnson. He was killed instantly. The case had dragged on. It was a court trial. It could not be determined with certainty whether the case would end on time. I requested a close friend of mine, Dominic Iamele, to be my co-prosecutor so that if the case was not over, he could finish it. I could then resign and be free to travel.

I withdrew from the case and left it in Dominic's very capable hands. A first-degree murder verdict was the result.

I arrived in Manchester on time and watched the rehearsal, and agreed not to reveal that one of the lawyers was my brother, or that I was a lawyer. I subsequently joined these volunteer jurors the next day for watercress sandwiches and tea. I pretended I lived in the Manchester area during the general discussion before we went on the set to listen to the evidence. My brother was taking the part of the prosecuting attorney. When the jury had retired to consider the verdict, I had kept my mouth shut during the deliberations until I saw it was not going my brother's way, and then I went into my prosecutor's mode and tried to convince the others of the defendant's guilt.

A scruffy looking man sitting across from me said in his North country accent "'Ere, you don't know what you're talkin' abou'. You can't convict somebody on circumstantial evidence!" I couldn't explain to him that that was the best kind of evidence, so I simply suggested that since the judge had not told us that, I thought that we could and we should. I was not convincing enough. The count was 9 to 3 for not guilty, and so we made it unanimous and delivered our verdict in open court "on the set." The television cameras recorded the verdict which was announced by the foreman for the first time in open court. Because this person was the only juror who got to speak on camera, he had to be a member of the Actors' Equity Association under union rules. The verdict was a genuine surprise to the acting courtroom participants and their reactions were consequently more lifelike. The rest of us jurors never said a word throughout the show. We were not polled!

My brother was disappointed with his "loss" and said to me "what good are you, you son of the bitch, you blew the only case I care about!" These folks were really taking their responsibilities seriously. Some cousins who had emigrated to Australia and South Africa saw the show, and also enjoyed the stunt when it was shown there.

*****

Almost immediately upon returning home, I became a Public Defender in the Circuit Court in Baltimore, representing people charged with serious crimes of violence, and my wife was also a Public Defender in the Appellate Division. We often worked on cases together—usually after I had lost. She was beautiful and brilliant. She did not get involved in the rough-and-tumble of trying criminal cases, but preferred the more academic exercise of persuading the highest appellate judges in the state that errors had been made. I felt that was rather like playing chess, one move a month, because appeals moved quite slowly. The contest there was, for the most part, in the research and writing of the briefs. The 20-minute oral arguments were very strenuous and difficult but mercifully limited.

As a staff public defender, I was assigned to represent a variety of violent criminals. Some I despised. James Frances Smith was a brilliant sociopath who victimized vulnerable women. For a period of over 40 years he usually stole their property, but sometimes sodomized and/or murdered them. He was repeatedly incarcerated, however he learned how to manipulate the parole system and gain early release. He spent his prison time on lock-up because he cheated other inmates in his gambling schemes and he was known to be a snitch.

Smith murdered Doris Martin in Hampden, Baltimore on November 12, 1973 while on work-release from a 1969 conviction for armed robbery. After a month-long trial, the jury found him guilty of first-degree murder. Because he was not tried within 120 days (the trial started on the 136th day) his murder conviction was reversed and dismissed.

During the course of his trial in Baltimore for the murder of Doris Martin, Smith testified to establish his own "Alibi" defense. He stated in substance that he could not have killed Mrs. Martin on November 12, 1973 because on that date he was in Alexandria, Virginia committing the crime of larceny. He stated that his victim was a woman named Virginia Sullivan, who had placed an ad in the November 9, 1973 edition of the Washington Post advertising a room for rent. While he was unsure of Mrs. Sullivan's address, he testified that she lived a few blocks away from a large Masonic Temple. Mrs. Virginia Sullivan was eventually located at 2400 King Street and was deposed under oath, and she was able to recall vividly that on or about November 12, 1973, (she was not certain of the exact date) the defendant did answer her Washington Post room advertisement and did remove $200 from her purse on the kitchen table and fled. Before he was released in Maryland, the State of Virginia prosecuted him for grand larceny, and he was incarcerated there until he maneuvered his release a few years later. After he was freed from prison, Smith went to California and victimized many elderly females.

Before Smith was permanently incarcerated he tried to rape a younger woman in her house in Sacramento, CA. He assaulted her with a screwdriver, but she stabbed him with a kitchen knife, breaking it off in his chest. He survived but was forced to leave. He was later arrested and convicted for the attack. He died in prison.

*****

Darnell Reid was a particularly unpleasant 19-year-old accused of murdering a man in a phone booth during a robbery. The State had three eyewitnesses and the police had reduced to writing a statement that he had made admitting his guilt. We argued about his chances of success and I had pressured him to take a second-degree murder plea. He insisted on a trial and then everything went right for the defense. Two of the witnesses backed out and the third was weak. The pen used to take the confession had run out of ink in the middle, and a new one was used. It looked suspicious. I jumped all over it.

The night before closing arguments in Reid's trial, Vickie and I went to Largo, Virginia—a three-hour drive—to see Mick Jagger and The Rolling Stones. We got home late. I got a few hours sleep but was still energized on the way to the Courthouse, a 10 block walk from our house in downtown Baltimore the next morning. "I know it's only . . . criminal law . . . but I like it, I like it, yes I do!"

Reid's trial lasted four days, and the jury deliberated for a couple of hours before returning a "Not Guilty" verdict. He was standing by my side and smirked to me "I told you chump!" He turned and walked out of the courtroom.

That same day in another murder case, another client of mine was about to be released directly from death row at the Maryland Penitentiary, located five blocks from our house. It was July 3, 1976, and Irvin Lee Wilson had been on death row since he had been sentenced to die in 1971.

Wilson was the top lieutenant of the major heroin dealer in Baltimore in the 1960s. Walter "Kidd" Henderson was notorious and dangerous. They both had many convictions. Henderson had murdered a woman in a bar in front of many witnesses and had been convicted. He was "Superfly" or "American Caesar." He was very popular locally because he gave away a lot of money. A dispute had arisen between them and Wilson shot Henderson to death.

Over 2,000 people viewed Henderson's body in the funeral home. He was dressed in an expensive black mohair suit with a pure white silk tie set off with a diamond stick pin, white shirt and matching carnation in his lapel. A choir sang "What a Friend We Have in Jesus" and "I Came to the Garden Alone." His 24-gauge mono seal olive bronze steel casket was extravagantly banked by flowers. An 8-foot wreath of evergreens was sent by a friend and many local businesses and organizations also sent flowers with elaborate designs. It was all then shipped to North Carolina along with his coffin in a big procession.

His murder generated a great deal of publicity—much of it was initiated by a rogue prosecutor, who had moved rapidly. Fearing retaliation, Wilson had walked into a local police station after the shooting. He was immediately interviewed by the States Attorney's Office and the next day was indicted. Within 10 days the case had been removed to the Eastern Shore. A jury convicted him of first-degree murder. The notorious "hanging judge," DeWeese Carter, sentenced him to death. He retained new counsel but his conviction was affirmed by the Court of Appeals.

Wilson contacted me from death row and I was intrigued by his situation. The only death penalty sentence that had been imposed in any case I prosecuted, was imposed by DeWeese Carter. (Willie Frank Brice had murdered three people and his case had been reversed three times when it was removed to the Eastern Shore. By the time it came to me, it was seven years old. Carter was a prick. He was the only judge in his small rural county and no one challenged him. He did not like me. The Brice case had been a very bad experience for me.)

Once I interviewed Wilson and realized I would have a great opportunity to attack DeWeese Carter, I agreed to represent him. It would have to be a collateral attack on the conviction in which it would be claimed that even if he was guilty he had not been treated fairly. I filed a Post Conviction Petition on his behalf, after I had assembled a small legal team and had accumulated all the documents in his case. It took nine months to prepare our 90-page memorandum and the States Attorney's Office to respond. A five-day hearing in front of a different judge on the Eastern Shore resulted in Wilson, several months later, being granted a new trial. The trial prosecutor—who actually testified in front of the jury that in his "opinion" Wilson was guilty of first-degree murder—was found to have given "careless and doubtful testimony;" the defense attorney was found to have been incompetent in this, his first jury trial. Judge Carter was found to have made many errors.

Since Wilson was incarcerated in Baltimore, we needed to get the order granting the new trial signed by a Baltimore judge to get Wilson released. Since I had to give the closing argument in Reid's case, I could not walk the paperwork over to the Penitentiary. I did not want to delay so I sent a law student there to perfect the release and film it with my movie camera.

I was still wondering what had happened to Wilson. The harried law student soon arrived and explained that Wilson had been freed two hours earlier. The student got there too late to get a movie of him walking out the front of the Penitentiary. I felt extremely lucky—two murder clients walked out on the same day. A few months later Wilson entered a guilty plea to manslaughter. He was sentenced to time served. He had gone from death row to probation!

Some of my clients had done horrendous things. However, they were sometimes naïve, pathetic and even likeable. One example stuck out. John Earl Williams was 18 years of age, and his girlfriend had left him. He was crushed, and wanted to die. He did not have the courage to kill himself, and so he left a suicide tape saying, "Goodbye to all the friends I never had," and he said he would start shooting at the police, hoping they would kill him.

It was Good Friday in Baltimore, April 16, 1976. Worshippers were returning from afternoon church services. Other folks, after cleaning up the dinner dishes, were preparing to attend evening services. Many others were participating in Passover observances. Still others spent the 90-degree afternoon in bars, tilting beer cans on their front steps, seeking relief from the humidity. It was not a normal April Friday. It was too hot—more like July than springtime. The sun was crimson as it settled over the western part of the city. Storefronts, church steeples and rows of houses created shadows which were lengthening quickly. It was getting cooler.

Officers were patrolling the streets, appreciative of the relief that the quickening darkness would provide. It wasn't really getting busy yet, not for a Friday night. Then bullets began to shatter the tranquility in the 1300 block of West Lombard Street. A volley from a high-powered rifle sent bullets ricocheting along the street. Officers from the Southern, Southwestern and Western districts responded, as did the quick response team of the Tactical Division. In the military, the incident would have been termed a fire fight. John Earl Williams had five high-powered rifles, and 1000 rounds of armor-piercing bullets, which he had legally purchased at Montgomery Wards. He fired over 200 shots in a 45-minute period. He then called Central Command and told them he wanted to surrender. When he, obeying instructions, came out of the house with his hands above his head, he was smashed to the ground by several angry police officers. One officer had been murdered, and six had been severely wounded.

I could only find one psychiatrist who would testify that he lacked the substantial capacity to appreciate the legality of his conduct, or the capacity to conform his conduct to the requirements of the law. The State produced nine psychiatrists who testified that he simply suffered from an "anti-social personality." The jury convicted Williams of first-degree murder, and all the other charges. At the start of the trial, the prosecutor said to me, "Anton, I'd like to introduce you to somebody." He presented me to the officer's widow, who was 6-months pregnant. I felt terrible for her, and a little ashamed. Every single seat in the courtroom was occupied by police officers in uniform throughout the ten-day trial. Even though I was working out a lot, I still felt the enormous stress I was under in my closing argument. The sweat rolled down my face.

Soon after I left the Public Defender's Office to go into private practice, I purchased a three-story office building located at 106 West Madison St. in Mount Vernon, Baltimore in 1977. A short while after moving in, I learned that a previous owner/occupant had been murdered nearby. It resulted in one of the most famous murder cases in Maryland history. In 1922, William B. Norris, a well-known and well loved building contractor, had conducted his business there for several years. On his way back from the bank two blocks away, he and his companion were carrying $6,800 for the payroll. A group of five gunmen robbed them, shooting them both. Norris died across the street from the office.

The brazen gang scattered. One of them was hidden by his lawyer, Harry B. Wolf, the leading criminal lawyer in Baltimore, who lied to the police to assist in this escape. Wolf was disbarred for his conduct. Three of the gang were arrested immediately, but Jack Hart got to Washington before he was captured. Walter Socolow fled to New York City, where his capture made a young Baltimore prosecutor a national hero.

Herbert R. O'Conor, son of Irish immigrants, had become an Assistant State's Attorney in 1920. He soon demonstrated his brilliance and tenacity in court. He was alerted by two local detectives, Charles A. Kahler and William L Murphy, that Socolow, who had been hiding in New York City, had been arrested and was being taken to court there. O'Connor joined them, traveling to the courtroom in New York City where a detention hearing was to be held. The judge there decided to delay the matter until some paperwork for the 19-year-old's extradition could be corrected. Just as the hard-nosed judge banged his gavel saying, "Writ dismissed . . . Prisoner remanded!", the three Baltimoreans rushed at the prisoner and took him out of the hands of the local police. They started to run with him from the courtroom, while the judge banged loudly with his gavel, ordering them to come back.

The trio dragged the prisoner through the courtroom door and down the hallway and then down a long flight of stairs. They were being pursued with shouts of "Bring back that man!" echoing through the corridors. "Don't listen to them," O'Conor yelled at the top of his lungs. Once outside, there was a mad scramble to get into their waiting automobile and finally clap handcuffs on their prisoner. They took several shortcuts and made their way to West Philadelphia and boarded a train for Baltimore.

Needless to say, the New York authorities were outraged at his conduct. It took letters from several Maryland officials including the Governor, who apologized profusely to his counterpart and the judge to placate them. The reaction in Baltimore to what Herbert O'Conor had done was almost universally favorable. He became a household name. He did not try the case, because his popularity convinced Gov. Richie to appoint him People's Counsel for the Public Service Commission. Six months later the five defendants were placed on trial in the courthouse and were all convicted. Two years later, O'Conor was elected States Attorney.

One major reform he instituted was to eliminate the so-called "fee system," which required the office to pay its own way. The budget depended on the criminal context of the cases which the State's Attorney might choose to bring before the courts. From out of these accumulated fees—for each felony, $10; for each misdemeanor, five dollars—the State's Attorney was supposed to pay the running expenses of his office. Hence, it was the usual practice for the prosecutor to bring as many legal charges as he could. Assuming for example that a murder was committed in the city, among other things, the killer would be charged specifically with violating a city ordinance, forbidding the firing of firearms within the city limits. In that way the State's Attorney was able to chalk up another five dollars to his credit. O'Conor helped abolish this practice. Six years later, he became the Attorney General of Maryland and in 1939 he became the Governor of Maryland.

After two terms as Governor, O'Conor resigned in order to take his seat in the United States Senate in January 1947. He served one term there with distinction. At his Requiem mass he was mourned as a man who "knew spectacular success as a prosecutor and politician."

Jack Hart, who was sentenced to life imprisonment for the Norris murder, escaped a year later. He was captured after a month. He waited patiently, and in 1929 he cut his way through the three locks of his solitary confinement cell and made his way to the roof of the Penitentiary, letting himself down from the wall with a rope made of sheets. He was captured four years later and was paroled in 1955 at the age of 68.

I practiced law in Norris' building for 40 years.

CHAPTER 13:
THE RIGHT TO COUNSEL

"The times—they are a-changing . . . "
— Bob Dylan, 1964

One of the most famous cases ever tried in Carroll County, MD was the prosecution of an indigent farm worker named Smith Betts, for robbery. His request to have counsel appointed to represent him had been denied, and Betts sought appellate relief. The U.S. Supreme Court affirmed his conviction in *Betts v. Brady* in 1942. It held that the 6th Amendment right to "assistance to counsel" was not applicable to individual states and that there was no constitutional right to counsel in non-capital cases.

Before Betts, in the 1930s, the United States Supreme Court had been outraged by the circus-like prosecution of the Scottsboro case, where seven poor black youths were convicted of raping a white woman in Alabama. It became obvious that to prevent such miscarriages of justice and protect the rights of people accused of serious crimes, if they could not afford their own private lawyer, one had to be provided to them at public expense. This concept started in the federal courts, and with the reiteration of the constitutional right to counsel in *Gideon v. Wainwright* in 1963, each state had to devise a mechanism to appoint counsel for indigents.

The prosecutor's job used to be much easier before the right to counsel was mandated, because the accused could be bullied into submission. Up through the mid 1960s, the prosecutors in the main courthouse in Baltimore would simply walk down to the bullpen in the basement, which held all the defendants to be tried that day. The pen usually contained between 30 to 50 men each day. The prosecutors would ask all those who wanted a trial to line up along one wall. They would then select some miscreant who wanted a trial, take him upstairs to a court and give him his trial without counsel, usually before a judge, convict that person, and then give him the maximum sentence. The prosecutors would then go back to the bullpen and ask what the rest of them wanted to do. Most would then seek a plea. Every day, this process was followed.

The selection of a trial by jury up through the early 1960s was considered to be a renegade act by the courthouse family. The effort and expense of a jury trial made work more difficult for everyone in the courthouse. At that time, most blacks and women were excluded from jury service. Rather than face any semblance of "a jury of his peers," a jury would inevitably be composed of the peers of the lawyers and judges and courthouse personnel. Consequently, most cases that were not disposed of by a guilty plea were tried with a judge sitting in effect as a jury of one, often referred to as a slow guilty plea. Most private practitioners could not obtain from their clients the legal fees necessary to thoroughly investigate and prepare, and then spend the energy and time involved with defending someone in a trial by jury.

In order to comply with the new right to counsel, Maryland judges would appoint private lawyers in court directly from the bench. It was this same judge who awarded a small discretionary fee, so these lawyers soon learned not to fight too hard or they would suffer the economic consequences.

Initially, the judge in charge of "arraignment court," which usually established motions dates and trial schedules, ensured that those entitled to counsel would have counsel appointed to them. The judge would assign a courtroom habitué, who was either there on some other business, or needed these appointments as a source of income. These lawyers were not usually the cream of the bar.

Consequently, the bench had total control over the defense bar. If a lawyer was too zealous in his representation, he might not be appointed to any other cases. If he needed a lesson in humility and "playing the game," he would be rewarded with a $25 or $50 fee for a trial that might have lasted a week or two. There were no standards. The trial judges had complete discretion in making this award, so if the judge was annoyed, he could punish the lawyer at the end of the case.

In 1970, I prosecuted a kidnap armed robbery case. The passenger in a taxi cab was going home with his Christmas presents, all neatly wrapped, when he was easily convinced to share a little holiday cheer with a long-legged attractive hooker who they chanced upon, and who happened to know the taxi driver. "The John" escaped a few hours later from a dingy apartment house. He got no sex, lost his wallet and his money, and all his family's Christmas gifts were stolen. He had lost all his clothes except for his white underwear and black socks. All of these items were found by the police in the apartment after they had discovered "Mr. Fruit of the Loom," as the police named him, when they first saw him walking down a main street at 3 a.m. The defendant's lawyer, appointed by the Court was not particularly impressive to the judge or me, but he certainly impressed the most important people in the case. The jurors acquitted the armed robber without much hesitation—some simple street justice from a black jury, unsympathetic to another white male seeking commercial sex in the black community.

The Judge, Anselm Sodaro, was a very kind and gentle man. Civility was very important to him. He was considered "a legal giant." He had an unparalleled 46-year legal career serving as an Assistant State's Attorney from 1938 to 1950 when he was elected States Attorney. He then served on the Supreme Bench for 25 years, the last five of which were as the Chief Judge. He was apoplectic—angry at the verdict and at the attorney. I did not respect the lawyer's ability, but I had been beaten fairly. I might not like it or understand it, but I had lost the case. I put on a good game face to hide my disappointment and congratulated opposing counsel. Judge Sodaro awarded him $50 as compensation for this four-day jury trial. I had a good friendly relationship with this judge, and I tried privately to convince him that the attorney had played by the rules during the trial, and that he had been a forceful determined advocate, who deserved a fair fee (which $50 was not.) It didn't happen. The judge would not increase it.

For several months my "team" of prosecutors was assigned to Judge Sodaro's courtroom and I got to know him well. We were fellow immigrants and bonded. He mentored me. He talked of his childhood in Enna, a scraggly village in Sicily, where life was hard and the family dream was to reach America. His father, Michael, a shoemaker, and three siblings scrimped for years to save enough liras. By 1914 they had enough for one steerage passenger. His father travelled to Baltimore where a cousin lived and he opened a shoe repair shop. It took four more years to save the money to transport his family from Sicily.

Although only six, Anselm remembered the excitement in the house when the tickets arrived. His mother cooked a farewell dinner and friends and family came over to say goodbye. Anselm, the youngest, standing tiptoe, tilted a pot to see its contents. He tilted it too far and boiling soup scolded his side, foot and leg. The village doctor treated the burns, but gangrene set in and it was feared the leg would have to be amputated. To take the boat trip as planned, would be fatal. So the Steamer Angona, for which they had four tickets, sailed from Palermo without them. It was in 1918 and Italy was engaged in World War I against Germany. When The Angona was a few miles from Gibraltar, a torpedo from a German submarine crashed into it. Everyone on board went down with the ship.

Nunzia Sodaro waited out her youngest son's recovery and despite what happened to The Angona, despite the knowledge that U-boats threatened every Allied ship, she arranged to use her precious tickets for passage on the freighter Italia. It had no Navy escort and it zigzagged far from normal routes. The passengers endured 31 days of tortured travel. They were met in Ellis Island by Michael who was ecstatic to see his family safe and healthy. They rented rooms in Northeast Baltimore and all went to work. The education of the three sons was the primary objective. One became a doctor; one started an insurance company; and Anselm earned a PhD from Loyola College and finished The University of Maryland School of Law as an honor student. He began his legal career as a prosecutor, and retired as The Chief Judge.

He was a very kind, quiet and unassuming man, but he could be quite dispassionate when he had to impose punishment. He had always approved of the death penalty. He was a seasoned prosecutor in 1952 when he teamed up with Harold Grady, who was also to later become the States Attorney, Mayor and the Chief Judge, to prosecute a notorious murder case which received national publicity: The Murder of Dorothy May Grammer.

There is a very long hill which descends from Baltimore County into the city. One cool moonlit early morning in August 1952, two police officers watched as a shiny Chrysler sedan rolled down the hill at great speed. It finally swerved out of control from one side of the road to the other, veered into a small embankment, struck a utility pole, tipped over and came to rest beside a tree. Inside the wreck they found a woman's body. It appeared to be just another road fatality, but it wasn't. Police were suspicious. The car was in fairly good shape and the woman, Mrs. Grammer, had strange bruises on her wrists and arms. Her eyeglasses, which she needed to drive, were missing. After beating her to death with a piece of pipe, her husband, Edward Grammer had placed her body in the car. Then he took a pebble, which was similar to those found in their driveway, and lodged it under the accelerator pedal to keep the car moving down the hill. The responding officers had immediately observed that the car was still accelerating and its wheels were still spinning when they had arrived at the accident scene.

The medical examiner concluded that the 33-year-old mother of three had been dead before the car ever toppled down the hill. She died from deep lacerations on her head. After initially denying any involvement or wrongdoing, Eddie Grammer then confessed. He said that he been drinking heavily and that he had become angry. Mrs. Grammer had been constantly nagging him about his job and she wouldn't stop. He was unable to control himself.

Life Magazine called it "The Imperfect Crime," since absent the moonlight, a change in direction and the unlucky arrival of the two officers, the car and its contents would have been demolished.

The Baltimore City Police Department investigated further, and soon discovered "the other woman." She was the attractive Mathilda Mizibrocky, a 23-year-old with whom he was sharing a "love-nest," and who did not know he was already married. Many love letters were discovered, revealing their long affair and plans to marry. Mathilda was a star witness at the trial. She was from New York, and carefully draped her fur piece over the witness stand railing when she took her seat. She testified she did not know he was married, and would have had nothing to do with him if she had.

After a nine-day Court trial, Eddie Grammer was convicted of first-degree murder and was immediately sentenced to death. After a number of appeals, Grammer went to the gallows in June 1954. He was calm the night of his hanging. He did not die easily. When he dropped through the trap door at the Maryland Penitentiary on June 10, 1954 his neck did not break and kill him. He dangled spinning and twitching so hard that his slippers fell off and he slowly strangled to death for 13 minutes. Outside of the Maryland Penitentiary a crowd of 300 then watched as the body of Edward Grammer, the man who wanted to commit "the perfect crime" was taken away.

Several years later Governor McKeldin said that he should have spared Grammer's life. He would always tearfully regret not doing so. Sodaro, however, did not regret the execution—even though it was botched—because he believed it was just punishment for the brutal murder.

One day in chambers while reflecting on how the male sex drive causes so much crime and harm, Judge Sodaro instructed that no one was immune to the difficulties that a strong sex drive presented. He was about 5'5", very slender and in his 70s. When asked how he was doing he often responded with a twinkle "Fit as a Fiddle and Ready for Love!" It was clearly still on his mind. He reminisced, with a cautionary tale about an interaction from many years before in 1938. He and another young prosecutor Doug Sharretts, had been at The Emerson Hotel, a block from the courthouse one evening, sharing some drinks with the lawyers and others who often met there. One particularly friendly defense attorney introduced them to the 2 young ladies that he was with. After a few hours the attorney left, and soon Anselm and Doug took their new best friends to separate hotel rooms upstairs.

The next day each of them, Sodaro and Sharretts, had the responsibility to prosecute all the cases in their respective courtrooms at different ends of the Courthouse. Doug was stunned to find that the friendly defense attorney had two prostitution cases on the docket for that morning, and as he looked at the people in the spectator section, he was sickened to recognize the two ladies from the night before. "His" lady gave him a smile and a small wave.

Doug left the courtroom to find Anselm Sodaro, who would know what to do. He walked swiftly down the corridor, hoping that Sodaro's judge had not yet come on the bench. He was lucky and strode up to his fellow prosecutor standing at the trial table. "I've got to talk to you. We're in trouble. Kaplan has fucked us . . ." Sodaro quietly asked what the problem was. Sharretts blurted out, "You know those women we met last night? They're on my docket! I've got those two women from last night on my docket! They're hookers!" Sodaro remained calm and simply said, "Don't worry about it! Just dismiss the cases!" So Doug did.

The Emerson Hotel, from Sodaro's story, located a block from the Courthouse, was a prominent "watering hole" for lawyers, judges and politicians. It contained only the finest furniture, marble, chandeliers and other fixtures. It was a well-known Baltimore landmark. The hotel became infamous when in 1963, a rich white "rural aristocrat" who owned a large tobacco farm murdered a black 51-year-old part-time waitress there. William Zantzinger, 24, 6'2" and 225 pounds arrived in his tuxedo, and wooden walking cane. "Billy's" father was a prominent developer and legislator and he was a fun-loving foxhunting, horse racing ne'er-do-well, who loved to drink and party. At the charity event for "The Baltimore League for Crippled Children and Adults", this patron struck the waitress with his cane several times, because her service had been too slow! She was a sickly mother of 10 children, who was just making ends meet. He was the first white man to be accused of murdering a black woman in the 350-year history of Maryland. The case became a symbol of white racism in Maryland.

The trial was removed to Hagerstown in Washington County, an overwhelmingly white jurisdiction three hours west of Baltimore. A judge convicted him of manslaughter, and Zantzinger served his six-month sentence on home detention and work release. The case was a dramatic demonstration of how the rich, white and powerful could prevail over the poor black and powerless.

Bob Dylan memorialized the murder and the trial in his song "The Lonesome Death of Hattie Carroll." He included it along with other protest songs in his album "The Times They Are A-Changing" in 1964. "In the courtroom of honor, the judge pounded his gavel, to show that all's equal and that the courts are on the level, and that the strings in the books ain't pulled, and persuaded and that even the nobles get properly handled!"

CHAPTER 14:
A REASONABLE DOUBT
AT A REASONABLE PRICE

"A Public Defender's lot is not a happy one . . ."
— Gilbert and Sullivan

In 1972, The Supreme Court ruled that counsel had to be available at all critical phases of a criminal prosecution that might result in a prison term of at least three months. On July 1, 1971, the Maryland Office of the Public Defender was established by the Maryland Legislature in anticipation of this decision.

The Governor at that time, Marvin Mandel, had been a private lawyer and had made a living representing small time criminals. His clients included pimps, prostitutes, bar owners, and those involved with the illegal lottery and other gamblers on "The Block" in downtown Baltimore. Obviously, none of these offenses was considered too important since they were occurring fifty yards away from the police headquarters and the Central District Court. The City Hall itself was only one hundred yards away. The Central Circuit Courthouse was located a block away.

Alan H. Murrell, Esq. had much the same clientele that Gov. Mandel had as a private attorney. Murrell had been a feared prosecutor for many years and was a formidable adversary. Most of the bondsmen, police, and many others in the criminal court arena, including the judges and prosecutors, held him in the highest regard as a litigator. Alan Murrell, at 69, was considered to be one of Maryland's most celebrated criminal defense lawyers in the 20th century.

*****

Alan Hamilton Murrell was born in the small town of Barry, Wales, in 1902, and came from a long line of sea captains. Murrell's father, Captain Hamilton Murrell, had first gone to sea at the age of 11 and had been a young skipper of an ocean-going transport ship dragging coal back and forth across the Atlantic for the Atlantic Transport Co. The Steamer Missouri departed West Hartlepool, England, on March 28, 1889. The 4,200 ton ship, with its distinctive three masts, black-striped red funnel, and green hull, had in its holds a cargo of cement, linseed oil, rags, wool, indigo, herring, and goatskins.

At about the same time, the emigrant ship Denmark was bound from Copenhagen for the United States. Fifteen days out, a boiler room explosion had killed the vessel's chief engineer, snapped a propeller shaft, and ripped open a large hole in the ship's keel. The Denmark's captain signaled for help: "I have 735 passengers on board." It was wallowing in the sea some 800 miles from Newfoundland, and there were no sails on the horizon. A heavy sea made it extremely doubtful whether lifeboats could survive. Slowly the vessel began to sink. For twenty-four hours, the passengers prayed and wept as the slashing sea swirled higher and higher about the ship.

Suddenly the next afternoon, the steamer Missouri of the Atlantic Transport Line, with 26-year-old Capt. Hamilton Murrell in charge, bound from London to Philadelphia, was sighted. A tow was attempted, but abandoned, and despite the heavy sea, lifeboats were lowered and the transfer of passengers and crew began. Twenty-two infants, sixty-five children, the women, and the men were taken off in that order. Not a single life was lost.

To accommodate the Denmark's passengers and crew, Murrell ordered that all cargo between decks be jettisoned from the Missouri. The rescue was recorded in a painting entitled "And Every Soul Was Saved" by Thomas M. Hemy. It commemorated one of the most graphic rescues at sea ever recorded in the history of maritime events.

Captain Murrell was given a hero's parade after the sixteen-day ordeal, and was honored by the Governor and Baltimore's Mayor. He was later given awards by the Kings of Denmark, Sweden, and Romania.

When Alan's mother, who was a beautiful debutante from Louisiana and a student at Notre Dame Prep School in Baltimore, went down to the triumphant parade in the Inner Harbor to see this handsome young Captain, love ensued. They were married two years later, and he took her back to England with him. For several years they traveled across the Atlantic as an inseparable couple, and then later with Alan aboard until Alan was 7. Captain Murrell then bought a home in Massachusetts, where Murrell learned to speak the King's English, with a distinct Boston twang that never left him.

In 1913 his family moved to Baltimore because The Captain had become ill and sought treatment at Johns Hopkins Hospital. Alan attended Boys' Latin High School and City College, but dropped out of both. In 1918 he enlisted in the Navy when his father died, just in time to serve as a seaman in World War I. He had spent his summers working as a lifeguard in Ocean City. He was always a strong swimmer. After the war, he sailed to Cuba in the merchant marine, but hated it—ending six generations of seagoing Murrells.

Between the wars, Alan worked as a door-to-door collector for a local insurance company. It was a fluke that he became an attorney. A family friend told him that only lawyers could collect money, so he earned his GED and went to work as a clerk in the office of J. Purdon Wright, then one of the top trial lawyers in Maryland. He later attended the University of Baltimore School of Law for 8 years at night. He obtained his law degree in 1939. At age 41, after the bombing at Pearl Harbor, he re-enlisted again in the Navy and was assigned to the Carrier Ranger. He was discharged with the rank of Lieutenant Commander.

He served as a defense counsel in many court-martials. After the war he became a special assistant U.S. attorney, and in 1946 he joined the Baltimore State's Attorney's staff as an assistant. He spent a somewhat uneasy four years prosecuting criminals, four of whom were sent to the gallows.

He then opened his own law practice and quickly became one of the most noted and accomplished criminal defense attorneys in Maryland. He pursued what he would later term a "down to earth, grass roots criminal practice," encompassing everything "from sodomy on up." A perfectionist in trial preparation, he personally investigated and researched all of his cases.

One of the highlights of Murrell's career was the successful defense of Anna Mae Pearson, the niece of famed Washington columnist Drew Pearson, who was charged with the murder of her paramour at her Annapolis home. Pearson, then proprietor of the Maryland Inn, claimed her intoxicated boyfriend had attacked her while she was cutting up a pork roast to prepare chop suey and had accidentally impaled himself on her carving knife. The skeptical police promptly discounted her story, but Murrell conducted his usual meticulous investigation, and uncovered the partially sliced pork roast in Pearson's refrigerator. He brought it into court to corroborate her claim of self-defense, and won her acquittal.

Murrell had an acerbic wit and method of questioning witnesses that would wither most people, yet he had the elegance of a gentleman. On one occasion during a trial, Murrell muttered something in an opposing attorney's ear. "Your Honor," the attorney complained, "Mr. Murrell just called me a rotten son of a bitch." "Mr. Murrell," asked the judge, "What have you to say to that?" "He must have been reading my mind," Murrell replied. He liked to say, "All we have is trickery and deceit," and was also fond of repeating "This man doesn't need a lawyer . . . he needs a priest."

In 1971, Governor Mandel created instant credibility for this new Office of the Public Defender when he persuaded Alan Murrell to become its leader. His reputation as an advocate in criminal cases was without equal. Because of it, he attracted a group of well-regarded lawyers to start the office on a solid footing. Several ex-prosecutors joined and added to the stature of the Office of Public Defender.

As head of the OPD, Alan Murrell was responsible for the appointment of the twelve District Public Defender's Offices, which were located across Maryland's twenty-four judicial circuits.

He was free to make whatever appointments were required throughout the Public Defender system, and made only one "political appointment." He was "sincerely requested" by Governor Mandel to give the ex-husband of his second wife, Jeanne Dorsey, a job as a Public Defender in St. Mary's County.

Governor Mandel had been in a serious car accident in St. Mary's County the year before, and had tried to explain his presence there as a political appearance. However, the press soon learned that the State Troopers assigned to protect him and to transport him had called the road from the Governor's Mansion in Annapolis to his girlfriend's (who happened to be Dorsey's wife at the time) home in St. Mary's County "The Road to Mandel's Lay." They had driven it many times. Alan Murrell was glad to oblige in this one instance, but for all the other appointments, he insisted on the autonomy of choosing experienced aggressive lawyers to staff his office.

A three-member commission initially assisted this new state agency in hiring the staff of sixty-eight lawyers and thirty investigators and all the other support personnel which would enable this new "law firm" to fulfill its assignment. They were to provide an attorney to all those charged with crimes, including juveniles, and mental patients in state hospitals. Initially, these attorneys were allowed to maintain a private practice. Because this inevitably interfered with their time and energy, though, several years later Public Defenders became full-time employees.

With the establishment of the Office of the Public Defender in 1971, the quality of justice in Maryland changed. The addition of minorities, such as African Americans and women reformed the system to a great degree. The Public Defenders were now on salary, and most soon became good seasoned lawyers. They could be required to take ongoing training, participate in seminars, and the discussion of effective trial techniques. Instead of taking a court trial in serious contested cases, the jury trial soon became the norm.

Defense counsel cannot refuse to fight for a client, even if he or she believes or guesses that the person they are representing is guilty. The system would not work if defense counsel were required to withdraw unless they actually believed the client to be innocent, since only the most gullible or stupid person would be left to participate as defense counsel in criminal court. Defense counsel's job is to fight the State, put it to the proof, and protect the individual, without suborning perjury. It is not an easy role.

The modern Public Defender's office is comprised of hundreds of seasoned lawyers who tend to stay for a career. Unfortunately, they are often too swamped with a high volume of cases to always be effective, but their knowledge of the system and how to best navigate through it cannot be surpassed. Those people who use the term "real lawyers" to distinguish the private bar from Public Defenders clearly don't know the system very well.

CHAPTER 15:
TRADEMARKS OF A DEFENSE ATTORNEY

"Untruthfulness . . . Leading others astray"
— Emanuel Punishment Book, 1955

It certainly helps a defense attorney to have a defiant attitude toward authority, or wanting to resist being controlled by others. It's also useful to be aggressive, domineering, confrontational and competitive. The Diagnostic and Statistical Manual (DSMIV) describes an oppositional defiant syndrome, usually observed in early childhood, lasting through the teenage years, sometimes continuing into adulthood. This can be a positive thing. A certain level of defiant behavior is to be expected, particularly from teenage boys. However, when it interferes or impedes adolescent adjustment and development, clinical intervention or criminal prosecution might be the next stage. In order to become independent and eventually separate from their family and develop an identity of their own, there is a certain expected behavioral chaos and instability at this age.

It's never simple, since most people don't fit perfectly into any single disorder, but are a combination of them. Oppositional defiant disorder often seen in children and adolescents may be a recurring pattern of negative, hostile, disobedient, and defiant behavior, which might well be channeled in some positive direction.

Persistent stubbornness, resisting direct action, unwillingness to compromise or give in, can be good if there is no serious impact on the basic rights of other people. It can be a good trait for those who like to argue. Failure to accept blame for misconduct and verbal aggression can easily lead to a prison cell however, if this behavior results in significant impairment in social, school, or work functioning. It can easily develop into a passive-aggressive personality disorder, or an antisocial personality disorder, whereby the basic rights of others are trampled and the rules of society consistently broken. However, it can also be the basis for a good career as a criminal lawyer.

It is difficult to sustain an adversarial posture all the time. It requires a great deal of energy to be confrontational in an effective way. There are no steroids that you can take to enable you to gain advantage over your opponents in this contest. It is difficult for the participants in this power milieu to remember that a great deal had been accomplished by a lot of talented people long before they were born. It's hard to assert one's modesty!

Most people's greatest emotional needs center around feeling worthwhile and appreciated. Very few want to appear "unfair." What are you scared of? Failure? We all are. Scared of screwing up? Scared of losing? Finding it difficult to be a Washington General as opposed to a Harlem Globetrotter? A chump rather than a champ? A contender always, and never the champion? If you can dare to be great you must dare to lose.

The three most important characteristics for a defense attorney are confidence, confidence and confidence. The personality of a litigator begins to change in law school while practicing skills intended to focus on effectiveness in court. It often results in more aggression, more impatience, more precision and more combativeness.

Most lawyers understand that big problems come with big cases, but they also brought big opportunities that often require you to swing for the fence. However, if you promise big, you will be compelled to do your best to deliver big. The lawyer facing a difficult case must be able to convince himself and act as though it is impossible for him to fail. Modesty never saved or cured anyone on the face of the earth. Negativity never succeeds and fortune always favors the bold.

Oscar Goodman, a well-known defense attorney before he became Mayor of Las Vegas, was presented with a plaque by some of his mobster clients. Two steel balls were mounted in the middle of it. They joked he had more balls than a brass monkey, underscoring the idea that a defense attorney does not want to win a Nobel Peace Prize from a judge or a prosecutor. "Life's battles don't always go to the strongest or the fastest person, but sooner or later the person who wins is the person who thinks he can." "If you think you are beaten you are, if you think you daren't, you don't, if you'd like to win but think you can't, it's almost certain you won't." It is a necessary outlook from either side of the trial table.

Also helpful to a good defense attorney is a "So what?" attitude. Confession? So what? DNA? So what? In-court identification? So what? Ballistics evidence? So what? Just as Marlon Brando responded in "The Wild One" when asked what he was rebelling against and he said "What have you got?," a good defense attorney must give the same response. If asked "What are you objecting to?" he must answer "What have you got?" Clients want you to be "a talking lawyer" and "a writing lawyer." They want to be able to brag that "you got objections," that "you got motions," that "you got argument," that "you got game" and "that you got case." Carry a "macro chip on your shoulder" but in a pleasant way.

A young prosecutor, who was stumped by a winning esoteric legal issue I had raised, once asked me angrily in open court, "Do you want to win this case on a technicality, or do you want the truth to come out?" I looked at the judge who was smiling and I responded "Give me a minute to think about that . . . okay . . . I think I'll go with the technicality!"

The use of humor as a release and as a weapon, should not be under-estimated. The British government during World War II made a concerted effort to have well-known comedians entertain on BBC radio broadcasts and it was well understood that making fun of their precarious circumstances and being free to laugh at the enemy as well as their own government, provided a tremendous release and boosted morale. Both sides in the war used music to stir the population, but the Nazi regime was too pretentious to allow any freedom to make fun of the way the fascists were running the country. If it were not for the inappropriate humor in criminal court, the impact of dealing with aberrant human behavior and tragic situations would be overwhelming.

The only thing that a defense attorney is in charge of is his own attitude, and you cannot accomplish anything or be effective without it. It beats talent, skill, experience and intelligence. It is usually the only thing you can control. Besides—a courtroom would be a very boring place if anyone could control everything that takes place there. The fact that everyone can be made to look like an idiot in a moment keeps you alert. If everything always went as planned and every performance was flawless, criminal court would be monotonous. Even the most routine matters are stimulating because of the chance that they can go drastically wrong. If you can make the right guess 95% of the time you're doing well in life. In court with its pressure cooker atmosphere, very high stakes, mistakes and bad judgment are sure to occur periodically.

The essence of the adversarial system is conflict. It is nurtured by conflict. You must live with conflict. You must be inspired by it. You must live with the competition and enjoy it and if you're not stimulated and challenged by it, you cannot survive long or thrive. It is a young person's game because a lot of energy is needed and you soon become addicted to the conflict but in order to stay effective, you have to know when to be adversarial and when to back away.

Much like a sporting event, it's easy to enjoy courtroom contests because they allow us to show off what we can do. It's nice to believe that we have left everything a little better than we found it. That is sometimes not possible, though, when by your competitiveness and skill, you have returned another psycho to the street.

Murrell used his deft trial skills in the courtroom on behalf of his clients, and in the Legislature to obtain adequate funding on behalf of his agency. He selected a lot of women for his staff because he believed they were detail-minded and very precise. He did not believe in the death penalty, because he said a lot of mistakes were made along the way, and he didn't want to be responsible for killing someone.

The system Mr. Murrell nurtured was created with liberal zeal to level the field of justice. He was worried it would grow into yet another overworked and bloated bureaucracy and Mr. Murrell—as combative in the courtroom as he was pleasant in private—often fought with legislators for the money he believed necessary to run a first-rate law office.

The legislators thought he was a pain. Murrell thought the legislators were "constitutional cretins." "I'm dealing with a bunch of morons. Would you yourself look at any member of the Legislature to represent you? Let's be frank about it. You'd be sure they'd sell you down the river at some point, wouldn't you?"

Although Murrell was of the legal generation that was inspired by the heroic courtroom battles of Clarence Darrow, he never developed much of a social conscience or sympathy for the underdog. Despite the aforementioned liberal zeal, he often referred to the clients as "bums," and openly condemned attorneys who treated their clients "as a cause." Such misguided dedication, in Murrell's view, obscured the primary role of a defense attorney—to get his client off. Murrell said that "criminal courts today are the garbage heap of humanity. Such a criminal, who has 'an adversary relationship' with his lawyer, hopes he can con his lawyer into committing some kind of reversible error, or attack him later on as being totally incompetent. The lawyer has to protect himself."

Murrell was an unabashed racist, and was undeterred by political correctness. He had been an Assistant State's Attorney in Baltimore City in the late 1940s, and since Maryland was a "border state," segregation was a way of life. The swimming pools and tennis courts were all segregated. Civil Rights protesters were starting to agitate. Several progressive lawyers, notably Harold Buchman of the A.C.L.U., arranged to play a prohibited integrated tennis match at Druid Hill Park in Baltimore. "Mixed, mixed doubles" they called it. This conduct was subject to criminal prosecution, for the crime of "integrated recreation" and carried a one-year prison term. Murrell had gladly prosecuted the case, and was frustrated that a sympathetic judge would not impose a prison term on Buchman and his allies.

As a student in the intern program to the State's Attorney's Office in the spring of 1968, I was assigned to the Trial Division where I helped prepare cases for trial. I was thrilled to be allowed to actually sit at the trial table during the course of several murder jury trials.

William J. Shotkowski, a mechanic, was tried for the strangulation murder of a 41-year-old home improvement salesman who was paying improper attention to his 19-year-old niece. The accused had been infatuated with her, and resented the victim dating her. Daniel Gary Baker was found dead in his apartment in August of 1966, having been strangled with an electric cord around his neck, his hands bound behind him with adhesive tape, and a handkerchief stuffed into his throat.

Shotkowski had quit his job two days before the murder, and was last seen a few days after Baker's body was found. A warrant was issued for his arrest three days after the gruesome discovery. He traveled through several states before he settled in St. Louis, Missouri, where he was living under an assumed name. He was not found until two years later by the FBI.

Hillary Caplan was the assistant State's Attorney that I was helping. He was very clever and articulate, but was clearly intimidated by Alan H. Murrell, who represented Shotkowski. Judge Solomon Liss presided over the jury trial.

The niece, Nancy Stokes, said the defendant came to her home in Baltimore County and exhibited a photograph of her, a membership card, and the driver's license he had taken from Baker. She quoted Shotkowski as saying, "This is what I got from a friend of yours. He won't be picking you up anymore. Keep them for whatever they're worth. Yes, he won't be going to work today." Shotkowski then fled from the city after he had argued with the young girl and her grandmother. The jury returned a verdict of murder in the 2nd degree, and Judge Liss imposed a 25-year prison term. I was surprised that the jury had compromised in the case. There was planning, and strangulation takes time and effort. First degree murder, however, had been rejected by the jury.

I approached Alan Murrell in the hall and said to him, "Mr. Murrell, this gruff attitude and manner you have in court, is that trial tactics?" He said, "That's just me, sonny!" Murrell intimidated everyone, and was a legend partly because of that, but at that point he was just being a bully to me and I knew well how to deal with bullies. Don't give them an inch. It was the last time that I called him "Mr. Murrell."

We later tried cases against each other when I joined the prosecutor's office. In one of them, I had overwhelming evidence. His 16-year-old client had held up a taxicab in the middle of the day, on a busy Baltimore street, and had ejected the driver, intending to steal the cab. However, he could not drive the stick shift and soon crashed it into several parked cars. The police arrested him there. Murrell took a court trial and made an earnest effort to assert that his client had just "happened" on the scene immediately before the police arrived. The "bum" was convicted. Not much of a feather in my prosecutor's cap!

Alan and I became fast friends a few years later. I joined his Office of the Public Defender in 1973, staying through 1978, and specializing in serious crimes of violence.

I understood that perhaps I did not have "The Sports Gene," but I did have "The Trial Gene." I had always known that it was not enough just to be clever, articulate and competitive—that "failing to prepare was preparing to fail." For some of my friends, athletic achievement and excellence seemed to come so easily and naturally. It was the same for me from the very beginning in Court.

In the boxing ring, everyone knew that "If you haven't got it, you might as well quit . . . put him in the ring, Joe, let me have a punch, put him in the ring, Joe, and then we'll go to lunch...we'll show him the ropes and destroy his hopes . . ." Similarly, in a courtroom it is much easier for the participants who possess some or most of these characteristics. Trial advocacy courses help, but, alone are no substitute. Neither is all the time and effort in the world . . . even ten thousand hours of it. No single characteristic or personality trait assures success, but a lawyer soon finds out whether or not he has "it," and if not, he might as well "quit."

CHAPTER 16:
JUDGES

"Appointed, not anointed . . ."
— Anonymous

It is often very hard to predict how a lawyer will act once he is sworn in and robed as a judge. If he or she is very energetic, flamboyant and combative, then the adjustment to the position can be difficult for all concerned. If he is at his core an insecure person, concerned with controlling every aspect of his life and therefore, also, a courtroom, he can do a lot of damage. If he feels it's a contest of wills between him and the lawyers and supporting staff the resulting damage can be substantial.

After I had been a lawyer for nine years I had a fantasy about being a Circuit Court judge. Thinking I wanted the stature and power that the position brings, I made my application and went through the rather vigorous vetting process. Those who passed went on to be interviewed by The Governor. I went to Annapolis and had a nice visit with Governor Harry E. Hughes in the Statehouse. We'd met before on the campaign circuit in 1978, when we were both running for office. He had been successful. The interview went well. He informed me he would appoint me to the District Court, and then, after a short while there, I would be elevated to the Circuit Court. I sat on the bench outside his office, feeling quite ambivalent.

For some, this would be the fulfillment of the American dream. Being a "WASP" made immigration easy. White society here welcomed someone from "the Old Country" who spoke the same language, only with a different twang. It was a nice ego trip to realize I had become a citizen in 1968 and now, a decade later, I could be a powerful judge. I'd always considered the District Court the farm league, though, and had never spent much time there. You always had the right to appeal the decision there to the Circuit Court for a trial "de novo." My experience was in Circuit Court, with bigger, more important cases. District Court, with its variety of less serious cases, seemed like a demotion. In actual fact most people derive their concept of "justice" in these courthouses, so it is critical to have competent, fair people dispensing it.

I reflected that perhaps all I had really wanted was the day I would be sworn in and "robed," with a bunch of people singing my praises. I also understood that perhaps I was not temperamentally suited for the position. It required great patience. I changed my mind and informed Gov. Hughes that I did not want the appointment.

*****

I first met Milton B. Allen a few weeks after I became a prosecutor in 1969. I had been assigned a double homicide, and he was representing Chicago "Al" Johnson. The gunman had walked into a nightclub just as it was closing, and opened fire—instantly killing one patron and fatally wounding another, who managed to live for 18 months. At the time, however, if the victim did not die from his wounds within a year and a day, a murder conviction could not be sustained. The lack of medical knowledge and certainty in earlier times had resulted in this common law principle.

The evidence was strong, since the assailant had waited until all the lights were on and the patrons were about to leave before making what was obviously a statement to all those present. "Chicago Al" was easily identified by several witnesses. He would have been difficult to overlook in his lime green suit and straw Panama hat.

Milton Allen was known as "The Black Perry Mason." He was a familiar figure in Baltimore City courts in the fifties and sixties, when there were fewer than 50 African-American lawyers in the entire state. He had prevailed over a rigidly segregated environment by first becoming a teacher, and then joining the Navy. There, as a Seaman First Class, he began teaching courses from remedial reading to college level courses. Upon his discharge in 1946 he focused on a legal career, financing this effort through the G. I. bill, his hobby of photography and work as a country club waiter. He attended the recently desegregated University of Maryland Law School, and was admitted to the Bar in 1948—a year before completing his law degree. Along with several others, he established the first African-American law firm in Maryland. This took place at a time when no black was allowed to eat at a downtown restaurant, or take a bar review course.

Milton favored expensive Trilby hats, and had soon become known as a consummate trial lawyer who was not afraid to stir controversy—but did so in an unassuming way, using his great sense of humor to get everyone to relax. He would sit back in his seat with his glasses perched on his bald head and mustache drooping, lulling the unknowing into a false sense of security.

He elected a court trial for "Chicago Al" and, astonishingly, managed to convince the Court that the first killing was not premeditated. Milton argued that the second one, under the law, could only at worst be assault with intent to murder, since the victim had to die within a year and a day for murder. Common law did not have modern medicine to help with "causation." I was startled with the result he had achieved. It was another early lesson for me that nothing was a sure thing in Court. "Chicago Al" was acquitted of first degree murder . . . maybe a favor from a friendly judge. He received thirty years and was incarcerated in the Maryland penitentiary, where I met him three months later, when in law school I had joined "The Seven Step" Rehabilitation Program.

The local Seven Step Program was started by a Greek convict, Angelo Tender. He was very clever and very dangerous. He had been convicted of the ransom/kidnapping of a member of the Hutzler family. It didn't end well. He got 40 years. After several years of careful planning, he became president of the local group whose goal was to get the attention of long-time convicts. He was eventually allowed to make speeches outside the prison. He'd been clever and patient. He made his escape one night, after giving a speech at a local hall. Nine months later, when he was captured and prosecuted, the sentencing judge quipped, "I guess he took the Eighth Step."

In this program, law students and other volunteers like myself would run focus groups once a week with convicts who were serving substantial sentences. We "square johns" were not even escorted as we walked across the yard to the school house, nor was there much supervision as each of us led separate groups of 10 inmates in discussions.

One night, I was approached by an inmate in the hallway. He asked if I remembered him, and I said I didn't. He became visibly angry and said, "You ought to you mother-fucker, you are the one who put me in here." He told me his name was Johnson—better known as "Chicago Al." I started to panic that he was going to attack, and started mumbling, "Oh, yes, of course, how are you doing? Hope you are well." Stammering and stuttering, I said it was nice to see him, and fortunately saw some other students nearby allowing me to make a hasty retreat. I realized, then, that I would not be able to lock them up during the day and play social worker at night. After that encounter, I never went back.

Milton was elected Baltimore's first black State's Attorney in 1970, when he challenged four white candidates. He benefitted from a vote split in the white community, and became the first African-American to hold a chief prosecutor's position in a major U. S. city. The 44 white prosecutors, including me and the two blacks already in the office Milton inherited, soon grew to love his unassuming manner, humor and quiet, gentle strength. He called us all either 'boyfriend or killer' depending on the circumstance.

Years later Milton was appointed a Circuit Court judge, and the lawyers in his Court for the most part welcomed his informal attitude. On one occasion during a rape-kidnapping trial, the new prosecutor observed that while he was giving his closing argument to the jury, Judge Allen was noisily eating a late lunch, a sardine sandwich, in open view on the bench. The prosecutor was offended and seething with rage during the defense summation. Immediately before he was to give his rebuttal the prosecutor asked permission to approach the bench and while there he complained that the Judge was detracting from the seriousness of the proceedings. Milton let him talk and then apologized saying, "You're absolutely right, I'm sorry. Please excuse me. Now let's finish up the case. Go ahead with your speech, boyfriend."

Apparently, Milton was still hungry, and had a large peach prominently displayed on the Bench. As a compromise to judicial decorum, he would remove it periodically and duck down below the surface of the bench to take bites from time to time. The slurping made more noise than the judge realized, nor cared to realize. I consoled the younger lawyer with the lines from T.S. Elliot's "Prufrock" about aging. "Do I dare to eat a peach? I shall wear white flannel trousers and walk along the beach."

Milton had lived through decades of racial segregation in Maryland and was very proud of his heritage. He had a dark complexion. In his chambers, he had a large mirror and to the delight of the court personnel, before going into court, he would often stand in front of it and gaze at his own dark complexion, and repeat "Mirror, Mirror, on the wall, who's the fairest one of all?"

Milton had a very easy-going temperament, and enjoyed the irony and humor inherent in many of the absurd situations into which people got themselves. Shortly after Milton went on the bench he conducted a trial where a white officer had stopped a black motorist for speeding. Things had spiraled out of control when the driver accused the officer of being a racist "motherfucker" and that his real offense was "driving while black." The officer maintained that those words supported the disorderly conduct charge which had been added to the speeding ticket. With a packed courtroom, composed of mostly African-Americans paying close attention, Milton gently explained that what had really occurred was a misunderstanding about the term "motherfucker." He said that there was a racial divide between the two that could easily be explained.

Judge Allen, who had been a teacher for more than a decade, gently explained that in the black community the word had many meanings. For example:

Said slowly, as a single word it could convey astonishment: *"Motherrrrrrfuckerrrrrrrr!"*
It could be used as a noun in a sentence: *"Check out this Motherfucker!"*
It could be used for emphasis: *"Motherfucker!"*
Or it can be used as an adjective: *"That motherfucking jerk!"*
Or it can be used as a sign of respect: *"He's a bad motherfucka!"*
Or can be used in a friendly way: *"How've you been, you crazy motherfucker?"*
Or used as an expression of disgust or contempt: *"Now, ain't that a motherfucker!"*

Judge Allen explained that while the term had led to many barroom brawls and street fights, it was not necessarily a sign of disrespect. As he had carefully enunciated each different usage, his mainly black audience let out loud shrieks of laughter and the white officer flushed with anger. The driver was given a small fine on the speeding case but was found not guilty of disorderly conduct. Judge Allen told the officer that he could be excused and wished him a good day. The officer said "Thank you. See you later motherfucker!" The spectators all gasped but Milton simply smiled and said, "Call the next case."

While a judge's informality often makes life easier for lawyers and other court personnel, it can have unintended consequences. Things were as casual and chaotic as usual in Judge Allen's court on one occasion, when I defended a client before a jury. He was accused of armed robbery. The States' case had been weak; the accused did well on the stand. There were smiles and laughter from the jurors and others during the two days of testimony.

On the third morning, Juror Number Seven was a no-show when closing arguments were to be given. The alternate took his place. At the conclusion of the arguments and the court's instructions, the jury was directed to get lunch and report directly back to the jury room to deliberate. In most courtrooms, the judge assembles the jury before sending them back to deliberate. In Milton's courtroom, he simply had them go straight to the jury room after lunch.

By the middle of the afternoon, after about an hour they informed the court they had a verdict and they were soon brought into the courtroom to announce it. There was not enough space in the jury box, however, since there were now 13 of them—including two Number Sevens. They were both claiming that seat.

The original Number Seven had been late, but joined the rest of them for lunch in the restaurant in the basement of The Equitable Building. He had then gone with them into the jury room for the deliberations. I knew of no precedent for this, and I did not want a mistrial because things looked good for the defense. Not knowing what to do, I meekly objected, in order to preserve a hip-pocket appeal.

The Judge ordered the foreman to announce the verdict. "Not Guilty!" The prosecutor polled them all individually and all 13 "harkened" to it. The local police had an expression: "Better to be judged by 12 than carried by 6!" referring to pallbearers. They say nothing about 13.

*****

David B. Mitchell had been a law student in the Public Defender's Office, and upon passing the bar briefly secured a position there. He got some trial experience but had limited talent, and he then started his own practice. He realized that the only way he could ever be appointed to the bench was to become involved in Bar Association politics. In the 1970s, The Monumental Bar Association, which specifically represented African-American lawyers, was growing in numbers and in power. After a few years he became its president and soon was appointed to the Circuit Court of Baltimore City. He was a petty tyrant and was not to be trifled with.

Judge Mitchell on several occasions locked up lawyers "for contempt" when they were simply trying to place objections on the record to protect their clients' interests. He took everything as a personal affront and a contest of wills.

He became a law unto himself, and unfortunately is not fully retired yet. He still sits frequently, and the stories still follow him. When spectators first began carrying cell phones and one would ring in court, he would scream, "Where am I in a phone booth?" On several occasions he had ordered every-body out of his courtroom and in one instance he was so angry that he ordered the prosecutor to start calling cases and then he issued bench warrants for each of the defendants who were in the hallway having just been ordered out. Hours later several lawyers convinced him to quash the warrants and he explained limply "I am only human."

For a long time, I had a friendly relationship with him. Then I appeared in front of him. On April 5, 1991 I represented Brian Watson, who was charged with rape, sex offenses and burglary. The trial was scheduled for a few days later, but the assistant state's attorney made arrangements to bring Brian Watson from the city jail so that his case could be dismissed. The prosecutor had just received the results of a requested DNA test and because these re-sults exonerated Brian Watson, she wished to secure his release from custody as soon as possible. He had been incarcerated for nine months, unable to post the $750,000 bail.

In the lockup while I was interviewing him, I had a young law intern with me. I explained to Watson that it was best for us to simply let the prosecutor "Confess Not Guilty" and get out as soon as we could. He argued with me that he was innocent, had lost his freedom, had lost his job and now his reputation. He wanted to complain in public. I argued with him for a few minutes. I was in the habit of trying to control the words and actions of people, who were usually guilty and I had become quite jaded. I rightfully became subjected to his scorn and the disapproval of the intern. Consequently, I apologized and told him that he should say whatever he felt he wanted to say when we got to the courtroom.

I exchanged pleasantries with Judge Mitchell and then the prosecutor called the case. She explained they had the wrong man and "confessed not guilty." I requested that I be permitted to address the court for "a minute." The judge cut me off, so I said Mr. Watson would like to address the court. Inexplicably Mitchell said "No, this is not the place for that!" I asked for permission to approach the bench with the prosecutor. Once there, I said "How are you doing, Judge?" Judge Mitchell replied, "I'm doing great, thanks, Anton. How have you been?" I said as calmly as I could, "I think that my client should be allowed to address the court. We all agree he's innocent!" I was trying to be as nice as I could, but he angrily responded, "Take it to the courthouse steps!" When I persisted and requested again that my client be allowed to address the court, Judge Mitchell again angrily and loudly denied my request. He said, "Tell it to Channel 13!" I told him this was an innocent man who'd been wrongfully held in the Baltimore city jail for nine months. It was difficult to explain to my client how we could call such a process "justice," or how we could share any pride in the system that could be so indifferent. A guilty person has the right of allocution. I didn't know a rule which provided the right of allocution for an innocent person, but I couldn't see how it could be fairly forbidden. He called the next case.

I wrote to Judge Mitchell a few days later in an attempt to share my insight into what happened to Brian Watson, hoping to sensitize Judge Mitchell and perhaps others on the bench. I told him that I had always found him to be a fair-minded and concerned person in the past, and that I hoped he'd accept this criticism in the spirit in which it was offered.

I explained that on June 25, 1990 at 4:25 a.m., the victim was attacked in her home. She had never seen her assailant before and described him as a black male, 5'7"–5'9", 140–160 pounds, brown skin, wearing a white jogging suit and maroon t-shirt. The assailant told her that somebody had paid him $10,000 to get her daughter for taking someone's money. He said, however, that his twin brother knew the daughter, didn't want to hurt her, and that the daughter had gone to Northern Parkway High School. The victim told the police that the rapist showed her a scar on his forearm claiming that it was done to him as initiation into a drug gang called the Bloods.

The police showed her photos a week later, yet none looked familiar to her. At that meeting the victim informed the police that she'd been looking through her daughter's yearbook and had seen a photograph of a black male that "resembled" the black male who had raped her. In the yearbook, Brian Watson was depicted in a portrait pose next to the victim's daughter's photo. The police immediately retrieved a photo of Brian Watson from the Baltimore City Police Department files. They added five more to it and showed them to the victim who positively identified the photo of Brian Watson. His photo was on file because he had been arrested for shoplifting a few years earlier. He had never been incarcerated before this.

Brian Watson was arrested at his home on July 5, 1990. At the time of his arrest, he had a large orange streak across the right side of his otherwise black hair. The police subsequently removed this orange streak, and Watson was placed in a lineup with four other tall black males. The victim identified him as being her assailant. The initial trial date was postponed to await the results of a DNA test being performed on the sperm discovered on the victim's sheets by the Crime Lab. Watson had given samples of his blood, saliva, head and pubic hair as soon as he was requested to do so. The State, for some unknown reason had not requested the specimens until four months after his arrest.

At the time of his arrest, Mr. Watson was working at Memorial Stadium as a cook. He was working six days a week, and during the two years he had been employed, he had impressed his supervisors with his dependability. His work records for the pay-period ending on June 27, 1990 showed that he had reported to work as usual at 7:48 a.m. on June 25, 1990. The victim had reported that the attack had taken place between the hours of 4:25 a.m. and 6:30 p.m. Brian Watson was a 6'2", 180-pound, dark-skinned man. He had no twin brother and no scar on either forearm. He did not own a white jogging

suit. He had a large gold crown on his front tooth that was not removable—
it had been applied in 1988, as medical records from the Baltimore Family
Dental Center demonstrated.

In addition, a photo taken on June 24, 1990 (the day before the rape)
depicted two other males standing with the orange-streak-haired Watson.
The photographer and the subjects were prepared to testify as to the date and
circumstances surrounding the taking of the photo. Mr. Watson's girlfriend
orange-striped his hair the first time in May 1990, and was ready to testify
that she renewed the orange application on June 24, 1990 just before the
photo was taken.

Brian Watson's mother, Linda Watson, had worked in the emergency
room at the University of Maryland Hospital for 15 years. She knew he was
home at 6:30 a.m. on June 25, 1990 because as was her habit, she called
him there. He was in his bedroom asleep when she called. Both Mr. Watson's
girlfriend and his sister were also with him at the time the rape took place,
and were prepared to testify as to his whereabouts.

It is fair to say that mistaken identification is one of the leading causes
of miscarriages of justice. This case represented such a miscarriage. Arrogant,
self-centered and insecure judges probably account for many more miscarriages.

In my letter, I complained that I understood that the entry of a nolle prose-
qui (or a confession of not guilty,) was completely within the discretion of the
States Attorney and that the accused has no right to object, yet it was also
clear that since fundamental fairness should be the ultimate goal of the proceedings, anyone who had been accused should be permitted the opportunity
to speak in court. I suggested that it was the responsibility of the trial judge to
safeguard both the rights of the accused and the interest of the public in the
administration of criminal justice. For that reason, I explained, I was requesting
the Maryland Criminal Defense Attorneys Association to propose a rule change
that would provide a defendant "the right to address the court" when the state
wishes to drop the charges it has brought against the defendant. Mr. Watson
would receive no compensation for his false detention; he lost his job and had
to expend money for legal fees. I wrote that the court has no power to redress
these grievances or to right the wrong done to him, yet prohibiting him or his

counsel from making a public statement in the appropriate forum, a court of law, added insult to his already substantial injuries.

Several days later I received a letter from him, with my letter included. He told me that there was a "certain cathartic effect in directing a missive regarding one's concerns, but in doing so, many have the good sense to recognize the benefits and then, once written, destroy it. Your letter of April 15 should have met that same fate, however because of our friendship over the years, I will not allow its contents to damage a more than 20-year relationship." This guy didn't get it. What kind of lawyer would I be if I didn't fight for an innocent client? There were not that many of them. Who needed or wanted a friend like him? He was a pompous jerk, and he had told me to stick it where the sun don't shine.

I wrote to the Maryland Criminal Defense Attorney's Association, sharing the correspondence and requesting that it sponsor "The Mitchell Rule" in the House of Delegates and in the Maryland Senate. Nothing became of it, but it was a good way to publicize what had happened.

Over the years, I had always respected a political columnist who wrote first for the News American and then The Sun. He also coincidentally appeared weekly on a Channel 13 Television News show as a commentator. He was the perfect person to contact. I telephoned him to explain that Judge Mitchell had "a case of the robes." He asked me to repeat myself, and I explained that Mitchell suffered from a bad case of "robitis," which occurred in some insecure people when they were "appointed," believing they had been "anointed" to the bench. The symptoms included serious swelling of the head, and certain bullying, detached, mean, and narrow-minded elements, which were all part of the disease. He was dangerous because if he was so wrong about this simple matter, his judgment had to be suspect all the time.

It was with great pleasure that I read Michael Olesker's column several days later. It was titled: "Silence Compounds Injustice of Jailing." Judge Mitchell refused to discuss the case with Olesker, and the prosecutor refused to accept Olesker's repeated calls. The column quoted an interview with Watson, who said, "I never saw the lady in my whole life and I didn't know what was going on. I got out of the bath tub and the police are at my door, and the next thing I know, I'm behind bars. I nearly went crazy at the City Jail. It was real bad. I was thinking of killing myself over something I didn't do. I mean, you see what goes on in that place. It drives you crazy and here I was locked up with nothing to do with it."

Several months later, I received a telephone call from Deborah Weiner, an investigative reporter from Channel 45, who was doing a series of programs on people who had been genuinely innocent and yet had been prosecuted. I was more than happy to go on her program. I explained what happened to Watson and provided Channel 45 with all the materials that I had accumulated. It made for excellent television. Before I was interviewed, I schooled myself to stay calm and be the voice of reason. I contemplated that the best way to handle this bully was to be temperate and even-keeled. I had earned my opportunity to speak on Watson's behalf and I was pleased with my performance when I watched it later.

I didn't appear in front of Judge Mitchell for several months and when I did see him it was clear that he was furious with me. I just eyeballed him (called eye-fucking, or reckless eyeballing in the Marines and prisons) and was very careful about what I did and said. I appeared in front of him several times after that. It was not pleasant.

In one instance, over a year later a jury convicted my spoiled brat of a client of disorderly conduct, disturbing the peace and trespassing. She had gone into a store—shoeless—in order to buy shoes (slip-ons costing five dollars) to wear to a High Holiday celebration. She was late. Impatient and frustrated with the line of customers ahead of her, she slapped a five-dollar bill on the table in front of the cash register and walked out. The security guard accosted her and an altercation ensued.

Judge Mitchell tried to punish me by making me wait in his court for two days until the case was finally called. He purposely dragged the case out, handling several other matters intermittently and forcing everyone, jurors and personnel alike to stay late. I was too stubborn to ever be beaten in this way, but this petty tyrant was willing to punish everyone, just to punish me. He knew such a case could only have generated a small fee. It didn't help that the client had not learned her lesson, and was totally obnoxious when she took the stand. She was convicted. The judge imposed substantial fines, a 30-day suspended prison sentence and 75 hours of community service! He refused to consider probation before judgment, which meant that this naïve, spoiled

19-year-old undergraduate would now always have a criminal record.

Over the years, Mitchell punished me at every opportunity, by making me wait endlessly to deal with postponement requests and other administrative matters. I was not the only forceful advocate he treated in this shabby and cowardly manner. Even in the most serious criminal cases, he often limited the prosecutors and defense counsel to 10 minutes for their opening and closing arguments. Even then, he would rudely leave the bench and engage in extensive dialogues with the court clerk. Many spectators commented that they did not think it was right for him to be joking and smiling with the clerk while the lawyers argued their case. To me, and most in the legal profession, it is a no-brainer to allow the innocent the chance to talk—especially if they've been punished unfairly. Judge Mitchell's feelings of inadequacy led to bad judgment, in my opinion, and to behavior more akin to a bully or tyrant than to a dispenser of justice. He was never sanctioned or reprimanded for his conduct because he had many friends with political influence. People were hesitant to complain about him or challenge him. After all, though, the defense attorney's function is to protect the client, and try to prevent him from being abused or treated unfairly.

*****

All court personnel are overwhelmed. There are some people who should be judges, and there are some who most definitely should not. Our adversarial, competitive justice system provides a stage for the very best and worst of human nature. Most of the people who apply this power daily, the judges and prosecutors, manage to keep the intrusion of their personal frustrations and failings to a minimum and attempt to achieve a "just" resolution of complex issues. This arena can be hectic or slow, stimulating or boring, tragic or comic. The struggle there is often exhausting, and is always important or critical to someone.

In some instances, the people who occupy those demanding positions, asserting their sense of fairness in terms of freedom, imprisonment or sometimes death, should never have been permitted to assume such power. They are dangerous. Even if these powerful people are fundamentally flawed, they have been successful in acquiring the judgeship. They can usually bring about the results they want. Judges are held in high esteem because they are perceived as clever, impartial and able to make fair decisions. These are the only occupations in our society which can exercise such power over other individuals. Sometimes it's life or death. On a routine basis, many make honest guesses about prison or freedom.

For the most part, judges attempt to do the right thing in very difficult circumstances. The more gregarious and impatient a judge is in his personal life, however, the more difficult it is for that judge not to act like he or she is the center of the show. Judges have much discretionary power, and sometimes become little more than petty, bigoted tyrants who are willing to bully everyone into submission. They can be very intimidating. They are in a position to do a lot of damage by locking people in noisy cages for long periods of time.

The average person on the street, and even most lawyers, do not know how a trial judge conducts himself, unless he appears in that courtroom. Most do not. Most trial judges get the benefit of the doubt, because they are performing a respectable public service: washing the country's dirty laundry. To paraphrase George Bernard Shaw, "When they are good, they are very, very good. When they are bad, they are horrid." Where a judge does not live up to expectations, the trial bar has an obligation to inform the public and the court. While many judges are unwilling to admit making a mistake, admitting their error will not make a judge look foolish. The robe itself did not make judges infallible super-lawyers.

Sgt. Charles Edward Keating.
London Metropolitan Police Force.
New Scotland Yard. 1930.

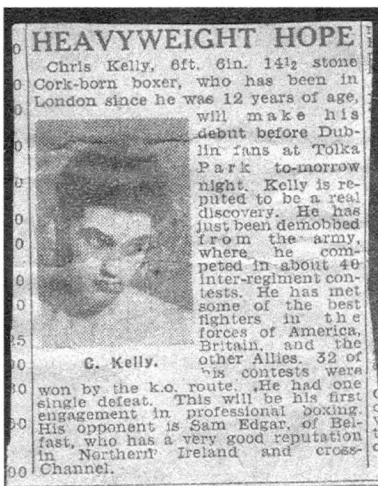

Article, The Irish Independent.
Dublin, Eire May 1948.
Chris Kelly was C. Keating's
"nom de ring"

After 3 knockdowns Chas retires with this first round knockout.
The Royal Albert Hall. London 1948.

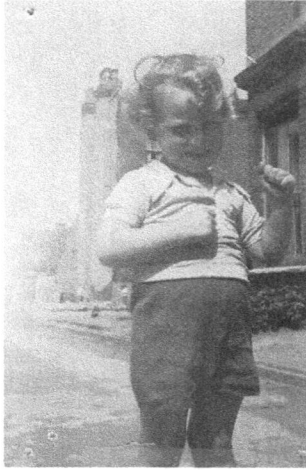

(Top, from left to right) Shaping up Seaside Holiday, Camber Sands 1948; Outside our home, Battersea, London 1946; In Battersea Park. London 1949.

(Below) A Saturday strut on King's Road, Chelsea, London,1950.

EMANUEL SCHOOL · RUGBY UNDER 14 XV · 1956-57

Back row: D. J. Denham · F. N. Reed · D. J. Miles · T. A. Tilley Esq. · K. L. Maddocks · A. A. White · P. R. Johnson

Centre row: P. E. W. Edwards · K. Dickson · A. J. S. Keating (captain) · K. C. Bennett · K. M. Brooner

Front row: J. D. Ainsworth · V. E. J. Roberts · G. Bilsaby

(Top) Emanuel School Rugby Team. Anton in the middle, with ball, 1956.

(Below) The Mantua St. Cricket Team. London. Charles—top left.
Anton—bottom right. 1953.

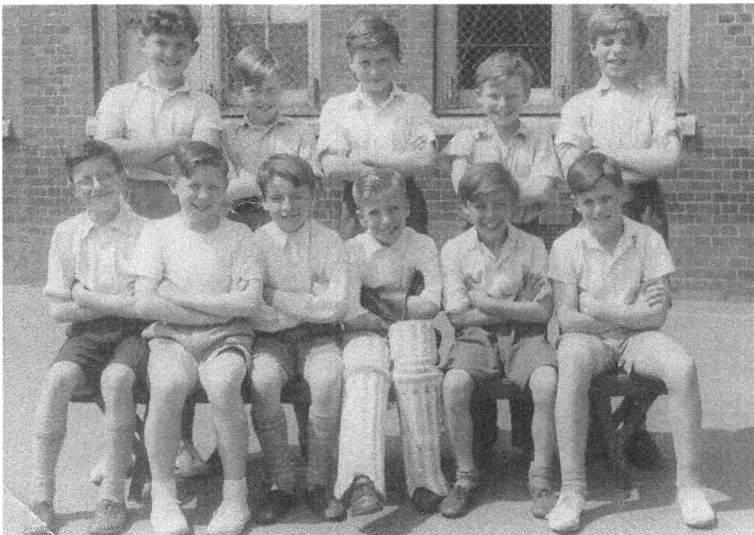

Name	Form	Date	Cause	Penalty	Given By	Witness
Olivier	1B	15.3.55	Deliberately throwing ink on wall	4	WSH	CBB.
Raeside	3A	"	Cutting work in Eng & Geo.	6	WSH	FOL.
Gamble	3A	"	" " " English.	3	WSH	FOL.
Roberts	3A	"	" " " "	3	WSH	FOL.
Lewis	3A	"	" " " "	3	WSH	FOL.
Noble	3A	"	" " " "	3	WSH	FOL.
Henton	4T	"	Cutting work.	4	WSH	W
Lamer	4T	"		4	WSH	W
Pollard	4T			4	WSH	W
Russell	4T			4	WSH	W
Smith B	4T			4	WSH	W
Smith D	4T			4	WSH	W
Fuller	4T			4	WSH	W
Tuckerig	4T			2	WSH	W
Clements	3L	29.3.55	Disobedience	3	WSH	FVB.
Scrase	5T	26/4/55	Cutting prep.	3		WSH
Whitfield	3.C.	2.5.55	Persistently talking in class.	3.	FVB.	WSH.
Banning	3.C.	2.5.55		3	FVB.	WSH
Keating	1B	2.5.55	untruthfulness; leading others astray	2	TBG	WSH.
Sweetsun	2A		Disobeying an order and cutting detention on Saturday morning	6	TVB.	WSH.
Wooldridge	2A	11.5.55	Persistently talking	3	FVB	WSH.
FERGUS	5A	13.5.55	Continual Lateness	3	G.B.S	FVB
Scrase	IT	13 May	cutting and forging	4	TBG	WSH
CARTER	5A	16.5.55	Continual Lateness	3	G.B.S	D.E.S.
HURRAN	4H	17.5.55	" "	3	G.B.S	BW.
BRADFORD	1C	17.5.55	Throwing stones & causing injury	2	G.B.S	WSH
NIXON	1C	17.5.55	" " " "	2	G.B.S	WSH
BILHAM	1C	17.5.55	" " " "	2	G.B.S	WSH
BROWNE	1C	17.5.55	" " "	2	G.B.S	WSH
EVANS	1C	17.5.55	" " "	2	G.B.S	WSH
RICKETTS	1C	17.5.55	" " "	2	GRA	WH

Emanuel Punishment Log, 1955.

A.N. Myer Discus Event, Niagara Falls, Ontario, Canada, 1961.

Rowing, Boston University, 1963, Freshman Crew.

Boston University Crew, Charles River, 1964.

Rowing, Boston University, 1965.

day Globe—May 24, 1964

B. U. Crew Elects Keating Captain; Three Honored

The Boston University crew elected a new captain and three awards were announced at a break-up dinner last night at the Smith House.

Anton Keating of Wayland was chosen captain for next year. James Stewart, the coxswain, was given the leadership award. Clark Breden of Assinippi the award for outstanding achievement and Ted A. Nash, a B.U. graduate of 1957, the Arthur W. Stevens Award for outstanding contribution to B.U. rowing.

(Left) **Boston Globe:** *B.U. Crew Elects Keating Captain, 1964.*

(Right) Boston University Varsity Crew, 1964.

(Left) Charles Keating The Barrister. Crown Court, BBC, Manchester, UK, 1973.

(Right) Brideshead Revisited, Charles Keating as Rex Mottram, BBC, 1993.

My father, Charles, at my campaign announcement,
running for State's Attorney, 1978, Baltimore, MD

FIVE ACTORS
of the
ROYAL SHAKESPEARE CO.

Left to right: Sebastian Shaw, Sheila Allen, Charles Keating,
John Kane and Ben Kingsley.

PRESENTS

NOV. 16-**LOVERS AND MADMEN**
NOV. 17-**GROUPINGS '78**
NOV. 18-**SIGH NO MORE LADIES**

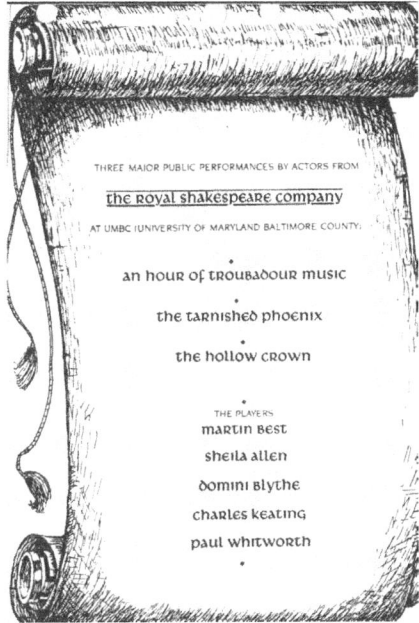

THREE MAJOR PUBLIC PERFORMANCES BY ACTORS FROM

the Royal shakespeare company

AT UMBC (UNIVERSITY OF MARYLAND BALTIMORE COUNTY)

an hour of troubadour music
·
the tarnished phoenix
·
the hollow crown
·
THE PLAYERS
martin best
sheila allen
domini blythe
charles keating
paul whitworth
·

(Left) Five Actors. The Royal Shakespeare Company Tour, November 1982.

(Right) Brochure, The Royal Shakespeare Company Tour, Fall 1982.

W

"LOOT"

BEST
OF THE
BEST

Joseph Maher, Zeljko Ivanec, Charles Keating and Zoe Wanamaker in "Loot"

Of the angry young men who burst upon the British theater scene in the Fifties and
Sixties few have retained their bite as well as Joe Orton, whose plays still seem
fierce and terribly funny. Listening to the dialog in "Loot," which is being given
a superb revival by the Manhattan Theater Club and will subsequently move Off-
Broadway, one has the sense of a latter-day Oscar Wilde. A cast that includes Joseph
Maher, Zoe Wanamaker, Zeljko Ivanec and Kevin Bacon, under the direction of
John Tillinger, find all the vitality in Orton's black humor.

Charles' Nomination for a Tony for "Loot," 1986.

(Top) Soap Opera Digest, April 1994.

(Right) Soap Opera Weekly, May 1995.

My mother, Margaret Shevlin, "Peg." London, 1950

(Left) My mother, Peg, in Caddyshack, with Ted Baxter and Chevy Chase, 1994.

(Right) Peg's Publicity Brochure.

Mr. Willie F. Brice #116777
954 Forrest Street
Baltimore Maryland 21202
March, 29, 1971

Mr. Anton J. S. Keating
assistant state attorney of Baltimore City

Dear Sir.
This letter is to let you know, I appreciate
your plea in mercy to the Judges for me,
I will always try hard to live in good
hope and faith that some day the truth may
come to light.

Sincerely yours,
Mr. Willie F. Brice #116777

Letter from Willie F. Brice on Death Row, March 29, 1971.

PART III

Carroll County Courthouse
Westminster, Maryland

Beber

CHAPTER 17:
MYERS AND I MEET

"Never trust the client completely . . ."
— Anton J.S. Keating, Esq.

It was Alan Murrell who assigned me to the Robert Myers case. He still headed the Office of the Public Defender, and I was in private practice, having left the O.P.D. four years earlier.

In cases where two or more people are charged in a criminal case, one Public Defender cannot usually represent more than one defendant because there is always the potential for a conflict of interest. The attorney may find him or herself in the position of having to decide which one is going to cooperate against the other. Consequently, when the Public Defender represents any one of several people charged with an offense, it is responsible for assigning lawyers who are not members of its office, but rather are members of the private bar, to represent any co-defendant.

On Christmas Eve of 1981, Alan Murrell had telephoned me to ask if I wanted to represent Robert Myers. He told me that Myers had no "assets" that were available because his debts were so great. Alan told me that I would receive a flat fee of $10,000, plus expenses. He knew I would give it my all and not concern myself with such a small fee for a capital case. I jumped at the opportunity. I thought, "This case meets my standards. There's a television camera and publicity involved. Plus a great challenge, and literally deadly competition!"

I had read about the brutal murder for months. It had been closely covered in the newspapers. The Public Defender's Office could not represent Myers, since Orrin Brown, the Public Defender for Howard County, was already representing Daniel Chadderton. Alan Murrell had been a mentor to Phil Sutley, thought highly of him, and in fact had sent him many private criminal cases in order to help Sutley establish his career.

Myers seemed very relaxed during our first session in the Carroll County Detention Center, periodically spitting the juice he was generating from the tobacco plug he was chewing, into a tin can. He did not appear to be a very clever accountant or a violent person. I've been fooled of course often before, but he seemed like a friendly harmless person. He told me "I'm not really guilty" a couple of times and I responded that I didn't want to hear him say that again, because he was either guilty or innocent. No one could be a little bit pregnant. He was not physically imposing; he was short and fleshy and not intense at all. He had a nice smile and a mellow disposition. Good. I would or should be able to control him. If the client would not allow me to make most of the critical decisions in the case, I would not participate. Technically a client makes only three decisions. To plead guilty or not guilty. To elect a court or a jury trial. To take the stand or not. The lawyer decides everything else otherwise the client is in charge. There are no bad ideas or suggestions however and as the Mossad, the Israeli intelligence service advises, "let the mashuganas talk . . ." Every now and then even they will stumble upon a great idea. Of course I listened to every client's opinion, but I never let them run the defense. I like to listen, debate, ruminate and then decide what to do or to say.

For the unknowing, a criminal case should be prepared backwards— there are about twenty-one rounds to be considered in a Maryland State criminal prosecution. A prosecution can be aborted during any one of these stages, much like a knockout in a fight. Think Courtus Interruptus.

You can never count on it, though, so you had better be prepared to go the entire distance before a jury and an appellate court, especially in a death penalty case. A court trial is usually a slow guilty plea, since many judges are premature adjudicators. Even if they are not, they usually aren't easily fooled.

A defense attorney, at a minimum, must prepare for the following stages, which must be contemplated in this reverse chronological order:

1. An Appeal from the Post Conviction ruling
2. The Post Conviction Hearing
3. The Appeal from the conviction itself
4. The Sentence Review by a three-judge panel
5. The Sentencing Hearing

6. The Motion for a New Trial

7. The Jury Verdict

8. The State's Rebuttal Closing Argument

9. The Defendant's Closing Argument

10. The State's Opening Closing argument

11. The Court's Instructions to the jury

12. The Defendant's Surrebuttal case

13. The State's Rebuttal case

14. The Defendant's case

15. The Defendant's motion for a judgment of acquittal at the end of the State's case

16. The State's case in chief

17. The Defendant's Opening Statement

18. The State's Opening Statement

19. Any Interlocutory Appeal

20. The Voire Dire

21. The Preliminary Motions.

Preparing a case in this way provides a total "big picture" and more chance of success. Each "round" must be prepared meticulously and consists of several parts—for example, the direct and cross examination of each witness, and the accumulation of potential exhibits relating to each.

The cardinal rule is never to trust the client, who, especially in the likely event he is guilty and convicted, has every motivation to attack you. He is definitely not worthy of your trust since he has likely already victimized someone else. If you do not win, the client will inevitably claim in a Post Conviction hearing that you mishandled the case. You and your representation will then be on trial. Count on it. Prepare for it.

From our very first meeting, Philip Sutley seemed distracted, disinterested, and had no energy at all. He never wanted to sit down and discuss the State's evidence or work on the preparation of the case.

I told Brown and Sutley that I had met Chadderton seven years before Mary Ruth's murder, when I was on the staff of the Public Defender's Office in Baltimore. I represented one George W. Smith, a.k.a."Chico," a dangerous bandit. He had two murder charges and several armed robbery cases pending against him. The prosecutor had offered a plea but Smith would not accept it. I learned from my visits with Smith at the Baltimore City Jail that he was in for severe punishment, and that he deserved it.

Judge Charles D. Harris was assigned the Smith case. A dignified, no-nonsense judge, he was always polite, yet could be stern and was considered "a banger"—someone who gave harsh sentences. He began his career on the bench as a strict law and order advocate and ended his tenure as a supporter of inmate programs. At this stage in his career, however, the State's Attorney's Office, which controlled the assignment of cases, would send bad guys to be tried in his court to meet their just rewards.

On the first day of court, Smith had to be dragged into the courtroom, his body limp. He sat half-conscious with his head on the trial table and his arms spread out. He had intentionally consumed medications, which he had hoarded.

I wished Judge Harris a good morning and suggested with a straight face, "Your Honor, I think there might be something the matter with my client." Judge Harris was furious at Smith because it was clear we could not proceed. He ordered that Smith be taken back to the Baltimore City Jail, strapped to a bench all night and kept away from any source of drugs.

The proceedings were continued the next morning. I met Smith in the "bullpen," the large holding cell in the basement of the Courthouse. Now he was sober, uncomfortable, and stressed. He said, "You must be pissed off at me, huh?" I told him to forget it, that we had to go ahead with the trial, and we should not waste any time worrying about what had happened.

The prosecutor in the case, Mark Anton Van Bavel, was tall, low key and very effective. He produced several witnesses after we had selected the jury. Ann Summerfield, 75, lived in the 3500 block of Auchentoroly Terrace in Baltimore. Smith had been renting a small room in her basement for several weeks. While the elderly landlady and Smith did not get close, they did see each other every day. Smith and two other unidentified men waited until Mrs. Summerfield returned from the bank one day with Daniel Chadderton, then 22, who was also a tenant in her house. The landlady and Chadderton were forced at pistol point to lie on the floor. They were tied hand and foot with clothing taken from a dresser. A ring, a watch, and $5 were taken from

Chadderton, and $17 was taken from Mrs. Summerfield's coat pocket.

The intruders then set fire to a pillow, and several clothing items in different places in the room. They then barricaded the door and locked both victims inside the room. Eventually, Chadderton was able to untie his bonds, and then climbed through the transom above the door and broke it down and carried Mrs. Summerfield to safety through the billowing smoke.

Both victims identified Smith. My cross-examination of Mrs. Summerfield was particularly difficult. She had a neck brace, thick glasses and walked slowly with a cane. She was a wonderful witness for the State. She was brave and indomitable. She had yelled at Smith, "Chico, you put down that gun! Now, Chico, put down that gun!" Smith took the stand. He said that he had been an intended victim of the robbery. The two bandits knew that he was a dope pusher and he was likely to have cash. "Chico" claimed Mrs. Summerfield and Daniel Chadderton were in error when they said that he was one of the perpetrators. In fact, according to his testimony, he was also one of the victims. The jury was not impressed and returned guilty verdicts on all the charges.

Judge Harris sentenced him to a total of 52 years and six months in jail for his crimes—including one charge he himself brought against Smith. He said, very deliberately, "Mr. Smith, if you will recall, the first day you were in this courtroom you had voluntarily taken drugs. I find that to be a direct contempt of this court. For that contempt of court I sentence you to 6 months. I rule, and I order, that the six months run consecutive to the 52 years, so your sentence is 52 years and six months."

I thought Smith had at least appreciated that I had fought for him and did the best that I could. However, I received a letter from him a week later that read, "I'm not impressed with the 52 years and 6 months I have to do, nor am I impressed by the way you represented me." He then instructed that I should go and check out this "perjury shit" and come to see him. He didn't quite understand that I did not sign up to be somebody's lackey, so I wrote him wishing him well in his other cases and discharging him from my life.

*****

The heroic witness from this trial, Daniel Chadderton, years later found himself a defendant in the murder of Mary Ruth Myers. It was a case with a more serious potential sentence if he were found guilty—namely, death. Chadderton's defense attorney, Orrin Brown, and I attended another meeting in late January in Phil Sutley's office. While we all discussed a general strategy, at the conclusion of the meeting, Orrin and I privately agreed that we should not expect Sutley to do very much work. I had never met Orrin Brown before the Myers' case, but I knew he was well respected. I mistakenly had hoped that the three of us attorneys could work well together. Initially I felt comfortable about the prospect of going to trial together if I could not get a severance of Robert Myers' case so that he could have his own trial—away from the other two defendants.

At another meeting in Phil's office two weeks later, I began to get a very uneasy feeling about Sutley's role in the case. I had called him a few days earlier and he explained that he could not properly represent Bobby because he was "too emotionally involved" with him. His whole attitude concerned me and I started to wonder what my position was to be in this case. It didn't feel right and I speculated, privately, that Sutley and Myers were trying to manipulate the situation. I had to be careful that even though Tina was not my client, I would not be involved in getting her screwed over by Sutley and Myers. Not for the first time in my life, I had it totally backwards.

During the course of these meetings with Orrin Brown and Philip Sutley, it became clear that Sutley had no intention of arguing any motions or putting up much of a fight. Brown and I had soon filed over forty preliminary motions contesting the law or the evidence. During our meetings, we were both energized and strategizing about our clients' dire situations. Sutley didn't seem that interested in any of it.

Orrin and I were determined to give the appellate courts as many reasons as possible to reverse potential convictions or death sentences, whether we felt our arguments on the motions were meritorious or not. We were determined to make it as difficult as possible for the State to kill our clients. At that time, there were ten people on death row. Even though no one had been executed for a long time in Maryland, we could not be cavalier. (We were proved to be correct. 5 executions were carried out several years later.)

I got Phil's permission to interview Tina at the Baltimore City Jail. It was important that the three co-defendants maintain communications, and that the three lawyers work together during the upcoming ordeal.

I waited half an hour in the attorney's booth. Tina had obviously been getting herself dolled up. She was coquettish, and flirting with me. She was behaving as if we were going on a date. Now, I had played the "come get me" game before, but never through a bulletproof glass window! She was five months pregnant, and still quite attractive. She had a very sexy voice and lovely big eyes. She had spent many years of her life using feminine guile to get what she wanted. I played along, because it might be in Robert Myers' best interest.

In our conversation, Tina explained to me that Bobby was a good man, but he was weak, and that he had given in to Leete and would often talk to him. He had not told Tom Hickman that he wanted to assert his Fifth Amendment right to remain silent. He wanted to please everybody. He had an inadequate personality and had significant sexual problems. This made him totally vulnerable to Tina's strengths. She was tough and would not break down under pressure. She had read a recent Baltimore Magazine article about me and told me that she felt I was "a special person." How sweet of her to tell me.

In the meantime, I had asked Robert Myers to write out the story of his life, requesting Sutley to pick it up from him the next time he visited the Carroll County Detention Center. Sutley told me he also had some other materials in his car that he would send to me. After two weeks, these items had still not arrived, and I called Sutley's law office and left several messages with his secretary, Linda. Still no response. This cavalier attitude was really starting to aggravate me, and when I called back a fourth time, Linda told me that Phil's dog "had eaten it." Finally two weeks later, the materials arrived. The pages were crumpled and looked a little worse for wear, but they had definitely not been eaten.

In early February 1982, Phil Sutley had told me that the prosecutors had offered Tina twenty years if she would become a State's witness, but he said she was "not the type of woman to do that." A few weeks later Phil told me that the State had offered her ten years. She was still not interested.

My doubts about Sutley grew stronger. He had not contributed anything at all yet that I had seen, but even if Sutley had no intention of putting up a fight, I'd be damned if he was going to prevent me from doing so.

CHAPTER 18:
REMOVAL TO GARRETT COUNTY

"This letter is going to be very hard to write . . . so please bear with me . . ."
— Tina to Robert Myers

The Chief Judge of Carroll County, Donald J. Gilmore had automatically grant-ed the prosecution's request to remove the case from Carroll County. Prosecutor Hickman had enemies there, and Robert—the accused—had many friends. The judge decided to send it to Oakland in Garrett County, the westernmost county in Maryland, nestled in the Appalachian Mountains, a four-hour drive from Baltimore. Seventy-five percent of the county is mountainous, with the remainder being a rolling plateau.

Garrett County was created from Western Allegheny County in April 1872—the last County in Maryland to be established. It was named for Balti-more and Ohio Railroad magnate John Work Garrett, because it owed its very existence to the coming of the railroad 21 years earlier.

On May 19, 1873, the first session on the Circuit Court for Garrett County convened in the Oakland Glades Hotel, and later sessions were conducted in stores and schools. A courthouse and jail were not built until November 1877. The current Garrett County Courthouse was erected in 1907, and has been modernized and expanded over the years. Oakland's selection as the new county seat drew lawyers to the Western Maryland town.

It had occurred to the grandson of John W. Garrett of Baltimore, Maryland that the 1896 Olympic Games in Athens could be a great personal challenge, and that the United States should be well represented there. 21-year-old Robert Garrett had been born into the third generation of the very wealthy Baltimore Railroad and banking family. Garrett was privately tutored in Baltimore at the family estate, Evergreen, before attending Princeton, where he immediately took a great interest in the track and field team and became its captain. He and several teammates decided they should compete at the First Modern Olympiad in Athens. Garrett established a fund to provide transportation costs for his needy teammates to enable many of them to go, without them ever knowing he was the donor. He wanted a team based on athletic merit.

While he was at Princeton studying the classics, he concentrated on the discus event and had a discus fashioned for himself. No one at Princeton had actually seen a discus, and it turned out to be heavier and more awkward than the standard one used by the Greeks in the Games.

The United States Olympic Team steamed across the Atlantic Ocean and arrived for a few days rest in Rome, and then they traveled south by train to Brindisi, at the boot of Italy. The team then clambered aboard a diesel-engine sailboat for the 24-hour trip across the Adriatic Sea to the Piraeus port in Greece. After another two-day trek by boat, rail, and horse drawn carriage, they arrived in Athens three days before The Games were to commence. The Athenians kindly lent Garrett a real discus and it turned out to be much lighter than the one he had been practicing with.

James Connolly and Ellery Clark were undergraduate students at Harvard, and were both exceptional athletes. They had met Garrett at an Ivy League track meet a few years before and they all agreed to go to Athens to participate. Clark had excellent grades and was encouraged to take a leave of absence to go to

Greece by the faculty but Connolly, a poor student, was warned not to go or he would be denied reentry. Connolly defied the faculty's orders and became the first gold medal winner of the Modern Olympiad when he won the triple jump event.

To the great disappointment of the host Greek nation, Robert Garrett won the discus event on his third and final throw. Before the Athens Olympiad was over, Garrett would add to his fame by placing second in the long jump and javelin and third in the high jump and the triple jump.

I had learned about Garrett and his achievements at The First Olympiad, and was intrigued to be trying a case in "his" county. I had been the top track and field athlete at my high school. I was proud to know I had jumped higher than Garrett, however the standards had improved a great deal over time. Now, here in his "home" venue, I would be competing not for a medal, but for life or death.

The Olympic Creed apportions glory to winner and loser alike. "The most important thing in the Olympic Games is not to win, but to take part, just as the most important thing in life is not to triumph but to struggle. The essential thing is not to have conquered, but to have fought well." However, for the defense attorney, moral victories don't count except in some remote academic sense if you need to make yourself feel better. Whatever you have to do to get suited up and fight again to stop even a guilty thug from being bullied and getting extra unnecessary time inside the cages we call prisons, you must do.

By 1980, the population of Garrett County was 22,420. It continued to have agricultural areas in its valleys and plateaus. Garrett County is the home of Deep Creek Lake, which has a shoreline of 65 miles. It attracts fishing enthusiasts and provides a broad array of water sports, including boating, swimming, and skiing.

This western part of Maryland is overwhelmingly rural and populated with self-reliant, mountain-country white conservatives. This is a part of the state with its own weather and its own attitudes. The region is generally socially and economically conservative, but with more of a libertarian streak than is found in other parts of Maryland.

In 1980, there were only eighteen lawyers practicing in Garrett County. The Circuit Court for Garrett County in Oakland has a central courtroom, situated in a small amphitheater, with a few rows of benches and chairs lining the pit-like area where the prosecution, defense, and jurors sit. The spectators literally look down on the players in the trial.

Fred A. Thayer, II was the trial judge, and had been Garrett County's only sitting circuit judge for nineteen years. He was born in Oakland in 1933, and received his law degree from Duke University in 1958. Within four years, he was elected State's Attorney. His grandfather had also been the Circuit Court Judge, and had been one of the pioneer lawyers in the county. Thayer was a tall, slender, balding man with white hair on the sides. As he puffed on his pipe, the jaw seemed more square, and the face more angular.

Judge Fred A. Thayer, at 49, gave the impression of a man totally at peace with himself, his job, and his environment. He liked the pace of life in Garrett County and he knew one could practice law in what he liked to call "the grand manner." The docket was smaller, which left a lot more time to be reflective. While others may have liked the clamor of an urban courtroom, he preferred the quiet of this turn-of-the-century courthouse where "renovation" often meant an occasional new coat of paint.

When he left Court for the day, he got into his pickup truck and drove about ten minutes to his home on Deep Creek Lake. In the winter, he and his wife skied constantly and in the summer, his passion was sailing a seventeen-foot fiberglass boat in the numerous races organized by a club to which he belonged. He had participated in the Annapolis to Newport race and several other offshore races. He enjoyed mastering the tricky gusts of winds on the long, narrow lake. In the autumn he hunted, and on alternate days he jogged a few miles. He and his wife enjoyed bird watching in the woods around their home.

Thayer had great pride in his Scottish ancestry, founding The Garrett Highlanders, a bagpipe and drum band, in the late 1970s. Thayer was the Pipe Major and used to practice his instrument at lunchtime in the church behind the Courthouse. He was so good at it that he gave lessons. Thayer took frequent trips to see operas and worked as a volunteer firefighter. He was always well prepared and lawyers knew that they'd get fairness and civility from him.

Garrett County had little violent crime. Welfare fraud, bad checks, and an occasional break-in at a Deep Creek Lake cottage were the routine felonies.

This resulted in a very small legal community. The longest trial Thayer could remember lasted nine days. The only full-time prosecutor was the elected State's Attorney.

In the Myers murder case, he really had done his homework. There were many motions filed in this case and some of them were very complex, but he had a grasp on every one of them. Judge Thayer had a very clear idea of the legal issues that were to be debated. He enjoyed the cases from other jurisdictions because they were a change of pace. It was invigorating for him to have an exchange with fresh lawyers. The Myers and Chadderton cases were the first death penalty cases ever to be heard in the county. Another murder case had occurred in Garrett County in which the prosecutors were seeking death, however it had been removed to the Eastern Shore for trial.

When the prosecution sought to have Robert Myers and Daniel Chadderton tried together, claiming the expense of transporting witnesses to Oakland and providing them with lodging added greatly to the cost, Thayer responded, "Time and expense are far down the line as considerations in a death penalty case." A week later, he ruled that the two would have separate trials. If convicted, both men had the choice of being sentenced either by the jury or by the judge. Sometimes a judge's known distaste for the death penalty leads a defendant to choose the judge, though Thayer refused to divulge his feelings on the death penalty. He had said, "I do not look forward to the sentencing portion for obvious reasons, but that goes with the territory."

The motions hearings were scheduled to start in Garrett County on Monday, March 22, 1982. I had never been there. It had taken four hours to drive the two hundred miles from Baltimore on the previous day. Orrin Brown and I stayed at the Will O' The Wisp resort, along with several reporters covering the case. It was nestled alongside Deep Creek Lake. The resort was deserted because of the time of year. The lawyers and the several out of town reporters were the only guests and we all enjoyed a good rapport during supper that Sunday night at the restaurant there. I had several meals with them over the next few days, and enjoyed their gallows' humor.

We all agreed that what made this such a sensational and unique case, apart from the nine bullets, was the likable, and flamboyant, open, and gregarious manner of Bobby Myers. Sutley told us that night that State's Attorney Tom Hickman had again suggested that Tina should take immunity. We laughed this off, because Sutley had led us to believe that "Hickman was way off base", and that Tina had no intention of taking any deal.

Chadderton actually wanted his trial to occur in Garrett County, since it was close to West Virginia, where he had been brought up. He had not joined in our appeal, contesting the legality of the removal. And he wanted his trial as soon as possible. Consequently I knew that no matter how Judge Thayer ruled on the rest our motions, I would not have to be ready to try the case, whereas Orrin Brown knew that within a few weeks, he would be going to trial and fighting for Chadderton's life.

The previous day I had a great three-mile run along Deep Creek Lake, worked out with weights, and had done a lot of calisthenics. I had quit smoking a few months before so I felt strong physically. As I ran, I thought about the hundreds of fights my father had engaged in. Of over 280 of them, he lost about 20. I could not afford to lose this fight. On the weekends he would go on his five-mile training run along the embankment of the Thames River, and would crisscross the Battersea, Albert, and Chelsea Bridges. He would often take my brother Charles and me with him, and I was always fascinated with the way he could run—throwing punches at the air, while snorting through his nose. He explained that this was to practice getting enough oxygen when blood caked the nose, since the mouthpiece prevented taking in air through the mouth. We had to take several steps to each one of his, and tried to imitate his combination of punches and the rage with which he seemed to be attacking the empty space in front of him.

On Monday, March 22, 1982 we were scheduled to be in the Garrett County Courthouse. No matter how I tried to distract myself from the task at hand, I could not deny the tension I was feeling. In my room before I traveled to court, I felt an uncommon stiffness in my neck and for a few minutes. I was concerned that the pressure would overwhelm me and incapacitate me. I wished it were only a physical fight. It would be easier. I calmed myself down by thinking about all the other difficult courtroom battles that I had been in and convinced myself that this was just one more, and since we would not be choosing a jury in the next couple of days I should relax because, "the trouble was not now. The trouble was before me."

I had been in a lot of tense trials, and under great pressure before. On the way to court I repeated to myself, as I had often done before, the lines from Henry V. "Once more into the breach, dear friends, once more. Or close the wall up with our English dead! In peace there's nothing so becomes a man as modest stillness and humility. But when the blast of war blows in your ears, then imitate the action of the Tiger. Stiffen the sinews, conjure up the blood, disguise fair nature with hard favoured rage." Then I switched to the Eagles, singing out loudly, "You may lose or you may win, but you'll never pass this way again, don't let the sound of your own wheels drive you crazy!"

*****

Tina was a prolific letter writer. During the entire time of her incarceration, she wrote daily to "Darling Bobby" on attractive flowered notepaper, with matching envelopes. Sometimes she wrote more than once a day. They winged their way from her cell to his. She professed her love and devotion to him, helping to keep his spirit strong.

In Garrett County in the early morning, before the motions hearing was scheduled to commence, she wrote to him:

March 22, 1982

My darling Bobby,

Hi sweetie, how did you sleep last night? I think my headache is from all the tension, can't seem to shake it. It's just a little after 5 a.m. & I'm bored, guess I got too much sleep yesterday. Last night on 60 Minutes it showed a woman having a baby at home, her husband was by her side & so were her other 5 children. I sure hope some how you're with me when Bobby Jr. comes. Phil said Hickman agreed to take me first if we're granted separate trials, but if I have the baby, it's declared a mistrial which means we have to start all over again. Keep your finger crossed Jr. doesn't make a surprise entrance!

Don't have any idea what time we go to court, do you? I'm wearing a black dress that mom sent me. Saturday was the

```
first day of spring. I have brought all winter clothes, hope
I don't roast! I thought Sherrie was coming to see me to-
night (last night) I figured by 8:30 she wasn't coming so I
showered & put my nightie on. Still wish you could wash my
back. Don't forget to ask Phil & Keating today about being
able to visit. I hope they can arrange it today? I just want
t hold you in my arms & love you! Well I think I'll try to
go back to sleep for a while. I love you sweetheart.

Your Loving Wife 4Ever & ever, Tina Myers OXOXOX

P.S. — I hope you read all your papers last night Keating
gave you, you're going to have to remember it all.
```

*****

Court convened. Tina, seven months pregnant, sat next to Myers and they were affectionate and loving to each other. Chadderton sat grim faced, while Orrin and I argued the motions.

Judge Thayer found me amusing and allowed me a great deal of latitude. He was a distinguished and polite gentleman. I was getting a little annoyed that Tina and Bobby were not paying attention to my arguments, but rather they were enjoying being together and holding hands under the trial table. We had purposely set up our seating arrangements so that this couple could sit next to each other. Though, who could blame them really? They hadn't seen each other for several months because while she was at the Baltimore City Jail, he had been incarcerated in the Carroll County Detention Center. Being distracted in the courtroom was the least of their sins . . . at one point, Myers ran his hand over her bulging abdomen, where he hoped a son was thriving.

Orrin and I presented several motions to Judge Thayer, who enjoyed our advocacy even as he knew that we realized there was little merit to what we were arguing. We needed to make a complete record of all our complaints about the constitutionality of the death penalty statute. This was a kind, considerate, and patient judge. I was developing even more respect for Orrin Brown because he was clearly articulate, intelligent, aggressive, and comfortable in court. He was a fighter and I felt lucky to have him on my side of the trial table.

Sutley, on the other hand, simply adopted our arguments and added nothing.

That Monday night, March 22, 1982, we had a group meeting in the large conference room in the Garrett County Detention Center. All three defendants and their lawyers were present. Since Tina had told me that she would testify that the prosecutor Tom Hickman had tried to date her, I had filed a motion to have the State's Attorney's Office of Carroll County excluded from the case. I asked her if she was still prepared to testify about his advances towards her, and she assured me that she was ready to take the stand.

Incidentally, Robert Myers had told me months earlier that Hickman had dated Mary Ruth. I was incredulous—dating the victim and later trying to date the defendant? Here's how that story came about:

Terry Lee Humple first met Robert Myers when both began sharing the same cell at the Carroll County Detention Center. He supposedly realized at that time that he had unsuccessfully attempted to have Myers prepare his 1978 income tax forms. He stated that in March of 1979, he was drinking a beer at the Spotted Horse Inn when the owner, Frances Baker, was talking with other customers about taxes. Humple asked where he might have his taxes prepared. Baker suggested a local accountant he knew, Robert Myers, and gave Humple directions to Myers' home. Humple hitchhiked from his home to Myers' home in Silver Run Valley.

He claimed he observed a white Lincoln and a green Corvette parked outside the home (Tom Hickman coincidently drove a green Corvette . . .) Humple claimed it was not until the fall of 1981, when he began sharing a cell with Robert Myers, that he realized his cellmate was the same person he had sought to prepare his taxes. Humple advised Myers of his visit to Myers' home in March of 1979, when he observed Hickman and a woman together.

Clearly complete simple-minded bullshit. I did not believe for a moment that Hickman had tried to date Mary Ruth. Terry Lee Humple was awaiting trial on an arson and attempted murder charge. He had recently received a twelve-year suspended sentence for breaking and entering. I decided to use an expert to conduct a polygraph exam of Terry Lee Humple to determine his truthfulness.

I had used William White in other cases. White was a genuine expert. He had worked for The C.I.A. Humple's polygraph report stated:

"On March 8, 1982, Terry L. Humple, born on 5/14/1960 in Carroll County, Maryland, an inmate at the Baltimore County Detention Center was interviewed and a polygraph examination was administered. Humple is presently awaiting trial on an arson and attempted murder charges."

"Humple alleged that he had actually seen Thomas Hickman with his arm around a woman in the house that Humple believed to be the residence of Robert Myers in March 1979.

"Humple alleged that he had been directed to the house in Silver Run Valley when he asked in a bar where he could have his income taxes prepared. He alleged that in March 1979 he actually went to a house that fit the description. A woman came to the door and she was accompanied by a man whom Humple recognized as being Thomas Hickman, the County State's Attorney. Humple alleged that the man had his arm around the woman and she had a glass of what appeared to be wine in her hand. In answering Humple's inquiries about having his tax returns completed, she told him that Mr. Myers did that work at his office and not at his home. Humple denied that Hickman said anything. Humple left, without entering the house. He had stayed at the front door as he talked to the woman.

"He recognized Hickman because he had seen his picture in the newspaper and someone had pointed him out in the Courthouse. Humple could not remember if Hickman had prosecuted him when he was tried on the breaking and entering charge.

"Humple denied that he had ever met Robert Myers before they became cellmates. "He denied that he and Myers had fabricated this story. All polygraph tracings were readable. There were significant and consistent changes in patterns at each of the relevant question areas. These were interpreted to be similar to those of a person who was attempting to deceive. When confronted, Humple stated that he was thinking about the fact that Hickman was going to be prosecuting his brother in approximately two weeks and he was afraid that he might take revenge on him if Humple testified for Myers."

This complete fabrication was too much even for me. I had the polygraph performed weeks before this hearing to get the upper hand. I didn't want Myers to be able to complain later that I had not explored calling a witness that he had asked me to present. I confronted them both several times about this and they both insisted it was true. It was clear to me Humple was being paid for this crap.

I issued a subpoena to guarantee Humple's presence, a four-hour drive from his jail cell. I had a strong feeling that a sentencing judge might be disturbed by this callous indifference to the dignity of the victim and the State's Attorney, diluting the sympathy that might otherwise be generated. I had shared the polygraph results with Myers and Humple, hoping that they would be persuaded to back off, but they did not. They knew the test results were inadmissible.

"Okay then," I thought, "More drama!" Humple was brought into the Court and was about to be sworn by the clerk. I asked the judge for a moment and whispered to Myers "I'm fucking telling you that this is going to blow up in your face and maybe get you executed! You want me to do it, trust me, I will," Myers stammered. "Okay. No, don't call him." I told the court that upon reflection, the defense did not want to call the witness. Humple looked over at us confused. He was clearly disappointed not to be able to embarrass Hickman.

I then focused on my attempt to have the State's Attorney Hickman removed for trying to date Tina Marco in the summer of 1979. I argued the State's Attorney had asked her to go out on six or eight occasions, and that two of these invitations were by phone—the others were in person. Tina told me this several times, and always insisted she would testify to it. I had placed a "corroborating" witness on the stand that Tuesday afternoon in support of the motion. This was a fellow patron in the restaurant where Hickman had been served lunch by Tina in the springtime, three months before the murder. That was the extent of the customer's knowledge: that he saw Tina wait on him. The session had ended before we had time to call Tina to testify.

The three defendants and lawyers met again in the Garrett County Detention Center, early Tuesday evening. I wanted to confirm that Tina would testify the next day, and said, "Tina, I'll put you on the stand tomorrow." To my great surprise, she responded that she wouldn't testify! I said, "What's going on?" and Sutley said, "She will plead the fifth." Brown and I realized that something very important was happening. It didn't require Clarence Darrow's ability to recognize that. Neither of them could be cajoled into discussing it further, and the meeting ended.

Orrin and I met for a late supper later that Tuesday night at the Willow O' The Wisp. I had gone out for my run along Deep Creek Lake and had worked out in the weight room again, so I was not feeling any tension, despite the strange happenings in the earlier meeting at the Detention Center.

Later we met at the whirlpool bath and since we had not seen Sutley for several hours, we speculated that he was probably with the prosecutors finalizing a deal for Tina, which could effectively put our clients in the gas chamber. Sutley did not come back to the Will O' The Wisp Lodge, and we both speculated we had been deceived by him, and all of a sudden, all his lack of advocacy or interest or energy made perfect sense. Why waste the time and energy if he knew all along Tina was not going to trial?

I was in a different mindset than Orrin. We sat strategizing, dissecting the case in that deserted lodge's whirlpool tub for a long time. We both talked about Sutley's absence. It loomed over us. I was not totally convinced that Tina would actually double cross Bobby, but I feared I had overestimated her feelings for him. It was becoming obvious that their relationship had actually been disintegrating for some time. All those letters to him expressing her love were looking like a charade.

The next morning, Orrin and I met for breakfast very early before court and Sutley was not there. He had slipped away from The Lodge. The prosecution team was staying in the Village Inn, the closest hotel to the Oakland Courthouse a few miles from us, so we could not get any clues from their activities.

As suspected, late at night on March 23, 1982, Tina Myers entered into an agreement with the State whereby, in return for her truthful testimony, she would not be prosecuted for the murder. Hickman, Coleman, and Leete, along with the local State's Attorney James L. Sherbin and his deputy, had all met Tina along with Philip Sutley and a stenographer that night. They had removed her from the Detention Center and they had negotiated the agreement with Tina in their hotel. It had taken until 3 a.m. the next morning to advise Tina of her rights, reduce their agreement to writing, question her, transcribe it, and get everyone's signature.

CHAPTER 19:
A LAWYER'S ULTIMATE
DOUBLE-CROSS

"You are pushing your own client into the gas chamber!"
— Judge Thayer's Chambers

On Wednesday, March 24, 1982 at 9:30 a.m. when Orrin and I arrived outside the Courtroom, Tom Hickman, Frank Coleman, and Jim Sherbin greeted us and joyfully told us that Tina had become a State's witness. She would be given immunity from the first-degree murder and welfare fraud charges. When we went inside the courtroom, Myers and Chadderton were sitting in their chairs. Tina was not there.

Myers kept looking at Sutley saying, "Phil, Phil what's going on?" Sutley, standing just a few feet away, did not look in Myers' direction, nor did he look at Orrin or me. Myers got tears in his eyes and turned ashen white. He was devastated by the outrageous double cross from his wife and the lawyer whom HE had paid, and believed had been representing him. The prosecutors came into Court and said we should go to the Judge's chambers to tell him what was happening. Chadderton did not react.

I had avoided looking at Phil as we entered the chambers. Once inside, Judge Thayer asked what was happening and Hickman explained that Tina had been given immunity and would testify against Myers and Chadderton. Sutley told the Judge that what Hickman said was correct. Sutley was sitting on the other side of the room, about twenty feet away, and I immediately confronted him. I turned on him and could not disguise my anger or disgust and, looking him in the eye, I said, "Then you've got a big problem now, don't you? You are pushing your own client into the gas chamber!" My face was red. He tried to ignore me, but I persisted. "You represented Bobby, so in effect you are trying to push your own client into the gas chamber!"

He responded, "What do you mean? I represent Tina." Sutley repeated him-self, saying, "What do you mean? I never represented Myers!" I was dumbfounded and stuttered, "I want to put him on the witness stand!" I looked directly at Sutley and then back to the Judge Thayer. No one else in the room spoke, and I looked at the judge and repeated, "I want to put him on the witness stand" as I sneered in Sutley's direction. Judge Thayer said, "Let's go into the court and you can put whatever you want on the record and produce any evidence that you desire." The judge assured me, "We can go into the court and you can put any witness on the stand that you want."

I had been most respectful to everyone up to that point, and I had gained some credibility with the court. Judge Thayer understood that there must be some truth to my allegations because my response had been spontaneous and I was visibly upset with Sutley. I said to the Judge, "Your Honor, I want to put him on the stand. He represented Myers all along until I got into the case, and it is totally improper for him to negotiate this plea . . . in fact, he's become a State agent." The judge attempted, in vain, to calm me down.

Outside the chambers I complemented Corporal Leete on his tenacity. He followed us into the courtroom. When we all got inside, Bobby and Chad-derton were still sitting waiting at the trial table. The two were huddled together, speaking in hushed voices with their heads inches apart.

They had guessed that there had been a major development because Tina was not there in court. Bobby asked me what was going on and I told him that Tina had fucked him, and that she was going to be a witness against him. Tears welled up in his eyes and he went from being flushed to being ashen grey as the blood drained from his face. He slumped back into the courtroom chair. Chad-derton shuffled his feet, and the phony grin that was almost always on his face disappeared. Chadderton stood up and he shifted his weight from leg to leg, looking out a courtroom window, and drinking a small cup of water.

His wife, Sherrie, left the court and returned several minutes later with reddened eyes. Myers had looked at Phil sheepishly and asked him, "Phil, Phil what happened?" Sutley ignored him and would not look in his direction. I thought Phil was a coward and that Myers, who was close to tears, was absolutely pathetic.

I had no idea what Sutley would say on the witness stand when he was sworn in five minutes later. I had to question him without any preparation, without having a chance to gather my thoughts or calm down. I could not hide my anger or my contempt for what he had done. It now all made perfect sense. Sutley had filed no motions, showed little interest in meeting about the case, and had little energy when we did meet. He had known all along that Tina would eventually testify against Bobby, and that if it meant Bobby was executed, then he would just be the collateral damage.

The proceedings were reconvened and Tom Hickman placed on the record the immunity agreement, and explained the reason Tina was not present in court.

I called Sutley to the witness stand and attacked him in the best way that I could. He denied that he had ever been Bobby's lawyer.

He admitted that Robert Myers had telephoned him on Friday, January 12, 1980 and that he had gone to the accounting office to discuss representing Robert Myers, but at that time there was no case pending. I showed him the letter that he had sent to the State's Attorney's office on Monday, January 15, 1980 and he agreed that he had sent it, and that it said, "I have been retained by Robert Myers." He testified that a couple of days later, he had received a call from the prosecutors and they had agreed to "get hold of him" if they wanted to contact Robert Myers.

Sutley maintained that he had never taken a fee from Robert Myers, but that over the next several months he had met with him on a few occasions, both at Myers' house on Turkey Foot Road, and in his law office. They had several telephone conversations over the next few weeks, and he talked to lawyer Alan Fox who had been down in Ocean City "checking a few things out." He had retrieved Fox's file containing notes and documentation concerning the Department of Social Services investigation and the potential bigamy charge. He had discussed all this with Robert and Tina Myers at their house. He earnestly maintained that he had not received a fee from Robert Myers, but when pressed, agreed that Tina Myers had paid him "a substantial fee."

He testified that he had helped Tina obtain local counsel in Bermuda and learned later about the murder indictments when he saw it on television. Sutley was being evasive and not forthcoming with his responses. Over the

State's objection, I delved into the financial dimension. He repeated that Myers had given him no money, but admitted that Tina had paid him.

He said that Thomas Stansfield, a local attorney who had represented Robert Myers in all his business dealings, had given him $30,000 in cash. Sutley weakly attempted to assert that this money was only for his representation of Tina on the bigamy charge. He claimed that Robert Myers was broke and that he did not know where Tina Myers had obtained this money to give to Thomas Stansfield.

He knew that he had signed in on many occasions to see Robert Myers at the Carroll County Detention Center, so he could not deny being there. Astonishingly, he asserted, "I live right near the jail. I'd go up and see him after he was indicted. I talked to him at length. But it really wasn't about the case."

I was now getting angrier and started to press him. "So when you say that you weren't really discussing the case, what you are saying is that you were discussing other things, but obviously the purpose of your going there was to discuss the case?" He said, "It really wasn't, no, it wasn't—it wasn't the purpose, no." I followed up with, "But on each occasion, would I be correct if I said that on each occasion that you did see Mr. Myers, you did discuss the murder indictment pending against him and the trial pending against him?" He answered "Yeah, I'd say so, not—not the facts though, not the facts of the case."

When we left Judge Thayer's chambers, I had not had an adequate opportunity to assemble my thoughts and decide how to counterpunch, or how I could possibly use this to Myers' advantage. Our defense had been significantly damaged or destroyed, but we could not fail to somehow counterattack if possible. Sutley would not agree that the money he received had belonged to Robert Myers. He did not agree that she had none of her own and that she had no claim on Bobby's property since her marriage to him had been fraudulent and was consequently null and void. Nor would he agree that he had been Myers' lawyer, stating that whatever few things he had done for Myers were on a "friendly" basis, and that he had always explained that he was not his lawyer and would be representing only Tina if they were charged with the crime.

It was bizarre. One day Tina Myers, seven months pregnant, sat with Bobby holding hands and whispering in his ear while we lawyers argued points of law. The next day when we came out of the Judge's chambers she knew she would soon be a free woman. He might be executed.

I was letting my frustration get the best of me. Judge Thayer correctly pointed out that I had not articulated to the court why this was relevant to this prosecution. It might be unfair and might be unethical, but what was the remedy? Since I knew that I would have a further opportunity to explore this dimension to the case once I had an opportunity to better prepare my attack on Sutley, I did not pursue it further. Knowing I would not get any relief from Judge Thayer, and that I would be able to renew my motion in this regard at a later time, I concluded my questioning.

I had lost my composure and had been unable to shake off my outrage. I optimistically told myself that this latest turn of events would further help me demonstrate that Robert Myers was weak and gullible, and that Tina Myers had manipulated him and, with the help of his attorney, had taken further advantage of him.

During the next recess, I had to explain to Bobby again that she had in fact double-crossed him, which meant she was in reality, signing his death warrant. Tears ran down Bobby Myers' face again as he contemplated the scope of his wife's treachery. He was in a panic and could barely control himself. As he sat next to me, his face was flushed and he had great difficulty in stopping himself from sobbing. I had always felt sorry for him because he was so weak and needy.

To be an effective advocate you cannot be judgmental or fail to recognize your client's humanity, or you'll never be able to present his positive qualities to the fact finder, the sentencing authority, or the public at large. With Bobby, it was easy to like him because he had a nice smile was not at all aggressive. He had done many kind things in his life. Even if a client was really despicable, as long as he treated me with respect and let me control the case, I would always try my very best to explain that he too was a "child of God" and that "we all fall short of God's grace."

I did not know Philip McKay Sutley very well. I had seen him in court over the years and he was a well-respected and experienced lawyer. He always seemed laid back and at ease. I had always thought that he must be clever and effective, based on his reputation, but I had never had any personal deal-ings with him. He had a boyish and charming manner, but the more I reflected on his betrayal, the angrier I became. He had clearly sold out his own client. I reflected on him telling me that he was too emotionally involved with Myers, and that a dog had eaten Myers' materials! I was furious that he had forced me into a position of having to either attack him, or else ignore what I knew to be the truth and become an accessory to this disloyalty. If he had expected me to back away and overlook his conduct to avoid unpleasantness, he had grossly miscalculated. I was not brought up to run away when confronted by some problem or person, no matter how big.

The Model Rules of Professional Conduct state that, "Loyalty is an essential element in the lawyer's relationship to a client. An improper conflict of interest may exist before representation is undertaken, in which event the representation should be declined. If such a conflict arises after the representation has been undertaken, the lawyer must withdraw from the representation. Loyalty to a client is impaired when a lawyer cannot consider, recommend or carry out an appropriate course of action for the client because of the lawyer's own the respon-sibilities or own interests. The conflict in effect forecloses alternatives that would otherwise be available to the client. The concepts of independent judgment and undiluted loyalty and the appearance of impropriety must be considered."

Whenever I had avoided a fight in my life, I always felt disgraced and cowardly. This case was already taking all my energy and focus and even though I felt physically and mentally strong, I did not need or want this extra personal dimension weighing me down. I rationalized that it would of course give me something else to argue about and file motions about. Furthermore, I knew that Sutley's conduct should cause his disbarment. For Myers, it could realistically make the difference between living in a prison or being executed.

During a pretrial conference later that morning in the judge's chambers, I told Judge Thayer and the lawyers what Tina Myers had told me about Hickman's dating attempts. Sutley said that his client would not testify about the incidents. I then proffered to the Court what Tina Myers told me: that she met Tom Hickman in June of 1979, when she was working as a barmaid in Westminster, and that in June and July of 1979, the State's Attorney had asked to go out on dates with her on six or eight occasions. Two of these invitations were on the phone and the others in person. I told the Court that I discussed this with Sutley and he informed me that if I called Tina to the stand, she would assert her Fifth Amendment rights.

The Judge allowed me to formalize my proffer in open court. I called Tina to the stand. She did not look in Myers' direction, and refused to testify. I had never actually believed that I would be successful in getting Hickman removed from the case on this basis, or that he actually tried to date Tina. I suspected that she had manufactured the story to cause his replacement, a mistrial, or a reversal on appeal.

The removal of the State's Attorney would have benefited all three defendants. Sutley, though, now had a different agenda. This tactic and her testimony in this regard had been discussed between the three lawyers on several occasions. Tina was now not going to lie since she now had no need to, and it would violate her agreement to tell only the truth.

To remove any lingering questions, Tom Hickman testified that he never tried to date Tina, but did admit that he met and talked with her once in John O's, during the summer of 1979, and about a month later in Angelo's, another Westminster tavern. Supporting Hickman's assertions that he simply talked with the barmaid were two State Police investigators who accompanied him to John O's, Charles H. Skuhr Jr. and Don A. Newcomer. Also confirming the nature of their conversation was Dean L. Minnich, the managing editor of the Carroll County Edition of the Hanover Evening Sun.

Tom Hickman said he "never considered asking Tina Marco for dates, and the whole idea was preposterous." "I never asked her for a date," he said. "Apparently, there are some people in Carroll County who believe all this," referring to the rumors that had persisted around Westminster.

The court took another morning recess and the newspaper reporters approached me for a comment on the situation. I tried to put a positive spin on this development and told them that the case was far from over, and that it had simply become more interesting.

We then returned to court, and I tried very hard to concentrate on the next motion, which was to have the judge declare that the death penalty in Maryland, on its face and as applied, was unconstitutional in that it was "cruel and unusual punishment." This was not a great argument. We also argued that the method of execution, the gallows and the gas chamber, had always been barbaric, and that lethal injection or a bullet to the head should be employed. Sutley was no longer at the trial table because his job was over.

I was further enraged when I read the next day's papers. Sutley was quoted as saying, "You're not going to believe what she says . . . It was shocking and I've been around long enough to have heard many stories. It was the kind of thing that really shakes you." He continued, "Tina's version of the August 29, 1979 murder of Mary Ruth agrees with that of the State Police and the Carroll County prosecutors. Even if all three of the defendants had been convicted, there still would have been a lot of doubts because of the circumstantial nature of the evidence. This way we'll know."

The Sun newspaper on the same day quoted Sutley as saying, "I think she wanted to do the right thing. Contrary to what may have been written about her, she's not altogether a bad person," and further stated, "Mr. Sutley lauded the work of Corporal James M. Leete, the principal investigator in the case, as well as Mr. Hickman and assistant State's Attorney Frank D. Coleman in putting together the case after a two and a half-year investigation." Sutley apologized for his earlier criticism of the investigator's handling of the complex murder case. "They handled the case in the most professional way I have ever seen," he said. The article continued quoting Sutley as saying, "Mrs. Myers' statements bore out the prosecution's theory of how the murder was committed. They were 100% correct in their theory." The article then detailed the State's entire case.

That same day, The News American quoted Sutley as saying, "She told me what happened the night of the murder. What she said is in complete agreement with what the State has said all along." Not only had Sutley double-crossed his client, taken his money, and totally deceived him, but he now had become part of the prosecution team and was gratuitously poisoning the public perception. It seemed malicious in the extreme. Sutley told the waiting press that "she is going to stay in jail. For one reason, she fears for her life and, for another, she is getting good medical treatment and she needs a month after testifying to decide where she is going."

He told another reporter, "I think the woman really wanted to get this off her chest. The look of relief on her face. She had been living in pure hell for two and a half years," adding, "I think it's important the truth be known. It's a very wise move by the State." He said that "the oral statement Tina gave police took more than two hours. It was so graphic that it was chilling," and added, "Tina Myers cried during much of the oral statement, recalling her involvement in the slaying."

The son of a bitch was gratuitously damaging Bobby for no apparent reason.

"She lies. She'll do anything to save her ass!" Myers told a reporter.

The victim's sister, daughter, and father listened to the announcement about Tina being given immunity before leaving for the return trip to Carroll County. They were pleased. "Two out of three is better than zero out of three," was their statement. Hickman said, "The victim's family is very happy with the way things turned out. We're all satisfied."

I knew, however, that if the trial of the case was moved back to Carroll County, I would be permitted to explore this conflict again. I would have a couple of months to prepare to confront Sutley. I resolved that the next time I had the opportunity, I would embarrass and punish him as much as I could. Perhaps some good legal issue could be made out of this, since in my experience it was unprecedented. Few would feel comfortable with a legal system that would allow an execution in these circumstances. This was a capital case, not some simple drug case where a lawyer had a conflict because he was representing two co-defendants.

Chadderton, though, had wanted his trial to take place in Garrett County, and would not waive his right to a speedy trial. He was prepared for his case to begin. Myers, agreed to waive his right to a speedy trial, and the judge knew we had an appeal pending on the viable removal issue. We still wanted his case returned to Carroll County. Thankfully, Judge Thayer formally severed the cases and I was greatly relieved. Not only would I be able try the Myers case alone, but I would also have the advantage of learning in more detail the evidence against Chadderton. Judge Thayer then excused me from the proceedings.

I could afford to be somewhat nonchalant about this latest turn of events. Brown and I agreed that the case had gone from a possible winner to an almost definite loser. We would now have to attack Tina. We both realized, however, that with her testimony all the loose ends of the State's circumstantial case could be neatly tied together, and that this change of events could very well mean our clients would be executed.

That night, Tina wrote to Myers while she was in her cell, fifty feet away from his in the Garrett County Detention Center.

```
March 24th 1982

Dear Bobby,
This letter is going to be very hard to write so please
bear with me. First let me say Bob I love you & had known I
always will. I am sorry that I did what I felt I had to do,
but let me say I did it for several special reasons. First
and foremost, the State has an over abundance of evidence
against this case and Bobby there are children involved that
are innocent of any wrongdoing. I can't picture us spending
our lives in prison and our children never knowing us. It's
not fair to them and I can't expect your family to raise
our family for us. One of us had to come forward. It's been
hell to live with for two and half years, although what I
felt I had to do is going to be even harder to live with
knowing I had to detach myself from the only person I have
ever loved. Regardless of you choosing to believe this or
not Bobby, I do love you & this is tearing my insides out.
Other than this terrible thing, I have loved you and expe-
rienced a lifetime of happiness with you for two years that
I will always cherish. As for our children, you are their
father; they will know what a kind, loving & decent man you
are. I will see you through this the best I can, please know
that I do care, have faith in God & continue to pray Bobby
as I will for you. I don't know what else I can say to ease
your pain and hurt, please forgive me for betraying your
trust, I will always love you with every ounce of me, more
than all the stars in the skies, more than all the marlin,
more that all the sand on every beach, more than every tear
```

I have and will shed. I love you. God only knows how much I
do, take care my love. May God bless you and keep you safe.
Forever is a long, long time.
Love,
Tina Myers

*****

Tina wrote another letter to Robert later that same night.

March 24, 1982

Dear Bobby,
I just wanted to drop you a note to say that if you want
to write me and keep in touch you should not have second
thoughts. I would like us to always keep our closeness, &
as we have always said we are the best of friends. I would
like to keep you informed of our children & as of now I have
made no plans to where I'll go or what I will do without
you. I wish you would swallow me so I would be with you,
but remember my heart will always be with you no matter
what. Thank you for making me feel like a woman and feel
loved for the first time in my life, I will always remember
the wonderful time we've shared, for providing for me and
treating me like Cinderella, the memories I have of us will
last me a lifetime. No one will ever take your place, Bobby,
regardless of how you feel towards me. I hope there is some
love for me left in your heart.

I just saw Phil and he told me how it went in court this
morning & Bobby I wish I could put my arms around you and
try to take your hurt away. Please know how I feel about
you, I have done nothing but cried all night and all day.
How I wish I could wipe this nightmare out of our lives and
we could start over.

Please try to keep your chin up and let me know how you are,
if there's anything I can do please don't hesitate to ask.
I will always be with you never doubt that. Please don't

feel I deserted you, I didn't, I just feel our children deserve a chance & although it won't be the same raising them without you, they will know you and in time will love you as I do, rest assured.

I told you before I would wait a lifetime for you and I meant it, if you still love me don't be ashamed to let me know, I don't have a crystal ball, it's up to you to let me know. Take your time, give it a lot of thought, but regardless you will always be my best friend & love.

I took our vows very seriously and to this day feel as though no one shall ever come between us.

I love you Bobby Myers with all my heart and if I have our most hoped for boy he will have your name if it's a girl she will be Robin Lee Myers, this I promise, and this child will be very special as Sabrina is, our child. I love you Bobby, always remember this, I will always wear my Bermuda charm since I don't have my wedding band.

I love you, May God bless you & keep you safe for me.

Forever and Endless Love OXOXOX
Tina Myers
204 S. 3rd St.
Oakland, MD 21550

I'm in you and you're in me, You gave me love I never had.

P.S. Bobby keep in touch with my parents. I didn't go into detail but they are concerned & worried & do care about you, what's done is done, we can't change it, all we can do is look ahead sweetheart, not backwards, shake it and let it go, if you have to be locked up, go to church, try & work, be good, the time will fly, if you want I will stay close so I can visit you, you have so much to give, maybe you would soon teach a class in accounting, but whatever keep your mind & body strong, think positive thoughts & pray Bobby, God takes care of us all, I won't let us down when we need him.

I love you, sunshine and always will.

CHAPTER 20:
ROBERT MYERS CONFESSES TO ME

"You marry me and take care of my kids
and I'll have your wife murdered for you!"
— Tina Gillen Marco

It had been a very dramatic day. For two days Tina Myers, seven months pregnant, sat with her husband holding hands and whispering in his ear while we lawyers argued esoteric points of law at the bench and in open court. The next day we all knew that she would soon be free.

Sutley's timing was excellent. He had waited until the last moment to catch us off guard and get Tina the best possible outcome. That evening, Orrin and I, along with Myers and Daniel and Sherrie Chadderton, met in the conference room in the Garrett County Detention Center. The guards stood outside. Sherrie told them both to "be honest" with us. She was acting so casually it was clear that she already knew everything, and a lot more than Orrin and I did.

Bobby was sobbing and repeated over and over, "Why did she do this? Why did she do this?" I said to him and Chadderton that they had better start leveling with us, and that this was very serious and they could both end up in the gas chamber. Sherrie said, looking at her husband, "You better tell them all about Tina."

Chadderton immediately blurted out that Tina had offered him $4,400 to kill Bobby back in 1980! I was inclined to believe him because at that moment we needed to have a united front, and I could see no motive for him to fabricate such a divisive comment. Myers started to sob more and appeared shocked. It was clearly the first time he had heard about this. Chadderton repeated it and then said casually that he had no intention of carrying out this killing, but he said he took the money anyway. Orrin and I exchanged knowing looks. We were both astounded about what we were hearing.

Myers then, looking straight at me, with tears streaming down his reddened face, shouted, "Okay, okay I'll tell you, I'll tell you, she said, 'You marry me and take care of my kids, and I'll have your wife murdered for you!'" I started to take careful notes. I knew that this conversation was critical and I would need to recall in detail what I was being told. The meeting ended after a few more minutes. It was very awkward. Chadderton and Myers did not look at each other or say another word to each other. Orrin and I joked cynically as we left the jail that their friendship was probably over. We both knew it would mean that they now had conflicting interests, which also meant Orrin and I needed time apart, to digest our respective obligations to our clients.

After this very long day, when I got back to the Will O' The Wisp, I telephoned Alan Murrell to explain what had happened, and I feared incorrectly that he might be sympathetic to Phil Sutley. He was furious and told me to, "Go get him!" He loved his lawyers to put up a fight just as he liked to do. I did not share with him Myers' confession to me. I was the lawyer, not him, and I was perhaps bound by the rules on confidentiality. He was the Public Defender for the entire State so, theoretically, he represented Chadderton. Myers had "confessed" to me in front of others—not in private. The rules concerning confidentiality did not necessarily cover such utterances. It was all getting really complicated. Too complicated. I erred on the side of caution, though, and withheld the information about the confession from Murrell.

Even though I was worn out, I needed to get away from all this and I got directions to some hillbilly bar up in the mountains somewhere. With some difficulty I finally located the place and, "it looked like a place to find some satisfaction, with a little less talk and a lot more action."

The people there were not very welcoming to me. To hell with not smoking, I decided. Who could have a better excuse to actively resume their addiction than I did? I was fully conscious that I was throwing away three months of abstinence as I walked over to the cigarette machine and purchased my pack of drugs. I had smoked about half of them by the time I left the bar around 3 a.m. No one seemed concerned about the 2 a.m. closing time. I had contented myself smoking and slowly getting drunk and listening to the songs blasting from the jukebox. "Hey, hey, you know what I mean put another dime in the record machine." I finally found my way back to my room and collapsed.

The next morning, I did not feel too well. I fired up a couple more cig-arettes, gathered my belongings so I would be ready to go home, and then I went directly to the courthouse. I had not shaved and I felt self-conscious sitting in the spectator section of the courtroom watching Orrin Brown argu-ing his few remaining motions. He clearly didn't need my help, but I think he missed my companionship and support.

I did not need to remain in Garrett County for the next couple of days while Judge Thayer considered Orrin Brown's arguments. Judge Thayer later continued the case for two weeks, which allowed time for Brown to get ready for trial.

I soon grew restless and after an hour I slinked away. I wanted to see my own kids—my nine-year-old daughter Erin and my three-month-old baby Chris. On the four-hour journey home, I amused myself singing the Alabama song, "Love in the 1st Degree," changing lyrics as I saw fit. "I once thought of love as a prison a place I didn't want to be . . . I never thought I would get caught. It seemed like the perfect crime . . . Baby you left me defenseless. I've only got one plea. Lock me away inside of your love and throw away the key . . . I'm guilty of lust in the 1st degree . . . Now babe I'm not begging for mercy go ahead and throw the book at me, if loving you'se a crime I know that I'm as guilty as a man can be . . . Oh yeah oh yeah love in the 1st degree." Then, "Hang down your head, Robert Myers poor boy you're bound to die . . .."

I stopped a few times on the drive back to Baltimore and picked up the newspapers. There was a lot of coverage about the case and the latest devel-opments. It made good copy, at least. The story of how Myers had confessed his guilt to me would not surface for three years.

In order to deal with the stress of criminal court and life in general, it is critical to develop some healthy safety valves and release mechanisms. Person-ally, I always relied upon physical exercise, sex, music, and "gallows" humor, as callous as that often seems to others. "But we're never gonna survive . . . unless . . . we get a little crazy, no we're never gonna survive . . . unless . . . we get a little crazy. In a world full of people only some want to fly . . . isn't that crazy?"

Over the next 3 months, on several occasions, Alan Murrell and I went to Westminster to meet Myers and review docket entries and other documents in the case. He actively encouraged his lawyers to be aggressive and thorough and would often personally participate in their cases. He drove his 1969 yellow Jaguar convertible, which seemed incongruous with his close-cropped crew cut, conservative suit and matching views. I enjoyed the smooth ride, and I welcomed his insights and his company.

CHAPTER 21:
THE CHADDERTON TRIAL

"You can't go home again . . ."
— Thomas Wolfe

The Chadderton trial started with jury selection on April 19, 1982. The prosecutors would accept no plea. They were determined to put Chadderton in the gas chamber because they believed, and had overwhelming evidence to prove, that he had brutally murdered a defenseless woman for a few thousand dollars. They knew he had subsequently offered to kill others in similar fashion, for a fee, and that he had threatened to murder Tina and her young children, in order to prevent her from telling what she knew in Court.

The courthouse in Oakland, Garrett County, was fifteen miles west of where Chadderton had been born in nearby West Virginia. He had grown up in one of the nearly one hundred homes that clung to the western bank of a mountain that the locals called "the backbone." These houses were painted drab shades of green and the town looked desperately poor. All day long dump trucks, laden with coal, roared through the town to leave their cargo at the train depot, where the black fuel was loaded into open train cars and shipped off. Dust and exhaust fumes cast a gray pall over the entire area. Most of the children growing up there moved to Baltimore for employment because there was little or no work nearby. They seldom returned.

The Chadderton family was large and well known in the area, since Chadderton's father had several sets of offspring. His father, Gerald Lyle Chadderton Sr., had recently committed suicide, but his grandmother, who was to be a witness in the case, lived just a few miles from the courthouse. Chadderton left school after the seventh grade and after working several menial jobs he had joined the military. He soon grew into a 6'4" muscular man with blond hair and tattooed arms, whose only passions seem to be riding motorcycles and chasing women.

Chadderton's military career had started well. He was stationed in Fort Bragg, North Carolina, Fort Gordon, Georgia, and then Fort Meade, Maryland. He enjoyed being trained to shoot and became an expert with 88 mm. mortars and other guns, but he soon tired of being told what to do and when to do it. His rebellious nature got him into one scrape after another. He was prosecuted in a civilian court for stealing a car and was sentenced to prison for eighteen months. After six months he was paroled, but the Army discharged him under conditions "less than Honorable." His grandmother, Goldie Wilson, who lived nearby in Kitzmiller, was told that he had been dismissed in 1967 because he opposed the war in Vietnam and that he refused to kill. She repeated that myth over and over to anyone who would listen.

Chadderton was a native son returning to Oakland to face sensational murder charges, in the first case to be tried in Garrett County in which the death penalty was being sought. This trial was to be the longest ever conducted in the County.

Chadderton had arrived in Baltimore in the early 1970s, and for much of the time was unemployed. He resented working in jobs that he considered were beneath him, but eventually adjusted to steady employment as a janitor and then a shelf stacker at the Pantry Pride Store on Reisterstown Road in Baltimore. He lived in a rented house with his wife Sherrie and their two young children. In court, however, he refused to wear his blue uniform, and instead he wore a dark three-piece suit with sharp cowboy boots and horn-rimmed glasses. He looked like television's stereotypical concept of a hit man.

The courthouse in Oakland has a central courtroom with a few rows of benches and chairs ringing the pit like area where the prosecution, defense, and jurors sit. These participants sit several feet below the spectators, who can peer down at the activity in the small amphitheater. When cases are removed from one jurisdiction to another, it is customary for the local State's Attorney to sit at the trial table with the prosecutor who has traveled there for the case, at least until the jury is selected. Even if he knows nothing about the case it always makes it clear to the local citizens that he is giving his stamp of approval to the prosecution of the case.

Each local State's Attorney is elected in his respective jurisdiction every four years, and consequently often knows many of the potential jurors, who must all be registered voters, personally. He knows the churchgoers, the "good" families, the law-abiding citizens, the petty criminals and the local drunks. He is therefore in a unique position to advise who to put on a jury and who to challenge. Local folks are not likely to reject him or the State's case, and it usually leaves a traveling defense attorney in an inferior position.

James L. Sherbin, the local State's Attorney at the time, had originally lived in Baltimore. More than a decade earlier he and I had been young neophyte prosecutors together in the Baltimore City State's Attorney's Office. He had a disarming "aw, shucks" persona, and he was a very effective advocate. After a short while, he left Baltimore and moved to Garrett County where he soon became well respected and well-liked. He earned the confidence of the people there and had been elected State's Attorney. "Jim" Sherbin was present for jury selection and spent a lot of time in the courtroom during the case. He had also been present when Tina confessed to her role in the murder a few weeks before.

Orrin Brown had arranged to have a local defense attorney assigned to help him with the defense of the case. James Watson was an experienced local lawyer who could provide some insight into the outlooks and sensibilities of the local citizenry and was a clever and industrious addition to Chadderton's defense team. Watson had immersed himself in the case so he could quickly catch up on its many nuances.

Fishing had become Brown's way to relieve the stress from the practice of law. As the Public Defender for Howard County, he was responsible for a staff of 24, but wherever he could, he delegated administrative tasks to others, to allow him to go to court as often as possible. Brown was an avid fly fisherman and hoped to get some quiet time casting in Deep Creek Lake and the many streams which fed into it. He had discussed his plans with several local lawyers who were happy to describe their many catches in their favorite places. Brown explained that he did not bring all of his favorite gear, but felt he could manage with the two rods and small tackle box that he always kept in the trunk of his car.

Incidentally, several months earlier, Brown represented a "contract killer" in two protracted trials. There was an ongoing hostility between Brown and the killer, and after the second trial's verdict of guilty, the killer exploded in the courtroom, threatening to shoot everyone. He gave a long rambling speech in which he accused Brown of being a government agent who had assisted the prosecutors in obtaining the conviction. He repeated several times that he would have Brown killed as punishment for his treachery. While people often make threats in court when they are angry, this individual was dangerous and had already murdered several people, so this conduct was taken seriously by the court personnel. For a short period, the police kept Brown and his house under surveillance.

At the time of Chadderton's trial, Brown was still apprehensive about this former client, who had continued to send him abusive and disturbing correspondence. However, he had several other serious cases that he had to contend with, including Chadderton's, and so he forced himself to forget about the death threats. For the most part he succeeded.

One morning after the jury had been selected, Brown decided to go fishing at 5:30 a.m. for an hour before court. He left his hotel room and went to his car which was in the parking lot. It was not yet daylight and the visibility was poor. As he approached his car the saw a large metal object underneath it, and the death threats he had repressed overwhelmed him. He was convinced that the object under his car was a bomb. Without going near it, he quickly went to the hotel lobby and telephoned Tom Hickman who was just waking up. The State Police were summoned, and soon arrived with two dogs and the "bomb squad." A helicopter also appeared and hovered while the bomb technicians cautiously approached the vehicle. It was now 11:00 a.m., and the courthouse personnel were informed that court was canceled that day.

As Hickman, Coleman, Cpl. Leete and other police waited at one end of the parking lot, Brown paced nervously, back and forward. The danger was soon over since the item that caused so much concern was actually a large metal tackle box that had been placed there late the previous evening. One of the local fishermen had talked to Brown a few days earlier and had kindly offered to lend him the use of his assortment of fishing hooks and other gear.

He had said he would leave it at Brown's hotel. Brown had forgotten. He was forced to overlook the inevitable smirks and jokes at his expense. Hickman and Coleman were more sympathetic to Brown's plight, though, because they liked and respected him.

The questioning of the jury panel, consisting of about one hundred people, lasted only two days before twelve jurors and two alternates were selected. It was apparent that most of these people were not particularly eager to serve on the first jury in the county to ever consider a death penalty case. Each time the prosecutors or defense attorneys exercised their peremptory challenges to excuse a prospective juror, the individual invariably smiled with relief. One man clapped his hands together silently. Throughout this process, Chadderton sat impassively, taking notes on a pad of legal sized paper. Once these jurors had been sworn in, they were ordered not to discuss the case and they were sent home and told to return four days later when the trial would start.

Several days later, crowds of housewives and retirees jammed the courtroom and overflowed into the four balconies. Competition was fierce for the thirty seats directly above the trial tables and the jury box, with spectators hurrying to get the best ones as soon as the room was opened. Many spectators carried notebooks and pencils, and many would take detailed notes as the testimony and legal arguments evolved. Some had copies of newspapers covering the trial tucked under their arms. One bystander, after getting a front row seat in the packed courtroom said, "This is like a soap opera. I've never seen anything like it in my life."

Chadderton's wife Sherrie had been present for the jury selection and had sat through the remaining pretrial hearings. Before the trial got underway, while the jurors were assembling inside the courtroom, Deputy Sheriffs escorted Chadderton to the back of the spectator's gallery. He knelt to embrace his daughters, Tracey, 7, and Danielle, 4, and kissed Sherrie. It was the first time he had seen the girls in five months, and the reunion caused Chadderton to cry. Orrin Brown had them walk around the wooden rail that separated spectators from the attorneys, so that the seven women and five men on the jury and the alternates could see the youngsters with their father.

Brown knew that he did not have a good defense. He would attempt to cast doubt on the time of the offense so that Chadderton's alibi would be more believable. He knew he had to attempt to discredit Tina and several other States' witnesses and then put Chadderton on the witness stand, hope that he could withstand cross-examination, and that the jurors would like their prodigal son enough to acquit him. In a separate trial such as this, a co-defendant can at least blame the other co-defendants for the murder. Such an approach in a joint trial would doom them all and make the prosecutors' job much easier.

Thomas Hickman gave a textbook opening statement, providing "a road map" so the jurors would know what to expect to hear during the case. He provided a detailed summary of each prospective witnesses testimony, often understating the emotional impact that he knew was sure to be achieved by them. He knew the case so well that he needed no notes. The jurors' attention was riveted on what he was saying and the exhibits he held up for them to see. He showed them a number of 8" x 10" photographs of the home and carefully described what they depicted.

Hickman stressed that while some valuable items had been taken, others had not. Bags containing about $100 worth of change were undisturbed. Also left untouched on the bedroom floor was Mary Ruth's wallet, which contained more than $100. He concluded his remarks after a half an hour by pointing at Chadderton and saying "I think you will agree at the conclusion of this case that he is guilty of premeditated murder!"

Orrin Brown declined the opportunity for a recess at that point, knowing that he had to respond immediately. He reminded the jurors about their duty to keep their minds open until they had heard all the evidence and the standard of reasonable doubt, which they were required to use to decide the case. He then began to argue about Tina's credibility, and Judge Thayer reminded him that the opening statement was only for telling the jury what he intended to prove, not for "arguing" the case. Brown resumed his presentation, telling the jurors that there were many questions to be resolved, including the actual time of death and who had been responsible for the murder. He blamed Robert Myers and Tina and her underworld contacts, and promised them that Chadderton would tell them himself where he had been that night, and that he had not committed this murder.

After a twenty-minute recess, the State called its first witness, Trooper Andrew Mays. He was the first State trooper to appear at the murder scene, and he explained what he had found there. His testimony concluded with his describing how the victim had been taken for a post-mortem examination. Dr. Ann Dixon, who had performed the examination, described her findings and her conclusions as to the time of Mary Ruth's death.

By the end of the first day of the trial, Mary Ruth's co-workers, who had found her, had provided tearful, powerful descriptions about their observations and feelings upon finding the bloody body of their boss and friend. The case had started well for the prosecution and all the participants were exhausted by the time Court was recessed at 6:00 p.m.

The next day, the trial resumed early at 9:00 a.m. Judge Thayer was determined to move the case along at a fair but steady pace, knowing that it would likely last for a few weeks, and that the other cases on the docket would, for the most part, be postponed until this trial was concluded. Six witnesses testified in rapid succession that long before the murder, Robert Myers told each of them that he no longer loved Mary Ruth, that he wanted to be rid of her, but that a divorce would ruin him financially, and that he could get a contract on Mary Ruth's life.

For several days, the State continued to add piece after piece to the picture that they were creating to lead to the overwhelming conclusion that Chadderton was guilty. The defense tried unsuccessfully to chip away at the presentation, but could not accuse any of these witnesses of not telling the truth, only of being mistaken about some minor details here and there. All the while, Chadderton sat expressionless, taking notes and staring at the judge and then the jury.

Kimberly Abbott, the daughter of Mary Ruth, pointed at Daniel Chadderton and said he was the man on the motorbike who was in Ocean City on August 28, 1979. He had attempted to see her mother when she was working at the beach motel. Chadderton appeared the day before the murder, but a stubborn maid prevented him from getting to her mother. Abbott said she later saw him walking on Ocean Highway while she was in her car.

Later the same day, Robert Myers had called the motel, Abbott said, and asked to speak to his wife. Abbott, who was working the switchboard, said her mother answered the telephone when she connected them, but that her stepfather was silent. "Bob didn't say anything for several moments," Abbott said. "Then he said, 'Oh, it was nothing,' and he hung up."

The maid, Mary Elizabeth Fooks, testified she was supervising the women who changed the bedding at the Northwinds Motel when a bearded man rode up on a motorcycle and asked, "Is the madam around?" Fooks said Mrs. Myers was asleep and that he couldn't see her. The man started up the steps to the apartment the Myers used when they visited the motel, but Fooks stepped in his way and prevented him from going farther. "I said, 'No, you can't go up there,' and he stopped," Fooks testified. "Then he went away." But the man Abbott identified as Chadderton from photographs early in the investigation returned later that morning, and again at 3 p.m., the maid said. Ms. Fooks herself was unable to identify him in the courtroom, but she did say a State Police photograph of his motorcycle was similar to the one she noticed the man was driving.

Hickman had contended that Chadderton made the down payment on the motorcycle with part of the first $5,000 payment. A receipt showing it had been purchased just a few days before the murder was introduced.

Fooks said she had told Mary Ruth about the motorcycle rider when she woke up, and that it provoked an extremely "nervous reaction" in the victim, who Fooks said was a close friend. "Her color changed," Fooks said. "She got some clothes together and drove off." She had driven to the couple's Silver Run home near Westminster. Hickman had told the jury that the murder was supposed to occur in Ocean City. He later elicited testimony from Tina that she and Maria Poulos had driven by the Northwinds motel the night of August 27 to see if Mary Ruth's car was there. It was, Tina said, and Poulos confirmed that fact.

Jerry Welch, who was the motel manager at the time, testified that the bag that was kept in the freezer of the Myers' apartment until the money could be deposited was missing several days earlier. Abbott said she went to the bank immediately and found Robert Myers there. She said he had made a small deposit but still had a lot cash in the bag.

Maria Poulos was the owner of the Electric Circus in Ocean City, Md. Robert Myers and Tina had stayed with Poulos. Tina had known Poulos through Jay

Gillen, one of Tina's ex-husbands. She said that Tina kept for herself some of the $30,000 in cash that the two had counted at Poulos's apartment while Myers was napping. "I've got so much money in my pocket book. I can't believe it," she quoted Tina.

Poulos testified that when Myers learned of the murder, he was "very upset. Very nervous, and he kept repeating, 'Why did she do such a thing?'" It had been rumored at that point that Mary Ruth had shot herself. Before the murder, according to Poulos, Tina bragged about Myers' house, the sunken bathtub, and beautiful bedrooms.

During their meetings following the murder, Poulos testified that Tina offered her some of Mary Ruth's clothes. "She told me 'You've really got to come up to Westminster. Mary Ruth had three closets full of clothes.'" Tina had said, "I don't want any."

Another witness, Adam Handschuh, who worked with the defendant, told the jury that in September of 1979, when he asked Chadderton if had killed Myers's wife, Chadderton responded, "'I'm not going back to the slam, but if I do I'm taking two people with me.' And I said, 'Who?' And then he just started sipping his coffee."

Tina was wearing a green maternity smock and slacks as she sat uncomfortably on the witness stand. She had put on a lot of weight during this seven-month pregnancy. She had tears in her eyes when she told the seven-woman, five-man jury of her firsthand knowledge of the murder. She began answering Mr. Hickman's questions in a weak, low voice, and apologized to the jurors, saying she had a cold. But by the end of the day, when she was answering Mr. Brown's questions, her voice was strong.

Under questioning by the prosecutor, she related how she had first met Daniel Chadderton in 1978, when she occupied an apartment in Reisterstown, and they had what she declared was a "brother-sister relationship."

Tina testified that she first met Robert Myers when she waited on his table in April or May 1979, while she was working at Johnny O's, a restaurant and bar in Westminster. She had no further contact with him until August 9, 1979, when she again served him and he joked with her about the dilapidated state of her car. On August 10, 1979 Myers bought her a used Ford Torino worth

$2600. Tina recounted how she and her two children spent that day with him, driving to his trailer in Mount Holly, Pennsylvania.

Tina told the jury about Myers calling her from Ocean City on August 12, 1979, asking her to come and spend some time with him. She drove to Ocean City in the Torino, first stopping in Reisterstown to show her new car off to an "acquaintance," Daniel Chadderton. She described this Ocean City visit. In his motel, they were intimate for the first time and he entered the room by crawling in through the bedroom window, so that his step-daughter wouldn't see him.

Tina testified that she returned to work in Westminster on Tuesday, August 14th, and that Friday, August 17th, she saw Robert at Angelo's during one of her shifts. Around 8:30 p.m., Mary Ruth Myers entered Angelo's and started arguing with Myers, who got up and walked away. Robert met Tina in the kitchen, hugged her, and asked her to meet him at Sharkey's Cove Restaurant and Bar when she got off work.

At the time, Tina was rooming at Horton's Boarding Home, which was located a few blocks from Sharkey's Cove. Because Mary Ruth followed Myers to Sharkey's Cove, Myers left and went to Horton's, where he met Tina. They spent the night at Horton's, and then began a two-week odyssey, which included stops at his trailer park in Mount Holly, Pennsylvania, Reisterstown, Maryland, Atlantic City, New Jersey, Wildwood, and then returning to Ocean City.

She told the jury that one night, on August 18, while the two were out for dinner, Myers asked Tina if she knew someone that would kill his wife, stating that a divorce would be too expensive. She replied that she did not, and Myers then asked if she knew someone who would "rough her up."

"I thought he was joking," she said, "and I said no, and he said, 'Well, you're from Las Vegas aren't you? Don't you know somebody?' And I said, 'No, I don't know anyone that would kill her.' I said, 'Why don't you just get a divorce?' And he said 'because she would take everything.' We had had this same conversation other than the killing part earlier that day. I believe we called Alan Fox first, an attorney that I knew, and he called an attorney that he knew.

"I kept asking him in this restaurant this particular night how much would it take just to divorce her. He said that he had lost everything from his first marriage, but he wasn't going to lose it again. Then he asked if I knew someone that would rough her up, to make her give him a divorce without asking for everything he had. I thought of Dan."

Tina recounted the story of the former boss had once assaulted her. She explained that Chadderton, in return, had offered to break the assailant's arms, legs, burn his house, or whatever, for Tina. Myers asked Tina to call Dan. Using a pay phone in Mechanicsburg, she called Chadderton and told him that she had someone who wanted to meet him, that he [Chadderton] could possibly make some money. Chadderton replied that Tina knew where he worked and to bring the person to the Pantry Pride, which she did in the early morning hours of August 23, 1979.

She described how the trio chatted for a while, and then Tina went to the car. Sometime later, Myers went over to the car and asked Tina to write down the name of his wife, address, her height, color of hair, and approximate weight. Myers had agreed to pay $10,000 for the murder of his wife.

As they were leaving, Chadderton said to Myers, "Don't forget. I want half down and half when the job's finished." Myers replied that they had to go on a trip, and that they would be back.

Tina told the jury that she and Myers then drove on to the Myers' North Winds Motel, then to the residence of Maria Poulos. When they arrived, Myers told Tina to get a bank deposit together with the receipt from the North Winds Motel and asked Ms. Poulos if he could lie down. Tina asked Ms. Poulos if she would help her make out the bank deposit. As Ms. Poulos was pulling money out of a white paper sack, Tina asked if she could freshen up. When she returned, Myers was standing, talking to Ms. Poulos. Myers said that the bank deposit was ready and the couple drove to a bank in Ocean City.

At the bank, the couple met Myers' stepdaughter, Kimberly Abbott, who was crying. She begged Myers to come home and to call her mother. Myers responded, "No, I'm not calling her."

That evening, Myers and Tina drove to a Howard Johnson's in Pikesville, Maryland. Myers took with him the same white paper sack, folded over. When the couple entered the restaurant, Chadderton was sitting at the counter. The trio asked for a table, ordered breakfast, and then Tina excused herself to use the restroom. When she returned, Myers and Chadderton were finishing up.

The trio went out to the car, where Chadderton opened the white paper sack and counted $3,000. Myers apologized that he did not have the whole $5,000, but said that he couldn't take it out all at once, but he would be back in couple of days. Dan said that was fine, and they left.

Her testimony continued that on Sunday, August 26, 1979, the couple drove from Ocean City to the Pantry Pride Store in Reisterstown, Maryland, where they again met Chadderton. When Chadderton got into the back seat of their car, Myers handed him a tin foil package. Chadderton counted out $2,000 and asked the couple if they were hungry. The trio went to a fast food restaurant in the same parking lot. As they were getting ready to leave, Myers instructed Chadderton "to make sure it looked like a robbery, just to make sure it looked like a robbery."

Tina then testified about their trip to Wildwood, New Jersey. She'd visited a friend who was a pit boss at the Resorts International Casino. When they'd returned to North Winds in Ocean City, they'd seen Mary Ruth's car, and stayed with Ms. Poulos instead.

On August 28, according to Tina, Chadderton "stalked" Mrs. Myers in Ocean City, but was unable to confront her. Myers was having a beer in the Electric Circus when the bartender handed him the phone. When Myers hung up, Tina recalled he had said, "Well, he blew it.' And I said, 'Who?' and he said, 'Dan.' And I said, 'What do you mean?' 'Well, he's in Ocean City.' And I said, 'Oh?' He said, 'We're going to meet him at Granny's restaurant.'" When Tina and Myers walked into Granny's, Chadderton was sitting in a booth. They joined him. Chadderton said that he wanted to get her in Ocean City. "He was playing with a knife in his hand," Tina said. Tina left Granny's to join Maria on a shopping trip. As they walked past the restaurant, Tina saw a new motorcycle and said to Ms. Poulis carelessly, "Well that must be his new toy." When asked who she was referring to she explained that they had been meeting with a man in Granny's who had been looking for employment.

She testified that around 7:00 p.m. on August 28, 1979, Myers asked Tina if she would try to get hold of Chadderton. Myers had talked to one of his stepchildren and had learned that Mary Ruth was going to Turkey Foot Road and would be home alone. Tina left word with Chadderton's wife.

On August 29, he left his job as a "night porter" at the Pantry Pride early, traveled to the Myers' residence, murdered Mary Ruth and at 5:20 a.m. called Myers and Tina in Ocean City to inform them that he had completed the job.

A few days later, Tina went to the Pantry Pride. Bob asked her to go there and pay Chadderton the balance of the $5,000, because he didn't want Dan at the house. Tina drove down to pay Chadderton, but it was right after the funeral, and Dan came out and told her to get off the property and to just keep going. Tina said "But I've got—" and Dan interrupted to say, "Just keep going, I'll get it later." Later, Dan told her that the reason he told Tina that she should leave was because there were police there.

Two weeks later, Myers and Tina were at home on Turkey Foot Road when they heard a motorcycle coming up the long driveway. It was Chadderton, accompanied by his wife. They knocked at the front door and Chadderton said that he had come for the balance of his money. Tina started to protest that she did not know what he was talking about but Chadderton responded, indicating Sherrie, "She's cool, she knows." The Chaddertons were invited into the living room and Chadderton repeated that his wife "knew all about it."

Tina served everybody drinks and Chadderton was smiling and laughing. She went to the master bedroom and removed $5,000 in cash from the bureau and returned with it to the living room where she handed the money to Myers. Chadderton told him to give it to his wife. Sherrie slowly counted it on the coffee table. After she had counted it a second time, she tried to put the money into her knee socks but it would not fit in, so she stuffed it into her jeans.

She told the jury that after Sherrie had counted the money a second time, Dan went into details about the murder. Before Dan could start, Bob said, "Did you have to mess up my door?" Dan responded, "Well, I didn't have a key. I had to bust the molding." Dan then said "Yeah you know, I had . . . that bitch was on the phone . . . and I had to stand outside, you know, and watch her talk on the phone and wait until all the lights in the house were turned off, except the bedroom lights, before I could break in."

Chadderton said, "You know, she sure could gab on the phone." Myers said, "Yeah, well what happened?" And Dan said, "Well, I waited until she got in the bedroom and then I went to the side and broke in." Dan continued, "That damn dog," and Bob interrupted, "Oh the poodle?" Dan said, "Yeah, I had to lock the dog in the bathroom." Then he said, "I went into the pool area—is that a family room? I tiptoed in there, and I sat down on the couch, and I could hear someone coming up through the house yelling, 'Bobby is that you?'" Dan said, "I just sat there and lit a cigarette. Mary Ruth saw the light from the cigarette and turned on the light in that room. Mary Ruth said, 'You're not Bob, who are you?' I told her, "I'm a friend. I'm a friend of Bob's, I'm waiting for him.' Mary Ruth said, 'Well I don't expect him back.'" Chadderton then said he got up and walked towards her, and Mary Ruth said, "Who are you?" Dan said, "Just a friend!" Dan explained he then told her, "I would like to see your house," and then "Are you alone?" And Mary Ruth said, "Yes, I am."

Dan asked, "Will you walk me through the house?" Mary Ruth walked through the room and turned on different bedroom lights to make sure there was nobody there. Dan said to her "Well, I thought maybe I could have a party with you and your daughter." To which Mary Ruth said quietly, "She is in Ocean City." They walked through the sitting room off the master bedroom. He originally had planned apparently to use a knife, because he didn't own a gun. When he walked into the sitting room, he saw the gun case. Chadderton said that he grabbed her with one hand, and with the other hand used his knife to pry open the gun case.

At that point Bob interrupted, "Why didn't you just turn the goddamn key? There was a key in the lock." Dan scoffed, "Well, I wasn't thinking about that!"

Dan continued, "I busted it open. There was a couch or something in there and I told her to sit down and I loaded two guns. I then took her into the bedroom and told her "If you believe in God better start praying . . ." Mary Ruth said "Who are you, why are you here?" and Dan answered, "Because your husband owes me money." Mary Ruth asked how much, and Dan responded, "It doesn't matter, I'll get my money!" Dan added, "Get on the bed," and he then fired a first shot. She turned and looked at him and said, "My God, you're going to kill me," and he said, "That's right, honey." The gun then jammed, so he put it down and used the other one. He continued to pull the trigger.

Bob said, "Where's all the money?" Dan said, "What money? And Bob replied, "I had a lot of money wrapped up in towels in the bathroom." Dan said, "I don't know what you're talking about." Bob said "Well, you know, you know my wife had about $2000 in her purse alone?"

Dan said, "I didn't see any money in her purse." Apparently there was a lot of jewelry that was never accounted for. Some pieces were there, but not all of them. Dan denied taking them and said he didn't take anything out of the house. That he just roughed up the house a little trying to make it look like a robbery.

According to Tina, she and Sherrie were just sitting there while Dan and Bob had this conversation. Bob asked Dan about the green vase from the mantelpiece that was broken in the poolroom and asked about the pills that were scattered around the floor. One of the State Troopers had told Bob there were lots of pills on the floor. When Dan went into the details of the killing Tina actually started crying and said, "My God, Dan, nine times? Did you have to shoot the woman nine times?" And Dan said, "I wanted to make sure she was dead."

Tina testified that at a later time Chadderton threatened her life and her daughter's safety if she ever revealed his role in the death of Mary Ruth. "One time in the house, Chadderton had his arms around my daughter and said that she was a beautiful little girl, and that he would hate to see anything happen to her." She described how she had had a special locked room in a closet built in the Silver Run home, and that it was intended to be secure against possible attacks by Chadderton.

Tina added that he said that if she agreed to turn State's evidence she "would never make it to the witness stand."

Tina explained that this new married life was enjoyable. "He was very good to me. He was always buying me things . . . In 1980, I got a Mercedes. That was my Mother's Day present. It had 'Tina' license plates and supposedly it was going to be replaced the next year by a Rolls Royce. She said she had spent about $150,000 on clothing and another $150,000 on jewelry. She admitted that she wore Mary Ruth's jewelry and clothing and that she had given some of these items to her friends.

Tina claimed that she did not know how Mr. Chadderton would earn his pay. On cross examination, while looking up at the courtroom clock, Mr. Brown read to the jury Tina Myers' version of what Mr. Chadderton supposedly had said over the phone in the early morning hours of August 29,1979. "Let the record reflect it took four seconds to say that," Brown said. He then turned to Tina Myers and demanded an explanation of what was said during the other 12 minutes of the conversation. "I rolled over and didn't pay any more attention," she responded. Then Mr. Brown asked Tina Myers whether she first heard of the murder during a call from one of her four former husbands, Jay Gillen, who owns a bar called the Tender Trap in Las Vegas. She denied discussing the murder with Gillen.

Brown also brought out in cross-examination that on the night of September 4, 1979, the night after Mary Ruth Myers was buried, Tina Myers slept at the Silver Run house. She agreed that she wore jewelry owned by her husband's slain wife and gained more than $150,000 worth of jewelry through her marriage to Mr. Myers. She testified that she asked Mr. Myers to buy her a Rolls Royce after he had given her a Mercedes Benz with "Tina" license plates.

After charging that Tina Myers lied under oath to obtain foster care services for her two children in Carroll County in April, 1979, Mr. Brown asked her if she would lie under oath to save her own skin. "No," she replied.

It became public knowledge that Tina had developed a close relationship with a Correctional Officer in the Garrett County Detention Center. The Garrett County Sheriff fired Roger White, 24, one of the jail guard's dispatchers because of his alleged relationship with Tina Marco while she was incarcerated there. White, who was married, had been working shifts as jailer and dispatcher there for a year and a half. Tina, when later confronted with a letter she had written to him, testified that White had just started flirting with her and referred to White in cross-examination as her new love interest.

The State then called Cpl. James Sherman, who had been in charge of electronic surveillance in the case for the State Police. He explained how after receiving authorization from the court, they placed wiretaps on the telephones in the Myers' house and office. The telephone in the office was activated by sound close to it, even if the phone is not in use, thereby capturing conversations taking place inside the office itself.

Cpl. Sherman told the jury that he and his small team had recorded over 1,200 telephone calls, but that it was clear the targets had figured out that the phones were tapped and so they were cautious about their conversations. Most were tapped in September 1981, two months before the indictments. Neither Chadderton nor Myers mentioned any involvement in the murder, but acted suspiciously.

Cpl. Sherman played several calls for the jury, in which Myers and Chadderton complained about police surveillance and particularly the activities of Cpl. James M. Leete, who was to be the State's next witness. "Leete's trying to put us in jail, because he scared," Myers told Chadderton in a tape made on September 18, 1981. "He's trying to fuck us all. Trying to play one against the other. Trying to get one wheel to go flat." "If one goes flat, it's permanent," Chadderton replied. "That's right," Myers said, laughing, "Any one of them."

In another call, Myers told Charlotte Horton, Tina's former landlady, that he was not running around on Tina and he added, "I helped Sherrie out with some grocery money, and Leete told Tina that Sherrie and I were having an affair. That's what the cops do, to try to come between people."

The prosecutors had supplied transcripts of these conversations for the jurors to read along while they were being played, because it was sometimes difficult to hear them, and while there were no outright admissions by Chadderton, he did seem to be guarded and picking his words carefully, giving an overall impression that he was not being honest and was acting suspiciously.

During Cpl. Leete's testimony he noted in his turn that weapons, and bags containing from $75 to $100 worth of change, were undisturbed. Also left untouched on the bedroom floor, he said, was the victim's wallet, which contained more than $100.

Cpl. Leete said that he found a cigarette butt in the soil of a potted plant in the den, and that he found the dog in a closet off the main bedroom, not a bathroom. However, the bathroom is directly behind the closet.

Leete and another Maryland State trooper went to see Chadderton on September 8, 1979, at the Pantry Pride. When asked to describe what occurred during that meeting, Leete said:

"[W]e parked our car directly behind the car of Daniel Chadderton, and when he came out [of his place of employment], we exited the police vehicle. He looked at us, and I in fact asked him if he had a gun in his car, and he replied no. And at that point, without any prompting, he went over and put his hands on my right front fender of my police car and assumed the frisk position."

Chadderton's assuming the frisk position without prompting might be viewed as indicating his prior experience of having been searched before by law enforcement officers, or knowledge gained from viewing television or motion pictures. However, even if the jury believed that Chadderton's assumption of the frisk position was based on his prior firsthand experience in being searched by police officers, it was not reversible error.

One of the key witnesses in the State's case, Eric Nettles, had been the cellmate of Chadderton's in the Anne Arundel County Detention Center January and February of 1982. Nettles had been convicted of murdering an 18-year-old girl and was facing a possible death sentence at his sentencing scheduled for July 26, 1982. Two days after his conviction, his lawyer contacted the Carroll County State's Attorney's Office and informed them that Chadderton had made several damning admissions to Nettles and, in return for a recommendation of life imprisonment instead of death, Nettles was ready to be a witness to what he had been told. Tom Hickman readily agreed.

Nettles testified in the Garrett County trial that Chadderton had bragged that he had murdered Mary Ruth Myers and that "he blew her fucking heart out." He testified that Chadderton had said Tina hired him for $10,000 and that he had met with Tina Myers and Bob Myers in front of the store at Tina's instigation with the purpose of signing up Bob Myers to pay for this murder. He told Nettles that he never dealt with Bob Myers but always with Tina, and that Tina had planned out this murder. He explained that after he killed Mary Ruth, he called Tina at the motel in Ocean City.

Chadderton also told Nettles he was a "contract killer" and enumerated the murders he had committed. He claimed that he had gone to California and murdered Tina Myers' second husband Botteron, who was a bail bondsman in Las Vegas. He said he had placed a pipe bomb in his car and connected it to a wire from a spark plug to the gas tank where the bomb had been positioned. Chadderton also bragged about committing "the Al Schaefer murder." He had provided details to Nettles about Tina Myers giving him a contract to kill Robert Myers for $30,000 once Tina and Robert had been married. Chadderton had also stated that he was to hire some of his friends to kill Tina Myers' father.

Finally, Nettles testified that Chadderton had threatened to kill him in jail. It was devastating testimony.

Thomas Bowman, another inmate and State's witness, testified about an incriminating conversation between Myers and Chadderton that he overheard in March of 1982, while all three were incarcerated in the Garrett County Detention Center. Bowman told the jury that Chadderton explained to Myers that Tina is "going to have to be shut up. She's going to have to be taken care of, got rid of, before she made a 'deal' with the State's Attorney." Chadderton, Bowman said, went on to say that he could arrange to have a hired assassin "take care of this and shut her up" if Myers "came up with some money, twenty or thirty thousand dollars." Meanwhile, according to Bowman, Myers stood by silently and nodded his head up and down. Obviously, a declaration by an accused that he intends to intimidate or procure the absence from the trial of a State's witness is admissible as evidence of the defendant's guilt

Bowman added that he heard Myers interject, "I knew we shouldn't have gotten into this mess to begin with . . . I knew we shouldn't have called her there to the house . . . I knew they'd know it was me." Chadderton then replied, "Well, that's the only place I could get a clean shot at her. That's the only place without any witnesses or anything that I could do it." Bowman testified that following that remark by Chadderton, Myers just looked at Chadderton without saying anything. Chadderton's remarks concerning the need to eliminate Tina as a witness were also admissible against Myers, to show Myers' reactions to the assertions. By nodding in the affirmative, Myers adopted Chadderton's remarks as his own. Patently, Myers by his silence acquiesced in Chadderton's declaration that the marital residence of Myers and Mary Ruth was the only place he could "get a clean shot at her."

This testimony led us to call the killer "Chatterbox Chadderton."

The State had presented a compelling case and rested after six days of testimony. Brown and Watson were granted an overnight recess so that they could alert the defense witnesses to come to court the next day.

Mrs. Dorothy Wilson, a neighbor of Mary Ruth's, was produced as the first witness for the defense. She said she had heard several gunshots at 7:00 a.m. on the day of the murder. She was somewhat confused, however, as to the exact day because she had not come forward and been interviewed for several months. She was an honest person, but could easily have been misled by the fact that this was an active hunting area and the season was already in progress, and gunshots were often heard early in the morning. Hickman carefully pointed that out on his cross-examination.

Dr. Rudiger Breitenecker, the associate pathologist at the Greater Baltimore Medical Center, had reviewed the autopsy performed by the Medical Examiner and contested Dr. Ann Dixon's conclusions as to the time of the victim's death. Based largely on her body temperature at that time, he concluded she probably died after 6:00 a.m. This doctor said he had performed about 3,000 autopsies in his career, and said that the victim's body temperature of 92°F at the time of the autopsy could only have reached that level if she had died later than the State contended.

His testimony was important because the prosecution had based its entire case on the fact that Mary Ruth was killed at a much earlier time, at least before 3:00 a.m. This timing would allow enough time for Chadderton to get home to Baltimore and make his phone call at 5:20 a.m. to Ocean City.

The defense also sought to damage Tina's credibility as much as possible and investigators had interviewed many people who knew her well. Among these were close family members who had bad experiences with her. Remarkably, they were willing to testify in public about their strong feelings towards her.

Even twelve-year-old Brad Myers, Tina Myers' son, told the jury that his mother is a liar. He said she had a favorite expression: "I lie, lie, lie, a whole lot." He told of the many times that he and his sister had been misled, lied to, and abandoned by her over the years. He was bright and articulate, but it was clear that he was bitter and angry with his mother because of her neglect of him. He was a powerful witness.

Ernest E. Butcher, Tina Myers' father was a Los Angeles television repair-man. He traveled the 2,500-mile journey to rural Garrett County to tell the seven-woman, five-man circuit court jury that he stopped trusting his daughter when she was 10 years old. Mr. Butcher, who said he had not seen his daughter in almost 10 years, said he separated from Tina's mother in 1955 and that the woman abandoned the little girl soon after. "I wouldn't believe anything she told me. She's bad news to anybody she comes in contact with." Tina Myers' father told jurors to disregard her testimony that Daniel Lee Chadderton killed Mary Ruth Myers because she could not be trusted. "We've been getting letters from her since it started," Mr. Butcher said of the killing and subsequent investigation by the State Police. "She's been saying she's not guilty right up to the night she turned State's evidence. She would lie to get out of trouble and to protect herself," he concluded, referring to the deal in which Tina Myers exchanged her testimony for freedom.

Carman Butcher, Tina's uncle, agreed she was not to be trusted. He said of his niece, who stayed at his home for three weeks in 1978, "If you don't know her, and you just met her, she could have you eating right out of the palm of her hand."

The defense called Sherrie Chadderton, who first described their family life and her battle with cancer, and was a sympathetic witness. She then testified that "Dan" had not gone to work that night but had stayed home nursing a cold, and that she knew that because she was with him the entire time. He had trouble sleeping and was up half the night. She recalled his interest in Tina's car, but they had decided not to buy it since he had just purchased the motorbike.

Frank Coleman in his gentle but effective way confronted her with Tina's earlier testimony, which asserted that she had counted the murder money. She was forced to make numerous denials and rather than humiliate or argue with her, Coleman kept his examination short. Short, but devastating. She had become a friend of Tina's, and had travelled to Bermuda with her to help her with her young daughter. She could not supply a logical reason that Tina would have lied about Sherrie being present to count the money while Dan was describing the murder. The fact that Tina was being given immunity did not explain why Tina needed to place Sherrie at the house receiving the payment and listening to Chadderton brag about his night's work.

Chadderton testified as the final defense witness. He agreed that Tina Myers had visited him at the Reisterstown Pantry Pride, where he worked as a grocery clerk, and said he discussed buying Tina Myers' car, but never talked about killing Mary Ruth. Chadderton said he went to Ocean City on August 28, 1979, the day before the murder, to break in his new motorcycle and to tell Tina he did not want to purchase the Ford Torino she was driving.

He was still wearing the same Western-style three-piece suit, and spoke in a relaxed voice, never stumbling over his words. Brown asked him on four separate occasions if he had inflicted the wounds on Mary Ruth. Chadderton loudly denied that he had shot her and on the last occasion he added that he had never even met "the lady."

Hickman had a lot of information to confront him with on cross-examination. His previous statements to the police and to the Grand Jury were kept at the ready, in case Chadderton tried to deny any of the damaging admissions he had made. Chadderton had been schooled by Brown and Watson, and they had coached him that he could not vary his testimony from what he had previously stated. He had agreed that a proven inconsistency would be more damaging than any statement he had made, no matter how implausible it might seem.

But Hickman was a skilled cross-examiner and knew that the jurors needed to see him be aggressive and harsh if he truly believed Chadderton was a cowardly killer. The jurors were not disappointed because the prosecutor challenged this bully with almost every question, often scoffing at the responses. Discussing car sales at 5:20 a.m.? Really? Not bragging how he had shot the woman nine times? Not telling other inmates he "blew her fucking heart out?" Not threatening Tina and her children? All a bunch of lies? Hickman was rightfully disgusted by Chadderton and what he had done, and was not scared to angrily demonstrate his outrage. His cross was textbook perfect.

After three days, the defense had concluded its case. Brown told the reporters he thought that Chadderton had done well on the witness stand. Orrin Brown was boyish looking although he was in his mid-40's, and had a slight slouch and he had worn a hangdog expression throughout most of the trial. This testimony had made him lift his spirits a little.

In rebuttal, the State recalled Corporal Leete and Trooper Mays, who testified that the room was very hot when they were there and it was so stifling that they both sweated profusely. Then Dr. Richard A. Jones, another pathologist, testified that as a consequence of the heat in the bedroom, the body temperature of the victim was not an important factor in determining how long the victim had been dead. This testimony seemed to resolve any dispute concerning the victim's body temperature and how that reading affected the pathologists' determinations of when Mary Ruth died.

The closing arguments were given a day later, on May 10, 1982.

To begin his closing argument, Frank Coleman pointed to a chart listing dates and locations. Coleman reviewed the series of phone records documenting telephone calls the State claimed corroborated the plotting and implementation of the alleged contract killing. Coleman highlighted that one of those calls, at 2:16 p.m. on Aug. 28, 1979, was placed by Myers to let Chadderton know Mary Ruth Myers was in Ocean City. A second call, later the same day, was placed to let Chadderton know the victim had returned to her home in Carroll County. It all fit together.

Coleman described the shooting—how the blood from the first shot flowed in a different direction than blood from the other shots because the victim was lying on her stomach. He explained how the bedsheets had twisted around her legs, proving she had rolled over onto her back and that the next eight bullets were fired into her back. Some of the jurors nodded in agreement.

Using a handful of pencils, Coleman demonstrated the overwhelming power of a circumstantial case. He easily snapped several individual pencils comparing each to an individual fact. He then bunched many together and showed that no amount of force could overcome their collective strength.

The thrust of Orrin Brown's closing argument was how could an amateur, a first-time killer, remember the precise number of times he had fired the weapons? His theory was that Chadderton was set up, and that the real killer or killers were contacted when Marco and Myers visited Atlantic City before their Ocean City trip. Tina Myers, Brown argued, had worked in Las Vegas and had contacted an acquaintance from that town while in Atlantic City.

When Orrin Brown described Tina, he asked the jurors, "Do you know that a black widow spider mates and then she kills? She wants to kill her husband and then she wants to kill Dan Chadderton!" alluding to the death penalty he faced if he was convicted.

Several witnesses had testified that $36,000 in receipts that had accumulated were kept in the freezer at the Myers' Ocean City Motel apartment and had apparently disappeared. No one could say what happened to the money, so the defense suggested it could have been used to pay another contract killer or that they there may have been more than one, who were more professional and more expensive than Chadderton. The prosecutor had documented that Chadderton had paid for a down payment on the motorbike and paid off some overdue bills, but the amount fell short of the supposed $10,000 fee. Where was the rest, the defense questioned?

Judge Thayer had agreed to allow attorney Robert Watson, who had joined Orrin Brown in the defense of Chadderton, to also give a closing argument to the jury on behalf of the defense. He also spent most of his thirty minute summation attacking Tina's credibility.

The defense closing arguments were both good. Both lawyers hammered on the definition of "reasonable doubt," and pointed to inconsistencies in the State's case. Tina had speculated that the murder had taken place at around midnight, but the impartial neighbor had heard gunshots at 7:00 a.m. Brown and Watson both spent much time stressing that the two medical examiners, one for the State and one for the defense, could not agree on the time of death. One said the victim died no earlier than 3:00 a.m., and the other said no earlier than 6:00 a.m. Both agreed that she could not have died at midnight.

Hickman, in his rebuttal, forcefully demonstrated that the defense had simply tried to pick little holes in the State's mountain of evidence, and that while Tina was not likeable, her testimony was corroborated for the most part by independent evidence and circumstances. He demanded that they do their duty and obey the oath they had taken and apply the law to the facts, which had been clearly demonstrated, and convict "this coldblooded killer of first degree murder."

A short while after the closing arguments, the case was submitted to the jury for their decision. It was already past suppertime, and the jurors' first order of business was to make their selections for food from the menu of a local restaurant that had been provided to them. An hour later, their meals had arrived.

Soon after they had finished their food, Chadderton was found guilty of first-degree murder. The jury returned their verdict at 10:15 p.m., after deliberating for just a little more than two hours.

Chadderton showed no signs of emotion when the jury foreman announced the verdict. He sat rigidly in his chair until he was handcuffed and led away. The victim's family embraced each other and vanished quickly from the courthouse after thanking Hickman and Coleman.

The next day, May 11, 1982, at 9:00 a.m., the sentencing phase was conducted before the jury.

In a hearing in Garrett County conducted before trial, Nancy Jackson, a Taneytown woman, had testified that Chadderton had offered to kill her husband for several thousand dollars and the travel expenses to New Orleans, where her estranged spouse was living. Judge Fred Thayer had excluded her testimony from the trial itself, ruling that it was not relevant to the merits of the case. It had been widely reported in the press.

During the sentencing phase, however, Nancy Jackson's testimony was permitted as relevant to what the appropriate sentence should be. She testified that she had complained to Chadderton that her husband had treated her badly during her marriage. She said the offer to kill him was made more than two years after Mary Ruth was murdered. Ms. Jackson was a Carroll County Sheriff's Department employee and was a very credible person. Brown did not ask many substantive questions on cross-examination, for fear of highlighting what she had said. Brown had earlier attempted to explain Chadderton's other statements about being a hit man by arguing that they were untrue, but that they gave him status among the inmates in the detention center. That same reasoning could not be applied to here.

Her statements were admitted to help the prosecutors establish that Chadderton had the potential to commit a contract murder again. The judge had instructed the jurors on the applicable law that they were required to apply. The aggravating factors had to outweigh any mitigating circumstances by a preponderance of the evidence, and this was certainly an aggravating factor.

Orrin Brown, in mitigation, had several members of Chadderton's family testify about his tough upbringing and stressed that he had to leave school after the seventh grade in order to work to help support them. His grandmother sobbed as she recalled his years as a small child, and how she had spent so much time with him after his mother had died. She had taken him to local churches where he enjoyed the music and the sermons delivered by travelling ministers and lay members of the congregation.

In his argument, Hickman said forcefully, "Do not go into the jury room thinking that you are determining the fate of Daniel Chadderton. Chadderton decided his own fate, just as surely as if he put a gun to his own head and committed suicide. I think you will agree that the punishment should fit the crime. And the punishment that fits this crime is the death penalty."

The jurors retired to consider the penalty later that afternoon. Only an hour later, the jurors sent a note to the judge saying they were hopelessly deadlocked. They had voted twice during their discussions on the sentencing, initially with a six to six result, and then with a seven to five tally in favor of the gas chamber. Chadderton waited to hear his fate in a small cell in the basement of the Garrett County Courthouse. Brown and Watson paced nervously in the parking lot outside.

The jury foreman informed the court after another hour that it was irrevocably deadlocked and could not reach a decision. Chadderton's lawyers were immensely relieved when Judge Thayer decided, over the prosecutors' strenuous objections, that two hours deliberation was sufficient. The judge then dismissed the jury after thanking them once again for their service. Most of the jurors went to the spectator section to watch what was to happen next.

Judge Thayer asked Chadderton to stand up, and then inquired if he had anything to say before sentence was pronounced. "No, your Honor," Chadderton responded after a slight pause. "Very well. Having considered the evidence as I have heard it, I sentence you to be confined to the Custody of the Department of Correction for the rest of your natural life," the judge said. "All right, Sheriff, you may take custody of the prisoner." Chadderton was handcuffed and led from the courtroom. Members of Mary Ruth's family, including her two sons and one of her daughters, stared intently at Chadderton as his sentence was pronounced.

CHAPTER 22:
RETURN TO CARROLL COUNTY FOR TRIAL

*"The right to trial in the place wherein
the crime shall have been committed . . ."*
— The U.S. Constitution, Amendment VI

At the time I was assigned to the Myers case, though, the trial had been transferred from Carroll County, where the murder took place, to Garrett County, located in mountainous terrain in the most western area of Maryland. It was over 200 miles from my home in Baltimore.

Under a provision of the Maryland State Constitution, a change of venue was automatically granted when either side requested it in any capital case. In January of 1982, then, when Prosecutor Hickman requested the case be removed to Garrett County, Judge Donald Gilmore automatically granted the request.

Initially, I did not understand why the Carroll County State's Attorney, Thomas Hickman, had wanted to remove the case from his own jurisdiction to a place four hours' drive away. I did know, however, that I did not want to be stuck in Garrett County trying the case for ten weeks. It was not only very far away, but it was a small, rural county filled with mountain people. A lot of these folks liked hunting, liked to kill bears, and other animals. I did not want to give them a chance to kill Myers.

I wrote a motion opposing the removal of the case to Garrett County, but it was after the case had already been moved. Judge Gilmore denied it.

However, a short time later The Court of Appeals, the highest Appellate Court in Maryland, involved itself in the dispute and granted our petition for a Pre-Judgment Writ of Certiorari. This meant, in plain language, "bring that issue here to us!" It is very rare for an appellate court to involve itself in a criminal case before there has been a conviction. In this case, though, The Court of Appeals had found merit in our contention that the case should be returned to Carroll County.

The question raised was: Is it unconstitutional to permit the State to have a capital case removed from the County in which it originated without making any showing of a rational need for such removal? My position held that it was. The United States Constitution, Amendment VI, states: "In all criminal prosecutions, the accused shall enjoy the right to a speedy and public trial, by an impartial jury of the State and district wherein the crime shall have been committed." Similarly, the Maryland Declaration of Rights, Article 20, says, "That the trial of facts, where they arise, is one of the greatest securities of the lives, liberties and estate of the People."

Next, I needed to file a Petition To Stay The Removal and file an Immediate Notice of Appeal. George E. Burns Jr., one of the best from the Appellate Division of The Public Defender's Office, agreed to help me. For the most part, the appellate lawyers were much better at handling appellate issues—they knew the law much better and were often legal scholars. Burns had almost total recall of legal precedents and was a great resource. Not only could he do a better job, but also regardless of the outcome, I would need all my time to prepare for the trial wherever it was to be conducted. I felt that since Myers had been so popular in Carroll County, it might help his case to have a jury selected in Westminster. Anyway, I would sooner be an hour's drive away from my home rather than four hours away.

I had argued to Judge Gilmore in my first appearance before him on February 9, 1982 that the removal was improper. I had pointed out that Myers was indicted for murder on November 23, 1981 and on December 23, 1981 he was notified of the State's intention to seek the death penalty. On December 31, 1981, the State filed a suggestion for removal and on January 21, 1982, the removal request was summarily granted. A hearing on Petitioner's Motion in Opposition to the removal was held. My Motion in Opposition was denied.

Judge Gilmore was clearly angry at my raising the issue. Since we had never met, he was determined to "put me in my place" and make me back away. The courtroom was packed with local people and he did not approve of my challenging his authority in front of them.

MR. KEATING: Well, my motion, sir, is in the opposition to the State's removing the case.

THE COURT: Well you, flat out, don't want it removed anywhere, is that—

MR. KEATING: That's my motion, sir, yes, sir, at this time.

THE COURT: Well how could I grant that-if that's the basis for your motion, how could I grant that in light of Article 4, Section 8 of the Constitution of the State of Maryland? Does that not create—I have in front of me. It says—quoting from subsection (b): "In all cases or presentments or indictments for offenses that are punishable by death, on suggestion in writing, under oath, of either of the parties to the proceeding"—with emphasis supplied, by the Court, or "by either of the parties, that the party cannot have a fair and impartial trial in the Court in which the proceedings may be pending, the Court shall order and direct the record of proceedings and the presentment or indictment to be transmitted to some other Court having jurisdiction in such case for trial."

MR. KEATING: I think the Court's got a delicate balancing decision.

THE COURT: I've got to call the Constitution unconstitutional if—

MR. KEATING: I think that may be very difficult, sir. It might be unconstitutional to have this applied in this case, to this Defendant.

I should not have interrupted him, but he allowed me to continue without comment. I said it is settled beyond question that no State law, whether promulgated by State constitution or otherwise, can be valid if it violates the Federal Constitution. It has often been noted that the right of removal in capital cases is "absolute." "However, a phrase in a judicial opinion must be viewed in the context in which it appears." Thus, in the ordinary case where a judge has merely the uncontested suggestion of a party that the right of removal may be absolute, it is a simple matter. However, removal should not be automatic when the suggestion that removal is necessary is challenged. A trial before a jury is one of the most cherished rights of the citizen. A denial of this right would destroy due process of law. A citizen should not be coerced to relinquish his right to a jury trial and submit to a trial before the court, in order to escape an intolerable situation of a trial before a prejudiced jury.

Arbitrary removal violates the right to equal protection because in all but capital cases, and the burden of persuasion as to the necessity of removal is upon the party making the suggestion. Thus, only in a capital case could an accused be moved to a different county merely on the basis of the charge. There is plainly no rational basis for the accused to have fewer rights than other defendants, because the State seeks a greater penalty.

Furthermore, the application of Article 4, Section 8, as interpreted by Judge Gilmore, would have deprived Myers of his right to a trial in the district in which the crime occurred. Constitutional rights may not be abridged without a demonstration of strong counterbalancing circumstances. Removal at the mere whim of the prosecutor does not provide for the demonstration of any such circumstance.

I argued to Judge Gilmore that I should be allowed to pursue these issues in front of the appellate courts if he did not agree with my position, because the public had a vital interest in the speedy resolution of the matter. He did not agree and refused to postpone the case. I, however, felt good because I had the chance to dominate the courtroom for more than an hour, impress the onlookers and get on the offense. The denial of removal in a capital case is immediately appealable.

I also argued Myers' claim—that removal over his objection violated due process and the right to have a jury of his peers—was wholly collateral to the impending trial, and had been finally resolved against him. The consequences of this issue are extreme in that the risk would be taken that it might require reversal in the future. Such a result is fair neither to the defendant nor the State. Specifically, in this case, I proffered that the trial would be complex and time consuming, with the possibility that hundreds of witnesses would be called.

George Burns reiterated my arguments to the seven-member Court of Appeals in Annapolis. The State's Attorney, Tom Hickman, did not agree. He believed automatic removal was the right of the prosecution and that Myers could not get a fair trial in Carroll County because of the wide spread publicity. That argument, however, was not up to him as the prosecutor to assert.

In capital cases there was, for the accused, an absolute right to request and be granted "removal" from the area where the crime occurred to avoid the inherent unfairness of having to be judged by jurors who might be prejudiced against the accused, and outraged by the crime that had occurred in their community.

The early colonists had bitterly resented the fact that they could be transported for prosecution and trial in England, thereby effectively denying them the opportunity to defend themselves in any meaningful way. The British Empire had controlled its domains in this manner. In the middle of the 17th Century for example, Oliver Plunkett, a Jesuit Priest in Ireland, had ignored the prohibition against teaching common people how to read and write in violation of the law, and had been whisked away to London, where he was imprisoned for 18 months and eventually tried and executed. His local Irish witnesses could not make that long trip, and consequently he was promptly and easily convicted. His head was cut off and displayed on a stake in Tilbury, England for a short while. It was then taken by his supporters and was preserved as a holy relic.

I knew about Plunkett because after his head had ultimately been blessed and pickled, it was returned to St. Peter's Church and Shrine in Drogheda, Ireland about fifteen miles from my grandmother's cottage in Co. Louth. While visiting her on many occasions as young boys, my brother and I were fascinated to see our cousins and other people on their knees praying to the grotesque "Head of The Blessed Oliver Plunkett." It is still a famous relic.

Many Americans had suffered similar fates.

People in England, historically, always had the right to be tried in the vicinity where the crime had taken place because the jury was composed of people who had knowledge of the facts, and of the accused, and were required when necessary to conduct their own investigations. As the adversarial system evolved, impartial jurors were selected and were required to make factual determinations based upon the presentation of the two parties to a dispute. However, it became an inherent right to be tried where the murder took place to safeguard against the unfairness and the hardship involved when an accused is prosecuted in some remote venue.

Theoretically, every capital case could be removed to a faraway county which, in a diverse state like Maryland, could mean trial where few people, if any, share the same ethnicity or heritage as the defendant. There was a dilemma to be resolved because no state law, whether established by a State Constitution or otherwise, can be valid if it violates the United States Constitution. Consequently, we theorized that because the right to removal of a case is "absolute" for the accused, the prosecutor must yield to the defendant's wishes in capital cases. In all other situations, a trial judge can remove the case from its jurisdiction if either party can demonstrate that it cannot obtain a fair trial.

Unfortunately, while the accused can insist upon removing a capital case, he has no control or input over to where a case will be transferred. There is no articulated method of deciding where the case should be sent, and consequently the removal can be subject to prejudices, personal preferences or individual whims. Again, in a diverse state such as Maryland, some counties are demonstrably more prosecution prone than others, and there are vast differences in the ethnic composition and heritage in these separate jurisdictions. It can be like the difference between day or night, or more accurately, life and death.

The death penalty in Maryland had not been mandatory since 1908. Consequently, it was up to the locally elected State's Attorney in each of the twenty-four separate jurisdictions to decide whether or not to attempt to execute an individual accused of the seven death-eligible crimes. Murder, both premeditated and felony, rape, assault with intent to rape, kidnapping, and carnal knowledge of an imbecile or a child under 14 all carried this ultimate penalty—at the whim of the local official.

Not surprisingly, the chances of the local prosecutor seeking and imposing the ultimate sanction differed drastically across the state, even when the crimes were indistinguishable. This disparity had been approved by the appellate courts. Jurisdictional bias ruled, but beyond that, there were great differences in the attitudes of individual prosecutors in the separate offices. In Baltimore City, the State's Attorney allowed individual prosecutors to decide for themselves.

One of my cases had been removed to a white rural county after the black defendant's two previous death sentences had been overturned on appeal. It was a gruesome rape murder and the jury convicted the murderer for a third time. I was unable to convince the jurors to return a qualified verdict, which would have prevented the racist "hanging" judge, DeWeese Carter, from imposing the death sentence. He refused to listen to my begging him for the life of the defendant, thinking it was somehow "unmanly" for a prosecutor to do so. Judge Carter imposed death for the murder and rape. He would have executed him twice if he could. The Supreme Court in 1972 found all the death statutes across the country unconstitutional as they had been written, and the defendant was consequently not executed, much to my great relief.

Other prosecutors in the office sought death wherever it was theoretically possible. Some would even *complain* they had serious crimes to present, but that "[t]here wasn't a pill among them"—shorthand for the cyanide pill used in the gas chamber. Other prosecutors were creative and in order to bring it about attempted to extend the felony murder rule in some situations. For example, a cabdriver had shot to death one of the two people who was trying to rob him. Under this theory, because it was a killing "that took place during the course of a felony," the surviving assailant who had been shot in the face, was death eligible. In another instance, the police had staked out a bank that they knew would be robbed and they killed one of the robbers. The creative prosecutor sought death for the other bank robber on the same theory. They ignored the fact that in this way, the police could make the case more serious and unilaterally increase the penalty by shooting the co-defendants to death. Hardly sound public policy.

In Myers' case, the legality of the procedure that removed his trial from Carroll County to Garrett County was argued in front of the Court of Appeals, on June 7, 1982. After weeks of court hearings in Maryland's Westernmost County in the Chadderton trial, it was recognized that it would be just as difficult to find impartial jurors there as in Westminster.

The Attorney General's Office of Maryland represents the State on appeal. It initially defended this change of trial site, and argued that the matter should be considered by the State's highest court only after the case was tried. George Burns argued that the case should be sent back to Carroll County. The issue, he maintained, should be resolved before Myers was forced to stand trial on the charges. The judges questioned the wisdom of Hickman's persistence in trying to keep the trial in Garrett County, because if the appeals court decided later that the trial should have remained in Carroll County, the whole case would have to be reversed and retried.

The Assistant Attorney General argued that while he did not necessarily agree with Hickman, he was merely representing the State's Attorney as required by law. He argued that since Hickman was willing to run the risk of a reversal, the case should be left in Garrett County. Judge Marvin Smith said, "When I was engaged in the practice of law, from time to time, I've told clients what they wanted to do was stupid." The Assistant Attorney General admitted that he had given this advice to his client, but that Hickman had insisted on the removal.

One of my goals in getting the case sent back to Westminster was to get a severance of the cases and get away from Daniel Chadderton. The Appellate judges were interested in the timing of the removal and focused on Judge Gilmore's decision to move the case out of the county without first holding a hearing. Ultimately, since the Court of Appeals had clearly indicated its displeasure with the removal, the State relented and agreed to move the case back to Carroll County. It was a significant victory for the defense. This prosecution would be the first in Carroll County history in which the death penalty was being sought.

*****

Judge Gilmore had led the effort to preserve the Westminster Courthouse, whose cornerstone was laid in 1838. By the late 1970s, the building was in a serious state of deterioration. He ordered the white paint, which had trapped moisture, stripped from the building's brick exterior and furnished the inside with period pieces. The restoration took about ten years to complete. Judge Gilmore said of the restored building, "It should command respect and this one does."

The two-story columned portion on the front and a tall cupola on top were later added to the building. The Circuit Courtroom has been rated as

"One of America's most beautiful courtrooms" by the American Bar Association. Its most distinguishing features are its original antique furniture, including oak Windsor chairs in the jury box. An assortment of jackets is stored in the clerk's desk, a reminder of bygone days when witnesses were required to be properly attired.

I thoroughly researched the background of the other available judges on the bench in Carroll County. Even though I respected Judge Gilmore and thought he was a fair person, since this was a life or death matter, if there was a better choice, I wanted to explore it. Gilmore had served in the Air Force for four years and was likely to be more authoritarian.

I learned about Associate Judge Luke K. Burns, who was born in Baltimore in 1934. After he graduated from Loyola High School in 1951, he planned to study for the priesthood and entered the seminary program in 1953 at Fordham University. When he graduated in 1957, he then attended several seminaries and finally withdrew when he was 26, in 1961, to pursue a career in law. In 1964 he earned his law degree from the University Of Baltimore School Of Law and was admitted to the Maryland Bar later that year.

He began practicing in Baltimore in a small firm. In 1972, a friend of Burns invited him to join his practice in Westminster. Burns wasn't happy in Baltimore, so this offered him the chance to move to Carroll County and practice law in a country setting an hour away. Burns was appointed to The District Court in September 1978, and in 1979 became a Circuit Court Judge. People felt he was a compassionate man. He was kind to attorneys, defendants, and all participants and personnel. He was considered fair-minded, thoughtful, and an even-handed dispenser of justice.

His favorite cases were adoptions. After completing an adoption proceeding, he would hold the baby and stand with the child and the new family while a photograph was taken. He would then add it to the gallery he kept on the walls of his chambers. He loved these cases because they were uplifting and happy occasions. Judge Burns would routinely call children into his chambers to talk with them and get to know them. He was very happy seeing children find a nice, loving home.

He was positive about life, so I guessed that this should make him less inclined to impose the death penalty. He was well-loved because he was completely free of phoniness.

Luke Burns was known never to upstage or scold a lawyer unnecessarily, and you had to work hard to make him angry. He had a very even temperament. It was clear to me that Myers would eventually be found guilty, no matter what I did or how hard I tried. Alan Murrell's cynical practical admonition, "This man needs a priest not a lawyer!" made it obvious I should put a lot of effort into having Judge Burns be the trial judge and then the sentencing judge.

When the Myers' case was returned to Carroll County, in order to request "the recusal" of Judge Gilmore and get Judge Burns, I argued that Judge Gilmore had presided over a civil suit in which Robert Myers had been a defendant. I also discovered that he had previously done some legal work for Mary Ruth's family and had met Myers socially. In the exercise of his duties as a Judge of the Circuit Court of Carroll County, he had reviewed several affidavits seeking search and seizure warrants, and the authority to intercept conversations on the Myer's home and business telephones. These orders were signed by Judge Gilmore. He had also signed the order authorizing the "bugging" at the Myers house.

I argued that in the event that Myers was convicted and elected a judge to determine the penalty, these facts might taint the entire proceedings. He was not happy, but he reluctantly granted my request that he remove himself, and Judge Burns was assigned the case. This was an important victory. In my experience, this new presiding Judge was a rarity —"a priesthood dropout!"

I had never met Thomas C. Hickman before the Myers case, but I respected him, because as a young lawyer he had moved from Baltimore City to Carroll County and almost immediately, at age 27, had become the State's Attorney. He had a good mind and a great booming voice, which made him a formidable adversary since it was coupled with a bulldog-like tenacity. I soon learned that I could make him angry. I knew he would never quit or back away, and thus I would have my hands full. A large part of my case would have to be attacking him, even though on a personal level he was quite likable.

I found out all I could about him. He was an athlete in high school, playing football, lacrosse, and was co-captain of the swimming team. As a college student at Virginia Military Institute, he co-founded the lacrosse team. He earned his degree in History, and graduated as Distinguished Military Graduate.

At University of Baltimore Law School, he was elected the Honor Court prose-cutor by his classmates. His graduating class had only 25 people, as the majority had flunked out early in the first year.

In November 1980, he had told about fifty members of the Carroll County Chamber of Commerce, in a speech at their monthly luncheon in Westmin-ster, that articles had appeared in the Hanover Evening Sun in October 1974 suggesting that he had taken a bribe. He said he had contemplated shooting the reporter. He told the audience that, "It is hard to imagine that I was led to seriously consider such an act, but I tell you now without shame and without regret that I did."

He was reading from a prepared text! "The spirit of revenge burns to some extent in all of us," he said. His hate-filled remarks were met with a standing ovation from all of the Chamber members present. *The Sun* papers in Baltimore and *The New York Times* reported the State's Attorney's bizarre comments in an editorial entitled "Pistol Packing Prosecutor."

I made a motion to have him removed from the case on the basis that I was scared of him, and that if he was going to shoot a reporter I was certain that he would shoot me if I were to win the case. I said to Judge Burns in open court that perhaps I should wear a bullet-proof vest while I made this particular motion. I requested that Mr. Hickman be placed on the witness stand so I could develop the idea that because of these comments, which had been made several years earlier, I, on some level had to be scared to effectively represent Robert Myers and therefore he was going to be denied his sixth amendment right to counsel.

The judge refused to allow me to put Hickman on the witness stand, and asked me why I wanted to do that when I had already presented the written speech as an exhibit. I replied that I wanted to demonstrate that Mr. Hickman had been drunk when he made these comments. Mr. Hickman jumped to his feet and said, "I was not drunk!" I looked over and said, "I was trying to give you the benefit of the doubt to try to explain why you would make such comments." He cringed because he knew he had been foolish to ever speak so recklessly, and this was the punishment—some jerk like me would taunt him with it.

He had mentioned the murder of Mary Ruth Myers in a subsequent speech, in which he had alluded to his previous remarks. This enabled me to argue, "It is significant that the mention of the Myers' investigation was made at the same address, in which the State's Attorney stated, 'I still have the pistol I intended to use,'" (i.e. to murder the reporter if he lost the election for county State's Attorney). The written motion continued, "Since this speech was delivered from a prepared text, there is little doubt that Mr. Hickman intended to impress upon the community in Westminster that Mr. Hickman was the type of individual who is capable of anything, including shooting a reporter to death if his views did not prevail." Judge Burns was mildly amused at my antics, but denied my request to have the prosecutor removed from the case. Hickman, however, knew how to counterattack, and was able to find out a thing or two about me.

Quaaludes had been outlawed in Maryland in 1971 and were difficult to get. I had visited a phony clinic in Baltimore to get a prescription for Quaaludes filled. I wanted them for recreational use only, since I'd learned first-hand that any mind altering substance prevents excellence in a courtroom. Baltimore pharmacists, however, had been alerted that the clinic was a charade and they refused to honor the prescription. So while I was in Westminster working on the case, I had gone to a local pharmacy and got it filled.

A few weeks later we were in chambers discussing whether or not Myers' Grand Jury testimony should be admitted into evidence. I argued that Myers had been drunk when he testified there. Tom Hickman said, "No, Mr. Keating, he was on Quaaludes, Mr. Keating! He was on Quaaludes!" He looked at me with a big grin. When I started to respond, he said with a huge laugh, "No, I'm just kidding you!" I should have been more cognizant of the fact that Westminster was a very small town.

There is no real way to avoid the pressure and anguish of a trial, because to do so appears unnatural. It is unnatural. People innately want to see you suffer for your client. You cannot avoid this price when involving yourself with serious matters. The temptation to numb oneself is great, but must be avoided if you really want to be as effective as possible.

In Westminster, I renewed my earlier motion concerning the Sutley double-cross. I argued that because the prosecutors had corrupted Myers' right to counsel, and in effect had manipulated the situation, they had essentially made Sutley into a State Agent. I could find no legal precedent and so I was just creating the best argument that could be made. I needed to introduce as many documents as I could to demonstrate beyond any question that Sutley had represented Robert Myers.

I filed a pretrial motion for "appropriate relief," in which I alleged that the State knowingly "cashed in" on this gross unethical conduct. I argued that Sutley was counsel to both Robert and Tina during the period of time when the "deal" was made and that the State abetted this professional misconduct and had interfered with and destroyed Robert Myers' sixth amendment right to counsel. Based on that premise, I asserted that the prosecution was so tainted that it should not be allowed to continue. Sutley had represented Myers and therefore it was unconscionable for him to negotiate a plea for Tina, which required her to testify against his own client. I requested that the court prohibit Tina from testifying, in order to deter the State from taking advantage of similar situations in the future. I argued that hopefully not many people had the misfortune of trusting a lawyer who had no reservation about pushing their own client into the gas chamber, but the State should not be encouraged to be complicit in such a gross betrayal.

Philip Sutley had assisted Robert Myers during the entire course of the investigation, and Robert Myers had paid Sutley a substantial fee.

Now I was appropriately armed with the documentary proof I needed. I prepared a long statement of facts with exhibits attached. On January 15th, 1980, Sutley had sent a letter to the State's Attorney informing that office that he "represented Robert L. Myers in reference to any possible charges that may be placed against him in Carroll County," and that if the police or prosecutors wanted to talk to Myers they should arrange it through Phil Sutley. This was a standard "letter of representation."

During the period August 25, 1981 through September the 18, 1981, the State Police were wiretapping Robert Myers and they were required to make a log of all the calls to or from his telephones. However, even though the wiretap had been lawfully obtained and approved by the court, the police could not eavesdrop on privileged, confidential conversations with a lawyer. To do so would jeopardize the introduction of all evidence discovered during the wiretap and, consequently, when the police heard a call commence between a lawyer and his client they had to stop the recording the interception and make a notation in the wiretap logs that such a call had been made and had been "placed on pause."

In that twenty-four day period, the State Trooper, James Sherman, the wiretap supervisor, noted that Phil Sutley and Robert Myers had actually talked on seventeen different occasions, and that attempts at communications between them were made in fifty-six instances. The logs showed another dozen references to Phil Sutley as the lawyer for Robert Myers. During many of her conversations, Tina had described Sutley as "our lawyer." There could be no real factual dispute.

On November 20, 1981, when Myers appeared before the Grand Jury on the record and under oath, Myers explained that Phil Sutley, who had told him not to testify, represented him. He said even though Sutley was on his way there, he wanted to proceed with his testimony. He was not interested in delaying so that he could consult with Sutley, who would be waiting outside the Grand Jury room. On nine separate pages in his Grand Jury testimony, Myers had referred to Phil Sutley as his lawyer.

The Carroll County Detention Center Attorney log showed that Sutley had visited Myers there on fourteen occasions between December 23, 1981 through March the 22, 1982.

Phil Sutley had prepared a "Power of Attorney" for each of them separately, and these enabled him to handle all their important affairs and literally gave him the right to end their lives if they were on life support. I introduced these as exhibits and later confronted Sutley with them. He was still adamant that he had never been Robert Myers' attorney.

Sutley had advised the couple that they should auction off all their personal property in the house, to generate more funds to retain Philip Sutley privately. On January 4, 1982, this auction was conducted and a thousand people attended. Sutley was present during the entire sale. Checks were made out to him. Approximately $30,000 was raised. There was no accounting made to Myers. Articles describing this auction appeared in several newspapers, and I introduced them into evidence.

Sutley had used The General Power of Attorney to allow him to collect all of Robert Myers' assets in order to help pay for Robert Myers' attorney's fees and investigative costs. Sutley exercised his powers under this document, and as a result, received and kept for his own use numerous items of personal property, including a ring valued at $3,000, a spinning wheel valued at $500, silverware valued at $16,000, a watch owned by Myers valued at $500, and a wedding ring belonging to Myers valued at $8,000. He also took from Myers' safe deposit box thirty or more pieces of jewelry that included rings, bracelets, and necklaces which had a value of approximately $20,000. Sutley had converted these items for his own use.

I produced in court dozens of newspaper articles demonstrating that Sutley held himself out publicly as Myers' attorney. He was quoted as speaking for Myers on numerous occasions, and was consistently identified as Myers' lawyer in the Westminster, Baltimore, Washington, and Hanover, Pennsylvania newspapers.

I carefully culled the clerk's file and retrieved other relevant written proof: the Bail Review form from the District Court clerk's case folder dated November 27, 1981, the Postponement Sheet in the Circuit Court (December 16, 1981), the Arraignment Form (December 23, 1981), and the Petition to have Myers evaluated (December 23, 1981).

I also introduced underlined portions from Tina's voluminous correspondence, showing that she considered Sutley to be "our" lawyer.

With subpoenaed telephone records from Sutley's law office and his residence, telephone records of the Carroll County Detention Center, and comparable ones from Myer's home and office, I carefully made a chart to match them all up. Scores of calls . . . Sutley was a very attentive and diligent lawyer for Robert Myers.

On February 8, 1982, after many requests, Sutley had finally sent me a list of character witnesses that Bobby had supplied to him to assist in his defense. None of them related to Tina. Sutley had told me that he could not properly represent Robert Myers because he was "too emotionally involved with him."

I argued to the court that the States' plan to negotiate with Tina to the detriment of Robert Myers had obviously been considered by the prosecutor before March 24, 1981. The failure to question the role of Sutley when he had entered his appearance on behalf of Tina on December 23, 1981, showed the prosecutors had, consciously or not, usurped the defense function. They had effectively made Sutley a State agent when they decided to negotiate with her.

I claimed that the State could not legitimately bargain with Tina Myers through Sutley, because Sutley also represented Robert Myers. "Essentially, the prosecution was bargaining and negotiating with Mr. Myers' own attorney in order to secure incriminating testimony against Mr. Myers. The State's intrusion and misconduct have made a mockery of the attorney-client privilege relationship between Mr. Myers and Phil Sutley." My motion accused Sutley of violating the lawyers' Canons of Professional Ethics in negotiating the immunity agreement.

For relief, I requested that Hickman be removed from the case, the notice seeking the death penalty be dismissed, and that Tina be prohibited from testifying. I could find no legal precedent for any of this, though, and the weakness in my arguments was recognized by all. I could not show that Sutley had provided the State with any information which he gained from representing Robert Myers, and therefore the prosecutors had no obligation to enforce the Canons of Ethics which Sutley had violated.

Judge Burns specifically found that Sutley was not a 'State Agent.' Additionally, he ruled, "the State met its burden of proving there was no taint, by showing that there was no disclosure to the State of information received by Sutley from Robert Myers." Although Judge Burns intimated that Sutley had been confronted by a conflict of interest between Robert Myers and Tina Myers, the judge said the prosecution was not tainted by that apparent conflict.

The judge went on to conclude, "The entire situation and relationship between attorney Philip M. Sutley and Robert Myers has possibly placed Mr. Myers in a compromising position, but there is no relief available to Mr. Myers in these proceedings before the Circuit Court for Carroll County. Relief possibly would be available to Mr. Myers in another forum or another tribunal."

Sutley had explained to Myers that for public purposes he would represent Tina, but he would get his close friend Alan Murrell, The State Public

Defender, to appoint an assigned public defender to represent Myers. Sutley assured Myers that he would make sure that both of them would ultimately be freed because he was in actuality representing them both. Myers trusted Sutley and went along with the scheme.

I had argued that the State had encouraged and facilitated Sutley's professional misconduct. Based on that premise, I argued that the prosecution was so tainted that any resulting conviction would have to be reversed. The Court did not agree.

Sutley testified again that he was representing only Tina. Judge Burns ruled it was clear that Sutley was representing both Tina and Robert Myers while negotiating an agreement that could send Myers to the gas chamber. The judge did declare that the conduct should be investigated by the State Bar Association.

The murder trial, destined to be the longest and most sensational in Carroll County history, was scheduled to begin September 20, 1982 in the midst of the election campaign for the State's Attorney office. I had hoped that the election would keep Hickman too busy to concentrate on the case. I was to be disappointed, as he devoted all his attention to the upcoming trial, and was easily elected without campaigning very much.

*****

During the motions hearings before the trial began, I received a large folder marked "Barrister" from the Rev. Buck R. Harris with an envelope in it stating, "Secretary! It's imperative Mr. Keating sees this immediately!" Inside was a letter from a group calling itself "Posse Comitatus," a right-wing, anti-tax extremist group operating on the belief that the true intent of the founders of the United States was to establish a Christian Republic, where the individual was sovereign.

They were part of a loosely organized national movement of fundamentalist Christians who challenged the legitimacy of most of the country's established political institutions. The Carroll County Posse had recently been formed and claimed that the only legitimate government is fundamentalist Protestant government and that most State and local authorities operated on laws that grew from "pagan" and "heathen" sources. Several members of this Posse showed up for the motions hearings and wanted to befriend me and Robert Myers, insisting that the entire prosecution was illegitimate. They dressed in jungle fighting camouflage uniforms, carried black leather riding crops, and wore combat boots. Harris was their Commandant, and he explained to me during a recess that he was also the pastor of the Church of the Holy Ghost, Pentecostal, in nearby Manchester. The "common law attorney" for the group, who all wore berets with the silver insignia of British Airborne Paratroopers, explained that because "the law itself operates on the principle of an eye for an eye and a tooth for a tooth, there is no room for love, no room for Christianity." They seemed angry at The State's Attorney and wanted to assist the defense.

They provided me with astrological profiles of the participants in the case, neatly typed from "leading astrologers." These detailed analyses had many pages of source materials attached to them. They contained physical, emotional, and intellectual biorhythmic compatibility profiles. For example, they concluded that Judge Burns was "sexually stimulated by Tina," "understood her to the max," and "wasn't emotional with her at all." Throughout these materials, the authors kept repeating, "Please Believe, Anton!" And, "For the record, what you see here is absolute fact." I encouraged them a little and was amused to see them challenging the prosecutors with all this bullshit on several occasions. I figured anything that distracted Hickman and Coleman, even for a few minutes, was okay with me as long as I didn't have to wear jackboots. They showed up on several occasions later during the trial. Although I could use all the help I could get, they were nut jobs, and I had no more time to waste indulging them.

Besides, I did not need them to help me to look foolish. I could do that on my own, made clear one day during motions hearings. I was being quite preachy and overbearing when, as the newspaper reported, "Proceedings were interrupted for several minutes when Mr. Keating missed his drinking cup and poured water on evidence he was about to present." Mr. Hickman gladly lent me his handkerchief to dry up the mess. Another reminder not to be too pompous.

*****

On one of Myers' trips to Bermuda to visit Tina, he met a baggage carrier named Sandy Clarke at BWI Airport. He struck up a friendship with her and they became pen pals. Later when she learned of his situation and he had been arrested, she visited him in the Carroll County Detention Center.

This was another example of the "Crim Dick" phenomenon that I had seen several times before: a basically inexperienced and unattractive woman being stimulated and intrigued by a male prisoner who was associated with a violent crime. Where possible, I encouraged these relationships, since it was usually in my client's interest to have as many ongoing contacts with people on the outside of the prison walls as possible. I was not a social worker and it was not up to me to let the woman know that she was being used and had no real understanding about the person she was communicating with. By definition, they had not known each other intimately before the incarceration. These women were usually very naïve and susceptible to the inmates' kindness and attention.

In April 1982 Ms. Clarke had written to Myers:

Hi Sweetheart! How are you? It certainly was great seeing you today Bobby! Honey, I love you. I know that it won't be much longer now until we are together forever. And who is Dan really? He's more than just a friend of Tina's, isn't he?

I got your letter today. And a beautiful Easter card. Thank you! Honey, you know my only hope and dream is to be able to share the rest of my life with you. I think we both really need each other and God is just waiting until the time is right to join us as one. God knows that you are innocent. And now that I know Marco [Tina's ex-husband] is around, I kind of worry about myself. You don't think he or Tina would have me hurt, do you?

It should be less than one month before we are together. I'm a Virgo too and I need a lot of loving. What does Keating know about me? We probably won't get any sleep for a month trying to make up for all this time we've been separated (Ha! Ha!) I didn't think you were going to stop talking to my Mom. But my Mom loves to talk. By the way, her name is Jeanette. You can call her Jeanette, Jeannie or Mom. I wish I knew what evidence you have to prove your innocence. And I pray all of the time that you can prove it. At least my Mom trusts you. She said that she thinks you'll be a good husband to me.

Honey, I pray that God is with you in court and whoever the guilty person (or people) is (or are) that He sees to it that they are hung. Babe, anyone to be guilty and to see them try to blame the innocent deserves to be hung. I know that you keep telling me you'll be free soon, but only God knows what I'll do if you aren't. Without you, I'm nothing. What does Keating seem to think?

I'll always be only yours. I love you Bobby, Sandy.

*****

Once Tina found out that Myers had flirted with the luggage carrier, she became very jealous.

On June 22, 1982 Tina had given birth to an 8 lbs. 14 oz. fair-haired boy. She was admitted to the Garrett County Memorial Hospital under an assumed name and under armed guard, because threats to her life had been made. Having learned of Robert's new lady friend that he loosely referred to as his fiancée, Tina was angry. Up until then Tina had sent Myers a nice Father's Day card and had constantly been wishing him well and telling him that she still loved him. At my direction, he had not written back to her.

She knew that Myers desperately wanted his son to be named Robert Lee Myers—after him. Angry about Sandy, and perhaps feeling vindictive, she wrote to him, "after nearly 2 weeks of careful thought and prayer, I felt my son should have a name all his own and not be forced to carry a name due to such a nightmare that has affected so many lives." She informed him that the baby's name was Jason Ryan Myers.

It was time to start his trial, and so on September 20, the ordeal began.

CHAPTER 23:
JURY SELECTION

"The Search for Fools . . ."
— Anonymous

The courthouse was guarded by deputies enforcing the tightest security measures anyone had seen. There had been a bomb threat a few days before, and so four deputies assisted by four bailiffs, and one plainclothes officer, guarded the ceremonial courtroom. Potential jurors, lawyers, and anyone else trying to enter the County's 145-year-old courthouse were greeted by a Sheriff's deputy, who searched them with a metal detector. Jurors, spectators, reporters, and even other deputies, were required to sign in and out as part of the security procedures.

The 300 registered voters summoned for jury duty were divided into groups of thirty-five, who were screened generally and then specifically by individual questioning. It took more than an hour to read the list of potential witnesses and to ask the potential jurors if they knew any of them.

It was decided that sixty-four jurors were needed for the final selection round. A juror's mere knowledge of the case did not make him biased and therefore an unsuitable juror. The judge told them however, it was necessary to ask each of them what knowledge they had about the case and whether or not that knowledge would affect their ability to impartially try the matter.

Only two people said that they had not heard or read about the case. Nine of the final sixty-four jurors dropped out because of medical or other personal problems, which all had to be detailed on the record. This questioning must be precise because there is no room for error. Under Supreme Court rulings, if a potential juror is improperly excluded, it can lead to a reversal of the conviction. It is a difficult and tedious process.

Jury selection is often a boring and mind-numbing process, but it is the most critical phase of any criminal trial. While the lawyer might suggest he is looking for an impartial and indifferent group of competent people who will obey their oath to try the case upon the evidence and the law, my definition of a fair jury is a group of people who will vote for my client. The prosecution and defense functions are not the same. The prosecutor must above all things be fair; while the defense attorney must also obey the rules, he is concerned only with advocating his client's position and must devote a great deal of his time, his energy, and his best work to this stage of the case. Cynically, defense attorneys call this process "The Search for Fools." Wealthy defendants can afford to engage jury consultants and body language specialists, in order to provide the most information to be able to make the best guesses possible.

The individual screening of the jurors was conducted in a very small room in the old courthouse, with the two prosecutors, the court reporter, the clerk, the Judge, Myers, and I all seated close together at a small table. I pushed Myers as close to the judge as possible. Workmen were noisily making renovations outside. Myers said loudly, "I feel as though they're building the gallows already." Myers kept pouring water for the participants at the table. Several times during voire dire, Myers said, "I'm beginning to smell the gas already."

The process was exhausting, since each prospective juror would enter the small room, be seated, and be asked the same questions. Individual questioning was allowed by each of the lawyers, and so we had to try to make a positive impression upon these individuals and at the same time attempt to discern who they were and what they were likely to do. In all, 280 people were interviewed over a period of two weeks in this fashion. The interviews continued every day from 10:00 a.m. to 6:30 p.m.

Some of the critical questions concerned their attitudes towards the death penalty, and some of the responses were brutally honest. I took careful notes on my impressions of all the prospective jurors so that I could ultimately make a best guess as to how to exercise my twenty peremptory challenges. (That is, potential jurors I could strike without having to provide a reason.) I was also seeking, through my questioning, to eliminate jurors that I felt would not be good for the defense by attempting to have them make statements which would allow me to challenge them "For Cause."

In the pressure cooker atmosphere of a trial it is easy get punchy and silly. The pressure gets debilitating for most everyone and makes the participants eager for any emotional relief. Consequently, some events at the trial of even the most heinous crime can become hilarious at times, and the Myers trial was no exception.

After several days of jury selection, we were all getting a little careless and exhausted. I kept reminding myself to stay focused. Choosing the jury was the most important part of the case. It was critical not to allow anything to interfere. I had taken all my white shirts to a local laundry in Westminster and just before voire dire when I retrieved them, they had all been inadvertently dyed pink. We all had a good laugh at my expense. I did not have the energy to replace them right then.

Late one afternoon the bailiff brought in a rather large, ruddy-complexioned man. He had a lapel pin on his jacket. He looked uncomfortable, wearing an ill-fitting tie, as though he was not used to such formality. I looked again at the shiny pin. It was a black and white cow. We had been questioning witnesses all day. I thought it was amusing when he said he was a dairy farmer, and then when he was asked his feelings about the death penalty he said, smiling, "Well," and then after a long pause, "as long as it's not me, I'm for it!" We all exploded with laughter. I could not stop the tears from rolling down my cheeks. This guy was absolutely honest. Even after all the other participants had calmed down, I still could not stop myself from laughing. All those seated around the table were staring at me, but I still could not control myself.

Judge Burns, clearing his throat, said, "All right now, Mr. Keating, please proceed." Every time I looked at the farmer, I started to break out in laughter again. Everyone in the room was uncomfortable and I could see the potential juror was starting to get angry. The judge called a recess and I went into the bathroom to wash my face and calm down. I realized that I was going to have to waste a challenge on this guy since he would probably kill my client in a minute and no doubt, since I had laughed in his face, he probably would have been more than willing to send me to the gas chamber along with him.

As monotonous and repetitious as this questioning process was, I kept making notes about my observations and how these folks had substantively responded to the questions, to the process in general, to the prosecutors, and to myself. Day after day we interviewed them. If I didn't like them, when they left the room, on the record, I made the best argument that I could that they should be challenged for "cause." The prosecutors did the same thing, especially trying to eliminate those people who expressed reservations about the use of the death penalty. If someone was adamant that they would not impose death, I would of course try to "rehabilitate" them, trying to get them to say that they would entertain the punishment in certain circumstances.

The information in response to these questions often provides materials to help in considering whether or not to keep the juror. This was a laborious process, rather like having a mini trial over each of them. Just as I wanted the prosecutors to use up their ten peremptory challenges, they in turn wanted to make me use up my twenty peremptory challenges.

This procedure inevitably results in a prosecution prone jury, since those who are against death as a penalty are more likely to be defense oriented, and those who are willing to impose it are more likely to obey the instruction from the court as jurors to "well and truly try the case, according to the law." Certainly, it was a lot of guesswork on everybody's part, even if all the potential jurors were telling the truth.

Once the 280 prospective jurors had been screened and the pool was reduced in this fashion, eighty people remained. There was a two-day recess during which time I studied my notes and tried to determine which folks I had to eliminate (like the ruddy farmer), which people the prosecutors would want to eliminate, and which people I preferred and the prosecutors might prefer. I had been involved with the selection of over 100 juries and knew that it was certainly a guessing game, and that inevitably people did not fit into rigid categories. They often did not even know themselves how they would respond to the evidence and the personalities of the participants. That could be used as a good excuse to not analyze and then reanalyze my thought process, however, it is always better to err on the side of putting extra time and effort into such a critical part of a case. I knew that I had been mistaken in the past, so I could and would make mistakes here. I needed to minimize them, if possible.

The actual selection process took place in the large ceremonial court-room. Each of the screened potential jurors was required to come to the front of the courtroom to be "Accepted" or "Rejected." The entire array of jurors watched this process. Both sides are trying to be likeable and gain the respect of those who actually end up being chosen. It is not helpful to say "Reject" when "Respectfully Challenge" will just as easily suffice.

Once the twelve jurors and three alternates had been selected, the rest were excused and there was a mass exodus from the room. It was customary, although not required, to name the person who was seated in the first chair as the foreperson of the jury, so that one of them could ostensibly be in charge. Judge Burns, however, designated juror number six as the foreperson. Up at the bench in private, I objected to this selection because it was arbitrary. I could not come up with a good reason, but if everything went wrong, perhaps an appellate lawyer could. I was overruled.

My notes reflected that juror number six was a lady named Marcia King, and that she was sharp, attractive, smiled a lot, had no fingernail paint, showed dogs, and had never discussed the case with anyone, did not know much about the case, and looked directly at Myers. The defense usually wants unattractive, weak, gullible, people who can be influenced, do not want to serve, and do not have strong convictions of their own. She did not know any of the participants in the case. She had said she would like to serve. She had moved to Carroll County with her husband, who was a salesman for London Fog, eighteen months ear-lier. She was quite feisty and self-confident. When Judge Burns got her name wrong, mistaking her for someone else on the list, she quipped, "Would you like me to leave and come back in again?" She was wholesome and outdoorsy. I guessed she would not like Tina. However, she was much too confident a person for me to want, except I only had a limited number of peremptory challenges. Many years later Judge Burns and Marcia King, the forelady would get married. Perhaps their mutual attraction started here.

I whispered jokingly to Myers that we should be really worried because his fate was to be decided by a jury composed of people who were too stupid to get out of jury service. But then I added that perhaps it was our best chance. He agreed. I told him I was thinking about objecting to the panel, because they were not a jury of his peers. They all seemed to be decent, law abiding citizens. He thought for a moment that I was actually going to do so. Because they looked intelligent, they were a jury of my worst "fears."

A criminal trial can be viewed as a series of attacks. If the defense attorney is not willing to attack, he might as well enter a guilty plea for his client. In this case I made many challenges, not only to the evidence and the applicable law, but also to the location of the trial and the people who were to participate in it.

Defense attorneys don't fight for principles. Rather, they fight for the person they are representing. You don't have to love your client. You only have to pretend that you do. People are very complex and cannot be categorized by one or two simple adjectives. Where there are such extreme consequences, you realize that you'll never do anything in your life that is more important than this.

Much like a boxing contest, when the words, "Seconds Out!" are shouted, all help is gone and you're on your own. You cannot confer with your corner between each and every punch anyway, and in this fight there is no one in your corner but you. As a criminal lawyer, your only companionship is that of the thief, murderer, or other criminal you are representing. Somewhere in the back of one's mind on some level is the idea that you are failing through success, when you help free some violent or otherwise dangerous person. Unlike a sport, this contest is usually rigged against you, and it's not going to be a fair fight in that the prosecution usually sincerely believes that it has the right person and is proceeding in a fair and just manner. They are usually correct.

The essence of the adversarial system is conflict. It is nurtured by conflict. You must live with conflict. You must be inspired by it. You must live with the competition and enjoy it, and if you are not stimulated and challenged by it, you cannot survive long or thrive. It is a young person's game because a lot of energy is needed. You soon become addicted to the attendant stress and the adrenaline high that comes with it. In order to stay effective, you have to know when to be adversarial and when to back away. It always helps to "pray for the heart and the nerve." Always.

It is hard to think of another profession where success amounts to getting more criminals off than other people can. Fortunately or not, in the final analysis, ours is a system of "justice by consent," since the disposition of most cases occurs through negotiation and guilty pleas rather than trial by jury. These negotiations are inevitably related to the proven trial abilities of the participants, and their willingness to fight and gamble. Incredibly, it is possible to effectively engage in the adversarial process and advocate a client's cause with wholehearted zeal, yet also maintain one's integrity. What becomes very difficult to deal with is a lot of rejection and failure. Like anything, when you put your whole being on the line in a quest for greatness, the common goal of always trying to be a winner or a champion, you can feel beaten up and used up if you lose all the time.

In a case where the State is offering nothing but death, it looms over every piece of evidence and every legal argument. Death if you ask the wrong question; death if you don't object properly; death if you haven't filed the right motion; death if you haven't selected the jury properly. You approach it like every other case except more so. You win it if you can. You must win it. You win it or else. Period.

Once the jury had been selected in the large ceremonial courtroom in the old courthouse, we moved to the new Courthouse Annex for the actual trial of the case. The small courtroom had room for eighty-four spectators. It had a tiny office at the end of it and I was allowed to keep all my materials in that office. I was given a key to it.

The night before the trial I got to Lee's Motel early. I was not going to waste my time and energy commuting to Court two hours every day. Lee's was five minutes away. I went over to the courthouse to take my files there and emotionally, to get ready. I had access to the courtroom, so I went in and sat in the jury box all on my own, the lights were dim. I was trying to visualize the action the next day. That process often helped lighten the pressure and anxiety before any meaningful contest.

While sitting in the jury box I heard a noise near the judge's chambers. It was Judge Burns, who then came into the courtroom. It was an odd meeting between the two of us. He sat down at the trial table and I stayed in the jury box. We chatted for several minutes and I then complained about the seating arrangements in the court. The way the courtroom was set up, it was a distinct disadvantage to sit at the defense table because the witness had to turn all the way around to see the defense attorney and then turn back to the jury.

I said that I was thinking of requesting that the defense be allowed to sit closest to the jury, as opposed to the normal tradition of the party who has the burden of proof, sitting closest to the jury. The State's trial table was just three feet away from the jurors. Whoever designed the courtroom had not had much practical experience watching or trying cases. I pointed out that I thought it was a distinct disadvantage to the defense.

I told him I might make a motion the next day to change the seating arrangements. He responded that he would be receptive to the motion because it would be prejudicial if the jurors saw something on the prosecutor's table which they were not supposed to see and which was not ultimately entered into evidence. While he did not go into detail, I had the sense that he had seen some similar problem in previous cases.

Later that night, in my motel room, I ruminated about the Viet Cong in the Paris Peace Conference in 1968, arguing for several months about the seating arrangements at the conference. It turned out to be a good ploy for them.

The next day I made the motion. We all went into his chambers and the prosecutors were adamant that our seating arrangement should not be changed. I wanted to get Myers over as close to the jury as possible so that they would not feel threatened by him, feel his humanity, and be less inclined to kill him. I was convinced he would be convicted, but I could not try the case with that mindset. In chambers, the judge granted my motion. I was having good fortune with this "removal" dimension to the case, I gloated to myself. I walked back into the courtroom first and immediately moved all my files and materials over to the "prosecutor's" side. Tom Hickman was furious and I was pleased. I had pulled this "seating" objection twice before, years earlier, once successfully. If it was not an equal distance from each of the parties to the jury, the accused should not suffer from this disadvantage.

I knew that I would never be able to cover up the nine bullets. I knew I would never be able to cross-examine the tape recordings, which helped demonstrate guilt. I knew I would never be able to put Myers on the witness stand. In short, I realized that he would be convicted of first-degree murder, and so I had to get ready for the second phase of the trial, where someone would decide "Death or Life Imprisonment."

I had learned long before this case that the best approach to trials, as well as life itself, was to eliminate the negative and emphasize the positive. I had to hang on to the affirmative. I couldn't always apply it to my personal life, but I was very good at it in Court. Just like a boxing match, I had learned to scratch and fight like the third monkey on Noah's gangplank. I would then have to concentrate on leaving the fight behind, and try to find some sense of normalcy in my life—sometimes an even harder task.

Robert Myers was an extremely likable, garrulous, and popular person in Carroll County. He greeted everybody with a smile and it was his personality that was mostly responsible for his business success. People liked going to him to have their taxes done. Consequently, when he was incarcerated in the Carroll County Detention Center located near downtown Westminster he had many visitors. His brother, Sterling Myers, and his mother, Elizabeth Myers, constantly visited him. As did his daughter Shelley Myers and some of her girlfriends. Sandy Clark and her brother also visited, as did several of his clients who could not believe that he was guilty of such a cold-blooded murder.

CHAPTER 24:
THE STATE'S CASE

"Let right be done . . ."
— Preamble to The Petition of Right, 1628

On the first day of the trial the courthouse resembled a fortress. Kevin Oleary, the spokesman for the Sheriff's department, said the heavy courtroom security was due to "the nature of the trial and the bomb threats that had been received. A lot of papers are not going to be served," Oleary added. Initially, seven Sheriff's patrol cars, a majority of the fleet, surrounded the courthouse, which was located two blocks from the Sheriff's headquarters.

During the motions, everyone had referred to my client as "Mr. Myers," but whenever I could, I soon began referring to him as "Bobby." Many people called him that, and I wanted to make the trial as informal as possible. He was a goofy, likeable kind of person and the more friendly, relaxed, and humorous an environment I could create, the harder it would be for anyone to want to execute him. However, I was mindful of the fact that I had to be careful not to look callous and disrespectful since the murder had been particularly brutal, calculated, and cold-blooded. Clarence Darrow instructed that jurors would not vote to execute where they had been laughing a lot during the case.

The prosecutors understood what I was trying to do and at first objected to calling him anything other than "Mr. Myers," but over the course of the motions hearings and voire dire, they had given up trying to correct me.

The courtroom was packed for the opening statements on October 6, 1982. Tom Hickman did an excellent job explaining the State's case and what rules and law would govern the proceedings. He was forceful and articulate. He said that more than a year before Mary Ruth was murdered, Mr. Myers had told a number of friends and business associates that "the only way to get out of the marriage was to get rid of her. To have her killed." He told jurors that "Ernestine "Tina" Myers, whom Mr. Myers married 28 days after his wife's death, introduced the defendant to the man, who last May was convicted of the slaying—Daniel Lee Chadderton. Robert Myers wanted his wife killed. He wanted it done through a contract. Dan Chadderton was the shooter. The role of Tina Myers was the introducer.

Hickman explained that Tina Myers had played a relatively small role in the murder plot and that, "in fact, the State had enough evidence to convict Myers without her testimony." But he said, "giving her immunity in return for truthful testimony was necessary" and promised the jury he would explain why later. Myers and I watched intently and both took notes as the prosecutor wrote names, dates, places, and times on a large artist's pad and outlined the State's case.

It is always a difficult time for the defense when the prosecutor is dominating the jury and telling them what he intends to prove. Jurors are curious as to how the defendant and his lawyer are responding to this and inevitably look over at them to gauge their reaction. I like to pretend that I am learning all this information for the first time, and try to make accurate notes and pretend that I have an answer for it all. Sometimes the evidence will not turn out as predicted, and in closing argument, the prosecutor can be challenged with this variance of proof. A poker face is essential.

Hickman said that "there was very little blood in the bed" where Mary Ruth's body was found. "The reason being, five shots had been pumped through her heart. On August 29, 1979, Robert Myers became the owner of everything."

Hickman described the "good life" the Myers couple had enjoyed. "Months before the murder, the defendant told one of his employees that 'he couldn't afford to divorce Mary Ruth. It would cost him more than a quarter of a million dollars to do so.'" Hickman said Myers hated his wife and wanted "to get rid of her." But he couldn't afford a divorce. "No, that would cost a lot of money," Hickman alleged that Myers reportedly told one witness. "There might be other ways . . . if I could get away with it, I would kill her." He promised that another witness would testify that Robert Myers told him in 1978 that he could "have somebody kill her and make it look like a robbery."

Hickman provided a detailed account of the slaying and the events leading up to it. He told them what they would hear from Tina Myers. In his opening statement, Hickman had charged that Myers knew details of the murder that he could only have known if he had taken part in it. Before the autopsy had been performed and the number of gunshots had been determined, Hickman claimed that Myers told a friend, "Yeah, they shot her nine times."

The opening statement by the defense to the jury is often critical. You've got to get in "fists and feet," even if you've got nothing to say. It is fairly easy for the prosecution to present a forceful and concise prediction about what the State's case will demonstrate. The prosecutors often spend time "wrapping themselves in the flag," telling the captive audience about our great system of justice and what procedures will be followed in the case. They can thereby gain immediate credibility with the jurors and, at the close of the entire case, are able to remind jurors that they have fulfilled the commitments they made in their opening statement.

If the defense counsel waives his opening statement, or reserves it until a later time, he will not be heard from until he starts cross-examining the State's witnesses. By then, the prosecutor might already have an insurmountable advantage and the defense counsel will simply look like someone who is "tricky" and an obstructionist. He will not have placed his own credibility and personality into the case, and since first impressions are often paramount, he will therefore probably not be likable, and the defense theory of the case will suffer. All studies about trial techniques conclude that in 80% of jury trials, the case is won or lost by the end of the opening statements. Even if the defense attorney has no good theory or idea what to do, he should still get up and give a limited "bullshit opening."

I did have a defense for Myers. I had researched carefully the instructions the court would give at the end of the case, so I could forcefully explain our defense to the jury. Before the opening statements, the jurors had only experienced minimal contact with the lawyers during the individual questioning on voire dire. Now I also could tell them what to expect the evidence to show, and what law would help them to decide the case, and thereby I could gain some credibility with them.

I told the jurors that my opening statement would take ninety minutes. I intended it to be specific and compelling. I had spent several days over the preceding months preparing it. I had practiced it in a mirror several times. If I could look at my own reflection, I had found over the years, I could deliver a good speech, no matter the intensity of the situation. The fact that I often used no notes always made me look smart and I looked like I actually believed what I was saying, which of course, I sometimes did.

In my opening, I carefully explained to them that murder in the first degree is the intentional killing of a human being with deliberation and premeditation and without excuse or justification. "Premeditation" meant that the intention to kill preceded the killing by some appreciable length of time, that is, time enough to deliberate. If the time was sufficient for the mind to think upon and consider the act and then determine to do it, it does not matter how brief the time is. People who themselves commit the crime, either by their own hand or by the hand of someone else are called "principles in the first degree." Persons who are present either actually or constructively, and who aid and abet the commission of the crime, but do not themselves commit it, are principles in the second degree. It really makes no difference since both are equally guilty of first-degree murder.

Myers was charged in the indictment with murder in the first degree, which included being an accessory before the fact. An accessory before the fact is someone that, although he is absent at the time of the actual perpetration of the murder, procured, counseled, commanded, incited, or abets another to commit it. If he aids or abets another in the commission of the crime, or willfully participates in it as he would in something he wishes to bring about, that he willfully seeks by some act of his to make the crime succeed, he is just as guilty of first-degree murder as the actual perpetrator.

An accessory after the fact, however is one who, knowing that a felony has been committed, accepts it, or relieves or comforts the felon, or renders him or her any other assistance in order to hinder his or her apprehension, trial, or punishment. In order to be an accessory after the fact: (1) the defendant must have become connected with the crime after its commission; (2) the defendant must have rendered assistance with the knowledge that the felony has been completed; (3) the assistance must have been given to one known to be the felon; and (4) the assistance must have been given in order to hinder the felon's apprehension, trial, or punishment. The mere failure to disclose the commission of the felony or to apprehend the felon or the mere approval of the felony is not sufficient to constitute an accessory after the fact.

I knew that Judge Burns would instruct the jurors at the end of the case that "if, after a full and fair consideration of all the facts and circumstances and evidence, you are convinced beyond a reasonable doubt that the State has made out a case of accessory after the fact only, you are instructed as a matter of law that it is impermissible to return a verdict of first degree murder under the indictment."

That would have to be the defense. If I could fashion the evidence to suggest that Myers became aware that Tina and Chadderton, and perhaps others, had brought about this murder, and that he was only an accessory after the fact, he could not be convicted. Myers' defense was that the State had charged him with the wrong crime. It is well-established law that where a defendant is charged with crime "A" and the State has proved crime "B," the defense must be permitted to make that argument to the jury. This theory was consistent with the facts. If Myers was not guilty of the murder, but he was guilty of being an accessory after the fact to that murder when he learned who had done it, he still had to be acquitted.

I then focused on Tina Myers in offering my version of the murder. I alleged that she and Chadderton had planned the crime and next they intended to kill Myers. "He was marked for death next. Chadderton was supposed to kill Bobby Myers after he murdered Mary Ruth. Tina's a predator. She knows how to use sex to get men. She was desperate about losing her children. That's how she gets by in life . . . Tina Myers is not the kind of woman who likes to be controlled by anybody. Her mind was set. She had her plump pigeon."

I charged that "Tina Marco" was the actual driving force behind the killing. She had masterminded the murder-for-hire scheme to acquire Myers' wealthy estate, and like a cuckoo, find a home for her children. "She'll walk away free, not only as an admitted murderess, but also with all my client's property. I described Myers, 40, as a weak and an easily dominated man, who fell under the influence of Tina after his marriage began to falter.

I told jurors that "Bobby" became infatuated with Tina. Soon after Mary Ruth's murder, he gave her $300,000 worth of expensive gifts including jewelry, fur coats, 200 pairs of shoes, and a new Mercedes Benz. But receiving expensive gifts was not enough for Tina, I told the panel of ten women and two men that she also wanted the assets Myers had accumulated from his accounting business and real estate transactions. They were valued at more than one and a half million dollars. "He was marked for death. Chadderton was supposed to kill Bobby Myers after they got married."

Hickman had characterized Tina Marco as a woman who played a minor role in the killing by merely introducing Myers to Chadderton, but I said, "As Mary Ruth Myers was being buried, Tina was moving into the hilltop home where the slaying had occurred."

Once Mary Ruth Myers was dead, Tina dominated Robert Myers, making him cook her meals and do the laundry "while she sat and watched TV." I also told jurors that Tina even tried on Mary Ruth's clothing and jewelry, a comment that drew gasps from the crowd of spectators in the courtroom. "This is the lady who merely made an introduction? Who's the dominant one here? Who's evil? Who's the heavy?"

It was important that I concede as much of the State's case as possible to reduce some of it's impact. "Is he the cold-blooded killer the State says he is . . . or is he a fool? Tina Myers is a cold-blooded killer. Tina Myers saw a good thing. Tina Myers has a way with men. She knows the power of her sexuality. I have a fool for a client."

I attempted to diminish the impact of Hickman's claim that Myers repeatedly expressed the desire to have his wife killed. "We have all made statements to that effect in our lives," I said, indicating that they are generally not serious thoughts. "Mr. Hickman has made statements that he would like to retract and didn't really mean, such as 'I should have shot that guy to death,' referring to the incident resulting in Hickman's nickname, "The Pistol-Packing Prosecutor." I was surprised when several spectators laughed loudly at my comment. I was not trying to be funny, since it was hardly an appropriate time to play the comedian.

I had to explain that the defense case would be developed by producing testimony from the witnesses which it called, the exhibits which it introduced, and also from questions it asked State's witnesses which the prosecutors, "for their own reasons," had not asked. I needed to alert the jurors what to expect and tell them about the importance of character testimony, since I would be producing many witnesses who knew Myers well and believed in him. They would testify "under oath" that he was a non-violent person, not likely to participate in such a brutal act.

I also had to let the jury know that no one accused of a crime could be forced to be a witness in their trial and the reasons why that was a critical part of our accusatorial system of justice. I had to cover the concept of "reasonable doubt" and "burden of proof." In this way, the jury would not be expecting that Myers would testify in the case, and so they would not be disappointed that he did not take the stand several weeks later. It was critical to reduce any false expectations that they might naturally have in this regard.

I omitted from my opening statement describing some of the testimony I knew that I would produce for them, such as the fact that Tina's son, father, and uncle would all appear to declare her untrustworthy. I hoped, thereby, that they would find that information more compelling. I also hoped to keep the jurors speculating as to what might come next.

Judge Burns recessed until the next day, cautioning the jurors as he would countless times over the next several weeks, that they were not to read about the case or listen to radio or television accounts or discuss the proceedings with each other or with anyone else until the case had been concluded. I was exhausted after this first day of the trial and I guessed everyone else was, too.

The prosecutors had given me the names of 160 potential witnesses. Even though I had vigorously protested and I had made a motion to the Court for clarification as to which of them would actually be used, I was not given any relief. The State was within its right to proclaim these were all legitimately "potential" witnesses, so I had to be prepared for each of them. I got some help from the investigators in the Public Defender's Office, but it was up to me to assemble a file containing information that related to each one.

In each witness folder, where available, I placed a police report, any statement given to an investigator, any grand jury statement (which I had obtained only because I had accused the prosecutors of abusing the Grand Jury pro-

cess,) transcripts of testimony from the Chadderton trial, a list of potential exhibits the State might use during their testimony, a list of exhibits the defense
might want to introduce through the witness, and my notes for potential cross
examination. These materials were kept in four large cardboard file drawers.
It was a bounty of riches, but it had to be organized carefully or it would all
be useless. I was grateful for the courtroom's empty office at the rear, to which
I had a key. Had I not been allowed to store my materials there, I would have
taken up much of the floor space around the trial tables.

On the first day of the trial, the prosecutors refused to let me know which
witnesses were going to be used during each session. As a consequence, after
the witness was sworn in, I left the trial table and with the Court's permission
went to the back, entered "my office," stayed as long as I could, and then
returned with the appropriate file. It slowed the trial down a lot. After two
days of these unnecessary delays, the prosecutors relented and gave me the
names of the upcoming witnesses ahead of time. This was a significant advantage to the defense, since I was then able to speed up or slow down my
cross-examination, stalling where necessary. I was able to use the luncheon
and overnight recesses to further prepare for the next witness—like holding
onto a boxer who had just dazed you . . . to get some respite and to be able
to regroup.

Cross-examination is the most dramatic and critical part of any case. It is
the most exciting and challenging because unlike most of the other phases of a
trial, it cannot be completely prepared. Unless a witness is somewhat damaged
or challenged, his testimony will prevail and compel the listener to accept the
substance of the facts presented as accurate, leading to inevitable conclusions.

The art of cross-examination rests in controlling the questioning, so that the
witness is requested to agree or disagree with the assertions contained in the
question. "I would be correct if I said that . . . wouldn't I?" "It would be accurate
to say . . . wouldn't it?" "It's true, isn't it, that . . . isn't it?" "It would be fair to say
. . . wouldn't it?" Some open ended questions can be intermixed sometimes, but
only where the answers cannot possibly damage the questioner's cause.

Possession of a prior statement made by the witness is a nice safety valve to
have, since impeachment with the use of a prior inconsistent statement can be

devastating. The witness can rarely escape being damaged by a prior written inconsistent statement, which can be offered as an exhibit. Like most things in court, obsessive preparation is a pre-requisite. Failure to prepare is usually preparing to fail. It is also necessary to realize however, that few witnesses can be totally destroyed and that it is not usually necessary to obliterate them. The attempt to do this can be fatal. Instead, the interrogator should be satisfied to diminish the effect of a witness and damage him as much as possible and quickly conclude the questioning, before the witness can recover. It is best to have designed the examination to end strongly.

It is usually best to avoid "Why" or similarly open-ended questions which call for explanations, or have the potential for serious damage. Consider these traditional examples that best make this point: after testimony that the witness did not actually see the accused bite off the nose of the victim, on cross examination, when asked why he was so positive that he knew the defendant had done it; the witness explained that he had seen the accused "spit it out." Or, after it was established that the witness had been 8 blocks away and 5 stories up on his roof, when he claimed that he had seen the defendant robbing the victim, he was then asked by the defense, "How are you so certain that it was this defendant when it occurred so far away from you?". The eyewitness explained he had been looking through his powerful telescope at the time.

I loved the challenge of cross-examination, since it is often the most critical part of a case, and requires a strong, bold, but delicate touch. Jurors do not often want to see people humiliated and crushed mercilessly, especially if that person is likeable at all.

They do expect some polite vigorous questioning, however. On one occasion while examining a supposed expert in a custody case, she responded to me, "These questions, young man, are making me look like a silly ass, which I am not!" Of course, it was her answers that were making her look that way.

The best moments in court seem to happen during cross-examination. Years earlier, I was defending a client in a robbery case where the victim had been shot and badly wounded. During a motions hearing on a Friday afternoon, before a judge, a key witness had explained that "she turned tricks for a living." I asked her, just as haughtily as I could, if that meant she "sold her body for money." She responded laughing "Yeah. Why, are you interested?" I immediately put my hand in my trouser pocket and said, "Sorry, I don't have any change!" The Judge exploded in laughter and the witness flushed and glared in my direction. She was being detained in jail over the weekend and was still seething with rage when the proceedings resumed the next Monday. We had then chosen a jury, and made openings and she was led into the courtroom as the State's first witness, and placed on the stand six feet away from me.

After the prosecutor had asked three fairly innocuous questions, I had objected, and the woman said, "I've heard enough out of you, you motherfucker!" and jumped off the stand raising her right hand, lunging at me and about to strike me. I remained seated, ready to absorb the blow and roll away from it to lessen the impact. I was ready to fall onto the floor to get as much sympathy as I could.

Just before contact, an alert courtroom deputy grabbed her and she was hustled outside, cursing. The jurors did not know what to make of her actions and even though she had later testified calmly, it was fairly easy to convince the jury to acquit my client since she was the prosecutor's key witness and had demonstrated how "unstable and unreliable" she was. When I asked the judge if I could be excused, he was no longer laughing and said, "You better get out of here before you're the next one who's shot!" He had always been a fan of mine when I prosecuted cases in his court, but when I joined The Public Defender's Office he often complained, "You're not going to make this the search for the Holy Grail, are you?" in ongoing attempts to dissuade me from always trying so hard.

In the Myers case, I had no intention of simply letting the State's witnesses repeat their entire direct testimony, thereby allowing them to reinforce it. I was going to get concessions from each wherever I could to help reinforce the defense case and diminish their impact.

As Hickman promised, several State's witnesses testified that during 1978 and 1979, Myers had exclaimed that he wanted to be rid of Mary Ruth and wanted to "have a contract put out on her," and that a divorce would ruin him financially.

Diane Amspacher, the bookkeeper at Maryland Business Service from February, 1980 through October, 1981, testified to details of the continuing cover-up by Myers, Chadderton, and Tina Myers, as well as the blackmailing of Myers by Daniel Chadderton following the murder.

A former employee of Robert Myers, she admitted on cross-examination that Myers had told her that his wife Tina had mafia connections, and could use them to have him killed. "Bob told you he was scared of Tina, did he not?" I asked her. She had been hired as a bookkeeper less than six months after Mary Ruth had been shot to death. Amspacher responded, "He spoke of her involvement with the mafia during the summer of 1980. He said Tina's family could have anything done they wanted." She understood from these comments that Tina could have him killed if she wanted. Myers also told her that Marco could take care of an employee who he thought was taking business away from the accounting firm. "He said if he told Tina, Tina could have her car blown up." On another occasion, he told the witness "if she wanted to go skiing, she can't do it with a broken leg."

Ms. Amspacher said Myers told her he could not divorce Marco despite their problems "because if he did, she would go to the police and say that he killed Mary Ruth and the police would believe her." She said, "All he ever told me was, 'You know I couldn't do anything like that.'"

Amspacher had testified that she believed Daniel Chadderton was blackmailing Myers during the two years after the murder. She said Chadderton or his wife would visit Myers' Westminster office at least once a week. She said she discussed the possibility of blackmail with State Police Cpl. James Leete, and later told Myers directly at a meeting with him. "He stood up at his desk very fast and said 'You're going to hang me,'" she testified.

Two of the witnesses had said that Myers asked them if they could help him find a contract killer to murder his wife. They were particularly compelling.

Joseph O. Browne, who was separated from Myers' first wife, testified that "he wanted to get rid of her, have her bumped off. He asked me several times to introduce him to several different people to do the job for him." Browne said that Myers alarmed him because he had boasted of his connections to underworld elements on Baltimore's "Block." Bobby had made these requests as they sat around Brown's kitchen table over the 1978 Christmas holidays. Brown said he would go on drinking binges by himself and with Myers. "I was consuming a gallon of vodka a day, 30+ pills, plus some more vodka," he said as he peered through squinted eyes at me as I was questioning him on cross-examination. He was a gruff man and contradicted himself several times. He had first denied he had ever been committed to a veterans' hospital, and then agreed that he had. He was treated for an emotional disorder.

He denied ever threatening Myers, but then said he "threatened to beat the hell out of him" for not visiting Myers' children by his first marriage. The children lived with Brown. The wizened man said in a gravelly voice, as he scowled at me, that he then became more satisfied with Myers' visits. "I don't know if he was concerned for his children or if he was concerned I was going to beat the hell out of him." He had tufts of gray hair sticking out from the sides of his balding head and his perpetual scowl made him appear more than his 50 years. I suggested that Bobby and he may both have been drunk when he thought he heard Myers' discuss contract killings. Brown admitted he had problems with alcohol, but said he had been sober for several months when Myers asked him about a contract killer.

Deborah Leibno and Margaret Buckingham, both of whom were employed at Myers' accounting firm when the murder occurred, were each called to the stand.

Leibno testified that about three months before the murder, "he mentioned to me he guessed the only way to get rid of her was to kill her." She testified that when she saw Myers the day after the murder he "just didn't look unhappy at all. It made me very disgusted. He didn't even ask me any questions about Mary Ruth." Buckingham's account was similar: "He would complain about not getting enough sex from Mary Ruth." She said Myers had claimed a number of times that "if he wanted to, he could get a contract on her."

Independent evidence, which corroborated Tina Myers' testimony, included the testimony of other employees of the Maryland Business Service and the victim's three children, who normally lived at the Turkey Foot Road home.

The State reproduced for the Carroll County jury all the witnesses that it had produced in the Chadderton trial, and then added many more. So for me, there were very few surprises and I could concentrate on my cross-examination of these witnesses.

Kimberly Abbott, Mary Ruth's step-daughter, described how she was working at the Northwinds Motel in August 1979, when a stranger on a motorbike had pulled up there. The prosecutors over my objection requested that Chadderton be seated among the spectators in the courtroom to see if Kimberly could identify him as that stranger she had seen. I strenuously objected because she had seen him in court in Garrett County where she had testified. I was overruled, and Chadderton—handcuffed and shackled—was seated dramatically between two plainclothes officers in the back of the courtroom. The jury was brought in and Kimberly Abbott was asked by Mr. Hickman if she could identify the person she had seen that day. Kimberly stood and gazed at the audience from the witness stand. She carefully looked around and when her eyes settled on the back row, she burst into tears and began sobbing uncontrollably. She composed herself and then pointed to him. The prosecutor requested Chadderton to stand and as usual, he smirked as he arose to his full height and gazed intently around the courtroom. The jury was excused for a short recess while he was removed from the courtroom. It was a good tactic creating great sympathy for the daughter of the victim, and supplying the jurors a sense of how big, dangerous, and intimidating this killer really was.

Mary Fooks, the housekeeper at the Northwinds Motel who had prevented Chadderton from getting near the victim, was the next witness and she was able to identify the motorbike from photographs.

Adam Handschuh told the jury that he was a coworker at the Pantry Pride and that in September 1979 when he asked Chadderton if he had killed Myers' wife. He responded, "I'm not going back to the slam, but if I do I'm taking two people with me." The witness asked "Who?" Chadderton did not answer but just started sipping his coffee.

Ronald Frampton testified concerning Myers's "sexual activity with women on The Block." Frampton's testimony was a repetition of similar evidence that had been admitted without objection.

Among the many States' exhibits produced was the motel registration for the Quality Inn in Randallstown for August 23, 1979, and the phone records of Charlotte Horton, Maria Poulos, the business office of the Pantry Pride store and several pay telephones in Ocean City.

*****

The trial was interrupted for several days. Judge Burns, Frank Coleman and I needed to travel to Las Vegas to question Jay Gillen about his relationship with Tina, especially about their interaction in August 1979. Gillen had emphysema and could not travel to Westminster, and the prosecutors wanted to refute my allegations that Tina had arranged the killing through her Las Vegas mob connections. Phone records had been introduced revealing that Tina Marco phoned Jay Gillen on August 29, 1979, the day Mary Ruth Myers was murdered. They had spoken for thirty-six minutes. In her testimony, Tina said she only chatted with Gillen about unimportant matters but never mentioned Mary Ruth Myers' death. I had no proof, but I could not be prevented from arguing this point. The prosecution needed to dampen this speculation.

The judge, prosecutor Frank Coleman and a State Trooper picked me up at my house in downtown Baltimore at 6 a.m., and we went to the Essex airport where a small, new, white six-passenger State Police Cessna airplane awaited us for the 2,400 mile, 12-hour flight.

Frank sat on his own, working on his potential cross-examination of Robert Myers. This amused me since it would be wasted effort in that I would never let Myers take the witness stand. Frank was a thorough, sharp lawyer who had lived with this case for over two years, and Myers was way too much of an idiot to survive the prosecutor's questioning. We were flying low, within sight of land the entire time and so the judge and I busied ourselves in the back seats with a map of the country, picking out landmarks as we followed Route 50 almost the entire way there.

The plane was not pressurized, so that when we got to a higher altitude over the Rockies we were forced to use oxygen masks. At one point, the Judge Burns needed to urinate and since there was no bathroom, this could only be accomplished by peeing into a tube. He asked me to excuse him while he knelt on the floor facing towards the stern. I stood behind him and told him that he did not look very judicial in that position and that he should put the robe on which he had brought with him to conduct the deposition. One of the reasons I really liked Luke Burns was because he did not take himself too seriously, and seemed to enjoy my humor.

We had to set down three times in small airports to get gasoline on the way there. When we flew over the Grand Canyon, the sun was setting. The beauty of the 200 miles of the Colorado River stretched beneath us and was awe-inspiring. The judge looked at me and said, "Should I tell them to bank?" I responded that he was the judge and that he should. The State Police co-pilots did not need any encouragement and gladly complied, banking the plane slowly from side to side for 50 miles or so at a couple of thousand feet. Glorious.

Three undercover officers from the Las Vegas Metro Police Department met us at the McClaren Airport in the Hughes Air Terminal. They were in two cars and had been waiting to meet the aircraft for three hours.

I was the first out of the plane and a man approached asking "Mr. Jones?" Since I had only imagined that organized crime was involved, not believing it at all and not understanding that this had triggered extra security to protect us, I had forgotten that we were traveling under assumed names. This undercover police agent looked befuddled when I said "no." The others then got out of the plane and responded appropriately. We all stayed at the Marina Hotel near the Tender Trap, a strip tease bar, owned by the witness, Mr. James Gillen, Tina's ex-husband. The Las Vegas Police Department had reserved three single rooms for us, listed under the name "Hoyt Jones," for security reasons. Each person was allotted $17 per day for meals.

It had been decided that Judge Burns would spend one evening with each of the lawyers. On the first night, he and I visited Jay Gillen's bar, and Gillen had a drink with us. He was quite likeable, but it was a little awkward since the strippers were dancing very near us, clad only in G-strings and tassles. They were quite aggressive, quite provocative, and quite naked. While I was not particularly comfortable with the place, the judge was clearly out of his element. I reflected that he was a long way from his Jesuit orientation.

We soon left and went to Caesar's Palace to get supper. We were seated in one of the very fancy, expensive, restaurants there, staring at menus, which detailed entrées for $75 a piece. After several minutes, before we had ordered, I asked Judge Burns if he really wanted to spend that much on a meal and he shook his head. We felt trapped but we had not yet ordered, so I suggested that we find a cheaper place. The other patrons and the staff seemed to wonder why we were leaving so soon and we tried to look like we were not cheap skates as we skulked out.

The four-hour deposition was to take place at the Las Vegas Police Department the next day, and I needed to spend some time preparing for it. Not only did I want to prove the trip justifiable and worthwhile, but I also wanted to interrogate Gillen and get as much information about Tina as I possibly could so that I could be fully prepared for her cross-examination. I knew that he could be a critical part of the case.

I was able to go on a "fishing expedition" with Jay Gillen to find out all I could about Tina's background. There was no jury present, so the Judge gave me a lot of latitude. Gillen said that there were two Tina Marcos. One side of her was thoughtful, intelligent, and considerate, a woman who was kind to her husband and children and friends. However, she was also an extremely moody, vindictive woman hooked on material possessions. "You couldn't want someone more and you couldn't want to run from someone more. It all depends on which shoe she was wearing."

When he was asked about his telephone conversations with Tina around the time of the murder, Gillen said Tina did not discuss the killing. "I pooh-poohed it. What interest in it did I have?" he asked. Gillen also called it "preposterous," the accusations that he was involved with the killing. "I don't know, or never have known, anyone in organized crime," he said. Jay Gillen stated that Tina had married Lee Hazelwood, the famous songwriter who wrote "These Boots are Made for Walking," in a Mexican ceremony in the late 1960s. The marriage was later ruled invalid because the couple never properly registered it in California, where they were living at the time.

Gillen also explained how Tina had a baby in April of 1973 which he believed was his, and then she later gave it up for adoption. Gillen said Tina gave the baby to an adoption agency because she could not do an adequate job with the two that she already had. He stated that she had received several thousand dollars for the baby. She was an inveterate gambler and could never hold onto money for any length of time.

At one point on the plane ride home, we stopped to refuel someplace in Kansas. Frank went ahead of us into the tiny office. I whispered to Judge Burns quietly, "You know what's going to happen don't you?" He responded, "What do you mean?" I repeated, "You know what's going to happen!" He replied loudly, "I never told you what I would do!" I said, "Do what you want to do, if you want to kill him . . . kill him!" We both understood that I meant Myers would be convicted by the jury, and after that, I would elect to have Judge Burns decide the punishment, rather than risk having the jury decide life or death.

I was dropped off at my house at about 10:00 p.m. and the trial was scheduled to resume in Westminster, an hour away, the next morning at 10:00 a.m.

When I got to court the next day, I was exhausted. I had gotten little rest. I'd been woken up by my 9-month-old son and he did not easily go back to sleep. I was greeted by a smiling Tom Hickman, who explained that there would be no session that day because Frank Coleman was ill, suffering from a gastrointestinal virus. I was angry that I had not been called so that I could have avoided this extra wasted commute to Westminster. I returned home. The more I thought about Hickman smiling, the sicker I got . . . so the next day, when court was supposed to continue at 9:00 a.m., I telephoned the Judge's chambers and when Judge Burns asked me what was wrong with me I explained that "I think I have the same thing that Mr. Coleman had yesterday." The Judge said, "Okay, we will resume the case tomorrow." I needed the day to recuperate; after all, Hickman had not traveled with us and had looked like he was well rested and full of energy.

The newspaper reporters were annoyed that they had no copy for the three days we had been in Las Vegas, the fourth when Frank was sick and the fifth when I was "sick." Judge Burns had convened court simply to make that announcement and to state that "we were not gallivanting in the West" and "it was not a pleasure trip." I do think most of us enjoyed it, however.

The videotaped testimony of Jay Gillen corroborated several aspects of Tina's testimony and was played to the jury when court resumed the next day.

*****

Tina was the 19th prosecution witness, and her direct examination was a perfect repeat performance, duplicating her testimony in Garrett County. She had been supplied with her initial statement, the statement she gave in Oakland and her testimony there. She had studied these materials well, knowing that I too had copies of them.

Hickman had asked her, "Do you see the man you have been referring to in this courtroom today?" And after a slight hesitation she raised her right hand and pointed toward Robert Myers. "The blonde haired gentlemen," she said, and then sighed heavily.

Tina's appearance had attracted more and more spectators. The public began to show up as early as 6:45 a.m., although court did not commence until 10 a.m. By lunch time, 75 people were in line, hoping to obtain a seat for the afternoon proceedings. The line, which ran about 60 feet, was roped off by blue crêpe paper, stretched across a series of traffic cones. Sheriff's deputies turned away dozens of spectators at the courtroom door.

Now that Tina was no longer pregnant, she could not resist dressing up in a stylish dark pant suit. She was adorned with jewelry. Tina was enjoying being the center of attention and she sighed deeply and often. When she dramatically pressed her hand to her forehead, her gold wristwatch sparkled under the overhead lights. It was worth $3,200. She enjoyed displaying her gold earrings, knowing that they jiggled when she moved her head. This was her premier performance and she was wearing more than $8,700 in jewelry.

On cross-examination, I confronted her about this display. As she sat on the witness stand, the light above her made it look as though she was a Broadway star. I requested that she hold up her hands to show the jury the expensive rings and watch that she was wearing, and then asked her to describe each and how much they had cost. At first she seemed to enjoy doing so. She had gold inlaid rings with diamonds and opals. After I had confronted her with the fact that she had recently been on welfare, she realized she had made a mistake by dressing so expensively.

The next day when I continued my cross-examination, I said, "I notice you are not wearing your rings this morning." She replied forcefully, "I was told not to wear them!" I followed up with questions about who had told her not to dress so expensively, glaring over at the prosecutors. On this day she looked frumpy and unattractive. She had to admit that the prosecutors had discussed this with her and had directed her to "dress down."

She was clearly angry with me, not only because she never responded well to being confronted but also because the deputies from the Carroll County Sheriff's office had seized her expensive jewelry the previous evening. She had amassed more than $6,000 in unpaid bills for medical treatment and "her housing" during the previous year. The County Commissioners had responded to the intense press coverage about her new wealth and wanted reimbursement for her "room and board." It was later determined that this seizure of "her" personal property was illegal and everything was returned to her.

Tina's cross-examination was going to require all my skill, and I knew she could not be destroyed as a witness, only somewhat damaged and made to look untrustworthy and totally unlikable. She was clever, worldly and resourceful. After all, she was now wealthy and was getting away with murder. Her direct testimony did not deviate in any material way from her previous accounts.

Fortunately for the defense, Tina was a prolific letter writer. I had assembled several law students to review the more than 100 letters Tina had written, with instructions to extract phrases I could use on cross. I used the same band of volunteers to review the hundreds of pages of logs made by the state police which summarized the wiretapped phone conversations, to look for similar information.

Tina was not expecting this line of attack. She was forced to make many admissions that made her look bad. She admitted that she had hoped to make at least a quarter of a million dollars from a book detailing her life and the contract killing. She had written to her friend Charlotte Horton saying that "her attorney Phil Sutley" was negotiating the contract. In addition, he was working to get her a guest appearance on Good Morning America, People Are Talking and Phil Donahue. She said she planned to publish a book in December while the details of the crime were "still fresh."

She was forced to answer some more personal and intimate questions. She said it pained her "very much" that Myers was facing the possibility of being executed. I produced a letter she had written to her father in July, on stationary on which was printed a drawing of a chaplain leading a man to the gas chamber. Tina only said that the writing paper was only a joke.

In another letter to a girlfriend she said that she liked the attention of the flirtatious jail guards and said "When this is over, you and I will get these guys, go get drunk, smoke all your pot and screw all night." Her testimony brought laughter from the spectator's gallery, and several of the jurors, while others had trouble concealing their smiles.

I introduced several photographs of naked men which had come from her wallet. "Why did you have pictures of naked men?" "I like to look at them," she replied. "And you like to blackmail them, don't you?" "No," she said.

Tina admitted that she had been irritated when a friend wrote to her that certain unnamed movie makers were planning a motion picture about her starring Tanya Tucker. "Tanya Tucker? Am I that ugly?" She told the jurors, "I didn't think I looked at all like that person." It certainly looked like she was enjoying herself, and that this was all some kind of meaningless game.

Her responses to my questions were sometimes evasive, but she knew she had to basically tell the truth, while she attempted to shade the facts to make her look as good as possible. "There is no question in your mind Mrs. Myers, is there, that you are guilty of first-degree murder?" I asked her. She responded, "I'm not sure about the law." I then asked, "What do you think you are guilty of?" "I feel that so what happened, I am just as guilty. I am guilty for being part of it." She said. I responded "That would make you guilty of first-degree murder then, according to the State?" Tina responded calmly, "Yes."

For two days, Tina had been calm as she coolly and dispassionately described the killing. On the third day, at one point however, she broke down and had to be led from the courtroom in tears, after reading love letters she had sent to Robert Myers. Some of the letters I read to her, and others I handed to her and requested that she read them to the jury. She had been somewhat detached during her direct examination but these letters discredited her and made her look treacherous. In one letter on December 8, 1981, Tina had renewed her marriage vows, saying she would love Myers "Till death do us part. Regardless of any legal problems, I feel that I am still married to you and no one will ever replace you in my heart. You are every breath I take and no one else will ever do."

In a letter dated February 5, 1982, she wrote, "I can see we live and breathe for the same thing; being together. I love you with all my heart darling and that won't ever change." As she read this letter, she trembled and her face flushed. When I asked her if she recalled writing the letter, she could barely answer. She began crying and had to be led from the courtroom again, tears streaming down her cheeks. Myers, sitting less than 10 feet away, was tight lipped and appeared close to tears himself.

When the two had been transferred to Oakland for pretrial hearings, she had written to him every day, sometimes several letters a day, and she got the jail guards to carry her letters to Myers, who was being held in a different section of the same jail. "Hang in there baby, and know I'm with you with all my heart and soul," she wrote on March 15, a week before the plea-bargain. "Sorry we can't share the same room. Those fruitcakes better keep their hands off of you or I'll call in all my hit men. Ha. Ha." She had written two days before the trial, signing the letter, "Your loving wife, Tina." I asked her, "That was just a joke?" She replied, "Bob and I often joked about that." "At this point the joke was on him wasn't it?" I quipped.

24 hours before she agreed to testify, she wrote to Myers, "You are my world Bob Myers. Sweet darling, there is no getting around it . . . Your face is what I see in my dreams."

She sniffled and clutched at a facial tissue and wept softly as I read to her the tender words she had written four hours before she agreed to betray him. On March 23, 1981, Tina repeatedly told him in the letter that she loved him: "Good morning, Bobby Myers. I sure wish you could've been here next to me all night. I love you. You are the only man I will ever love and you are my best friend." She called him the "father of my children." "Do you recall writing that?" "Yes," she said softly, her face flushed and her eyes red. "And then some four hours later, according to your testimony, a deal was offered to you that you could not refuse." "Yes," Tina said, even more softly her voice breaking.

Robert Myers sat grimly looking on as she acknowledged the steady stream of love letters that she had written to him.

Tina described how she had converted a sitting room into a large walk in cedar closet. She kept her furs, jewelry and Myers' gun collection there. Only she had a key to it, and no one else was allowed in there. Tina said that Mary Ruth "had a lot of costume jewelry," but that all of Tina's jewelry was genuine. She bragged that Myers kept buying her jewelry. "It was a monthly, almost a weekly thing." I foolishly asked her "You're very fond of jewelry aren't you? Her quick and obvious response was, "Most women are!"

I showed her photographs from her wedding in Bermuda and asked her whether or not she had been married in a white dress. She responded "No, it was off-white." I stated "Off white, uh,huh!" The spectators in the courtroom and the jurors burst into laughter.

She had written to her parents on June 30, 1982: "I know you and daddy still find it hard to believe, but I hope you two have really thought about it. I was very happy with Bob, he gave me anything I wanted and in my eyes he was perfect. And at times I sit for hours and wonder how it would have been, if I'd kept my mouth shut. I'm confused most of the time, and I think all of the times people had hinted he was running around—it hurts and hurts bad. I guess I really don't owe him anything. I wouldn't lie about anything like this and I know because Bob was so highly reputable and wealthy that most people just can't believe it, but I swear it's true and I look at my own four children and that it could have been me." Mary Ruth also had four children.

In a July 5th letter to the same friend, Tina wrote, "I never dreamed I'd be sitting in jail. I spent Christmas, New Year's, Valentine's Day, Easter, Mother's Day, all of my children's birthdays and my own as well (all for the love of a man) in jail." She continued "there are a couple of really cute guards that come in and flirt. At first I cried because it upset me (constantly thinking of Bob) but now I guess because I have no ties to anyone I'm starting to enjoy the attention. One just started, he has blond hair, is about 6 feet tall, has a nice body, and is only 24. He's really sweet—is a little young, though who knows (keep your mouth shut)."

Tina admitted on the stand that she was having a love affair with this 24-year-old guard at the jail named Roger White. "He lights your cigarettes for you, does favors for you, doesn't he?" I asked. "Yes," she responded. "Most of them, the jail guards, do."

In a July 13 letter to Charlotte, Tina wrote, "I wrote Radio Bible Class in May and asked if they would put Bob on the mailing list, explained he was facing the death penalty and that I was expecting our second child. I told them I read their "Our Daily Bread" every day and it was helping me get through this painful ordeal, and that perhaps it could help Bob, too. I feel that since he won't write me and isn't interested, anyway, there's no point in me worrying about him any longer. I wish him the best, but I have to get on with my life and so does he. I'm getting sick to my stomach. Just the thought of looking at Bob and having to tell what I know."

In a July 26 letter to her parents, Tina complained about the newspaper coverage: "I got a stack of clippings the other day," she wrote. "Really making me out a cold bitch, aren't they? If only they knew I had feelings too."

Tina denied my contention that she had supplied Chadderton with a key to Myers' house. She continued to maintain that she had ended up in Washington D.C. after getting lost on her drive from Ocean City to Westminster, just after the murder. I had suggested that she actually met Chadderton during the three hours in which she claimed she had been lost.

There was still much to cover on cross examination:

- Tina had a juvenile record for theft,
- Tina engaged in a credit card "flimflam" in California for which she had received a prison sentence,
- she had been a prostitute in California and in Las Vegas,
- she had lied on several occasions to social welfare agencies regarding her domestic and financial affairs,
- she had deliberately started a false rumor that the State's Attorney had asked her several times for a date, the only purpose of which was the disqualification and embarrassment of the prosecutor.

Tina admitted that she had a "very close" and "intimate" relationship with Chadderton, and said she had stopped dating him several months before the killing. However, she admitted to stopping by The Pantry Pride store on August 12, 1979, two days after Robert Myers had bought her a new car. This was helpful to the defense because I had alleged that once she had her "plump pigeon," she conspired with Chadderton to kill both Myers and his wife in order to get the rest of his money and his estate. "After you had your car, you, on your way to Ocean City, you just happened to think of him, and you just happened to drop in? Did you tell him about the new fellow you had?" She responded, "I was very proud of my new car, and I felt he could appreciate the fact that I had gotten a better car." "I imagine he asked you about the new guy who bought you the car?" She answered, "actually, he wished me a lot of luck." "I'm sure he did," I responded. "You knew that Chadderton planned to assassinate Mrs. Myers didn't you?" She said, "I think it was in the back of my mind." I said, "you knew someone was going to die and you were able to push it into the back of your mind? Do you suggest your credibility is to be trusted?" She said "Yes."

Before the beginning of the resumption of the trial, her third day on the stand, nearly 100 spectators—some from as far away as Pennsylvania—started lining up in the hallway. One woman standing in line was heard to say, "Why stay home and watch *The Young and The Restless* when you can watch it here?"

Tina had a record with the identification division of the FBI under different names. On January 2, 1969, "Dana Layne Richards" had been charged with being a vagabond and loitering with the possession of burglary tools. She was also arrested under that name in Las Vegas, Nevada on September 24, 1969, for the possession of dangerous drugs. "Ernestine" had been arrested on January 19, 1972 in Los Angeles, California for passing a check knowing she had insufficient funds to cover it.

Despite hours of damaging personal attacks, for the most part she remained calm and answered questions in a soft, controlled voice. But when I introduced another photograph from the wedding, her cool demeanor seemed to finally crack. I showed her the snapshot taken on September 18, 1979, which depicted Tina dressed in a wedding gown clasping her hands in prayer. I asked her to read the inscription scribbled on the back of the photograph and she looked startled, and her eyes welled up with tears. Finally, after a long pause, she read the inscription in a soft halting voice. It read: "Dear God, Please Bless this forthcoming marriage till death do us part. I love this man. Amen."

A photograph of her fifth husband, James Marco, on which was written "The Godfather" was the subject of a different line of cross examination. Hickman had

Tina simply explain that Marco was the godfather of her two oldest children, but I used it to further my contention that she was an untrustworthy liar. Tina did not deny my allegations that she had used the photograph to intimidate men who bothered her, when she was working as a barmaid. She finally agreed that she had been lying when she told customers that Marco was a Godfather who watched over her.

I questioned Tina about statements that she had made to Myers, that while she was living in Nevada, she had been involved or had knowledge about individuals who'd been taken into the desert, murdered and buried. She simply denied it all and I had no independent proof.

Hickman was still trying to portray her as a loving mother, who felt remorse about her participation in the murder, and on redirect examination he introduced several letters that she had written after she had negotiated her agreement. "Well, they brought Bob here on Tuesday and he was placed next to my section in the Garrett County jail," Marco had written to a friend on April 23. "He wouldn't look or speak to me until last night, when we finally started talking. We talked from 8 p.m. until 2 a.m. He's hurting, all he can remember is our life together, and we both cried. In fact all I've done is cried. I know it's over, but God knows in my heart I love him and always will. Sometimes, I wish I was the one that was shot, I don't know how much God thinks I can handle, but I think I've reached my limit. Sometimes I just pray and pray."

Hickman asked her to explain the remark she had made previously in her direct examination, which I had not questioned her about. "What did you mean when you said that Myers "was not the goody two shoes that everyone thinks he is?" She responded "it wasn't just Mary Ruth that he wanted killed." The prosecutor asked "why do you say that?". She answered "Because I overheard Dan Chadderton and Bob discussing killing Cpl. Leete and yourself!" I immediately objected and moved for a mistrial. We went up to the bench to place this objection on the record. Myers was then just 4 feet from where Tina sat on the witness stand. She looked straight ahead, ignoring him. Judge Burns instructed the jury to disregard Tina's testimony concerning Myers' plans to commit future murders.

Tina was excused from the courtroom and returned to a holding cell in the basement of the courthouse.

During Myers' trial, my mother, Peg and father, Charles traveled to Baltimore. My brother, Charles, was a member of a cast of five touring the U.S. with the Royal Shakespeare Company, an awe-inspiring galaxy of talent and unique programs, mostly of Shakespeare's scripts and plays. They were winding up their North American Tour at two Universities between Baltimore and Washington, DC. By coincidence, in the courthouse in nearby Westminster, this widely publicized murder trial was reaching its climax.

Even though people lined up early at the Courthouse each day to ensure entrance, and there was limited seating, I arranged through the Judge and the Sheriff's Deputies to get my parents seats in the front row of the spectator section. As I was cross-examining Tina, from time to time I glanced at them and recognized the pride they were taking in my performance. They were now listening to an actor in a vastly different field. My background had been so different from my brother's. Dealing with modern criminals is somewhat seamy compared to Shakespearean portrayals of human frailties. We were equally articulate and quick-witted. After my parents watched me perform in court, in the murder case, we all traveled to watch Charles perform with the Royal Shakespeare Company.

The next day, I continued to cross-examine Tina for hours. There was a cat and mouse feeling in the hushed courtroom with everybody on the edge of their seats not wanting to miss a word. Then we made a mad rush for a quick meal and then on to the University of Maryland's Baltimore County show. I was still feeling flushed and heady after the court case. It took only a short time to change gears and become fully engrossed in the "Hollow Crown" and the bloody history of Great Britain's royalty. Charles' performance was spellbinding. My father's adulation and raving was now for his eldest son. My brother looked ten feet tall on stage and had a masterful presence, a wonderful performer. This visit of my parents to see Charles and myself perform on stage and in court was a day for us all to remember.

The fact that my parents had been in court for a few days still cheering me on, after all these years seemed to highlight the early experiences and values which had been so carefully nurtured. Their presence made me reflective. I had not realized my childhood ambitions, to become The World

Heavyweight Champion or compete in the Olympics, so this competition would have to do. It would do just fine.

During the trial, a 21-year-old thief, Terry L. Romano, testified that Chadderton said, "You better tell that bitch Marco to keep her mouth shut or she'll get herself hung." Romano said Myers merely nodded during that part of the conversation. Myers shook his head and took notes as Romano testified. Romano said Chadderton had described the murder: "The way he took care of her was Bobby and Tina was supposed to have left the state—and Chadderton went up to the victim's house and asked where Bobby was. She turned up and went upstairs to make a bed and he turned up and followed her and took a pistol and shot her once and she said, 'My God, you're going to kill me," and he said 'If you know the Lord you'd better start praying,' and then he emptied the gun." Romano added that he is kept in maximum security at the jail because he won the reputation as a "snitch."

A second Garrett County Jail inmate, Thomas Bowman, testified the he overheard Myers and Chadderton discussing the murder while they were staying at the jail in the spring.

Bowman testified about an incriminating conversation between Myers and Chadderton that he overheard in March 1982, while all three were incarcerated in the Garrett County Detention Center. Bowman related to the jury that Chadderton told Myers that Tina is "going to have to be shut-up. She's going to have to be taken care of, got rid of before she made a 'deal" with the State's Attorney. Chadderton, Bowman said, went on to say that he could arrange to have a hired assassin "take care of this and shut her up" if Myers "came up with some money, twenty or thirty thousand dollars." Meanwhile, according to Bowman, Myers stood by silently and nodded his head up and down. Bowman narrated that he heard Myers interject, "I know we shouldn't have gotten into this mess to begin with . . . I know we shouldn't have called her there to the house . . . I know they'd know it was me." Chadderton then allegedly replied, "Well, that's the only place I could get a clean shot at her. That's the only place without any witnesses or anything that I could do." Following that remark by Chadderton, Robert Myers, Bowman testified, just looked at Chadderton without saying anything. Myers then said, "I'll call and see if I can get some money together."

Bowman said he was approached by a State Police investigator just two days before jury selection. Cpl. Leete told him that he knew he had overheard Myers and Chadderton talking. He said he had agreed to testify in exchange for immunity from charges of withholding information. He was serving an 18-month sentence for larceny and weapons charges, and facing the possibility of being sent back to prison for violating parole on a 16-year sentence he had received in 1973.

I suggested to him on cross-examination that he would do anything to get out of jail, and when he said that was not true, I made him acknowledge that he had glued his eyes shut with "super glue." He denied it was just a ploy to get out of jail, and when I asked, "If you weren't attempting to get out of jail by doing that, then why on earth did you do it?" Bowman explained that he had marital problems on-and-off and he was always in fear of his wife leaving with his children. As he gazed out of the jailhouse window one day, he said he happened to see his family. "I see my wife and kids and her new boyfriend, who was supposed to be my best friend," Bowman said. "I just couldn't stand it anymore. So I took the superglue and poured it into my eyes," he said. He had recovered, and the glue did not permanently damage his eyes.

Bowman also testified that Chadderton had tried to break his way into the women's section of the Garrett County Jail where Marco was being held. He said Chadderton broke into the ceiling and pulled out some ductwork in an attempt to crawl through to the women's side. After he tore them out, he found he couldn't get through.

Chadderton's remarks concerning the need to eliminate Tina as a witness were admissible to show Myers' reactions to the assertions. By nodding in the affirmative, Myers adopted Chadderton's remarks as his own. A declaration by an accused that he intends to intimidate or procure the absence from the trial of a State's witness is admissible as evidence of the accused's guilt. Myers, by his silence, also acquiesced in Chadderton's declaration that the marital residence of Myers and Mary Ruth was the only place he could "get a clean shot at her."

Myers had explained to the police that he thought that this was a burglary because various items were missing from his home. He had first described some guns which were missing, but later recalled that some of them had been sold, but he said that there was packet of $2,700 in cash wrapped in tissue. It was missing from its hiding place under some towels in the bathroom at his home at the time Mary Ruth was murdered. No one had believed Myers about the missing cash—no one believed that it was a burglary.

I requested the opportunity to review all the items that had been taken from the murder scene by the police, including a red overnight suitcase that was being held at the State Police barracks in Westminster. When I went over there, the police were incredibly aggressive and hostile to me, though I had no idea why. A huge State Trooper ordered me to sit down behind a desk and threw the suitcase on the desk and said, "Anything you touch in here, you will have to mark your initials on it." I was furious at the way I was being treated.

The suitcase was full of all kinds of sexual objects, pornographic movies, suck machines, every sex toy you can think of, and then some. This had been found by the bed where the victim had been shot to death. She had been in her bikini underwear at the time of her murder. In any event, as I went through the objects I discovered $2,700 dollars in one hundred dollar bills near the top of this suitcase.

I immediately called the State Trooper's attention to the money and wrote down the serial numbers of the bills. It became clear to me that the State Police had been so angry with me because they had intended to pocket this $2,700 in cash. The prosecutor never intended to put the suitcase into evidence—he knew it was irrelevant. So, after the case was over, the police would be able to simply remove the money. That was now impossible. The prosecutors knew nothing about this deception.

In any event, of course, when I got back to my office, I documented what had happened from the notes I had taken there. I was amused by the fact that the State Trooper said he was sorry that we had gotten off on the wrong foot. He knew that my discovery would soon be revealed.

In court, Leete had previously testified that Myers told him his new wife, Tina, would refuse to have sex with him whenever she found out he'd been talking to Leete. For that reason Myers had asked to meet him in his Westminster accounting firm office instead of the Silver Run home he shared with

Tina. "He told me that when Tina found out he talked to me, she would cut him off sexually," Leete testified.

It was in one of those conversations, shortly after the murder, that Myers suggested that Tina had arranged the murder. He was to continue suggesting that over the next couple of years. "He told me once again that Tina had been the one to do this alone," Leete testified about a later meeting.

Leete sought to keep his cordial and friendly relationship with the usually affable and talkative Myers—whom he almost immediately considered a suspect—"on a strict law enforcement basis." "In fact, I told Bob that the day would come when I would have to arrest him and testify against him in court," Leete said as he gazed at Myers, sitting a few yards away at the defense table.

During their conversations after the murder, Leete said Myers would always deny his own guilt and sometimes offer contradictory explanations of incriminating evidence that Leete would present. An example, Leete said, was Myers' explanation of how he allegedly knew how many times Mary Ruth had been shot at the same time that police were trying to keep that information secret.

First, Myers told him one person told him this detail, and then changed the source to another after Leete checked the first one out. And finally, Leete testified, "He told me that whoever told me that he said Mary Ruth was shot nine times was lying." Leete was a calm witness, with a cool demeanor. He had, though, on a couple of occasions, lost his composure when he interpreted some of Myers' remarks as an offer to bribe him. "He asked me what it would take to get me off his back, and I interpreted from the tone of his voice that he was attempting to bribe me. He then said that if he knew a professional, that he would have me done in, have me hit." Leete further testified that he attempted to isolate Myers, Marco, and Chadderton—the three suspects—and tell them different stories is an attempt to win their cooperation.

For example, Leete told Myers that Tina could be planning to kill him. "I would tell Bob that he should be careful of Tina," Leete said. "That's probably the only reason something wasn't happening to him, was because there was such intense police pressure." When he talked to Tina, he said, he advised her to cooperate and disassociate herself from the other two. "I think I told her something to the effect that she was on a sinking ship and if she wanted to get off, it was up to her," Leete said, "or she could go down with the ship."

He implied to Chadderton that he was getting information from the other two suspects. Leete testified that on one occasion a few days after the murder, Chadderton saw Leete and another State Trooper outside the Reisterstown Pantry Pride store where he worked. Leete asked him if he had a weapon in the car, and without prompting, Chadderton assumed the frisk position against the police car. Leete said he took advantage of the situation to search Chadderton, but he assured Chadderton he was not under arrest. Chadderton agreed to go with the troopers to the Westminster barracks for questioning. When they arrived there, Chadderton telephoned his wife to check on her progress in getting him a lawyer. At that point, Chadderton discovered that a State Trooper was there interviewing her and he became very agitated. Leete testified that Chadderton then angrily said he no longer would talk to them and wanted to leave. Leete said Chadderton strode to the door and stopped. "He asked me if I would give him a ride back to his car at the Pantry Pride," Leete said, adding that he gave Chadderton a lift.

When he was confronted with the money that had been discovered in the suitcase, Leete agreed that he had not believed Myers' claim that the money had been stolen. Leete testified, "I did not see the $2,700 laying in the top of the suitcase in the many times I went through it," Leete said. I asked, "I would imagine it came as a surprise to you, that is, finding the money?" and Leete said, "Yes sir, it did." The Corporal offered no explanation as to how the money suddenly appeared in the case that was being held in the State Police's custody for over three years. "There's an investigation taking place." Leete said it was under the direction of the barracks commander. I pulled a larger red suitcase from behind the clerk's desk, Leete sighed softly. He'd obviously seen the suitcase before.

I had set the red suitcase in front of Cpl. Leete and asked him to open it and describe the contents. With some difficulty, Leete opened the suitcase and paused for a moment as he delicately look through the items. He took a deep breath and said, "the suitcase contains pornographic films and various sexual devices such as vibrators, dildos, joy cream, etc. etc., etc., etc."

Maryland State Police officials said they have solved the mystery of the bundle of cash that turned up in an overnight bag more than three years after the bag was collected by police while investigating the murder of Mary Ruth

Myers. The money, $2,723 in cash, originally was hidden behind a mirror in the woman's overnight bag, said 1st Lt. Richard Janney, commander of the Westminster State Police barracks, where the property was inventoried. Janney said, "That's why it was overlooked when investigators collected the bag and other valuables. The money, wrapped in pink tissue paper, turned up September 13, 1982, one week before the start of the Myers trial. It was found inside the small bag at the Westminster barracks when the attorney for Robert Myers was looking through the property." "We did a full investigation and in our opinion, the man missed the money when he inventoried the property," Janney said. At some point during the transportation of the property, that mirror was jostled loose and fell out with the money behind it." Janney said he had no evidence to indicate the money ever had been stolen from the bag or that it was planted in the bag to embarrass the police investigation.

During Mr. Myers' trial in Westminster, Corporal James Leete said Mr. Myers had more than once suggested he wanted to have Leete murdered too. "There were times I was concerned about my safety around Mr. Myers," Leete testified Friday. The tall, veteran State Police officer was asked if he had been physically afraid of Mr. Myers. "I have no fear to face the defendants in this case," Leete responded. "It's when they're behind my back, sir, I worry about them." On Friday, his third day and final day on the witness stand, Cpl. Leete concluded reviewing for jurors the details of his investigation. He testified on Thursday that eight days after the murder, Mr. Myers had brought up the possibility that Tina Myers was involved in the killing.

Leete said Mr. Myers had told him he suspected her because the day before his wife was killed, Tina Myers had made a telephone call to her ex-husband in Las Vegas and had asked Mr. Myers to leave the room during the conversation.

Leete explained that James D. Palmer, a federal agent, testified that his investigation into Skip Botteron's death for the Bureau of Alcohol, Tobacco, and Firearms revealed that Tina had been a prostitute while in California, and she had worked as a prostitute for Mr. Botteron when she was 20 years old, before their marriage in 1971. The agent testified that she may also have worked on The Block when she first came to Baltimore in 1978.

Palmer testified on cross that Tina and Botteron had a bitter divorce after their 11-month marriage had ended, and Tina was extradited from Nevada by Californian authorities to face bad check charges. Botteron had supplied the information that led to these charges.

In order to get her out of the way, Skip Botteron gave information to Californian authorities about Tina's involvement in a check fraud scheme. She was arrested in Las Vegas and extradited to California to face the charges. Skip Botteron took custody of Tracey and Brad, Marco's children, and moved them back to California. Tina showed up a few months later "with two tough guys from Vegas" at a house in Turlock, California where the children were staying with one of Skip's friends. "She brought these two toughs from Vegas and demanded the children. She did not have to threaten Skip's friend. When you get two tough guys looking down your throat, you'll backup."

The bitterness of the divorce was one reason authorities wanted to question Tina about Botteron's death in Ceres, a community in central California. A bomb had exploded in his car, killing him instantly.

I showed Cpl. Leete a "little black book" that had belonged to Tina Myers. He testified that, "Most of the people I called in that book were not happy to hear from me." The small black address book contained the names, addresses, and telephone numbers of men Tina knew throughout the nation. He explained he obtained the address book from a car that Marco had abandoned in August 1979. As part of his investigation, he had visited many and had called most of the men in the book. I questioned him as to why, if he knew, Chadderton's name was not in the book? He had no response.

After Leete's testimony, two Westminster insurance adjusters testified Mr. Myers had submitted $18,000 worth of damage and loss claims resulting from the murder of his wife. The claims listed several items, including jewelry Mr. Myers had said was stolen from his home by his wife's killer. Police ruled out robbery as a motive because cash and other valuables had been left in plain sight at the murder scene. The insurance companies eventually paid Mr. Myers a total of $8,500 for his losses.

They testified that on October 2, 1980, Robert Myers was contacted again by the State Farm Fire and Casualty Company with reference to the personal property he had listed as either being destroyed or stolen from his property on August 28, 1979. Myers had submitted a detailed list alleging that guns and jewelry had been taken during what he termed was a robbery. He listed diamond cufflinks, diamond tie tacks, a pearl necklace, and an Indian jewelry necklace he said he had purchased in Shockey's restaurant. The casualty company had been in touch with the state police. Myers also made a claim for the damage to the house and the cleanup after the "robbery." He even included the king-size bed, the sheets, the bedspread, and the cost of cleaning the carpet. The insurance company requested more proof of the origins of these items. Myers claimed that several jewelry boxes containing items such as a diamond watch, six diamond rings, a marquee diamond ring, a small pinky ring with all diamonds, three Bulova diamond watches, and 14-karat gold Onyx earrings had been taken. Myers did not claim that any of these items were particularly expensive; in fact he wrote next to some of them, "(cheap)."

In the fall of 1979, Myers had also contacted the Equitable Life Assurance Society to cash in the $100,000 life insurance policy on Mary Ruth. They stalled payment pending the results of the State Police investigation.

On the stand, Trooper Andrew G. Mays said that eleven months after the murder, Myers had complained that he was not happy with Tina. In July 1980, Myers stated he was not going to make the same mistakes this time. He said Tina's name was not on the house or in his will. He said that "Myers was very jovial. There was some small talk and then he became serious and told the trooper he was not getting along with Tina and that he was not having the amount of sex he wanted. He was only getting sex twice every two weeks. He said he would have gone to the block if Tina didn't keep such close tabs on him." In a later conversation, he also suggested that when his 17-year-old daughter had run away in April 1981, she might have gone away with Dan Chadderton, but Myers had refused to discuss it any further.

On cross-examination, I asked Trooper Mays whether or not he had had a conversation with Myers about the people who were invited to a Christmas party. He confirmed that he had, and that some people had been specifically excluded. I asked him if Myers told him why Alan Fox, the lawyer who had helped Tina in the juvenile proceedings, had not been invited. Trooper Mays had obviously reviewed the reports that he had made in the case and knew that they had been turned over to me in discovery. He knew what was about to be revealed. He started to flush with embarrassment and I enjoyed his predicament. He responded, "Yes." I followed up with, "And what was that reason?" He answered, "Because he was one of the guys that Tina blew." I then said, "Blew? Blew? You mean orally gratified?" He responded yes. Everyone in the courtroom was quiet and as I looked at the jury, they seemed about ready to break into laughter. Just my way of keeping them amused, but more importantly, making Tina look as sexual and provocative as possible. Trooper Mays was relieved to step down from the witness stand.

Eleven wiretapped conversations were played to the jury. They were chosen from about 1,200 calls that were recorded from August 25, 1981 until September 24, 1981. The recordings were made under the supervision of Maryland State Police.

The jury was provided with transcripts to read as the tape of the conversation was being played. Six of the conversations were recorded from the telephone at Myers' home, and the remaining five were recorded from the two phones at Myers' accounting firm.

Wiretapped telephone conversations between Robert Myers and others did not directly implicate him in his wife's murder. In most of the eleven conversations. Myers indicated that his business and home phones were tapped, and he arranged to talk with the callers in person. The majority of the calls were recorded in September 1981, just two months before Myers was indicted for allegedly arranging the murder.

Several of the recorded phone calls showed the effect of Leete's investigation on Myers. Leete began investigating the case on the day of the murder. According to the Corporal's earlier testimony, he told Myers about 24 hours after the killing that he would probably be arrested for his wife's murder.

"I got my right mind and all from, you know, this past year. But they're trying to drive me back crazy again," Myers was recorded as telling a friend on September 5, 1981.

Two days later, wiretaps recorded Myers saying, "This is gonna drive me to drink. But I know that's the worst thing to do. That's what Leete want me to do. Bastard."

After 65 witnesses, the State rested.

CHAPTER 25:
THE DEFENSE CASE

"Be a good fellow . . . let me do the talking!"
— Rex Mottram Esq., Brideshead Revisited

In Maryland, character testimony is sufficient in and of itself to create a reasonable doubt, the idea being that someone who possesses a relevant character trait, is likely to act in conformity with that trait. He is therefore less inclined to have behaved otherwise and to have committed the crime. The character trait has to be relevant to the charges. For example, if it can be demonstrated that a person was nonviolent it would be less likely that that person would commit a violent crime. If an individual can be shown to be honest, it would be less likely that that person would commit a fraud or theft.

Character testimony can be developed through a witness' "opinion" or that witness' knowledge concerning the "reputation" of the accused for possessing that relevant trait.

When I was a Public Defender representing individuals accused of crimes of violence, they had often previously violated the law and did not have good reputations in the community. I never had much opportunity to use this kind of testimony. However, later when I served as the Chief Counsel of the Medicaid Fraud Unit of the Attorney General's Office I was responsible for the prosecution of healthcare professionals and learned the hard way just how effective character testimony could be. I arrogantly told a lawyer representing a thieving doctor that I would simply stipulate to the statements of the character witnesses he wished to call on behalf of his client. This physician/defendant that I was prosecuting had billed for "seeing" 230 patients in a nursing home during a five-hour period.

This lawyer, rejected any stipulations, and insisted on calling these character witnesses to the stand. A day and a half later I understood why. A cross-section of humanity was basically vouching for the accused, in effect saying that they did not believe he had committed the crime. They were patients, employees, fellow doctors, neighbors, friends and relatives. Some were nuns, some were young, some were older, and one was blind. They all testified that he was honest and truthful and law-abiding. The physician was acquitted and I had learned a valuable lesson.

I soon developed my own "character questionnaire" which I could send to prospective witnesses and thereby reduce the amount of time necessary to produce this powerful testimony. After a mass mailing and receiving their responses, I could select the best ones, arrange to meet all these folks en masse, prepare them generally for court and then interview them individually. These witnesses are allowed to give the basis for their opinion, including their knowledge of the defendant, to show their familiarity with him and give specific examples to explain the basis for their opinions.

I developed this dimension in some white collar crime cases to such great effect, that in one instance where I was representing a dentist, accused of overbilling, the Judge surreptitiously sent me a note "When are they serving the strawberries?" It was very much like a retirement banquet.

For Myers who had been law abiding and nonviolent, generous and truthful, likable and popular, it was easy to unite support for him in this fashion. This testimony can also be used sometimes to mitigate the sentence to be imposed.

In this case there was to be an added benefit. I had sent out a form letter with a questionnaire that had to be returned to me, I had then rented a hotel conference room, talked to everyone en masse and then interviewed each individually. In addition to saving time, it helped build "a team mentality."

Robert Myers was a friendly person, who liked to joke and make people smile. There were many people in Carroll County who could not believe that he was guilty of this brutal murder. Many were willing to testify on his behalf. I requested the character witnesses complete a five page questionnaire and return it to me. This was a cross-section of the community: business owners, clients, healthcare providers, fellow church members, old school mates, relatives and neighbors.

I gave a 30-minute speech to energize these 40 potential witnesses and create a team spirit on behalf of Bobby Myers. I explained the situation he was in, what they could expect from me, in Court and then on cross-examination by the prosecutor. I then read out a schedule that I had prepared, explaining that I would need about 20 minutes with each of them, individually, and that I did not want to waste their time so that they could leave and return at different times during that day and the next day.

I then took them into a separate room and interviewed them privately. I stressed to each of them that they were to tell the truth to me and on cross-examination. If they were asked what they had been told to say, they were to respond "The truth."

During this interview process, a precocious, tall and attractive 22-year-old woman, who was a friend of Myers' daughter, flirted with me. Her extra squeeze during our handshake provided a final clue. I decided she could be more useful to the case by meeting me in the evenings to help me release the pressure I was under, and later during the trial, she would often join me, late at night where I was staying at Lee's Motel. I followed my regular routine. After I left Court, for the day, I would get coffee and doughnuts, make notes on the day's proceedings, get supper, prepare for the next day's witnesses, and then invite her to my room. While we chatted I did my ablutions and then we had our adult play. She would then leave. I needed my rest and I slept well. I kept my mind on my priorities and winning the case was always paramount.

On one occasion, when my parents came to Westminster and stayed in the next room, my 22-year-old "petite amie" and I were forced to drive into the country so that we could have at each other in my car. She said "I feel as though I'm back in high school." Me too! And it hadn't been 3 years before, at least for me. I serenaded her with "I've got a couple more years on you baby, that's all, I've had more chances to fly, and more places to fall. It ain't that I'm wiser; it's only that I've spent more time with my back to the wall. And I've picked up a couple more years on you baby, that's all!"

At another meeting, I was giving half a dozen character witnesses last-minute instructions several days before the trial. Each one of them belonged to a church. All were Protestants. The Church of the Assembly of God and The Church of the Open Door seemed to be the most popular. They were all dressed casually in shorts and T-shirts and one of them asked me "How should we dress to go to Court?" I responded that they should dress like they were going to church. "This is the way we dress to go to church!" "Well dress like you're going to Court!" I immediately replied. I had not believed in any religion since my Chapel choir days, but I thought long pants at the least should be required to attend.

The defense case started with Marianna Wilhelm who was a cosmetologist in Westminster, and therefore knew a lot of people. She had been singing Bobby's praises in the community. I examined her at length knowing that after a few days my questioning of these witnesses would have to be curtailed somewhat. She testified he was nonviolent, honest, truthful and law-abiding. Each of these witnesses was allowed to describe any anecdotes or facts which led them to form the basis for their opinion. They were also allowed to discuss his reputation for these character traits and who they had discussed it with.

The defense produced 26 witnesses in all and most of them were character witnesses. Friends relatives and former clients of Myers who testified to his law abiding, honest, truthful and nonviolent nature.

Robert Kalman, Edward Bauerlein, Alan Becker, Herman Moffit, William Ebaugh, Paul Meyer, Andrew Shaw, John Hyde, Wayne Hatfield, Mary Schaefer, David Hess and others all testified in similar fashion. They were all well known in Westminster. Some added other helpful information, such as he always had a weakness for girls and women, and that in school and bar room situations he would always back away from any confrontation, physical or otherwise.

Some witnesses said that he seemed scared of Tina and that she seemed to dominate him. One particularly good character witness, Gilbert Abbott, was an ex-police officer.

Linda Charnock Hill, also testified that Bobby was mild mannered. In contrast, while she was negotiating with Tina to buy her car, Tina had threatened her with her Mafia connections and suggested that she should read the California papers, an apparent reference to the Botteron bombing murder.

Elsie Thomas, a Westminster businesswoman, also verified these positive character traits and said she was shocked when she learned he had married Marco in 1979. "I said, 'Bob, why did you marry her?' and he said, 'What would you do if you had a gun to your head?'"

Paul O. Meyer Jr., said he had known Myers since the first grade and that "In school he was a real likable person. Prior to this episode, I've never heard anything bad about him in the community." On cross-examination when Hickman asked what bad things he had heard about Myers concerning "This episode," Meyer seemed to get angry. "You've been putting out all kinds of stuff, he responded. "From the newspaper . . . Mr. Hickman said this, Mr. Hickman said that."

Several character witnesses reiterated that he was "A fool when it came to women and that he would shower women he fancied with gifts."

Melanie Haines, a county social worker from the Department of Social Services, explained that in November 1978 she was assigned to investigate the living conditions of Tina Myers' children.

Tina telephoned from Ocean City in July on one occasion explaining that she could not get back to Westminster for her scheduled appointment. On other occasions Tina broke her appointments without any notification at all. She was not trustworthy. When Tina had arrived at the children's school late in the month to pick them up she learned they had been moved to a Carroll County school. Mrs. Haines described the living conditions of Tina Myers from April through September 1979, while her children were in foster care, as meager and not adequate for them to live with her.

She testified that her agency was considering going to court to gain custody of Tina's two children because she seemed unable to provide for them. Melanie Haynes also told the court that Tina had disappeared for 10 days, leaving her son and daughter with a friend and not telling them where she was going, or if she would even return.

Tina Myers had met with Mrs. Haines twice in March 1979 to discuss her financial situation. The social worker told her the agency was considering going to court at that time to gain temporary custody of the children but decided to leave them with their mother. In April 1979, Tina Myers agreed to place the children in temporary foster care. During the 10 months they were in foster care, Tina Myers failed to show up or call to schedule visits with her children. She missed three of six appointments with the social worker.

In an August 7th court session Tina asked for her children back, but the County Department of Social Services sought to retain them because of Tina's financial situation. The Juvenile Master decided to keep the children in foster care for 30 more days. By her next court appearance on September 9th, it was observed that "Mrs. Gillen's situation had changed drastically", because by then she was living with Robert Myers in his $250,000 Silver Run Valley home. Master Speaks would not allow the children to stay there unless Tina was married. The Master gave social services 45 days to investigate living conditions at the home. During that time Mr. Myers and Tina got married.

After 45 days, it was decided the children would remain in foster care while being allowed to visit the Myers couple on the weekends to get used to living in the new environment. The social agency was reluctant to return the children immediately because of the publicity surrounding the murder. The children eventually went to live with Robert and Tina Myers full-time in February 1980.

Melanie Haines also said that Robert Myers told her of a continuing deeply romantic relationship with Tina after they were married. They danced and had romantic dinners at night and he bought her flowers almost every day. She said Tina on the other hand, told her she married Myers because, "Basically, it was Mr. Myers' ability to care for her and provide her with material things."

Haines was a good witness because she had kept detailed records and clearly did not approve of Tina. She elaborated by explaining that Tina had lied to her several times and had claimed she was getting back together with Jay Gillen. At another time Tina said a new boyfriend, Steve Sommers was going to help her care for the children. Tina also claimed she was waiting for a large money settlement from a law suit she had pending. When she had broken her appointments, sometimes she provided elaborate explanations for doing so and at other times, she simply did not show up. What was left unsaid was that while the children had a better home, an innocent victim had been murdered to provide it.

On cross-examination Mrs. Haines agreed that Tina Myers teenage son Bradley had problems in foster care because the boy had lied, cheated and stolen.

The defense recalled Corporal Sherman. Rather than developing exculpatory information on cross examination when he had testified in the State's case in chief, I preferred to recall him as a defense witness. All the wiretap logs and the 1,200 conversations themselves were offered into evidence. Four of these conversations were played by Cpl. Sherman to the jury. They all demonstrated that Tina was in complete control and dominated Robert Myers. It was my intent to demonstrate that Myers really had nothing to hide.

Myers had telephoned Chadderton on August 28, 1981: "Well, I gotta get there (home) as soon as possible, you know Tina," Myers said. "The minute I call and tell her I'm coming home she expects me home." "Did you tell her you were coming?" Chadderton asked. "Hell, no, not yet," Myers said. "I gotta call her, though." "All right," Chadderton said.

"Cause if she calls here and I ain't here, I catch hell again," Myers said.

"Okay, well call her and tell her you're going to stop with a client," and "you'll be on your way home", Chadderton said.

Myers said "Yeah, I'll have a beer or two. Maybe I can try and talk her into letting me pick her up some food, see, and I got an excuse to be late." "Okay," Chadderton responded.

During several telephone calls, Myers cautioned the other party and said he knew the line was tapped. "You know I got a lot to tell you, but I can't tell you over the phone," he told Chadderton in another conversation.

Myers complained about Cpl. Leete constantly. During a September 7, 1981 call to the mother of Sherrie Chadderton, he said, "And that damn state trooper went over to my wife in Bermuda over there and told her that Sherrie and I was having an affair and this kind of crazy shit." "She wasn't brought up like that," her mother said. "No, well I'm just trying to tell you, what the cops do and how they're trying to come between my wife and I," Myers said. "Oh, yeah, they figure you get one against the other, they'll say things they won't say other times," Sherrie's mother replied.

On another occasion, Myers lamented to Charlotte Horton, the owner of the boarding house, "Oh God, this is going to drive me to drink," Myers said. "But I know that's the worst thing to do. That's what Leete wants me to do." "That's exactly what he wants you to do," Horton said.

Myers said, "Well . . . I did meet Dan a couple of times, but not drinking. You know what I mean? But that didn't look good . . . We'd meet about court things and we'd meet at different places every time. Because the cops . . . but I didn't drink or anything," Myers continued. "Hell, I don't drink since I met that girl. But you, but you know even before I met Tina, I never fooled with any women, did I?"

In another conversation with Chadderton, Myers said "Leete told Tina you were blackmailing me . . . Can you believe it? Just because you help a friend without a job . . . People say this Leete's getting pretty desperate. He's been spending money for two years."

These conversations were played in open court on November 10th. The jurors were also supplied with transcripts so that they could read along and listen at the same time. The spectator section in the courtroom was hushed as everyone strained to hear what was being said by these co-conspirators. The next day was November 11, Veterans Day and the Court was in recess. I welcomed the break so I could work on my closing argument which would have to be delivered in a couple of weeks.

I recalled ATF Agent Palmer, who testified when he had interviewed Jay Gillen, he was told that Marco "boasted" about her prostitution activities. He quoted her as saying "You can't step on me. I've been all the way down. I've been a whore." My attempt to have him link Tina with her ex-husband Botteron's bombing murder was thwarted when the agent said that insufficient information was developed to charge Tina with that killing.

Tina's closest relatives came to court to testify against her and they didn't have anything good to say about her at all. The three Marco relatives had testified as defense witnesses for Chadderton. They all repeated their testimony that she had a history of lying and untrustworthiness.

Tina's 13-year-old son, Bradley, repeated that his mother, who had been married at least five times, used "a lot of different names." The boy also said she told him "I lie, lie, lie, lie, lie a whole lot." The youth testified forcefully for his stepfather. He referred to the formerly wealthy accountant as "Dad." "He acted to me more like a father than any other father I ever had."

Myers wept as the young boy read a letter he had written to him in the previous month. In it he chastised Mr. Myers for not writing him. He said he did not mind not making his school basketball team because "you wouldn't be there to see me." "I wish we could start everything over again," and concluded the letter signing it "Your son." Bradley also wrote a letter to me offering to testify in his stepfather's behalf, which I shared with the jury.

"I wouldn't mind being subpoenaed to let everyone know about my life with Bob," he said, reading the letter he had written in pencil on yellow paper. Bradley said that Bob loved his mother and that she had always treated him well. But he said, she had lied to him on several occasions. He said his mother told him his father "was part of the Mafia in Florida."

He said Tina had promised he could be in the wedding ceremony when she and Mr. Myers were married, but when they returned from a trip they were already married.

Before Bradley testified, I had taken him into the Courtroom a few days earlier to make him feel more comfortable. I had put him on the stand and had a dress-rehearsal with him. He was a compelling witness. Bradley described how he had found cocaine in his mother's room. She had talked about Dan Chadderton a lot. Once they started to live with Bobby, Chadderton was around all the time. He described how Tina was quite secretive and had converted a closet into a room for herself. Only she had a key to it. It contained clothes, guns and jewels. Bradley said that Bobby sometimes acted scared.

Judge Burns had requested the child not be identified by name out of court to protect him from the taunting of classmates. The youngster, who hugged Myers on his way out of the court during a recess, told of his love for the man with whom he had lived for two years. Bobby encouraged the youngster to do his homework. He recounted the good times together, including fishing trips: "You caught them and told mom I did." Some of the jurors appeared near tears as the engaging youngster read the lengthy letter.

Ernest Butcher, Tina Myers' father, was the next witness for the defense.

He testified he had not been able to control Tina since she was about 15. He said she got into trouble with the law and ended up in a juvenile home. He said he agreed to her marrying a 19-year-old when she was 15 because he said she was out of control and had kept threatening to run away. He said the marriage lasted a week. "I don't think you can believe a word she told you" Butcher said. He had traveled from his California home for this appearance in court. "She just lies all the time." He said she could be a convincing liar. "Talk to her and you'll believe everything she says within five minutes." Butcher said that when he learned Marco had asked his brother, Carmen Butcher, for help some years later in Florida, he tried to warn him "that if you continue to help her, you'll have the same problems."

Ernest Butcher was a slender, sad-looking television repair man in his early 50s. He spoke about his daughter without the slightest trace of affection in his voice. "I wouldn't believe anything she said," he repeated, adding she'd been a compulsive liar since she was 10. He was not angry, but whatever love he once felt for his daughter had long since vanished. "I got letters from her all the time saying she wasn't guilty right up to the night she turned State's evidence. She always made sure she protected herself." He described how he and Tina's mother separated when she was 3 ½ years old and he had remarried 18 months later. His testimony was terse and lasted only 15 minutes, but this melancholy individual gave the lasting impression he never wanted to see or hear from Tina again.

Carmen Butcher, Tina's uncle, was next and testified that he soon had big problems when he took Tina into his house. She lied and stole from him, and finally he had to kick her out. In turn, he said he tried to warn James Marco, a Florida plumber who eventually married her. "I told him, you don't know what you're getting into" Butcher said. "He couldn't see it any other way. He was crazy about her."

It was unprecedented in my experience to have such close family members castigate someone in this fashion. These people presumably had known her the longest, and better than anyone else.

Thomas Stansfield, Myers' attorney for his civil matters, testified as to his assets in August 1979, and how by the time of the trial Myers had been bankrupted by lavish spending on Tina. He said that there had been an assignment for the benefit of creditors on December 4th, and that he and Sutley suddenly had powers of attorney. They conducted the auction. At one point Myers was worth $1.6 million and now he was $150,000 in debt. He only had one suit. Stansfield testified that he had set up a safety deposit box in Pennsylvania, but that Tina had control of it.

He was a totally believable witness. He was quite prissy and proper and favored conservative bow ties. He described the rumors he had heard regarding the number of shots that had killed Mary Ruth, thereby providing an explanation as to how Bobby knew so soon there had been 9 shots. This point had been stressed several times in the State's case. Stansfield explained that the information had been discussed "all over town" and that he had told Bobby about it at Mary Ruth's funeral.

He testified that Chuck Holman had told him that there were nine shots and that Holman said he had asked Cpl. Leete. He said that Diane Babylon had told him that it was nine shots. Her husband, Guy Babylon, was one of the gravediggers.

Next, I called Dr. Rudiger Breitenecker, the associate pathologist at the Greater Baltimore Medical Center who had reviewed the autopsy performed by the Medical Examiner. He had contested Dr Ann Dixon's conclusions as to the time of the death. Based largely on Mary Ruth's body temperature at that time, he concluded she probably died after 6.00 a.m. His testimony was important because Hickman had based his entire case on the fact that she was murdered much earlier, at least before 4 a.m. The doctor said he had performed about 3,000 autopsies in his career and that the victim's body temperature was 92° at the time of the autopsy. It could only have reached that level if she had died more recently than the State contended.

I knew that Orrin Brown had disputed the time of Mary Ruth's death in Chadderton's trial and that it was critical to his alibi defense. It was not important to our defense whether the victim died at one time or another, but I wanted to cast any doubt that I could on any prosecution theory.

The time of death was not relevant to the argument that he was only "an accessory after the fact." However, since there was no real downside, this was helpful testimony since it tended to question the reliability of the State's case in general. The prosecution had produced telephone records showing a call was placed from Chadderton's house at 5:20 a.m. to where Tina and Bobby were staying. It was during that call that the State contended that Chadderton told the couple he had murdered Mary Ruth.

Myers did not testify in his own behalf. If he had testified the prosecutors could have asked him to explain much of the States' evidence and he would have failed to do so miserably. I had attempted a practice session with Myers to prepare him for cross examination by the state. I started with the old "trick" question, "Have you ever discussed this case with your lawyer?" Myers responded "No!" I then stopped and I asked him why he had said no to that question and he said, "What do you want me to say?" I told him to just tell the truth.

I then asked Myers why he had appeared at Angelo's restaurant in Westminster with Tina on his arm three days after the murder, information I was sure the state knew. Myers looked at me, confused and said, "I didn't, did I?" I didn't need to waste anymore of my time. He was an uncontrollable and un-coachable witness.

In 1981, in another classic example of art paralleling life, my brother, Charles had appeared in the extremely popular BBC series *Brideshead Revisited*. He played Rex Mottram, a Canadian lawyer who moved to London and married Julia. My brother's character was central to the plot and in one episode he was required to go to a local police station to represent Sebastian, who had been arrested. The aristocratic protagonist was drunk and giving the local constables a piece of his shallow mind. My brother rather artfully said to his client "Be a good fellow. Let me do the talking!" I often shared this advice with clients, and it was particularly critical in this case.

The last jury trial I prosecuted in 1973 appeared on the docket as a routine rape case. The name Norman Winegan meant nothing to me. One could never rely on the accuracy of the information available about cases or defendants in this pre-computer era, and the crush of preparing cases for trial did not allow for non-critical research. I called the case for trial before Judge Charles D. Harris, who was my "home judge" in that I was responsible for all the criminal cases prosecuted in his court.

Winegan had accosted the victim, an 18-year-old Morgan State College student, who was waiting for a bus in downtown Baltimore. He had threatened her and forced her to walk 3 miles to an apartment, where he raped her and forced her to perform oral sex. He then took two dollars from her and let her go. He had threatened to kill her with his gun, but he never showed it to her.

Once she was allowed to go free she made a prompt complaint to the police. She was traumatized by what had happened to her. She was crying and screaming as she attempted to describe her assailant. She kept washing her mouth out and needed medication to calm her down.

Four months later, Winegan telephoned the victim at the movie theater where she had told him she worked as a ticket seller. Two other employees testified that Winegan or someone who looked just like him had come by the theater and asked for the victim. He said he wanted to return the two dollars to her. She was frightened and astounded to hear from him. An arrangement was made for a meeting and then the victim called the police, who staked out the area where they were supposed to meet, and arrested Winegan.

The States' witnesses were all compelling, and this freshman college student who had been victimized was particularly sympathetic and believable. Defense counsel informed the court that he needed more time to determine whether or not his client would testify. The court clerk asked me if I knew that Winegan had been prosecuted on a previous occasion for rape and perverted practice. I didn't, but I thanked him profusely for the information. The investigating officer and I scrambled to locate any information on this other case. After two hours reviewing files in the clerk's office we came across it. Winegan had indeed been convicted before, but his case had been reversed on appeal, in a reported opinion. I rushed to the law library and made a copy of it on the old mimeograph machine there. The factual scenario in the reported case was identical to the scenario I had just presented to the jury. A 17-year-old girl had been walking on a downtown street in Baltimore, when Winegan accosted her, forced her upon threat of death to walk with him many blocks, after which he sexually assaulted her.

The Court of Special Appeals had ruled that, where it could not be corroborated by wounds or bruises or disturbed clothing, the lack of consent could be shown by fear that was based upon reasonable apprehension of bodily harm. In their analysis, the court observed that this victim testified she had intercourse with him only because she thought he had a gun and that there was no evidence that she made any outcry while accompanying the defendant along the public streets. There had been no proof that Winegan at any time, claimed to have a gun and none was found by the police. The court ruled that the fear, even if actually present, was so unreasonable as to preclude a conviction for rape!

Based upon that analysis, the court reversed the conviction. Winegan had taken the witness stand, and on cross-examination said he had met the victim on the street, that the meeting was friendly, and that she went with him because she wanted to, not because she was forced to accompany him. He had denied that fellatio had occurred. However, he was forced to admit he had five separate convictions for minor assaults on women, an assault upon a police officer, and several convictions for the unauthorized use of motor vehicles. The court found that there was sufficient evidence to sustain the perverted practice conviction, and they allowed that 10-year sentence to remain. He had served four years. The precise holding in the case was that where sexual intercourse occurred without actual force, and without any physical resistance because of fear, that fear must be a reasonable one.

I ran down to the clerk's office to see if I could locate the transcript from this previous case. I was in luck. I signed it out and returned to Judge Harris' courtroom, and told the defense attorney that he was to be congratulated for having won this previous case on appeal, but that if he attempted to put the defendant on the witness stand in this trial, I would find some way to bring up the previous case, to show that there was a pattern or scheme that Winegan used to attack women in this same manner. I didn't actually care whether or not he took the stand because if he did I would have the opportunity to cross-examine him. After a brief consultation with his client the lawyer informed the court that the defense was resting and that the defendant did not wish to testify.

The court looked to me for my opening closing argument. I had looked over at the defense table and had seen the attorney was just starting to make notes for his argument on an empty yellow pad. He was going to prepare it while I was making my speech. I stood up and for the only time in my career, I recklessly said to the judge, "I see no reason to argue this case. If it please the court, I submit without argument." The defense was caught completely by surprise. He then gave a rambling, rather incoherent speech, trying to read some notes that he had taken during the trial. He was totally discombobulated and one of his trouser legs was caught up in his sock, so it looked as though one pant leg was six inches shorter than the other. He terminated his incoherent remarks after just a few minutes.

It was my turn. I stood before the jury and carefully gave my forceful rebuttal argument. When the State's case is not contradicted in any way it must be very weak in order for a jury to acquit, especially when there's a young vulnerable sympathetic victim. The jury returned guilty verdicts after one and a half hours of deliberation. The court could now impose a term of life imprisonment—serious stuff for only two days in court. Well, serious no matter how long the case takes.

Winegan asked the court if he could address the jury. This was unprecedented in my experience. Judge Harris gave me a knowing look and said "Well, by all means Mr. Winegan, if you wish to say something to the jury, the Court will not prohibit that." When Winegan pulled himself up to his full height, the defense counsel began to pose an objection, but Winegan insisted on continuing with his statement. He denied his guilt and said to the six-man, six-woman jury, "I just wanted to tell you that I have raped many women's 'minds' but I have never raped any 'body.'" The judge and I exchanged slight smiles. He had in effect admitted that his MO was to place his victims in fear and mental anguish thereby overbearing their will. The judge immediately imposed a 20-year sentence on the rape charge and a 10-year consecutive sentence for the perverted practice. The conviction was affirmed on appeal. A little knowledge can be a dangerous thing; so can a lot of knowledge.

If a defense attorney plans to put the client on the stand, the client is usually the last to testify. This way, he will have the advantage of first listening to all the evidence. It also helps to build interest in his testimony. In Myers' case, since I was not going to put him on the stand, it was important to have discussed this issue in my opening statement so jurors do not expect to hear from him. I had told the jurors in my opening in an oblique manner about the right not to testify so they were not really expecting to hear from him.

Unless you are positive as to what you are going to do, best to keep them guessing. Years earlier, I had committed to putting a defendant on the stand. Then the State's case had crumbled, so I re-thought it and I changed my mind. It was a 20-year mistake, paid for by the defendant. The prosecutor berated me over and over in his summation for not fulfilling my promise.

By not putting Myers on the witness stand, he avoided being confronted with the previous statements he'd made to Corporal Leete, Trooper Mays, and other police officers. Many of the things he had said to them were unkind and spiteful. He would have been confronted with his Grand Jury testimony and would have looked like an insensitive liar who had no remorse for what he had done. The petite jurors (and of no little concern to me, the general public,) would no longer think of him as a gullible, weak-but-kind and likable "good old boy Bobby." Instead, he'd be seen as the self absorbed, selfish, crude and insensitive killer that the evidence had clearly demonstrated.

Of course jurors must be given an explanation as to why someone would not testify if they are innocent, so this problem must be addressed in both the opening statement and the closing argument. A short discussion about an accusatorial, as opposed to an inquisitorial system, usually helps. Most people know that in the Spanish Inquisition an individual could be tortured so that a confession could be extracted from him and that alone was sufficient to prove them guilty.

Knowing exactly what the judge is going to say in his instructions can also be critical. I knew that Judge Burns would instruct the jurors that:

"The right to silence is absolute because an essential mainstay of our accusatorial system of criminal justice is the right to a free choice to admit, to deny, or to refuse to answer. It is the recognition that it is unfair ever to require an accused to testify if he does not choose to, not only because he may thereby be forced to admit his guilt, but it is not everyone who can safely venture on the witness stand though entirely innocent of the charge against him. Excessive timidity, nervousness when facing others and attempting to explain transactions of a suspicious character, and offenses charged against him, will often confuse and embarrass him to such a degree as to increase rather than remove prejudices against him. It is not everyone, however honest, who would therefore willingly be placed on the witness stand."

Paraphrasing these ideas before the judge has articulated them in his instructions at the end of the case is an easy way to gain and maintain credibility with the jurors and reinforce the concept. The State, however, must be careful since the prosecutors are not permitted to make even an indirect reference to an accused exercising the right to remain silent. Prosecutors will rarely spend much time discussing the defendant's failure to testify since to comment on it inappropriately risks a mistrial or reversal on appeal.

In England, because there is no written fifth amendment, it is permissible for the prosecutor to argue that the failure of the accused to make a statement to the police or in Court is indicative of guilt. In America, however, the right to silence is definitively expressed in a written constitution. Therefore, the prosecutor cannot argue that the assertion of that right to remain silent was a sign of guilt without effectively eliminating or diluting that right completely.

The State presented several witnesses in its rebuttal case. The prosecutors were a little fixated on the importance of Myers' statements about the number of times Mary Ruth had been shot. They called three people who had been at the gravesite and had them try to recall the conversations there between Myers, Stansfield and others. Their confusion, however, was easily demonstrated on cross-examination.

*****

During the last week of the trial my right testicle had became enlarged and was very uncomfortable because of a hydrocele. I had been holding my young son around the waist with his back to me when he kicked his heels into my scrotum some months earlier. I had survived boxing, rugby, soccer and Canadian football only to be hobbled by a baby. It would cause me pain from time to time. Now I was in agony and finally in the judge's chambers I explained my problem and noted that while I was willing to sacrifice a lot for Myers I was not willing to give my "right nut."

The judge referred me to the only doctor he knew who was available—a pediatrician. I waited for my turn along with several other little kids. I had fun playing with them while we waited to be seen. I was referred to Carroll County General Hospital. The attending physician diagnosed my problem and asked whether I had been injured recently. He joked that such a condition could occur from stress or vigorous intercourse with an 18-year-old. Close! Now everyone would know my problem but I was given some anti-inflammatory drugs and a scrotum holder. I was to deliver my closing argument wearing it! I was wearing the most solemn, dark and conservative business suit that I owned. Underneath, I was daintily secured by a white scrotum holder.

*****

Dale Abbott, Mary Ruth's son, was a strong rebuttal witness. He explained that there were tally sheets inexplicably missing from the Motel's financial records. These pages reflected the number of occupants and the cash receipts that had been received. Among others, the sheet from August 11th was missing. Because the motel had been crowded, much more cash would have been received than had been accounted for. A lot of cash had been siphoned from the business. I attempted to limit the impact of his testimony by getting him to admit that the record-keeping had been chaotic and that often they did not make new entries for every day an occupant had stayed, but rather, they just put them down the first day that they arrived at the motel.

The State's case ended with Mary Ruth's son gazing at the jurors several feet away, in essence demanding justice for his mother. It was a powerful way to conclude the presentation.

The jury heard 10 hours of closing arguments. During the course of the eight-week trial, over 200 pieces of evidence were introduced in addition to the many court authorized wiretaps and dozens of love letters. 91 witnesses had taken the stand.

One secret to an effective closing argument is to understand that few cases are won because of it. Close cases can be affected but to think that jurors are often steamrolled at that point in the proceedings is naïve. In any event, preparation for it must begin very early—ideally before the trial has even started. This enables the lawyer to easily gain credibility by knowing what the jurors will inevitably be told or shown during the proceedings. In the opening, a defense attorney can predict what evidence will be presented by the State, and then remind the jurors in his closing argument that he had already told them what to expect.

A lawyer is not allowed to define what a reasonable doubt means in Federal Court. In State Court, however, detailed explanations of the term and practical examples are permitted, and they can be compelling. It is always helpful to explain the different standards for the indicia of reliability of information. They span mere rumor, probable cause, preponderance, and clear and convincing. Reasonable doubt is a doubt based upon a reason. It is always effective to emphasize that if a juror cannot act in a most important affair in his or her own life "without hesitation," he or she then has a reasonable doubt about that act. The same standard applies in Court—if he or she cannot decide guilt "without hesitation," he or she has a reasonable doubt, and therefore must acquit.

You can then articulate examples of those important affairs . . . deciding whether to marry, have a child, to get divorced, adopt, move across country, accept a new job, leave a job etc. One or more of these things will resonate with one or more of the jurors. It is also worthwhile to embolden each individual, by explaining that their vote is theirs alone, and that they should have the courage to maintain their position after they have listened to and considered the concerns and conclusions of their fellow jurors. The goal is to stave off conviction. A hung jury is also a victory for the defense.

It is important and helpful to handle, review and explain all the exhibits, or else in its rebuttal argument the State will emphasize those that you did not discuss.

The prosecution is permitted not only a closing argument, but a rebuttal to the defense's closing argument. The State's closing closing argument must be anticipated and contemplated. Furthermore, the defense should always stress that while it might look grossly unfair to allow the prosecutors to argue twice and the defense only once, this procedure is fair (wink, wink)—because the State has such a heavy burden of proof. A good prosecutor will often make a strong "call to duty speech," and will have reserved some special energy to rebut the defense' closing argument.

During Hickman's argument, the prosecutor twice made statements which could be viewed as an attempt to bolster the credibility of Tina by placing his own credibility in issue. Moreover, he implied that Judge Burns' ruling with respect to a particular evidentiary point was erroneous. The prosecutor overstepped his bounds, and Judge Burns properly and promptly admonished him in the presence of the jury. Judge Burns refused my request to grant a mistrial when I objected to the improper closing argument by the prosecutor.

The judge immediately instructed the jury to disregard the State's Attorney's improper comments. "It is unprofessional conduct for the prosecutor to express his personal belief or opinion as to the truth or falsity of any testimony or evidence or the guilt of the Defendant."

I, however, strenuously argued that the prosecutor's remarks were totally improper and had been unfair. I had used the tactic so often I had the speech almost memorized:

> "A prosecutor's duty is to see that justice is done for both the individual and the community. Attorney General Robert Jackson in 1940 admonished Federal prosecutors that 'a prosecutor has more control over life, liberty and a reputation than any other person in America and that while the prosecutor at his best is one of the most beneficent forces in our society, when he acts from malice or other base motives, he is one of the worst.' He stressed prosecutors should be controlled by the 'spirit of fair play and decency that should guide every prosecuting entity, and that although technically the government might lose its case, it has really won and justice has been done if they have acted accordingly.'"

A prosecuting attorney occupies a superior position because the trier of fact knows that he is not simply an advocate. He occupies the responsible position of prosecuting attorney whom the people have chosen because of his ability and character. A jury may well suspend its own power of judgment in reviewing the evidence and defer to the experience and prestige standing behind the prosecutor's office, the police department and ultimately the person who is making the comments in the courtroom. If either counsel were to be allowed to express their personal opinion on the merits of their case a trial would turn on the status of the person vouching or endorsing for their side of the case.

If the expression of personal belief were permitted, it would give an improper advantage to the older and better known lawyer whose opinion would carry more weight and it would give an unfair advantage to an unscrupulous lawyer. Furthermore, if it were permitted, when counsel failed to make such a positive assertion in his belief in his case, it would be taken as an admission that he did not believe in his case. The assertions of personal knowledge or insinuations of personal knowledge often carry too much weight when they should properly carry none. An astute juror once remarked that he had not seen either the prosecutor or defense counsel take an oath, so why should he believe anything they said.

The defense lawyer's art of advocacy, however, is in persuading the jury that you really do believe what you are arguing. This is done indirectly and without ever saying so, and without providing a basis for the opposing lawyer to object to what you are saying or doing. Criminal court is not a sports arena where the result is simply winning or losing a game, a medal or a championship. The consequences are often "scored" by years in a cage, or life or death itself.

Before the case was submitted to the jury for their consideration, at the conclusion of the arguments, it took the lawyers three hours to review all the exhibits, which had been introduced into evidence. This too was a critical part of the case because all these items would be sent back into the jury room and a mistake concerning just one exhibit could cause a mistrial.

The jurors worked very hard to reach the correct verdict. They were in constant conversation. Many of them had notebooks filled with their observations. Every time someone brought up a point, they tried to see both sides. Later on in the second day of deliberations the jurors had finished reviewing testimony and evidence and began to argue and discuss the case. The vote was nine in favor of conviction and three for acquittal. It had been a long day, and a little after 10 p.m. and after 12 hours of deliberation the jurors decided to retire to their dormitory rooms at the New Windsor Brethren Service Center, where they were sequestered.

It had been very hot, very stuffy and very smoky in the jury deliberation room. It was nerve-racking. Everyone wanted to get out of there and be finished with the case. However when most of them retired for the night, facts kept spinning in their heads even though they tried to leave it in the courtroom.

On the second day of deliberations, nearly 20 reporters and photographers sat outside the empty courtroom, but the jury asked no questions and remained behind closed doors. Judge Luke K. Burns, Jr. said the longest time a county jury has been out in the last 10 years was 16 hours. The Myers' jury spent seven hours deliberating the first day and 11 hours the next. The 11-woman, one-man jury scurried out of the courthouse about 10:15 p.m. most of them hiding their faces with briefcases, hoods and folders. A mass of cameramen was waiting for them to make their exit from the Courthouse and board the bus waiting to transport them to the New Windsor Center, where they were sequestered for another night.

After three days of jury deliberations, the more than 30 spectators waiting on the wooden benches outside the 2nd floor courtroom became aware around 3:45 p.m. that something was happening. There was a flurry of activity at the end of the hall leading from the waiting area to the grand jury room and the entrance to Judge Burn's chambers. Reporters clustered around a sign reading "No unauthorized persons beyond this point," watching the judge pace in the doorway. After a wait of more than an hour, sheriff's deputies opened the courtroom to press and spectators.

For the three days of the deliberations Hickman and Coleman and I roamed the courthouse halls. They often went back to their offices. These deliberations were now longer than any other in Carroll County history. By Thursday afternoon Hickman and Coleman were starting to look worried and the newspapers reported that I had begun to look a little more chipper. However, on that third day, when the jury took another vote, the last undecided juror began to agree with the others. This young woman was concerned that Myers might get the death penalty and was saying "This guy could be dead and it's my fault because I sent him to the gas chamber." But by 4 p.m., all agreed that Myers was guilty. One of the jurors, Erin Connors, had filled more than four notebooks during the trial. A final unanimous count had been taken. Juror Helen Uttermahlen, who was 68, said "It was the heaviest responsibility of my life. I am okay physically but mentally and emotionally I'm very tired. I never want to go through such an experience again. We considered all of the evidence and all our notes matched, which was a great comfort to me."

It took an hour to assemble the lawyers and personnel after the jurors had knocked on the door to let the bailiff know that they had reached a verdict. As the time dragged on, some were worried that perhaps a juror would change his or her mind, and everyone was wondering what was taking so long. They had sent their note to the judge at 4 p.m. At 5 p.m., spectators and reporters assembled in the courtroom. Four plain clothes officers stood by the rail and gazed towards the gallery.

Hickman smiled, and then sat in his deep-cushioned trial chair. He slumped in the chair. I looked over at him and gave him a wink. A loud knock came from the door beyond the courtroom. As I had many times before, I reflected to myself the lines from *Macbeth* . . . "Hear it not Duncan, for that is the knell that summons thee, To Heaven or To Hell!" At 5:10 p.m., the door on the left swung open and the clerk said, "Silence in the court, all rise!" Judge Luke Burns stepped up on the bench and sat down.

Myers had told me that he wanted to wear his three-piece light green suit, to bring luck. He looked pale and was smiling weakly. I put my hand gently on his shoulder to calm him.

As we stood at the defense table. The Judge asked. "Are you gentleman ready to proceed?" Hickman and I both said "Yes, your Honor." The judge nodded. The door to his right opened, and the only male member of the jury appeared. He stepped up and took a seat at the far end of the jury box, then looked out at the gallery. The 11 women on the jury went to their seats following behind him. Most of the jurors were casually dressed, some in jeans. None of the jurors looked at the defendant as they came in and Myers only glanced in their direction, even though they were less than four feet from where we stood.

The judge, cautioned the audience against any reaction and then the clerk asked the jury, "Are you agreed upon a verdict?" A woman's voice came from the jury box. "Yes." The clerk responded "And what is that verdict?" Foreperson Marcia King said quietly, her voice barely audible. "He is guilty."

As King announced the verdict one of Mary Ruth's sisters broke into tears. She had to be helped from the courtroom. Dwayne Abbott, the victim's son, clenched both his fists shook his head up and down and said "Yeah yeah!"

Tears streamed from the eyes of 19-year-old Kimberly Abbott as she congratulated members of her family, seated next to her. Dale Abbott, 26, put his arm around his grandmother Ethel Fowble, Mary Ruth's mother who cried softly when she heard the verdict. "We just feel better," said Grayson Fowble, Mary Ruth's oldest brother, a short while later as he wiped tears from his eyes as he stood outside the courtroom.

I requested that the clerk poll the jury. "You have heard your foreperson's verdict. Is her verdict your verdict?" Mr. Myers looked at them as each one replied, "Yes, it is." Myers was ashen but gave me a weak smile. A reporter observed that while Myers appeared to be calm and in good spirits, I had looked sullen and chagrined.

After Court was dismissed the prosecutors embraced each other. Hickman beamed broadly as moments later he shook the hand of Cpl. James M. Leete.

After the verdict as Myers was led from the courtroom by a Sheriff's deputy, I walked over and congratulated Hickman and Coleman. And as I turned to leave the room I said. "Nice case!" I then strode from the room to meet Myers in the basement holding cell. Several members of the victim's family burst into tears as they left the courtroom.

Leete was visibly happy with the verdict but did not want to comment on the case until the sentencing was over. Throughout the lengthy investigation, Leete had crisscrossed the country pursuing leads, including stops in California, Texas, Las Vegas, North Carolina, and Pennsylvania and he had also travelled to Bermuda three times. "I'm just glad we could do it" The case interfered with his personal and professional life and had caused him "many sleepless nights."

A local columnist, Dan Rodericks, reported, "And just like that, all the drama was gone. The Myers' case shrank from the stature of sensational passion play back to small-town tragedy. The Myers' case fit most of the plot of 'Body Heat.' Ned Racine ended up in jail. Matty Walker ended up behind sunglasses on some tropical island. Perfect casting—stupid men, and a woman who liked them that way." For me, though, the drama was not completely "gone" since there was still the matter of whether or not Myers would be executed.

It was just past 5:30 p.m. when Tina Myers received word that the jury had convicted Robert Lee Myers of first-degree murder. "I was up all night. I looked through our wedding pictures. I cried and I cried and I cried." She said she was "a basket case," her voice breaking with emotion. The verdict shocked and saddened her and left her weeping. "It was not supposed to end that way," despite the fact that it was her testimony that had doomed her former husband. Tina Myers said she had no choice but to turn state's evidence against him. "I was facing the gas chamber." She said, "I've got four children to think of." The jury had deliberated for 25 hours over three days. Frank Coleman had called her on Wednesday saying he was concerned about the outcome of the case.

Tina said, "He was concerned it was going to be a hung jury and so was I." "I told Bobby before the jury went out whatever he got, whether he was set free or whether he was found guilty to Thank God for it because it was his will. I told him that I feel that maybe God has some work for him behind bars. Maybe he can do some good." Throughout the trial, I had repeatedly attacked Tina, her testimony and her credibility. I called her an "evil predator" that consumed, and easily dominated men. Despite all the personal attacks, she said that she held no grudge against me, and that I was just doing my job. Tina said, "There's nothing personal, I know that. By God, if Bob had some fly by night flunky up there that didn't have any questions, who didn't try to put me down, then what chance would he have had?"

In an interview the day after the verdict, Tina continued to profess her love for Bobby, but said she was tired of being publicly portrayed as the evil black widow spider luring men into her web. She said that I had crucified her. For the interview she was wearing designer jeans and a fashionable gray sweater. Her facial expressions ranged from serious to mournful to amused and it took her 15 minutes before she would agree to have her photograph taken. She said she didn't love Myers when she married him but she slowly grew to love him. "I love Bob" she said blinking back tears. "I still love Bob. But I have four children, and I wasn't sure I wanted to die for him."

She said that the wait for the verdict was unbearable as she sat in a jail cell in Oakland. She said she was praying for a miracle. "Whatever happens to

Myers this week," Marco said she hopes he one day will forgive her. "I still love him very much. I hurt for Bob. My feelings are for him." Tina said it started as a storybook romance, filled with kind words and thoughtful gestures. "He treated me like a queen at all times. If I looked at something in a store, just looked at it and walked away, he went running back to buy it. It was a story with a tragic ending. But I hope someday, someday the story will have a happy ending for Bob and I. The man that had Mary Ruth killed was not the man that I lived with, that's not the man I know. The man I know is very kind, he's very sensitive and he's very gentle. He brought me flowers almost every day. He always brought me home fresh roses. Three, always three."

"One day I came home, and he had big holes out in the front yard. And he said to me, "go back into the bedroom until I call you." So about two hours later my kids came in and they were filthy and dirty. And they say, mom, dad wants you. I walked out and he had built me a heart shaped rose garden. He and the kids did it by hand. He was so proud of that."

"I could have gone to the gas chamber with him, but I have four children. It's a very tough decision to choose between four children and the only man I've ever loved" she said in a television interview. She added she still writes to her husband and hopes for a reconciliation.

Tina claimed that she had become a born-again Christian since she had been taken into custody. "I've always believed in God. For the past year I've become a lot closer to him, and Bob also. I think if we had both really been living for God before, that this would never have come about. Mary Ruth would still be alive."

She was unsure what she would do when she was freed from jail after Myers had been sentenced. She didn't know if she would be reunited with her 13-year-old son Brad. "I love him and I understand why he did what he did during his testimony calling me a chronic liar, but I think he is better off where he is. The people looking after him in his foster home really care for him. I think that at the age of 13 it's a very difficult time for him after all he's been put through. It's going to take a long time to heal, so maybe he's better off there.

"As far as the babies are concerned they are both under two and once I'm on my feet they'll be with me. Now they're being taken care of and provided and they are very happy babies. So is Tracey, my 11-year-old daughter who is also in a foster home. I wouldn't dare get out of this jail and then pick up my kids and say "Okay let's go." Tina said, "I have a lot of business to take care of when I get out which I hope won't take too long. I'll make my plans later, although I will move out of the state. It'll be a period of adjustment for all of us. I have two young kids who don't even know who I am. I also want them to get to know their father. There are a lot of questions being asked. I hope in time to visit Bobby with the children. A lot of parents are behind bars and kids get to know them."

Tina Myers had testified she was working on a book and arranging television and movie deals, but now said she has stopped that work and didn't know if she would complete the book. "I was urged to write a book even before I moved to Maryland and married Bobby. This murder case publicity just added to it. But I've decided I don't want to live through it a second time." Instead she has been crocheting, reading, writing a lot, and exercising. While murder mysteries had been her favorite kind of book, she now enjoyed Harlequin and Silhouette romances and magazines.

She also spent time reading the approximately 3,000 letters she had received since April. She said they came from all over Maryland and many people still write to her. "I have gotten some hate letters, but most have been positive. That surprised me at first, for I thought everyone hated me, but not everyone does." She wrote to Robert Myers once or twice a week. "I talk about the kids, give him words of encouragement and send him religious materials." She said her decision to testify against Bobby cost her a lot of so-called friends and that many people are very judgmental. "I like simple things, contrary to people's beliefs. I like kids, picnics and walks on the beach." She said she thought Bobby needed a doctor instead of imprisonment and expressed hope that the conviction would be reversed on appeal.

Erin Connors, one of the jurors, said she was impressed with my antics and strategies. "I thought Mr. Keating was the greatest," she said, "I thought he should win an Academy Award." (Wrong Keating . . . my brother Charles won an Emmy for Best Actor in a daytime soap opera years later, in 1996, playing a sophisticated villain whom the viewing audience loved to hate.)

She liked my method of reacting to prosecution points. "He'd go (making an exhaling sound) and then stare (up and down) the jury box," she said. "When he had his own point to make," she continued, "He'd look at every juror like, 'Did you hear that?' "I thought he was very amusing," said Connors, who during the trial appeared to be the juror quickest with a smile during light moments in the courtroom. She said "she was convinced Myers had a good defense from Keating."

After the jury had returned their verdict, I had pretended Myers and I needed a couple of days to make the election on who would decide the punishment: the jury or the judge. Two days later everyone was then assembled again, and on the record I explained to Judge Burns that Myers "has elected to have you make the decision" and the jury was finally excused. The jurors were visibly relieved.

They had suspended their own personal lives for 10 weeks and the trial had been hard enough. Some had speculated correctly that since they had found Myers guilty, he might believe that they would also sentence him to death. Burns was such a kind and courteous man and was clearly compassionate, so it made sense that he would be requested to impose life or death. The jurors were dismissed with the thanks of the court and with a stack of the newspaper clippings from the case that the judge had requested his staff to prepare for each of them.

The judge then suggested to me that I should go back with him to the jury room and thank the jurors for their service. This placed me in the awkward position of basically thanking them for rejecting all my great bullshit and for convicting Myers, making me look totally insincere. The judge and I went into the jury room and I prefaced my remarks by telling them that I in no way agreed with their conclusions, but I did understand the amount of effort and the personal sacrifices they had made to obey their oath to "Well and truly, try the case." One of the jurors, a female in her late 60's with blue hair, a member of the Church of The Open Door, a popular local institution, said "Mr. Keating would you give Bobby a message for us?" After I had said that I would, she responded "Would you thank him for taking the judge on the death part?" I said that I would, thanked them all and left . . . thinking . . . "Feets, don't fail me now!"

The prosecutors and Cpl. Leete dined later that night at Maggie's restaurant along with about 15 members of Mary Ruth's family. Not surprisingly, cheers and animated conversation dominated their celebration. Although under a gag order not to discuss the trial publicly until Myers had been sentenced, the trio who sat at a long table with the victim's relatives was free to savor their victory among their friends. Coleman, a gleeful smile on his face, sauntered up to the bar and stood behind Thomas Stansfield, Myers' civil lawyer and a key defense witness at the trial.

At the restaurant bar, when Stansfield turned to face him, Coleman smashed a pile of whipped cream in Stansfield's face. As Mary Ruth Myers' family shrieked with laughter, Coleman whipped out a Polaroid camera and began snapping shots of the white-faced lawyer, clad in pin-striped suit and bow tie, and covered in whipped cream. No sooner had he wiped his face clean than Stansfield found himself facing another prankster. Grason Fowble, the murder victim's brother, handed Stansfield a white paper bag containing a bottle of Pepto Bismol, which Fowble apparently thought Stansfield needed to cope with defeat. That brought another round of laughter and applause from Hickman and relatives of the victim. Stansfield took the ribbing good naturedly, exchanging barbs with Coleman and callously telling friends about bets he'd have to pay off because his client had been convicted. Community sentiment ran heavily against Tina.

The newspapers had been covering this notorious case with front-page articles almost every day. After this wild celebration at Maggie's, details and photos of it appeared in all of them. I was back in Baltimore reading about the festivities in my home when my phone rang and to my surprise it was Judge Burns. "Have you read about that party in the newspapers?" I said I had, and that I thought it was pretty outrageous, and that I thought I would raise the matter before the court at the next session on Monday. He said he thought I should. There was no question that I would, since it would allow me to get back on the offensive.

Mar 24, 82

Dear Bobby, this letter is going to be very hard to write so please bear with me. First let me say Bob I love you & God knows I always will. I'm sorry that I did what I felt I had to do, but let me say I did it for several special reasons. First & foremost the state has an overabundance of evidence against this case & Bobby those are children involved that are innocent of any wrongdoing. I can't picture us spending our lives in prison & our children never knowing us. Its not fair to them & I can't expect your family to raise our family for us. One of us had to come forward. Its been hell to live with for 2½ years & although what I feel I had to do, is going to be even harder to live with knowing I had to detach myself from the only person I have ever loved is the hardest thing I've ever had to do. Regardless of

Letter from Tina Myers to Robert Myers. March 24, 1982

you choosing to believe this or not
Bobby I do love you & this is
tearing my insides out. Other than
this terrible thing I have loved you
& experianced a lifetime of happiness
with you for 2 years that I will
always cherish, as for our children
you are their father, they will know
what a kind, loving & decent man you
are. I will see you through this
the best I can, please know that I do
care, have faith in God & continue to
pray Bobby as I will for you.
    I dont know what else I can say
to ease your pain & hurt, please forgive
me for betraying your trust, I will always
love you with every ounce of me, more
than all the stars in the skies, more than
all the marlin, more than all the sand
on every beach, more than every tear I have
& will shed, I love you, God only
knows how much I do, take care
my love, May God Bless you &
keep you safe.
          Forever is a long, long time.
               Love,
               Tina

THURSDAY, APRIL 29, 1982

Myers kin identifies defendant

By Peter Ruehl
Evening Sun Staff

OAKLAND—Kimberly Abbott, the daughter of Mary Ruth Myers, pointed at Daniel L. Chadderton and said he was the man who went to Ocean City in August 1979 and attempted to see her mother.

Abbott, one of three children the murder victim had during a marriage prior to that with Robert L. Myers, testified yesterday that she was working at the beach motel owned by her mother and stepfather when Chadderton appeared Aug. 28, the day before her mother was killed.

Abbott's testimony and that of several others yesterday corroborated Tina Marco's account of the events leading up to the Myers murder.

Chadderton, Marco said Tuesday, stalked Mary Ruth Myers at the beach but a stubborn maid prevented him from getting to her.

The maid, Mary Elizabeth Fooks, testified she was supervising the women who changed the bedding at the Northwinds motel when a bearded man rode up on a motorcycle and asked "if the madam is around."

Fooks said Mrs. Myers was asleep and that he couldn't see her.

The man started up the steps to the apartment Robert and Mary Ruth Myers used when they visited the motel, but Fooks stepped in his way and prevented him from going farther.

"I said, 'No, you can't go up there,' and he stopped," Fooks testified. "Then he went away."

[Continued Page D6, Col. 1]

By Walter M. McCardell—Evening Sun Staff

Daniel Chadderton arrives at the courthouse for his trial.

(Left) Evening Sun *news article, Chadderton arrives for trial, Oakland, MD.*

(Below) The News American *news article*

The News American 10

Wednesday, April 28, 1982   Baltimore ✦ Maryland   20 Cents

Tina Myers testifies on details of slaying

By Camille Fecchia
News American Staff

OAKLAND — Recalling the predawn hours of Aug. 20, 1979, Tina Marco Myers said she asked Robert Myers who was telephoning so early in the morning. She said she put the phone to her ear and heard the voice of Daniel Chadderton saying, "The job is done. Label her nine times. She's dead."

Tina Myers were shook and she sobbed Tuesday as she related her story to a Garrett County jury that is expected to decide whether Chadderton, 31, is guilty of the contract slaying of Robert Myers' wife, Mary Ruth Myers.

After the phone call, she testified, she rolled over in bed and slept late that day.

Tina Myers, originally charged in the Mary Ruth Myers killing, was given immunity by the state in exchange for testifying against Chadderton and Robert Myers, 40, whom she married less than a month after his wife's death. Robert Myers also is charged with the killing, and the state is seeking the death penalty for both men.

In Tina Myers' nearly five hours on the witness stand Tuesday, her wide brown eyes focused directly on whoever was speaking to her. She smiled shyly at Garrett County Circuit Court Judge Fred Thayer, who repeatedly admonished her to speak loudly enough so that the jury, sitting a few feet away, could hear her. She raised a handkerchief to her eyes at almost every mention of Mary Ruth Myers' death.

Mary Ruth's body was found Aug. 29, 1979, in the master bedroom of the Myerses' Silver Run Valley home, with nine bullet wounds. She was 43.

Tina Myers said the state contends that her role was limited to introducing Chadderton and Robert Myers to each other.

She is spending her time beneath the courthouse in the Garrett County jail. After the trials, she said, she will move to California to live with her father.

She testified Tuesday that Chadderton told her he would "never make it to the witness stand" if she turned state's witness. She also recalled an incident in which Chadderton put his arms around her 10-year-old daughter by a previous marriage, saying he would "hate to see anything happen to her."

By the time she takes the stand against Robert Myers, whose trial date and location are being decided by the Maryland Court of Appeals, she will have given birth to her second child by Myers. Her first, Sabrina, is 10 months old.

She appeared before the seven-man, five-woman jury Tuesday wearing a dark turquoise maternity suit. She is eight months pregnant.

The defense attorney for Chadderton appeared completely surprised Tuesday by Myers' appearance on the witness stand, and he seemed to have no organized plan for cross-examination.

See MYERS, 5A

ACCUSED: Daniel Chadderton

Robert Myers outside the Carroll County Courthouse on the first day of trial.

Start of contract-murder trial

Robert L. Myers (in checked jacket facing camera) shook hands with his lawyer, Anton J.S. Keating, as he arrived at the Carroll county courthouse yesterday for the start of his contract-murder trial in the August, 1979, shooting death of his wife, Mary Ruth Myers. Prosecutors are seeking the death penalty. The once-husky Mr. Myers reportedly has lost about 80 pounds since being jailed last November. Article, Page D2

The Sun/Lloyd Pearson

9/21/82

ONE HELL OF A MARRIAGE

A BUSINESS tycoon faces ruin — and perhaps death — in a bizarre scandal of sex, sin and murder.

Robert Myers, 38, allegedly hired a hitman to kill his wife so he could run off and marry cocktail waitress Tina Marco, who police say has a lurid past that includes a trail of husbands.

Investigators probing the case claim that:

● Myers paid grocery store janitor Daniel Chadderton, 29, to break into his home in Westminster, Maryland, and murder his wife, Mary Ruth.

● Just one month later, Myers and Tina flew to Bermuda to be married.

● Tina was legally married to another man when she wed Myers.

● One of her three former husbands died mysteriously when his car blew up.

The shocking case took an even more bizarre twist when Tina, 31, agreed to turn state's evidence — threatening to send Myers to the gas chamber while she walks away scot-free.

The couple met and fell in love in August, 1979. Just three weeks later, Myers' wife was gunned down during an apparent burglary.

State police launched an investigation, but even though Myers married Tina before Mary Ruth was cold in her grave, the newlyweds appeared to be in the clear.

However, Tina was arrested last fall and charged with bigamy.

James Marco, a plumber in Florida, claimed she was still his legal wife. During her trial, it was revealed that she had had three other husbands, Anton Keating, Myers' attorney, told GLOBE: "She married some guy named Layne when she was 15 or 16. After that, she married Jay Gillen and then Skip Botterorod, who died around March, 1979, when he was blown up by a bomb

Police say tycoon had wife killed to marry bigamous waitress whose ex-husband died in car bomb blast

in his car. Then she married Marco, and it appears she was still married to him when she met Myers. It's hard to sort out the details of her life."

The State Attorney's office in Carroll County dug deeper into the death of Ruth Myers and eventually indicted her husband, Tina and Chadderton for murder.

Myers and Tina hired Baltimore attorney Phillip Sutley, but the lawyer later decided to defend only Tina.

Keating says: "At that point, prosecutor Thomas Hickman offered Sutley a deal to let Tina go free if she would help send Myers to the gas chamber.

"Maryland law states that the prosecutor cannot engage in negotiation of this sort when the defense represents more than one client. So my contention is that there is an appearance of impropriety in this case."

Myers was a well-respected businessman in Westminster who earned around $100,000 a year. Restaurant owner Terry Burk describes him as a pleasant

but not overly sociable man.

"He used to drop by here occasionally," Burk told GLOBE. "I didn't know him well, but the charges came as a shock to all of us. There has been a constant buzz of rumors and speculation. Everybody's talking about it — it's like a soap opera."
— BLANCHE HODDER

MARCO (left) gets police escort on way to face justice.

MYERS... well-respected.

The National Examiner: *One Hell of a Marriage. Businessman and Stripper/Lover Ended in a Hit Murder of Wife.*

NAME *Mr George W Smith* NO *128298*

ADDRESS *954 Forrest street*

Baltimore, Maryland

Mr Anton Keating

STREET *Office of the Public Defender*

CITY *800 Equitable* STATE *Md*

DATE *1-26-74*

Mr Keating

im not impressed at this 52 years and 6 months that i have to do, nor am i impressed by the way you represented me. However that stage has passed now, and i would like to see you at your earlier convenience concerning my Appeal!

Letter—"I'm not impressed at this 52 years and six months I have to do . . . nor am I impressed by the way you represented me . . ."

Tina Myers to testify against husband for her freedom

By JOHN BILLMYRE
Staff Writer

Newspaper Article. "Tina To Testify Against Husband . . ."

STATE vs. Robert Myers   Nov 1982   Westminster md.

Sketch by Susan R. Bloc

TINA SHOWS JURY HER RING

(Top) A courtroom sketch of Tina being cross-examined.

(Left) Sketch of Tina holding up an expensive ring in court.

Seats in the court-room were limited, so spectators at the trial lined up early.

The interior of the Maryland State police plane. Frank Coleman and I with oxygen masks.

The Maryland State police plane.

"The Night Watch." The jury on the second floor of the courthouse behind the local cemetery deliberates Myers' fate for a second night.

The Evening Sun, *Myers Gets Life Imprisonment.*

Article. Keating: Courtroom Counterpuncher.

Carroll County Times

Year 74, Number 65   Westminster, Maryland   Wednesday, March 19, 1986   30 cents — 42 pages

Myers: I was framed

By LYNDA MAPES
Staff Writer

It's fishing that Robert Lee Myers of Westminster misses the most, he says, now that he is serving a life sentence in the Maryland State Penitentiary for the contract murder of his wife Mary Ruth.

While winning the softball tournament this summer as the star pitcher in the pen's ball team was a good time, it doesn't stack up to life on the outside, he says.

Myers was convicted of first-degree murder in December 1982 in connection with the contract slaying of his wife in August 1979. After a 10-week trial and 25 hours of deliberation, a Carroll jury found Myers guilty of paying Daniel Lee Chadderton $10,000 to shoot his wife at her Silver Run home.

It is a conviction that Myers insists was unjust, and one that his former defense attorney, Anton J.S. Keating of Baltimore, has called inevitable because of overwhelming evidence that Myers committed the crime.

Myers, nonetheless, says he will continue to fight the conviction until his death.

"I am the victim of a conspiracy. The prosecutors, the police, the public defender, they all were to on this together. I was framed," Myers said in an interview at the county detention center Tuesday night.

"To this day I have not heard one piece of evidence that proves that I'm guilty," Myers said.

"If I could be convicted with what they had on me, then anyone walking down the street could be thrown in jail," he said.

Myers accused State's Attorney Thomas Hickman of "going after" him because Hickman was jealous of his relationship with a barmaid named Tina Marco that Myers married 28 days after the death of his wife.

"He was jealous because she was dating me and not him," Myers said.

Myers' assertions that Hickman had wanted to date Tina were discredited during Myers' trial in 1982 and again on Tuesday when Keating called the allegations "nonsense" during testimony in Carroll Circuit Court.

Myers said police investigators planted evidence in Myers' Silver Run home and "framed" him because they did not want to be embarrassed at not being able to convict anyone for the murder of Mary Ruth.

"This kind of thing happens more often

Robert Myers peers through the glass at the visitor's area of the Carroll County Detention Center.
George Welty photo

Please see From jail, A6

Carroll County Times, Myers "Still proclaiming his innocence."

BALTIMORE   SECTION B

The News American, Sunday, March 23, 1986

Keating takes off gloves in Myers case

By Christine Stutz
News American Staff

The dramatic three-month trial that resulted in the contract-murder conviction of Carroll County businessman Robert Myers in 1982 was resurrected last week, as Myers took one last chance at vacating his life sentence.

About 40 spectators sat in the quaint Westminster courthouse for the four full days of Myers' post-conviction hearing. The 44-year-old former accountant, convicted of paying a man $10,000 to kill his wife

Mary Ruth in 1979, is seeking a new trial on the grounds that he was poorly represented by his attorney Anton J.S. Keating.

Carroll County Circuit Judge Donald Gilmore is expected to rule on the petition the week after Easter.

Almost all those who attended the hearing also had attended the trial, where they heard lurid details of Myers' relationship with his girlfriend Ernestine "Tina" Marco — an affair that involved infidelity, bigamy, drug and alcohol abuse, murder-for-hire and thousands of dol-

lars in gifts to Marco of jewelry, furs and luxury cars.

Among the many ironies in the proceeding were that Keating, who worked so hard to put forward an argument of innocence on Myers' behalf four years ago, now sat on the witness stand explaining why he was convinced of Myers' guilt early in the case.

Carroll County State's Attorney Thomas Hickman, who in the 1982 trial was a bitter enemy of Keating, now was an admiring ally, as the two labored to keep Myers in the Maryland Penitentiary.

And Myers' present attorney Morris Kaplan, 76, who has a reputation as an effective criminal lawyer but not as a scholar or orator, had come into court to criticize the work of Keating, 42, known for his glib tongue and meticulous preparation of cases.

At the 1982 trial, Keating presented 23 character witnesses to attest to Myers' reputation for truthfulness and kindness in the community.

Yet, at last week's hearing, Keating described Myers as "cold-blooded," "ruthless" and "insensitive."

Among those attending the hearing were Westminster neighbors of Mary Ruth Myers, who are still shocked and outraged at her violent death. In that close-knit community of 12,000, the Myers family was well-known and well-liked, and Mary Ruth Myers was widely admired.

Also in court at various times were Mary Ruth's mother, sister, brothers and four children from a previous marriage, who sat close together on a front bench. When

See MYERS, 3B

Article. Keating Takes Off The Gloves.

Carroll County Times

Year 74, Number 64   Westminster, Maryland   Tuesday, March 18, 1986   30 cents — 22 pages

Keating goes public

Calls Myers 'not credible'

By LYNDA MAPES
Staff Writer

Baltimore attorney Anton J.S. Keating went public Monday in Carroll Circuit Court with what he called "damaging information" about Robert L. Myers, after Myers went ahead with his request for a new trial.

Myers has claimed in a hearing on a motion for post-conviction relief that he is entitled to a new trial because Keating represented him incompetently.

Throughout the two-day hearing, Myers' attorney, Morris Kaplan of Baltimore, has claimed that Keating should have put Myers on the witness stand during his trial.

"What jury in the world is not

"If I were to put him on the witness stand, he simply would not be believed," Keating said.

Myers was convicted of first-degree murder in December 1982 by a Carroll jury after the longest and most expensive trial in county history.

Keating told Gilmore he spent 1,200 hours on Myers' case and gave up his personal life and all other work and moved into Lee's Motel in Westminster for three months in order to devote all of his time and energy to Myers' case.

"This feels like a divorce proceeding," Keating said, after a look at Myers during a break in Monday's hearing.

Keating brought four boxes of files and notes into court Monday

Carroll County Times, Keating Goes Public.

Christmas Card from Tina Myers, Dec. 1983 from Houston, Texas, 2 weeks after she had been released.

PART IV

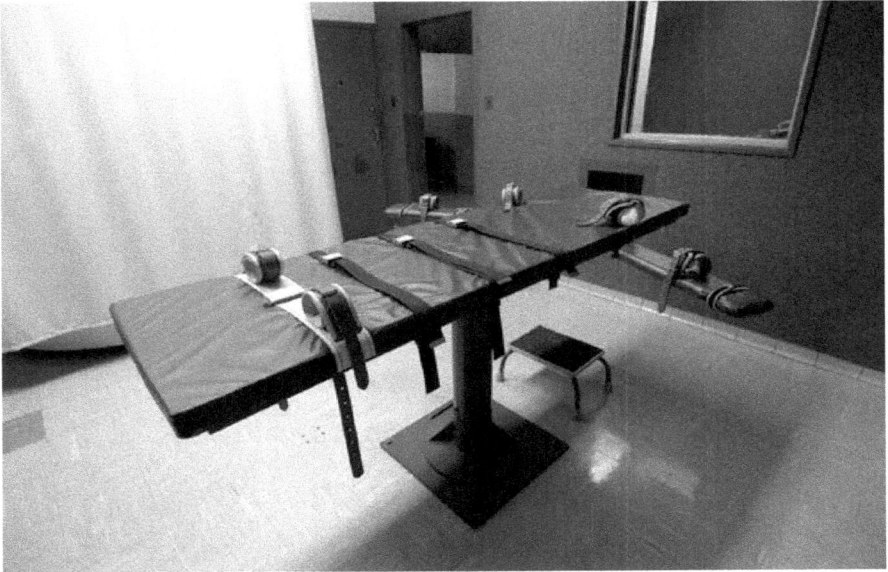

CHAPTER 26:
THE SENTENCING

"This man needs a priest not a lawyer!"
— Alan H. Murrell, MD State Public Defender

I had filed a detailed motion for a new trial, listing 20 reasons why one should be granted. All of these matters had already been ruled upon, so I did not expect the court to change its mind, however this process would allow me to complain that the verdict of the jury was suspect. It also allowed me to go on the attack, reiterating the objections I had raised to the prosecutors' closing arguments. I had objected that Mr. Hickman claimed that "he personally believed" that the testimony of Tina Myers was truthful. Judge Burns had reprimanded him at the time. None of this effort was wasted, because it made the public statement that Myers had not been treated fairly regardless of the result. I, of course knew differently. It was not a perfect trial, but it was a fair one.

I complained that "Mr. Hickman struck at the very heart of our system, usurping all the rules and all the work we had done." I suggested that his conduct had been so gross that it would require a reversal of the conviction. I argued that on a different day, with different jurors Myers could have been acquitted. I stressed that it was improper for Hickman to tell jurors to disregard evidence concerning Tina's past and that the court had ruled that such testimony was admissible. The judge, in denying my motion, correctly stressed again he had ruled on all these matters previously.

I had arrived in court early and had several copies of the newspaper articles about their "celebration" with me at the trial table when the prosecutors walked in. "He has the article!" Frank Coleman said to Hickman. "You bet your ass I do," I responded, "And I have several copies for the court." When the session started, I argued at length that the undignified conduct of the prosecutors, treating their victory as if they had won a high school football championship and celebrating so childishly in such a public fashion, was totally uncalled for, had demeaned the entire process, and should be considered "a mitigating factor" and in and of itself was a reason that the death penalty should not be imposed. The prosecutors squirmed in their seats as I offered the articles as exhibits after I had read extensively from them.

To illustrate this supposed mitigating circumstance, I looked over at the prosecutors and said, "Yes, this is the party," glaring over at Hickman and Coleman as I overheard them whispering at the prosecution table. "While I can understand their relief, only barbarians would party in public and be glad and be happy." I asked the judge to consider "the lack of dignity at that party" to be a mitigating factor and one more reason why Robert Myers should not be executed. The judge lectured the prosecutors.

My strong feelings about the death penalty had been the product of many childhood experiences which when I reflected on them always energized me.

I could not be cavalier. I had never made the argument against death from the defense side of the trial table before this case. Many years earlier, a Circuit Court Judge had chided my attitude about the death penalty, and scoffed that when he had been a young prosecutor, a notorious hanging judge had warned a defense attorney in a death penalty case, "Now I don't want to hear that he hated his mother or when this guy first started to jerk off!" It was indeed a different day, and it was now a more complicated process to execute someone. And it was my job to make it as difficult as possible.

Under the new "death" statute, a sentencing judge or jury had to make specific findings about whether "the mitigating factors outweighed the aggravating circumstances by a preponderance of the evidence." If they did, a life sentence had to be imposed. There were no comprehensive definitions as to what these "factors" or "circumstances" were, and so the defense could basically introduce anything remotely relevant to punishment. No trial judge wanted to be reversed later because he had improperly excluded some evidence, no matter how inconsequential. A mistake at this critical stage would mean repeating the entire laborious process, so the judge inevitably allowed great latitude to the defense.

Several months before this trial, I had initiated the "mitigation" part of the case, knowing it would certainly be needed. The State's case was just too overwhelming. As The Queen had dictated in Alice in Wonderland, "First the sentence, then the evidence!"

Lawrence Donner, a PhD and licensed clinical psychologist from The University of Maryland School of Medicine, was also a diplomat in clinical psychology (ABPP) and testified about his observations and testing.

He produced a confidential psychological report that he had written at my request. It was intended to be unassailable, but helpful to the defense. Very helpful, since it demonstrated that Myers was easily manipulated and posed no actual threat of violence.

In one part, he wrote that "Mr. Myers is a man of average height and somewhat overweight, who has bleached blond hair and a rather fair complexion. He related in a most personable and friendly manner, appearing outgoing and quite spontaneous, showing an absence of reservation as he spoke without editing or monitoring his thoughts. He seemed unusually candid and direct, responding to the examiner's questions although his answers tended to ramble, volunteering more information than had been initially requested. His behavior seemed unusual in terms of lacking the outward manifestation of anxiety and dysphoria one might expect with the charges of first-degree murder and facing the death penalty. Throughout the interview he showed good eye contact."

As for test findings, "Bobby received a 'low-average' range of intellectual functioning. A combination of both emotional factors (i.e. underlying anxiety and depression) and organic factors have significantly attenuated Mr. Myers' functioning.

Myers' test results "showed a naïve, insightless man who has a rather hysterical world and self-view. He is quite sensitive to others, and the impression he makes upon them, working hard to ingratiate himself and to be liked. The test results show him as sensitive, emotional, softhearted and prone to worry."

His personality structure shows a basic passivity and dependency, although he seeks high social visibility and tends to be viewed as a sociable, energetic, open, and forward individual. He shows a remarkable lack of insight and self-understanding."

These test results indicated "Mr. Myers is extremely impressionable and easily influenced by others. He tends to have an overly trusting attitude and is quite suggestible, especially to a strong authority figure who he thinks can provide a magical solution to his problems. Particularly in the relationship with the opposite sex, he shows a constant demand and need for support and reassurance because of his longstanding underlying helplessness and dependency. He is quick to form such relationships, as has been reflected in his three marriages."

The report concluded under Diagnostic Impression: Alcohol Abuse/Dependence, Histrionic Personality Disorder, Severe with Dependent Features, Organic Brain Syndrome Secondary to Alcohol Abuse, Dominated completely by Tina.

Specifically, under "Relationship with Tina," Dr. Donner wrote "Robert Myers drank heavily day and night, and continued this pattern of drinking throughout his entire relationship with Tina. Mr. Myers became "Tina's slave" (his words): "I did the wash, laundry, cooked. I don't know why I became her slave. I loved her." He turned his financial affairs over to her, as he had done with Mary Ruth. He spent money on her without any thought to limits or logic. He married Tina shortly after Mary Ruth's death to help her get her children from her previous marriages back from foster homes. Even when she turned State's witness against him, he tried to find some reason to justify her doing so. He went along with almost anything that Tina requested.

The Mental Status Examination revealed "Mr. Myers was cooperative, articulate, not at all introspective, but very pleasant, almost cheerful. He appeared to be very naïve and almost childlike in his demeanor. He was not euphoric, but he did not display the expected anxiety or anger when he discussed his marital history. He realized that death is a possibility, but he discussed this almost blandly." He described a religious conversion that started in December 1981. "God came into my life," he said. "It is God's will that I am in jail." He spends his time reading the bible and praying. His hobbies included golf, puttering around the house, and lifting weights. Soon after meeting Mary Ruth, he said his life turned around completely. Like a very young child, he idealizes whoever is the important woman in his life at the moment and sees her as very powerful, exciting, and gratifying. He is overly trusting of others, very suggestible, easily manipulated by a female authority figure, and unable to use communication and compromise as ways to solve problems."

"Alcohol also increases impulsivity, and Myers' chronic abuse rendered him even more dependent on whomever was the designated caretaker. When not under marked pressure, Mr. Myers functions as a responsible, conventional, law-abiding citizen. Under severe stress (divorce, problems with children) he does not have the maturity to deal with the situation in a way that is productive, rather than destructive. Tina came along to "rescue him," and he immediately grabbed onto her, finding her both exciting and domineering, and ultimately destructive for him. He became a pawn in the subsequent drama of Tina's, going along with the script as long as he was bolstered by Tina's attention and the heavy use of alcohol."

Dr. Donner was a compelling "expert" witness. He explained that he had tested Myers and analyzed his background and personality and concluded that Myers was a gullible man incapable of violence, and that he became a slave to his third wife Tina Myers.

He testified "that Myers wouldn't hurt a soul. Even though he made threats, no one took them seriously because everyone knew Bobby." He concluded that while Myers was not insane at the time of the murder, Myers suffered from a personality disorder, a histrionic personality. His ability to reason, to be introspective, and to look at things in depth were impaired. He was an extremely gullible individual, to a fault. He looked for magical solutions to his problems and showed an absolute lack of insight into his own personality. It was easy for him to become infatuated. With people, he wasn't very smart at all. He was stupid, as a matter of fact, because according to the tests, "Myers was good with numbers but had little sense concerning people. He is a dependent and naïve man who is always trying to get others to like him."

He continued "the women Myers had known had somewhat dominated and directed him. He had great difficulty in standing up to any of them. He cannot behave in an aggressive fashion. For example, Myers did not want to buy the Turkey Foot Road home, but he did so at the request of Mary Ruth. With Tina, he explained, "He was very much like a child that she was carrying here and there. Myers would go to almost any length to gain approval and was incapable of being independent." He pointed out that Myers dated Mary Ruth while he was still married to his first wife, and began dating Tina while Mary Ruth was still alive. "He could not leave a woman without someone to replace that woman. Tina apparently did all kinds of disparaging things to him after they were married, but he could not leave her. Tina and Bobby were both drinking heavily, but she was a barmaid who could drink Bobby under the table. She always did most of the driving. He was very much like a baby at this point."

Donner described Myers' life as a boy. "He was a well-behaved student who played the tuba in the high school band and who, at 15 years old, saved the life of his drowning friend. He had never achieved top grades in school because he worked from the time he was eight years old."

Hickman knew that he could not effectively cross-examine this expert. No one could, without a great deal of caution and preparation. When he was questioned by the prosecution about the threats that Myers had made, Dr. Donner replied, "That was a way to ventilate his anger. He threatened people but he was all talk and no action." After a few perfunctory questions, Hickman wisely decided not to try to press him further.

The next witness was a forensic psychiatrist, Ellen G. McDaniel, M.D. She was an Associate Professor of Psychiatry at the University Of Maryland School Of Medicine in the Institute of Psychiatry and Human Behavior. Her detailed report was also offered as an exhibit.

She had concluded that Myers had continued his pattern of drinking heavily day and night throughout his entire relationship with Tina and only detoxified when he was jailed in November 1981. While he never became abusive when intoxicated, he did become very silly and would act in an indiscreet, uninhibited, and socially inappropriate way. She also concluded that he became "Tina's slave." He did the wash, laundry and cooked. He maintained that he married Tina to help her get her children back from foster homes. Soon often meeting Mary Ruth while still married to his first wife, Pat, his life turned around completely. Following his 13-year marriage, he went through a separation, divorce, and remarriage in rapid sequence. His compulsive drinking happened within a year.

In the area of interpersonal relationships, it was Dr. McDaniel's opinion that "Myers had always had difficulty, particularly with women. He was exceptionally dependent on a woman's interest in him and would do whatever was required to maintain it. Like a very young child, he idealized whoever was the important woman in his life at the moment and saw her as very powerful, exciting, and gratifying. Any problems, negative aspects or unpleasant attributes were always denied. Thus, unlike in a more mature relationship, these factors about the individual were not given consideration and did not become a part of the decision to pursue the relationship. Myers was thus eventually bound to be disappointed. He was able to see the negative side of the picture only if another woman that he could idealize was available to meet his emotional needs. Only then could he permit the heavy curtain of denial to be lifted. His disappointment with the woman with whom he was having problems was then sudden and considerable.

"When Mary Ruth came on the scene, he left Pat and their sexual problems. When Tina arrived, he left Mary Ruth and the problems with the children. These defects (immature object relationships, massive use of denial) which are considerable ones in his personality, made him overly trusting of others, very suggestible, and easily manipulated by a female authority figure. He was unable to use communication and compromise as ways to solve problems in relationships."

Echoing Dr. Donner almost verbatim, Dr. McDaniel observed that "Myers was very pleasant, almost cheerful. He appeared to be very naïve and almost childlike in his demeanor. He did not display the expected anxiety or anger when he discussed his marital history, Tina turning State's witness against him, the possibility of a death sentence, or a long prison sentence. He realized that death was a possibility but he discussed it almost blandly."

He had also repeated to Dr. McDaniel his religious conversion that had started in December 1981. "God came into my life, and it is God's will that I am in jail. It helped me straighten my life up as I was going astray," he said. He spent his time reading the Bible and praying. He had no fantasies of revenge. Dr. McDaniel reported he had above average intelligence but his judgment was extremely poor, and he had no insight into his behavior. Until his marriage to Mary Ruth, he had lived a productive and responsible life. He had worked hard, even as a child and had functioned as a responsible conventional law-abiding citizen.

Dr. McDaniel also diagnosed him as having alcohol dependence and a severe histrionic personality disorder. While he was sane at the time of the crime and competent to stand trial, she concluded that mitigating factors included his chronic state of alcohol intoxication around the time of the crime, and that this substance abuse severely impaired his ability to conform his conduct to the requirements of the law. She stated that he had a decidedly submissive role in a relationship with a woman who played a major role in the murder, and that Myers was under the domination of Tina. She observed that there was no past history of violent or illegal behavior.

Dr. McDaniel had been qualified as an expert witness in similar situations in Maryland Courts many times before and was consequently considered a "professional witness." She was very intelligent and polished and responded to my questions by initially looking at me and then turning to Judge Burns and delivering the rest of her remarks to him. Wisely, Tom Hickman did not question her at all, but rather profusely thanked her for taking "the time to come here today." He knew that any attempt to challenge or refute her in any way would only have served to allow her to repeat and re-emphasize her conclusions.

One morning, while incarcerated and awaiting trial, Myers had saved the life of a cellmate in the Carroll County jail who was attempting to hang himself. Cecil L. Redman was a 16-year-old charged with murdering a 17-year-old female neighbor. He later asserted an insanity plea but he was deemed responsible and received a life term.

On December 16, 1981, Myers had awoken in his cell and discovered his cellmate hanging by a bed sheet. He had to step up on the bars to release the loop around his neck, administered mouth-to-mouth resuscitation, and pounded on Cecil's chest. The youth began breathing.

The inmate left a suicide note to his parents which read, "Dear Mom and Dad, I am sorry it had to end this way, but I have no reason to live. I never did. I am just putting myself out of my own misery. Even my lawyer don't care. He never came to see me." He left a "Will" in which he wrote: "I leave everything in my possession outside this here cell to my family and everything I own inside (pack of cookies, sheets, clothes, blanket) to my only friend Bob Myers."

Myers testified in Redman's defense, to this supposed suicide attempt, but a guard had observed that the mouth-to-mouth ministrations were not necessary since the youth was breathing. This obviously made the suicide attempt suspect. It was still worth raising in the sentencing phase of Myers' own trial, however. It helped make the prosecutors look a little inconsistent and harsh, another distraction from the brutality of Mary Ruth's murder. I wanted to humanize Myers as much as possible.

In 1776 America, suicide was a crime, which meant attempted suicide also was a crime. At the time of the American Revolution, suicide was punishable by forfeiture of the dead person's estate to the Crown. Additionally, a person who committed suicide could not be buried in hallowed ground. Under common law, his body was subject to desecration. But the British Parliament, as well as the General Assembly, later repealed the laws requiring the forfeiture of the estate.

Much more recently, there had been two attempted suicide cases in Carroll County. One charge of attempted suicide in 1979, months before the Myers murder, was dropped. However, another had occurred after the Myers murder and Thomas E. Hickman had argued that the act still must be a crime, because the Legislature never formally outlawed desecration of the body of a suicide. District Judge Donald M. Smith had found Robert L. Humple guilty of attempted suicide and sentenced him to 90 days in jail to be served concurrently with a sentence for assaulting an officer. Hickman had said he used the threat of criminal prosecution to get people who have attempted suicide to seek counseling. David Burke, Esq., Humple's attorney, complained publicly, throwing Hickman's treatment of Tina Myers back in his face: "This Hickman is the same guy who granted immunity" to Ernestine (Tina) Gillen Myers, charged in the contract killing of her husband's then-wife, "and he puts this kid through the ringer for attempted suicide,"

Humple had taken an appeal to the Circuit Court and Judge Burns listened to expert testimony from psychiatrists stating that prosecuting someone who attempts suicide does more harm than good. Hickman's position was that suicide attempts were a real headache for the police because they are listed as the kinds of events police have to investigate. Burns ruled that while the Legislature had never specifically abolished the English common law crime of suicide, it had "implicitly done so" by abolishing, in 1809, imprisonment as one of the penalties for the crime. Without this penalty there could be no crime. Hickman got the Attorney General's office to appeal the decision to the Court of Special Appeals and it was ruled that Judge Burns was correct.

Once I learned that this "suicide case" had occurred just a few months earlier, I thought that it was helpful to stress Myers' actions in saving his cell-mate from that fate since Judge Burns and Hickman had been on opposite sides of the issue. In this case, Hickman was seeking death and in the other, he was arguing that a person who was unsuccessful in killing himself should be punished. The irony and hypocrisy couldn't be missed, nor should it be.

CHAPTER 27:
THE TESTIMONY OF
FATHER TOBEY

"There is no chapel on the day on which they hang a man . . ."
— The Ballad of Reading Gaol, Oscar Wilde

Father Meyer Tobey had been born into a Jewish family, but had converted to Roman Catholicism when he had attended an old Jesuit seminary, Woodstock College, as a young man. His family at first threatened to "sit shiva," demonstrating that they believed he should be shunned, and was "dead" to them, but eventually accepted him in his new faith. He ministered to the general population in the Maryland Penitentiary for 11 years and also comforted those who were scheduled to be executed. At every opportunity, Father Tobey would attempt to persuade all who would listen that the death penalty was repugnant. He often testified before the Maryland Legislature, and also in the sentencing phase of capital cases, sharing his recollections and observations of the executions he had witnessed in the Maryland gas chamber. In addition to his anti-death-penalty work, Father Tobey was active in prison reform, and helped found one of the first Halfway Houses in Maryland. It was formally named "The Dismas House" after The Patron Saint of Thieves and other sinners, but in the prison system, it became known as "The Dismal House," to the priest's great amusement.

St. Dismas is also The Patron Saint of death row prisoners, penitent criminals and prison chaplains.

I had met Father Tobey ten years earlier when I was a young prosecutor. I had traveled to Annapolis to testify against the death penalty. We both appeared before The Maryland Senate Judiciary Committee, which was supposedly considering the repeal of the death penalty in 1971. We were both adamant in our opposition and we struck up a bond. He had a lot of practical experience and his testimony was riveting. I had shared with him the fact that I had sat in the gas chamber, when we had been on a field trip to the Maryland Penitentiary, a few years earlier. I was one of about 20 law students who were being given a tour of Death Row. The door to the gas chamber was open. I seized my opportunity and went inside it, pulled the door closed and sat down. I did experience a moment of panic, but it was not long before the Guards reacted and ordered me out. I was made to apologize to everyone, which I did profusely, and I was given a big lecture by the Dean. Father Tobey had been in the Chamber right after executions and explained to me that the gas lingered there for hours. He understood that my way of dealing with the enormity of it all was to play the clown. He understood.

Judge Luke Burns had been a candidate for the priesthood. He had spent several years in a Jesuit seminary as a young man, and had met Father Tobey there. At the time of the Myers' trial, I had not seen Father Tobey for several years and he had retired. I was able to locate him in Washington D.C., though, and he eagerly agreed to travel to Westminster to testify on Myers' behalf. He told me that he remembered Judge Burns from the Seminary.

When I was a teenager, my uncle, Paddy Shevlin, insisted that we learn "The Ballad of Reading Goal." Oscar Wilde, the Irish playwright, had written it there while he was serving his own two-year prison sentence at hard labor. The poem describes the impact of an upcoming execution on other inmates and staff. "There is no chapel on the day on which they hang a man; the chaplain's heart is far too sick, or his face is far too wan." I had read it again in Lee's Motel. I was fully prepared. This penalty stage would now determine whether Myers would be executed or be imprisoned for life. I felt confident that my two chaplains would come through.

When Father Tobey arrived in the courthouse just before the noon recess, I took him back to the Judge's chambers. They had not seen each other for many years and hugged as soon as we walked in. I sat with them for a few minutes. There was no prosecutor present. They started to reminisce about various "Fathers" they had known. "Do you remember Father so and so?" and, "Do you remember Father so and so?" I soon left them alone to chat while I went to get lunch. I felt smug. "This man needs a priest not a lawyer!" Hell, I would provide two priests!

We had decided that apart from his personal observations about executions, Father Tobey could use the opportunity on the stand to summarize the history of the barbaric practice nationally, but more particularly, in the State of Maryland.

When I returned for the afternoon session, Father Tobey was to be my next witness. He made a powerful impression with his gray hair, wire-rimmed glasses, dark black vestments and white clerical collar. We had the stage and the captive audience was fresh after the luncheon recess.

Father Tobey began with the earliest recorded execution in Maryland. In 1773, four convict servants were hanged in Frederick for murdering their master. No standard method was used, and no special training was provided to the "hangman." He was often the local sheriff or warden, who rarely got a lot of experience with the difficult task. Some of these executions were protracted and gruesome affairs with the convicted man often strangling to death over a long period of time.

The State Legislature began debating the appropriate punishment for murder in 1809, and noted that killings "differ so greatly from each other in the degree of their atrociousness, that it is unjust to involve them in the same punishment." It was decided after much debate, to create "degrees" of murder, reserving the death penalty only for the killings characterized as first-degree murder. Nearly 100 years later in 1908 the General Assembly rewrote the law so that judges could impose a sentence of life in prison and not death, which had been mandatory until then.

Father Tobey described the mobs that often turned out to watch these hangings. He explained that the last public hanging in the USA occurred in Owensboro, Kentucky in August 1936. The man was hung in a field in the presence of a crowd numbering between 10,000 and 15,000.

"The curious mobs" who showed up to watch these hangings in Maryland often got out of control, creating huge public spectacles. Consequently, in 1922 the Maryland Legislature centralized all executions at the Maryland Penitentiary in downtown Baltimore.

Because little thought was given to the length of the rope, the distance of the drop, the weight of the individual or the size and strength of his neck, executions were still bungled. Miscalculations sometimes resulted in ripping the head completely off, or necessitated swinging on the prisoner's legs to hasten the breaking of his neck. It was disturbing to watch someone dangling for many minutes while they slowly choked to death.

Father Tobey noted, "In Maryland, with the passage of The Toleration Act in 1649, blasphemy and the denial of the divinity of Christ or The Holy Trinity were added to stealing over 12 pence and witchcraft among the list of capital crimes. That always seemed a little odd to me!"

The priest then got emotional when he said, "Do you know that the last execution in Wisconsin occurred in 1851?" He took from his notes a single page and read from it. "The last agony is over. The crowd have been indulged in its insane passion for the sight of a judicially murdered man. McCaffary murdered his wife without the sanction of the law and McCaffary has been murdered according to the law. We do not complain that the law has been enforced. We complain that the law exists. The prisoner we know received from the law all the mercy and lenity that the law and its faithful execution could give . . . We hope this will be the last execution that shall ever disgrace the mercy-expecting citizens of the State of Wisconsin."

Father Tobey carefully looked around the courtroom as he explained that there had been 15,000 sanctioned state killings from 1608 to 1972. Maryland had kept up with the pace, recording 309 executions in that time period. He quoted a favorite saying on death row: "those without the capital, get the punishment."

In explaining its history, he noted the early practical reason for the penalty. Governments did not have enough prisons to safely restrain violent people for a long period of time. Rather than set them free, they were executed.

He argued that the system used to identify, isolate and condemn the guilty was based on the false concept that we would have 100% accuracy. Recent history and the development of new technologies, however, has demonstrated that at least a few hundred innocent people have been executed.

Father Tobey noted that it costs about eight times as much to bring about a death sentence, but that was not his real concern. One reason the court in 1972 had abolished the old death penalty was that there were no guidelines or standards for deciding who should die or who should live. The priest cited

Justice Harry Blackmun's conclusion: "that by debating the combination of chemicals which should be used to bring about a 'more humane' death, the country was 'tinkering with the machinery of death,'" and he wanted nothing to do with it.

Finally, Father Tobey argued that the imposition of the penalty was so arbitrary that it had become "unconstitutionally random." In 1972, there were 600 prisoners waiting to die in the United States, but their cases were all reversed. Even among those convicted of murder, there was a greater chance of being struck by lightning than of being executed.

Father Tobey explained that one is quickly made aware of the relationship between political absolutism and the heavy dependence upon capital punishment as a vital instrument in maintaining political stability or the status quo. Prior to the rise of Mussolini's Fascism and Hitler's Nazism, both Italy and Germany had abolished the death penalty. Of course, during their respective regimes, capital punishment was reintroduced on a grand scale. He said, "There should not exist in the United States a collective attitude conducive to the exercise of capital punishment that in any way reflects an acceptance of the theory of the expendability of human life. History has taught us what the result of such an attitude can be."

Father Tobey was giving a loving sermon now. "Vengeance should have no place in modern society. Vengeance cannot be an atonement between the individual and the State but can only be a private balance. The State must act rationally and deliberately and justly. It is difficult to see how a gentler nonviolent humane society can be created, since executions only serve as a brutal throwback to the full horror of man's inhumanity in an earlier time. We stress the sanctity of human life and condemn those who would intentionally deprive another of his right to live. The function of the criminal law is to protect the law abiding—not to satiate societies' lust for revenge."

Father Tobey gave some specific historical anecdotes about some Baltimore judges who had served several decades before. Samuel King Dennis was from an old line Worcester County family. When he was appointed The Chief Judge of the Supreme Bench in 1928, he dictated that no longer would judges sit in their business suits as they had throughout the entire state of Maryland since the Revolutionary War. As a reaction to the imposing gowns and wigs that

English tradition had dictated, the colonists as soon as they had the option, discarded these judicial robes. They then wore business suits.

Dennis was the first Maryland judge to adopt the British tradition of wearing a robe. But he had a cruel streak and enjoyed his reputation as a "Hanging Judge." He knew that capital punishment would never solve the crime problem but he liked to joke that it would "Put a dent in it!" He imposed death whenever he could. Courthouse habitués laughed, "Swing and Sway with Sammy K!" He refused to follow the modern concept of suspending a sentence or any part of it. He declared, "I have no faith in suspended sentences as a deterrent! The only deterrent for some of these people is to suspend them on the end of a rope."

Other judges wanted to use the death penalty to project their individual strength and toughness. One bragged that "the death penalty may not be a deterrent to the public at large but it would sure as hell deter this particular son-of-a-bitch who is about to be executed."

Father Tobey described a bizarre execution which took place in 1906. Eugene O' Dunne was an associate judge in Baltimore from 1926 to 1945. Before that, though, when Dunne had been a young prosecutor, he arranged for the execution of George Scott Lee, who had raped two Somerset County women. Lynchings were prevalent at the time, and to avoid this risk, Lee's trial was transferred to Baltimore. Lee was convicted in a court trial and sentenced to death within three hours. There was great fear that Lee could not be peacefully executed because the citizens were angry and had organized lynch mobs. The Governor directed O' Dunne and others to hang Lee off the coast of Somerset County, in the middle of the Chesapeake Bay.

The gallows at the Baltimore County jail was packed up and transported with Lee, The Baltimore City Sheriff, his deputies, several prosecutors and others, in the middle of the night aboard a steamer. The sealed envelope containing Lee's death warrant was opened and it called for Lee's execution on Smith Island the next morning. O'Dunne read the warrant to Lee in the moonlight. Lee confessed his guilt. The deputy sheriffs went ashore in skiffs to erect the gallows. A short time later, Lee was rowed there and hung. The coffin which contained Lee's remains was left on the dock at Princess Anne, much to the surprise and consternation of the angry crowd that had gathered there.

Thomas Hickman objected several times that this testimony was irrelevant because hanging was no longer used. He realized that I was attempting to put the facts of the Myers case far into the background while stressing the unstated theme that there have been lots of murders and few people were executed. Hickman was not surprised when Judge Burns overruled him, "Please continue, Father Tobey."

The priest resumed the history lesson explaining that 75 people had "stepped onto the gallows" in Maryland over the previous 34 years. 55 were executed for murder and the rest for rape. After Edward Grammer had been executed in 1954, one more person— William C. Thomas—was to be the last in 1955. He was executed for rape and murder.

The gas chamber was installed in 1956 as an alternative to hanging and in an attempt to make the killing process more humane and reduce the trauma for the correctional staff and other witnesses. Four men were asphyxiated in the gas chamber before it, too, was abolished in 1993 in favor of "lethal injection."

Father Tobey described how he would discuss prisoners' cases with them since there was no Public Defender's office at that time, and even in death penalty cases, there was no right to counsel once the conviction had been affirmed.

He saved the life of at least one inmate on death row. John L. Brady, then 25, had been sentenced to die in the gas chamber for robbing and killing a disabled man. Brady's accomplice, Charles Donald Boblit, had given the police five confessions. In the fifth one, Mr. Boblit admitted he had strangled the victim. An investigation revealed that the State had improperly not provided Brady with these facts, which could have been used to mitigate his sentence. Brady, while not innocent because he was involved with the robbery, should have been given this evidence. It was exculpatory as to the appropriate sentence.

Father Tobey was also a professor of criminology at Loyola College. He asked Clifton Bamberger, an attorney who had once studied sociology under him at Loyola, and Elsbeth Bothe, who later would become a Baltimore City Circuit Court Judge, to represent Brady. They took the case to the Supreme Court of the United States. In 1963, it ruled in a landmark decision that prosecutors have a duty to disclose exculpatory material. The result was "one of the most important cases in criminal jurisprudence"—a 7 to 2 ruling that Mr. Brady was entitled to a new sentencing. Brady received a new hearing and avoided execution.

Father Tobey testified about the executions he had actually witnessed, and the trauma caused to everyone involved. He told of the sometimes difficult nature of killing another human being. He described a hanging where the inmate's neck had not been broken with the fall and that a prison official had pulled on his legs until he strangled to death.

Father Tobey recalled the four people who were executed in Maryland's gas chamber: Daniel Kier on January 23, 1957; Eddie Lee Daniels on June 28, 1957; Leonard M. Shockley on April 10, 1959; and Nathaniel Lipscomb on June 9, 1961. Father Meyer Tobey was the Chaplain at the Maryland Penitentiary during that period and in any debate on the death penalty, Father Tobey would share his recollections and observations of the executions that took place there.

Eddie Lee Daniels was the first to be gassed, on July 28, 1957, for the murder of the owner of a Silver Spring Montgomery County car wash during a robbery. Daniels was led to the death chamber and was strapped into the chair. As the leather straps were tightened around his arms, legs, and chest and he sat passively with a look of disbelief and terror in his eyes. Father Tobey, standing outside looking in through the clear glass, had instructed him that he would say prayers for him as soon as Daniels looked him in the eyes and that they would both say prayers together. As the cyanide pill was dropped into the sulfuric acid and gas began to rise, both the condemned man and the priest started repeating, "My Jesus I love you, My Jesus I love you."

Daniels kept his eyes on Father Tobey through the window and the two repeated together, "My Jesus, I love you," as the gas began to take effect. "His whole body twisted and jerked and then his head dropped," Father Tobey recalled. Although he was believed to be dead, "He lifted his head up and looked me straight in the eyes and he began to form the words, 'My Jesus, I—' and his head dropped again." The testimony was riveting.

The fumes started to engulf Daniels and he began gasping for breath. The veins in his neck were standing out and seemed as though they were about to burst and his face began to turn blue. Daniels head fell back and he started straining against his straps and his eyes began to bulge out. After his head had dropped several times, the attending physician said it was finished, but just at that point Daniels lifted his head one more time and looked at Father Tobey. Their eyes met and as Father Tobey began to repeat the words "My Jesus . . ." Daniel's body went into convulsions, his head began to drop and white frothy saliva ran from his mouth and he stopped moving. Father Tobey said the State of Maryland had done its job. Daniels had suffered for three or four minutes after the pellets had been dropped. Those present agreed that he had to be suffering, and he had to know what was going on. Death by lethal gas is a lingering, painful, and terrifying death.

Carl Daniel Kier, at age 23, was the second to meet his fate in the chamber on January 23, 1959. He had been on parole in June 1956 when he murdered a Towson woman in her hillside home on Charles Street. It was one of the most vicious crimes of that time. Kier was tried and convicted twice. The Court of Appeals had overturned the first jury verdict. It upheld the 2nd verdict and sentence, imposed by a two-judge court trial after the case had been removed to Frederick in October 1957. Governor Theodore R. McKeldin, who had commuted 16 of 21 death sentences during his eight years in office, reprieved Kier once before finally denying executive clemency. His term ended before the execution, and the newly inaugurated Governor J. Millard Tawes conducted a final review and also denied clemency. Years later, McKeldin expressed his great regret for not granting clemency in the five cases that he had refused it. At the end of his life he reflected that these decisions had been the biggest mistakes he had ever made.

Kier wore only white shorts as four uniformed guards led him into the steel gas chamber just before 10:00 p.m. on January 23, 1959 and strapped him into the perforated metal chair. For the witnesses who were peering into the hexagonal steel chamber through the large observation windows, it was like watching television without the sound. Kier sat quietly, his lips moving in silent prayer as he stared out at the Jesuit chaplain who had spent the day with him in the nearby deathwatch cells. With Kier secured, the guards backed out through the door. The last one turned the mechanism to seal the chamber airtight, leaving Kier as alone as a human being can be.

The telephone line to Annapolis was open; there was no last second call. A few ticks past 10 o'clock, Warden Vernon L. Peppersack signaled. A lever lowered a bag of potassium cyanide crystals into a pan of sulfuric acid beneath the chair. There was a quick puff of fumes, then nothing, at least nothing visible. The chamber filled quickly with deadly hydrocyanic gas. Although Kier flinched at the hiss of the crystals reaching the acid, he did not struggle against his bonds. His face remained impassive. He breathed; his chest heaved once and then again.

One minute and forty-two seconds later, the Chief Medical Officer, listening to the monitors attached to Kier's body, nodded and said, "He's dead." Kier's head slumped forward, and then rose again in an apparent postmortem nerve reaction. This happened several times and the electrocardiograph continued to register heart action for several minutes, but it was over. Kier was dead—quickly, quietly, and efficiently. The guards hustled the silent witnesses down the stairs from the prison hospital building and back across the yard, through several clanking barred doors, and out into the black winter night. Outside there were no vigils or news conferences for the witnesses to describe the execution as inhumane and barbaric. There were no sign waving demonstrators. The death sentence had been carried out quickly, quietly, privately and completely without passion or public outcry.

Nathaniel Lipscomb was the last to be put to death by gas. He had raped and murdered three women and during this series of crimes, East Baltimore was gripped in a reign of terror. Women fearing attack stayed home from churches, night school and civic meetings. Judge James K. Cullen pronounced the penalty after a court trial. "In the case of the murder of Mrs. Lottie R. Knight, the sentence of the court is that you, Nathaniel Lipscomb, shall be taken by the sheriff to be delivered into the custody of the penitentiary, there to remain until the time of your execution." Lipscomb who had desperately relied upon a plea of insanity mumbled, "I'm not guilty of these crimes."

The priest's testimony left Myers red nosed and teary eyed. I cynically thought, "The preacher looked at me and he cried, he said, come and walk with me down that long last mile . . . now for once in my life I'm alone, Oh, I gotta get a message to you for in one more hour my life will be through."

Father Tobey made an excellent witness. As I suspected, Tom Hickman was most respectful and almost apologetic, asking mostly innocuous questions. He was profuse in his thanks for the witness having "taken the time" to come to the court.

Judge Burns took a 20-minute recess before the closing arguments.

CHAPTER 28:
A PLEA FOR LIFE

"Murder by legal sentence is immeasurably more terrible
than murder by brigands . . ."
— Crime and Punishment, Fyodor Dostoevsky

The prosecutors had waived their right to an opening statement concerning the sentencing that would lead Myers to the gas chamber or life in prison. I again went on the attack and complained about their strategy. "They don't see fit to name the reasons why this man's life should be snuffed out. I must look upon them as cold-hearted and unfair because I am forced to guess at their arguments and respond to my own guesses." I pointed to my pale, blond client who was taking notes on a legal pad and I said, "These two men seek to execute, to kill, this human being. But they don't even see fit to stand up in this court and enunciate to you the reasons this man's life should be snuffed out."

The night before, I had gone to Maggie's Restaurant in Westminster for supper, and when I finished, I asked the waitress to prepare the same thing I had just eaten for me to take out. A steak, baked potatoes, and salad. We were to appear the next morning in court for the judge's decision on "life or death." I smuggled it into the jail—his "last meal." I let him eat it while I walked back and forward, pretending that I was him begging for mercy from the judge. He pissed me off when after several minutes he put down his knife and fork and said that he thought the *food* was really good. I was trying to spoon-feed him the words to save his life but he hadn't really been listening and instead had been enjoying his meal.

Myers asked me to write it out or repeat it for him. I refused. I had reminded him a little earlier that while I had said he was innocent throughout the trial, he needed to say it for himself. He insisted on writing that down! He wrote some notes. I sang him that Patsy Cline song, "Will Your Lawyer Talk to God for You?"

"We all face that final judgment and it's very strict they say, When your time comes, I wonder what you'll do, Will you bow your head in shame or will you turn your head away, or will your lawyer talk to God for you?"

The next day, I went down the back elevator to meet him in the bullpen. We were then accompanied by three guards. The five of us got on the small elevator from the basement to go to the court on the second-floor. All the evidence had been presented and this session was for our arguments.

I used Father Tobey's descriptions of executions to argue that the emotional impact of knowing the moment of your own death was so alarming and all-consuming that the process and this damage should be considered a mitigating factor in and of itself. Tobey's had been a powerful voice against the death penalty.

I decried what I saw as an absurd checklist to be used by judges in totaling aggravating and mitigating circumstances to determine if death is warranted. "As though were dealing with some IBM punch card and you just entered death, and that'll be the end of Bob Myers."

With an execution, all that last hope, which makes dying 10 times as easy, is taken away. Death is guaranteed. An additional awful torture lies in the fact that there is certainly no escape. There is no torture in the world more terrible.

At one point I mocked the State's attempt to get executions back on track. "That's right! We must put some life back into the death penalty to show that we really, really, care about life."

The criminal law revolution of the 1960s and 1970s made it much more difficult for the individual States to be able to execute its citizens. Between 1972–1978 there was no workable death penalty in Maryland. Although capital punishment was resurrected in 1978 it was still a complicated process. The Public Defender's Office became experts at seeking post conviction relief. There were many rounds involved. An automatic appeal; post conviction; habeas corpus; appeals; writs of certiorari to the State and the Federal courts; to the Supreme Court back and up again. All free for the convicted murderer.

In my closing argument, I cited Dr. Karl Menninger, the distinguished psychiatrist who concluded that under no circumstances, should society condone the taking of a human life. "To a physician discussing the wiser treatment of our fellow men, it seems hardly necessary to add that under no circumstances should we kill him. It was never considered right for doctors to kill their patients, no matter how helpless the condition. Similarly, capital punishment is morally wrong, even though punishing and even killing criminals may yield a grim kind of gratification. There are times when we are so shocked at the depredation of an offender that we persuade ourselves that this man should die. We had better correct this mistake. However, playing God in this way has no conceivable moral or scientific justification."

I cited the factors that should mitigate against the death penalty: the lack of a criminal record, the fact that his two codefendants did not get the death penalty, and that Tina would be freed within a few days. I also delivered a scathing attack on the prosecution team for the post verdict party at Maggie's, and produced another copy of The Evening Sun newspaper which detailed Frank Coleman hitting Tom Stansfield with a plate of whipped cream. I glared at the prosecutors while they sat, heads down, taking notes, and launched into my attack. "Barbarians would not have a system of justice to determine the fate of this man. Barbarians would have a party. These two men knew that they would be coming into court to ask for this man's execution and the lack of dignity shown by them should be a mitigating factor and another reason why Bobby Myers should not be executed."

I argued that Myers' drinking had substantially impaired him and that he was unlikely to commit any future crimes, and that he was "provoked" by another person, namely Tina. I also added that since the statute did not delineate what youth is, that even though Myers was 40, I felt that he was of "youthful age." I included Myers' numerous charitable acts and his concern and love for Tina's children.

I summarized what I claimed were thirteen mitigating circumstances that I believed should serve to keep Myers out of the gas chamber. "The State is relying on only one aggravating circumstance, the nature of the crime itself." I argued that the State should not even have considered seeking the death penalty. "The mitigating circumstances easily outweigh the aggravating circumstances, even if the defendant had the burden of proof, which he does not." I facetiously added, "Hopefully, the state will see the error of its ways or, in my opinion, they stand in the same place as Daniel Chadderton. They use their legal education and position instead of bullets."

I kept my eye on Judge Burns, waiting to see if he wanted me to sit. I couldn't tell. So I kept going. I invoked Dostoevsky, who himself once faced the firing squad and was reprieved at the last minute and described the cold-blooded horror of execution. "The chief and worst pain may not be in the bodily suffering, but in one's knowing for certain that in an hour and then in 45 minutes and then in half an hour and then in 10 minutes and then half a minute and then now at this very moment, the soul will leave the body and one will cease to be a man and that that's bound to happen; the worst part of it is that it is certain. To kill for murder is a punishment incomparably worse than the crime itself. Murder by legal sentence is immeasurably more terrible than murder by brigands. Anyone murdered by brigands, whose throat is cut at night in the woods or something of that sort, must surely hope to escape till the last minute. Some want to use death to solve social problems. They want to promote and use death as their ally or tool and seem quite proud of themselves." I quickly added "Their chests are all puffed up like bullfrogs in heat."

I argued that not only is the death penalty cruel, it is ". . . unusual . . ." in a constitutionally significant sense. In reality the penalty is exacted against only a small and erratically selected proportion of the persons convicted of similar crimes. Those chosen for execution have been the victims of a haphazard process. Normally, the decision to impose life or death lies in the unguided hands of the jury. In some States, the judge has the discretion to reduce a jury imposed death sentence to life imprisonment, also without any standards or criteria to guide him. These sentencing bodies are free to act on grounds of impulse, prejudice, or recent public outcry; they need give no reason for their life or death decision.

Other discretionary elements enter into this vital decision. The prosecutor may charge a capital offense or a lesser included one; in many jurisdictions he has the choice of asking for the death penalty or not asking for it. If the death penalty is rendered, the executive has total discretion on whether to commute the sentence. Each of these discretionary devices is more likely to work to the benefit of a defendant who has influence, money, or a good attorney. Therefore, the present criminal justice system leaves the poor, the uneducated, and members of minority groups with the ultimate penalty of execution. Each of these factors plays a large role in determining the ultimate decision of who will die.

The reason for the increasingly infrequent and arbitrary use of the death penalty is that society will no longer tolerate executions resulting from convictions in capital cases. In many States this has led to the complete abolition of the death penalty. In others it has led to the wider use of discretionary sentencing measures, particularly granting the jury the authority to render by its discretion a verdict of death. The public is apparently not sufficiently appalled by the few executions that do take place, to force the death penalty to be completely abolished. If, however, the death penalty were applied in all capital cases, the penalty would definitely be eliminated.

You can go to any institution and pick out many prisoners serving life sentences or less for crimes just as atrocious, and sometimes more so than most of those men on death row.

It is not surprising that those few executions performed in the name of society are carried out clandestinely, out of public view. The State is so ashamed of its process that it has to kill in the dead of night in private. We hide our executions because we are ashamed to show them, because they make men sick, and the only way that our civilization can accept them is if they are hidden from sight.

A premeditated crime is usually considered more serious than a crime of spontaneous violence. Capital punishment is the most premeditated of killings and cannot be equated to any one criminal's deed. For them to be the same, the criminal would have to have warned his victim of the date on which he would be murdered, and who for several months confined the victim until a horrible death is inflicted on him. (Incidentally, a decade later, the State's Attorney had failed to persuade a jury to execute the inmate who I was representing, and was confronted at the sentencing. My client had warned me that he was going to let the prosecutor know that he had the heart of a killer. As promised, during his allocution he placed one hand on the trial table, in front of me and with the other pointed in the prosecutor's face. "You tried to kill me! You're guilty of attempted murder!")

The death penalty looms over the lives of not only the inmate and his family and his lawyers, but also the correctional officers that house him. A defendant's friends, social workers, minister and others spend years with him before the actual execution. Notably absent are the prosecutors and judges who have determined that this judicial killing is appropriate. These participants in the death process ironically have had minimal contact with the defendant. In fact, they have the least contact. They have been insulated from the defendant's humanity, never having had a real opportunity to see him or "feel" him, as an individual or a human being. He is merely a set of facts and a face in the courtroom. The prosecutors and often the judge have determined very early on in the evolution of the case that he is to be killed. The defendant has become a target. To accept him as a human being like the rest of us would interfere with their ability to annihilate him.

I had questioned Father Tobey about new interpretations of the law on a national and statewide basis, and how that had thrown the entire death penalty apparatus into complete disarray. The US Supreme Court had invalidated 40 death penalty laws across the nation in 1972, but allowed its reinstatement in 1976. Maryland enacted its new death penalty statute two years later.

In order to further show how arbitrary the death penalty is, I referred to the many hundreds of murder convictions which had been reversed by two landmark cases: the Schowgurow case in 1966, and the Evans case ten years later. These two appellate opinions prevented and forestalled the Maryland death machine for many years.

In the case of Edward Evans, my wife, Vickie happened to be the appellate attorney arguing the case which made new law in Maryland. Evans, 18, received a 10-year sentence upon his conviction for second-degree murder. Evans had stabbed the victim during an altercation. The judge had instructed the jury that all homicides were presumed to be second-degree murder, with the state obligated to prove first-degree murder by a showing of willfulness or premeditation, and with the defendant obligated to prove the lesser account of manslaughter by showing mitigation or justification. Vickie filed a brief which complained that these instructions placed an unfair burden on the defendant and required him to produce evidence necessary to reduce the crime charged from first-degree murder to either second-degree murder or manslaughter.

The Supreme Court had recently decided a similar case from Maine, ruling that a defendant does not have to prove anything in that situation. The prosecution had to prove that mitigating factors were absent. So the Evans case was reversed by the Maryland Court of Appeals, but because the decision was made retroactive, it affected over 500 murder cases which had been prosecuted under the previous law. The ruling did not affect first-degree murder convictions because the elements necessary to prove first-degree murder had often already been produced by the state in those cases.

The Evans case necessitated the filing of hundreds of post conviction petitions and then the trial transcripts had to be obtained, memoranda written, and oral arguments heard by another court. The Evans opinion—100 pages long—contained a detailed history of homicide law. "The Ghost of Homicide Future," explained that it had been "but a matter of time before the common law's crazy quilt of murder and manslaughter—800 years in the making would come under the cold glare of latter day due process." Appellate lawyers and judges (unlike a trial attorney who is concerned with only one case,) sometimes have the opportunity to make sweeping changes which can have a profound impact on the quality of justice. It would take years to resolve all the cases seeking relief, citing "The Evans Case" as precedent.

Everything worth saying had already been said. Myers in his turn rose to address the court and he pulled from his pocket a 4 x 5 card. He looked down at his notes and said "Judge, I just want you to know I am innocent of the charges." He read it word for word, and then rambled on some more for what seemed like an interminable period of time. I tried not to squirm in my seat. I had admitted to the court that unlike most of my other clients, I liked "Bobby" Myers despite "his failings." I said, "All advocacy aside, he's a kind person and a gentle person." I often hate those I defend! I thought, 'I know, hate the crime, love the criminal!'—but I was starting to change my mind!

I was stunned that he would consider reading from a card to a packed courtroom that he was "innocent." I had repeatedly explained to him in our preparation for this sentencing hearing that he should keep it short and not use notes. Generally, a speaker who seems to be talking spontaneously appears genuine and has a greater impact than a person who seems to have prepared his remarks. Having to remind oneself to declare one's innocence and needing to read it before expressing it certainly lacked sincerity. This man really didn't have a clue.

Myers said, "The jury was wrong. I am innocent. I didn't want Mary Ruth to die. I didn't plan it, I didn't pay for it." He read these comments from his notes, his voice showing no emotion. He said he had faith that the Judge's decision will be guided by the will of God. Myers went on to say that he was shocked to learn of his third wife, Tina's, part in the murder and said, "I was a fool. I was a fool many times in my life, but I never hurt anybody." "Judge, you may wonder about my jovial nature," Myers continued, "but it's based upon my faith that God has determined all things. I want to thank you Judge Burns, whatever the sentence. I feel strongly and believe that you will do it with the will of God."

*****

The wait for Judge Burns' decision was not long. He took a recess for an hour to deliberate, while Hickman, Coleman and I passed the time chatting with our respective supporters. A number of jurors had returned as spectators. They wanted to hear the sentence pronounced in the case that occupied so many weeks and their hearts and their lives and their minds. Finally, Judge Burns returned to the bench with his decision. Myers smiled when Judge Burns sentenced him to life in prison. It was over.

*****

An hour later, the lights were out in the courthouse, and the spectators had gone to their suppers. Shelly Myers was stunned. Her father, Bobby Myers, had just been sentenced to life imprisonment for murder. She was having a hard time accepting the fact that he would not be around to share Christmas with her or to provide grandparental love should she have children. Shelly remembered a happy childhood when the whole family would go camping on weekends, or go out on Friday nights together or going to dinner, or shopping, or spend Saturday night at the stock car races.

She explained to reporters that it was a happy childhood until she was 12 years old, when things started to unravel between her mother and her father. They were not happy anymore. Shelly had to face choices she did not want to make. Her loyalties were towards her father, as he was so soft hearted. He was a gentle and pliable Dad; a man people called "Bobby." The good times did not end abruptly when her mother and father divorced. They slipped away gradually, and although she was placed in the custody of her mother, she came back to visit her father whenever she could.

When Robert married Mary Ruth, she didn't hit it off with Shelly. There was enough tension between them that when Shelly visited, she stayed with a friend. Mary Ruth did not like sharing any time with Shelly. When Tina first entered their lives, she was very charming, treating Shelly sweetly—like a princess. Gradually, though, Tina began to let it be known that Shelly was not welcome. Tina started to assert herself. Bobby and Tina would go out on Friday nights, and they would not allow Shelly to go with them. Bobby would say, "Well come on, let's bring Shelly with us," and Tina would say, "No, she must stay home to babysit." Bobby often suggested they could get a sitter, but Tina always insisted, "No, I said she stays here and she's the sitter."

When Mary Ruth was murdered, Shelly knew during investigation that her father and Tina were suspects. It was very difficult for her. When they arrested her dad, she was sure it was a mistake and that it would all go away. It had been two years of torment not only for her but also for others in the family who loved Bobby Myers. Every other Saturday since they arrested Bobby, she traveled from her home in Pennsylvania to visit with him for twenty minutes through the bars.

After the sentencing, Judge Burns agreed to let her spend some time with her father in a room in the courthouse. She sat on his lap and they just hugged each other and wept. The visit meant a lot to both of them and she felt that Judge Burns, who might give many gifts over this holiday season, would have none of them appreciated more than letting her see her father and be with him, where there were no bars between them. She wanted to make sure that Judge Burns understood her gratitude. Even though she only had a few minutes with her father, she felt that he was a fair and compassionate man allowing her this last extra taste of childhood.

Mary Ruth's relatives were satisfied with the life sentence given to Robert Myers. They had sat through the eight weeks of testimony in the trial and were glad that the three years of investigation and trial were over, even though they knew the appellate process would take several years more. They gathered briefly in the States Attorney's office after the sentence was announced. Mary Ruth's sister-in-law patted Coleman on the back and thanked him for his work; she said, "We won't ask you to go to Maggie's." Mary Ruth's brother, Grayson Fowble, said that his family had been close and will never again have a normal life. He said Mary Ruth was a lot of fun and that the family was not vindictive. "If you had killed all three co-defendants, it would not bring Mary Ruth back."

On the day Bobby Myers was sentenced to life in prison, Tina Myers told a *Baltimore New American* reporter that, "I'll be there when he gets out (of prison), I'll wait as long as it takes." More bullshit.

In December of 1982, Tina continued to express her love for Bobby Myers and complained she was tired of being publicly portrayed as an evil, black widow spider who was luring men into her web. She said that I had crucified her on the witness stand.

She said she did not love Myers when she married him in September 1979, but that she slowly grew to be in love with him. She was housed in the Garrett County Jail complex for more than 8 months and maintained, even after his conviction, "I love Bob" as she blinked back tears, stating that "I have four children and I wasn't sure I wanted to die for him." Tina could not wait for this interview with the reporter and allowed a new photograph to be taken of her. Myers was still waiting to be sentenced and faced the gas chamber while Tina, whose release from jail was imminent, wore designer jeans and a fashionable gray sweater. Her facial expressions ranged from serious to mournful, to amused, and she talked for fifteen minutes before allowing the photograph to be taken.

Tina Myers claimed to have nightmares that started immediately after the murder. She said that it was always Dan Chadderton stalking her in the middle of the night, and that the dream varied. She would go to bed and outside the room she would hear footsteps in the hallway and a man with a husky voice would say to her, "If you believe in God you better start praying," and he would shoot her nine times. Tina stated that it was awful, since there was not a day that went by that she did not think of it. She would lie in bed and close her eyes and see Dan Chadderton come to the foot of her bed and start shooting her.

Tina, who had been behind bars since she was arrested December 1, 1981, was in high spirits during the evening press interview she gave in Sutley's law office. As a reporter waited to speak to her, she was busy on the telephone announcing her release. "Jim, Tina. I'm out!" one conversation began. She also placed a call to homes of friends who were caring for three of her children, including a baby son and daughter fathered by Myers. Her fourth child was in foster care.

She arrived in Baltimore at 7:30 p.m. after a four-hour car journey with Philip M. Sutley, her attorney. Sutley said she was to spend the night in a downtown hotel. She was a free woman after more than a year in jail and was spending her first full day of liberty in Baltimore.

In an interview, Tina said she was considering staying in Maryland despite her earlier pledges to leave the state as soon as possible. "A lot of people want me to stay. I might stay," but she promised she would not settle in Carroll County, where the murder occurred and where public sentiment seems especially strong against her. "I don't have any friends in Carroll County," she said. "You could open a boutique in Westminster," Sutley suggested with a laugh. "Or a dating service," Tina said giggling.

As she was giving this press interview, Robert Myers was adjusting to his new life in prison in the reception and diagnostic center, less than a dozen blocks from Sutley's office. He was to remain there for several weeks until the state Division of Correction assigned him to one of the States' prisons.

Tina, who professed she still loved Bob Myers, said she would not attempt to visit him in prison, but she added that she hoped he would have some say "eventually" in the rearing of their two children. She had repeated in several jailhouse interviews that she would faithfully wait for Myers—"the only man I've ever loved"—to be released on parole, and that he could be out as early as 1993.

After nine months of protective custody in the Garrett County Detention Center, she was released on December 16, 1982, after prosecutors formally dropped the first-degree murder charge and the unrelated welfare charge against her before Judge Fred A Thayer. The proceedings took ten minutes while Hickman recited the agreement between Marco and the State and said that "the State was satisfied that she fulfilled the agreement."

On December 23, 1982, a Garrett County judge ruled that Carroll County had no claim over her jewelry despite the government's argument that Tina Myers owed compensation to the county for expenses incurred during her recent incarceration. After the suit had been filed, she threatened to move to Carroll County and "go on welfare" if the property was not returned to her. She made the threat in hostile letters to the commissioners who she labeled "bastards" after they had filed the suit. The judge had ruled that prisoners in jail under indictment are not liable for their living expenses, which he said should be paid by the indicting County.

In Montclair, California, Tina's father, Ernest Butcher, said, "I think they're releasing the wrong person." Butcher said he believed his daughter masterminded the matter and said, "I feel she is capable of having done it. They're taking her word for everything. To me, Bob Myers is not proven guilty of anything." The additional welfare charges against Tina Myers were dropped on January 18, 1984.

I filed an appeal immediately after the sentencing. The newspapers stated, "His wife, attorney Victoria Keating, probably will be handling Myers' appeal as an appellate public defender. She is the most qualified because she's been 'living with this case for the last year.'" It was not to be.

Michael Braudes, another excellent member of the Public Defender's Appellate Division, briefed the appeals. I met with him several times to give my input, but I felt strongly that there were no winning issues, and I did not need to devote any more of my energy to the case. The conviction was affirmed on Appeal the next year.

CHAPTER 29:
THE POST CONVICTION HEARING—
FREEDOM FROM THE PRIVILEGE

"I guess you'd really call it more of a trial against Mr. Keating"
— Morris Lee Kaplan, Esq.

After the Myers' conviction had been affirmed by the Court of Appeals, he then directed his attention to the representation I had provided him. Myers filed a Post-Conviction Petition challenging my competency as his attorney.

My representation during the trial was now going to be judged. His latest lawyer, Morris Lee Kaplan, had alleged that Myers had been denied genuine and effective representation and that therefore he had been denied a fair trial. In his opening statement Kaplan said, "I guess you'd really call it more of a trial against Mr. Keating." However, a bold naked claim of such a denial will not suffice. Kaplan and his son Michael Lee Kaplan filed the Petition on October 30, 1985.

At 79, Morris Kaplan was one of the last of a vanishing breed of criminal defense lawyers. With his soft voice and loud attire, Kaplan managed to win over juries and jurists alike. Respected for his keen mind and loved for his gentle humor, he was a legend in the courthouses in Baltimore City and County. Kaplan shuffled in, sporting garish, polyester clothes, the pockets of his flashy sports jacket bulging with papers. In most courtrooms, the tables in front of attorneys become cluttered with files and books. But Kaplan's table remained bare. He was frail looking with wisps of white hair clinging to his scalp, and the mismatched clothes hanging loosely on his bony frame. Kaplan obligingly pulled up the cuffs of his bright green slacks up over his scuffed brown shoes to display diamond-patterned socks of red, gray, and blue.

He sometimes favored a peach colored sports jacket, lemon pants, sky blue shirt, red socks, and a wide purple tie right out of Guys and Dolls. He stood on spindly legs, hands in his pockets. Kaplan spoke softly and approached everyone with a gentle, solicitous humor. He always rose early. He was in court by 9:00 a.m. every weekday, moving from case to case and courtroom to courtroom throughout metropolitan Baltimore all day long. He had so many clients, though, and so much volume, he was often late to his appointments. He went to bed late. He was fond of saying, "At my age you're afraid to go to sleep."

"You look smashing as usual," a smiling spectator had said before the hearing as she eyed Kaplan's gaudy yellow pants and frayed orange jacket. "I like 'em," Kaplan said of his clothes. "I hope to be buried in them rather than the undertaker's traditional black." Kaplan believed, "You can't take notes and absorb what the witness is saying. To me, most motions are silly and idiotic." He often sat quietly, sometimes with eyes closed, as prosecutors built their cases against his clients. But he never missed a chance to make an objection. Kaplan delivered his arguments in a folksy manner with a minimum of gestures and histrionics.

Underestimating Kaplan was a serious mistake for an opposing lawyer. Kaplan graduated from The University of Baltimore School of Law in 1929, and won his first case. His client was a woman charged with prostitution, and after the trial, the two disappeared for a week while Kaplan collected his fee. "My mother reported me missing," he recalled. "In those days, money was scarce."

Morris Lee Kaplan went to law school when the tuition was $250 a year—$50 down and $5 a week. He finished at age 19. He waited two years to take the bar exam. In Kaplan's early days, there were no plea bargains, the volume of cases was manageable, and there were very few jury trials.

Kaplan lived in Baltimore nearly all his life. He was born in New York City a couple days after his parents stepped off a boat from Lithuania. As an attorney, he would never become agitated at a trial's outcome. Guilty, not guilty, life in prison, death in the gas chamber—he took them all in stride. Around the ancient Baltimore City courthouse, he was known as "The Dean." Criminal practice, which once attracted the best and brightest legal minds as well as the most flamboyant, was not nearly as lucrative as corporate or business law. Kaplan was often late for trials, always drifting in 10 or 20 minutes late. At one time, he held the record for contempt citations. The stories about him abounded throughout the court system. In one, it was said that prisoners at the Maryland Penitentiary named a wing of the prison after him.

As a young lawyer, I had prosecuted a murder trial in which he was the defense lawyer. The killing had taken place at a drunken party with many witnesses, supplying different versions of the event. I had many pages of notes to help me give my summation. He had taken none. I spent some time describing the applicable law and he dismissed my presentation by constantly referring to the law I had accurately described as "Mr. Keating's law" in a derisive tone. He was effective and salvaged a manslaughter verdict from what I had thought in my naiveté was a strong murder case.

If Kaplan was late for Court, everyone resigned themselves, deferring to his years and his unfailing cheerfulness. Judges impatient to see Kaplan usually contented themselves with what was known as The Morris Watch. The deputy sheriffs responsible for courthouse security were instructed to find Kaplan and to radio his whereabouts as soon as he was spotted. He was a lifelong gambler. In less litigious times, he went to the track nearly every day with his mother. "When horses run, I certainly will bet them. That's what life is all about."

Every weekday evening and on Saturdays he visited clients in jail. He would often meet several of them at a time. He was fond of saying to them, "If 80% of what you are telling me is true, you won't have any problem at all." Kaplan would walk through tough city neighborhoods collecting his fees on Saturdays and Sundays. But it was not safe. One summer night in 1984, on Kaplan's 75th birthday, he was robbed of $240 by a kid on a bike, ironically, outside the City Jail.

With Kaplan representing Robert Lee Myers, the Post Conviction Hearing was held before the Honorable Judge Donald J. Gilmore in the Circuit Court for Carroll County, Maryland, from March 13–19, 1986. Such a hearing usually assumes the guilt of the defendant but is conducted to determine if he had been treated "fairly."

There are three steps involved in such a proceeding. Step One: Determine if defense counsel erred; whether defense counsel was wrong in failing to object or in failing to offer appropriate evidence or instructions. Step Two: Analyze the reasoning behind counsel's erroneous action to determine whether it was justifiable or non-justifiable, and whether it was a legitimate "trial tactic." Step 3: Upon the facts of the case, determine if any incompetent representation existed and if it contributed to the conviction or the sentence.

Tom Hickman, Frank Coleman and Cpl. Leete traveled to Baltimore to interview me, so that they would be prepared for the hearing. We went to lunch to discuss the upcoming proceedings. It was good to see them. I had grown to like and respect the three of them. They had conscientiously and cleverly investigated the brutal murder and had brought the three accomplices who were responsible for it to account. Myers, had been brought to justice and had been prosecuted fairly. Great work on their part.

If they had not used Tina as a witness, we all believed that Chadderton and Myers would have avoided convictions and justice would have been thwarted. It had taken great courage on their part to dismiss the charges against Tina, because they knew that many citizens would not understand or approve of their sound and pragmatic decision.

Hickman and Coleman reviewed each of the bald claims that Morris Kaplan had creatively asserted. Kaplan had not been able to find any expert to testify that I had done anything that could be criticized. No legitimate "trial tactic" could be a reason to provide relief in a Post Conviction proceeding, as long as it was based on sound reasoning. Competent lawyers can legitimately approach cases differently.

I had known that this stage would eventually come, and so I had carefully set aside my four cartons of materials containing all the work that I had gathered to be ready for trial. I had kept the folders for each of the State's 160 potential witnesses. I also had my folders for all potential defense witnesses and potential defense exhibits, and my trial notes. I had acquired the 7,000-page transcript which had been used to prepare the briefs to the Courts in Annapolis. During the hearing, I displayed in front of me the materials I had used in the case.

Every State's witness' folder contained the statement to the police, statement to the grand jury, testimony from the Chadderton case, my trial notes with potential questions, my trial notes after the witness had testified, and any police reports pertaining to the witness. I also had copies of the State's potential exhibits, the exhibits from the Chadderton case, and the exhibits introduced at the Myers trial. I had accumulated 150 letters from Tina Myers to Robert Myers and others, as well as the logs and some transcripts of the 1,200 wiretapped conversations.

I was called to the stand by Tom Hickman. I was determined to demonstrate that I had provided effective representation. Now I was under attack. It was now personal. It was important to the prosecution team that they demonstrate that I had done an effective job. The prosecutors were now my lawyers. If they were not successful, Myers would be given a new trial and they would be forced to try the case again. Once they saw all my materials, they realized we did not have to spend a lot of time preparing for the hearing—all they had to do was ask me what I had done, and I could take it from there.

Their job was made easier because of the fact that I had been subsequently qualified as an expert in the prosecution and defense of criminal cases in Maryland, and I had been called as a witness to give my opinion as to the quality of the representation provided by other lawyers in murder cases.

Initially I was asked to describe my background. I explained that while I was in law school, I was fascinated by the many murder cases that were being tried at the courthouse in downtown Baltimore just a few blocks away. I knew that if I wanted to participate in these contests, there was no reason why upon graduation I shouldn't. I became an intern in the State's Attorney's Office for Baltimore City in 1967 and 1968 and was appointed an Assistant State's Attorney in December of 1969 when I passed the bar.

I testified that six weeks after being sworn in as a lawyer, I prosecuted my first murder case in front of a jury and after a weeklong trial, Alfred Jerome Streat was convicted of 1st degree murder. I then went around to the older, veteran prosecutors and asked them if they had any old "specials" they didn't want. At that time, all murder cases and rape cases were known as "specials," and the assistant kept them and personally supervised the prosecution of each case.

I soon accumulated and prosecuted over 30 murder cases during the next 18 months, in addition to the regular docket. During my service in the State's Attorney's Office, I tried over 60 murder cases. Many were won, others were not, but I learned much from the lawyers I battled.

Execution was the potential sentence for seven separate offenses at that time, including: first-degree premeditated murder, first-degree felony murder, rape, assault with intent to rape, kidnapping, child-stealing, and carnal knowledge of a child under 14.

I explained to the court that I had personally prosecuted 70 individual cases where the potential penalty was death. In only one instance was I unable to prevent a sentencing court from imposing that sanction.

In that one case, notwithstanding my best efforts, a death sentence was imposed. I had begged the judge not to execute him . . . I was not surprised when the court pronounced a sentence of death. Brice had murdered 3 people and had received death twice before. Much to my great relief, the sentence was vacated, but the conviction was upheld by the U.S. Supreme Court. Brice appreciated my efforts on his behalf. He sent me a note from Death Row.

I recounted how I had attended The National College of District Attorneys in Houston, Texas. Before I resigned from the State's Attorneys' office in 1973, I had become a Chief Prosecutor and had conducted a 6-month Grand Jury Investigation of the Baltimore City Jail. I had also prosecuted three police murderers.

I was then appointed an Assistant Public Defender for Baltimore City. I represented people charged with serious violent crimes. I had just moved from one side of the trial table to the other. From 1973 to 1978, I represented defendants in many major cases, including over 40 murder trials, and won acquittals in over sixty percent of my jury trials. While there, I defended an individual accused of murdering a police officer and shooting six others.

I testified that while for the most part I concentrated on jury trials, I had filed briefs and argued cases before The Maryland Court of Special Appeals and The Maryland Court of Appeals. I also represented a client, Irving Lee Wilson, who was already on death row when I was assigned his case. It was to be a protracted Post Conviction Proceeding. His death sentence had been affirmed by Maryland's highest court. After my representation, he was granted a new trial on the bases of prosecutorial misconduct, defense attorney incompetence, and judicial racial bias. He was released from death row on minimal bail. I then negotiated a guilty plea, which guaranteed his freedom. His case was unique in Maryland jurisprudence because during the course of my representation, his sentence changed from death to probation.

Alan Murrell assigned me to another capital case where the state had offered nothing but death. An inmate housed in the South Wing, Segregation Unit of the Maryland Penitentiary, serving a life sentence for the murder of a taxi driver, was considered to be incorrigible and was brutalized there. He struck back, attacking correctional officers and killing one of them. When I went to visit him the first time, a long line of guards greeted me with angry stares and comments. I couldn't blame them—my client had murdered one of their peers. The trial lasted five weeks. The States Attorney of Baltimore City Kurt L. Schmoke personally prosecuted the case. I was successful in preventing my client's execution. The guards who had beaten him were all subsequently prosecuted in State and Federal Court.

I had appeared in serious and petty criminal cases in all of Maryland's 24 local subdivisions. For many years, I had been on the Faculty of the Maryland Institute for The Continuing Professional Education of Lawyers, specializing in jury arguments, cross-examination, and trial tactics. I had also been a guest lecturer at both local Law Schools for a long time.

I continued my testimony. I had also represented clients in Federal Court in Maryland, South Carolina, Pennsylvania, and Washington DC., and had argued before The 4th Circuit Court of Appeals in Richmond, Virginia and had been sworn in before The Supreme Court of The United States.

Myers was now complaining that I did not allow him to testify at his trial before the jury. Trial tactics of counsel are not to be "second guessed" on post-conviction review. "The defendant must show that there is a reasonable probability that, but for counsel's unprofessional errors, the result of the proceeding would have been different."

In order to demonstrate that a lawyer is ineffective or incompetent, it is necessary for the client to waive the privilege of confidentiality and once that is done, the lawyer is free to tell everything he knows about the case.

The Rules of Ethics, statutes, and court decisions have created exceptions to the general rule requiring confidentiality and have raised questions that often have few simple answers. They state a "lawyer shall not reveal information relative to representation of a client." This edict does not apply when you attack that lawyer's performance.

The privilege of confidentiality has an ancient history, and was recognized in the common law of England by the time of Elizabeth I in the 16th Century. The common law had as the basis for the privilege the quaint idea that the lawyer as a "gentleman" should not reveal any secrets of his client. It was called "The Point of Honor." The modern view, of course, is that the privilege belongs to the client alone. The current basis for the privilege is that, when providing legal services, the lawyer must have a complete understanding of all the facts of the case, particularly all the information known by the client. To acquire this information, the lawyer must be able to assure this client that their private conversations will always be confidential.

The lawyer cannot simply ignore his client's contemplated perjury. The lawyer is required to remonstrate with the client, seek to withdraw, and finally, make disclosures to the court. It is then up to the court to tell the fact finders (the jurors or judge) of the perjury, order a mistrial, or do nothing. In a capital case, for example, where it may be critical to save his life for the defendant to take the stand and deny his guilt, should the lawyer reveal his perjury? Can the lawyer rationalize that his client's 5th and 6th Amendment rights would be jeopardized if the lawyer told the court of the perjury?

Assuming the lawyer's belief is considered reasonable he is protected from discipline, but would he be protected from the criminal charge of suborning perjury if he assisted the defendant in his false denials? Lawyers involved, particularly in criminal cases, can be enmeshed in difficult ethical questions that involve their duty to the client as opposed to their duty as an "officer of the court." The overwhelming majority of lawyers want to be "ethical," but they also want to give the client the most competent representation that is possible.

Morris Kaplan insisted that it was incompetent of me not to have put Myers on the witness stand. I responded that I had conducted a practice session with Myers, with me taking the role of the prosecutor. To the question, "Have you ever discussed this case with your lawyer," Myers replied, "No." I then stopped and asked him why he answered "no" to that question, and he said, "What do you want me to say?" I then asked Myers why he appeared at Angelo's Restaurant in Westminster with Tina on his arm three days after the murder, information I told him the State was sure to know. Myers looked at me and said, "I didn't, did I?" I insisted that Myers would be an uncontrollable and un-coachable witness. I testified that I did not believe Myers could "survive" cross-examination because of the many prior statements that Myers had made to the police, in his deposition and to the Grand Jury.

I described the scene in the Garrett County Detention Center immediately after we had learned that Tina was going to be a State's witness. Daniel and Sherrie Chadderton and Orrin Brown were there at that meeting.

Myers was very upset and I pressed him, "You've got to tell me what happened!" Myers had tears in his eyes and was almost hysterical and I was very aggressive with him, repeating, "Bobby, you've got to tell me what happened!" Then he said to me, "Okay, I'm going to tell you, Tina said to me, 'If you marry me and take care of my kids, I'll have your wife murdered for you.'"

Myers never repeated that statement and later consistently denied knowing that Mary Ruth was going to be murdered, and denied putting up the money to pay Chadderton for the murder.

I testified about Myers' appearing before the Grand Jury. He'd been drunk, and his testimony was rambling and bizarre. He had been invited to give "his side," and the Grand Jury was eager to hear from him. Myers had described his and Mary Ruth's use of sexual devices in their marital relationship. He testified that she used sex as a weapon, often putting her fingers between her legs and then putting them under his nose and saying, "You're not going to get any of this." Corporal James Leete had testified that on the day after the murder Myers had said, "I'm going to miss her. She's one of the best pieces of ass I ever had."

Myers had accused Corporal Leete of being a vicious police officer who had been trying to frame him. When asked by one of the Grand Jurors in what way he was vicious, Myers said that "Leete went around farting in people's faces." Myers had told the Grand Jury that Leete was trying to get him convicted just to earn a promotion, and that the trooper was fabricating evidence.

Myers also told the Grand Jury that Mary Ruth had pulled knives on him, and, "I just couldn't take it no more."

I testified that I did not place Myers on the witness stand because some of the comments he had made could have sent him to the gas chamber, and that only by keeping him off the stand could I prevent the jurors from hearing his crude and outrageous remarks.

The Grand Jury testimony and his other damaging statements had been excluded from the State's case because Myers had not been clearly advised of his rights against self-incrimination. However, if he were to take the stand, all these previous damaging comments could legitimately be used to impeach him. As his defense attorney, I wanted to avoid that.

I also testified that I felt some of his comments were so mean, indifferent and callous that if I had put him on the stand, he would no longer look like a sympathetic goofball, but cold and sinister—and perhaps in some people's minds—worthy of execution. Comments like, "Yes, I did say I wished the bitch was dead," and that he could have murdered Mary Ruth on the couple's $140,000 boat if he chose to ("If I wanted to do her in, the Captain would never had known it. There were slippery seats. I just had to give her a little nudge. But I don't kill anyone. I'm a lover.") might not go over well with the jury in his trial.

I read from his grand jury testimony and from his statements to the police, which up to that point had not been revealed publicly. The grand jury minutes had been the subject of a motion to dismiss the indictment on the basis of prosecutorial misconduct in that the prosecutors had allegedly abused the process. I had cited seventy-five instances of "bullying, interrupting, double teaming, and making improper statements by the prosecutors" during the testimony given by Mr. Myers.

Myers had sued Mary Ruth's children six months after her death in order to recover $8,000 that Myers had claimed she had improperly taken a few days before she was murdered. Mary Ruth had left this money with a neighbor for her children in case "something happened to her." When Myers was asked in a deposition, "Where is your wife now?" he replied, "She is in Hell."

In that civil suit, he denied that he had ever met Daniel Chadderton or even knew Chadderton's last name. He had perhaps forgotten that Chadderton and his wife Sherrie had attended Brad's birthday party at the house on Turkey Foot Road and had also celebrated Christmas there in 1982. Chadderton had also been chosen as his daughter Sabrina's "godfather." Myers had committed perjury by denying that he knew Daniel Chadderton. Many witnesses had seen the two men together and knew they were friends.

The large ceremonial courtroom in the Carroll County courthouse in Westminster was packed with 200 spectators who were quite shocked by my testimony.

When Kaplan asked me a trick question, I responded, "Don't try to trap me." "Don't use the word 'trap!'" Kaplan said. "We're lawyers," and I responded, "That's why I'm using it," and everybody laughed. Morris kept repeating, "This was just an ego trip for you wasn't it? This was an ego trip for you?" He was making me feel shabby, but I soon responded that he was correct and that is why I had done all that work and I had tried so hard, because I wanted to look good to the public and to other lawyers! I was thinking, it is not enough to just fuck, pray and get high or drunk. Life should be more than that! I read aloud the cards and letters Myers had sent me during and after the trial thanking me and praising me for the work I had done on his case.

Kaplan cross-examined me for two days and was now really starting to piss me off. Judge Gilmore was giving him great latitude, and Morris asked me repeatedly whether or not the trial had just been a "huge" ego trip for me and suggested I was ineffective because I refused to let Myers talk. Myers would have had to contradict many people. Morris Kaplan kept on at me and at one point said, "I've got ya going now, your eyes are blinking Mr. Keating." The truth was he was getting me going—getting under my skin. I responded, however, by saying, "It's your socks Mr. Kaplan. They are shining in my eyes." Kaplan was wearing blue, red, and yellow argyle socks with black and tan checked trousers. The courtroom exploded in laughter and Morris had lost his advantage. Kaplan insisted that I could have explained away the Grand Jury statements by showing that Myers has been drinking the day he went before the Grand Jury; however, I maintained that I didn't think the Petit Jurors would forget Myers personal attacks on his murdered wife.

Morris accused me of dragging the case out and spending more time on it than necessary so that I could increase the fee I was earning. I explained that I had been told that the arrangement was a flat fee of $10,000 and no more. I had kept detailed time records and produced them. They showed that I had expended 1,200 hours of my time up through the end of the sentencing hearing. Eight dollars and thirty-three cents an hour before the time I expended consulting on the Appeal, and at the Post-Conviction proceedings lowered it some more! It was indeed a labor of love. Love of competition.

Morris criticized my efforts to get the case removed back from Garrett County. My theory was that Myers was a popular businessman in the community—well-liked—and that he probably would stand a better chance of getting, not what I would call a fairer trial, but a better result in Carroll County than in Garrett County. The State's case was based on circumstantial evidence, so in effect, what Tina Myers did by testifying was to corroborate in every detail, and in every respect, the circumstantial evidence that had been developed.

There were over 100 exhibits produced by the defense and offered into evidence. There was no complaint about them, but Morris chastised me for not producing a map of the Eastern seaboard to show where Tina and Robert had traveled.

Morris had alleged that I had gone to Las Vegas where a hearing on the case was held, and that Myers had wanted to go but I had insisted that he remain in jail. Judge Burns had clearly advised Myers of his right to go there with us and Myers clearly waived that right on the record.

At the end of my second day of testimony when the court was to be recessed for the day, the young female clerk said "The Circuit Court for Carroll County is now in recess, All Rise!" Indicating to the packed courtroom that they should all stand while Judge Gilmore left the bench. Morris Kaplan, who had his hands in his pockets appearing to play pocket pool with himself, visibly moved his hands around, and grinning from ear to ear said loudly, "I wish I could!" Morris flashed me a smile as I was standing in the witness box. The young clerk flushed with embarrassment and I looked to the judge to see his reaction. Judge Gilmore kept a straight face, pretended he had not heard the remark and walked from the bench to the side exit.

Robert Myers did testify at this Post Conviction hearing. He said that he had lied during "most" of his testimony before the Carroll County Grand Jury in November 1981. Myers testified that he did not remember making any of the disparaging remarks that I had carefully highlighted in the 150-page transcript of the Grand Jury proceedings.

Myers said he had taken drugs and got drunk, consuming "four to six beers" the day he testified before the Grand Jury and said things he "never would have normally said." He told Judge Gilmore. "If I was in a normal state of mind I never would have talked like that." States Attorney, Thomas Hickman, asked Myers why he had said during the Grand Jury proceedings that he had not consumed drugs or alcohol that day and in fact, he had stated under oath, that he never drank or used drugs.

Hickman asked Myers, "Are you lying today or were you lying then before the Grand Jury under oath?" "I was lying then," Myers said. "That is perjury. You are testifying today that you lied that day to the Grand Jury," Hickman responded. Myers maintained that he did not know the difference between the truth and a lie at the time of his testimony to the Grand Jury.

Myers claimed that I refused to put on an alibi or other defense witnesses because I felt it was too much trouble. He sounded like an idiot, because he could not name any possible "alibi" witness that he wanted produced. He overlooked the 25 witnesses I had called on his behalf. "He was having trouble with his wife. He had a newborn baby. He said he was spending too much time on my case," Myers said of me.

Throughout the post-conviction hearing, sitting quietly in the front row, was Robert Myers new fiancé Elizabeth "Libby" Sriyapant. She was a private nurse and had been involved with Myers since September 1982, shortly before his trial began. A mutual friend gave Myers her phone number with the invitation that if he was lonely he should call her.

She only rarely called attention to herself during the hearing—when she stepped forward to pass notes to Morris Kaplan. She came to the hearing in a state of exhaustion one day. She had spent the whole previous day in court and was up all night, caring for a patient. Early that morning, as was her routine, she drove to Kaplan's Owings Mills home and chauffeured him to the courthouse.

This, despite the fact that at that time he was "engaged" to Sandy Clarke, the 21-year-old luggage carrier at the Baltimore-Washington International Airport, whom he had met when he dropped Tina off for a flight to Bermuda two years earlier. Myers called Libby on his birthday, September 16. He wanted someone to wish him a happy day. And then, he called almost every day after that, and they began daily letter writing. She made weekly visits to the various prisons where he was being held. They would be allowed to hug and kiss, but nothing more, and they apparently fell in love. She wore an engagement ring on her finger and was optimistic that Myers would be released from prison soon. "I think he's innocent," she said. "Hopefully he'll get this straightened out and he'll be permitted to come home and we'll resume a normal life. If not, he's eligible for parole in about seven years." Libby, who was in her 50s, said she was not disturbed to hear the disparaging sexual terms in which Myers described his second wife, Mary Ruth. "I've heard it before," she said. "I have probably said worse things in anger."

Myers testified that he spent most of his time working on his case. "I am obsessed with it. I never knew until I started studying law how wrong I had been done by Mr. Keating," Myers said. "I'm sure from the cases I've read that I'll get a new trial."

Myers testified that, "Every night I lie in bed trying to figure out who really killed my wife. I've got to figure it out. Otherwise I will spend the rest of my life in prison. I've only got one life." Myers said further that "Tina was the one that killed her. She and a couple of guys. But I don't know who. Tina was going to kill me too. I'm absolutely sure about it. I started to really get scared when she kept asking me to buy more life insurance." Myers added, "That woman has no love in her. She does not know what love is."

Myers told the court that Tina sent him a Christmas card every year. "I think she does it just to be smart, I wish she had never come into Maryland. It was a nightmare meeting that woman. She did me in."

Myers pushed his straight, straw-colored hair from his eyes and leaned closer to the microphone as he explained that he was not bitter. He said the other prisoners at the Penitentiary had been "perfect gentlemen" to him through his stay there. He said he had a cell to himself with its own radio and TV and that he spent most of his time working on his case. "Maybe God will give me an extra long life so I can get all this straightened out!"

Judge Gilmore found that I knew Myers would be impeached by his previous statements, and knew of the potential damage to Myers if he testified. He concluded that I had hoped that Myers could either be acquitted outright or found to have only been an accessory after the fact to murder. This gave him a chance for acquittal since he was not charged as an accessory after the fact.

Myers also complained that I had not put Chadderton or Charlotte Horton on the witness stand during the trial. They both testified during this hearing to demonstrate what the jury had missed.

Mrs. Horton was called to tell the Court she could have portrayed Myers in a positive light. She started her remarks with a warning to the courtroom participants to avoid upsetting her because of her brain damage. She then launched into her detailed medical history. "Mr. Kaplan, is this really relevant?" Judge Gilmore asked the lawyer. "Yes, it's relevant," Mrs. Horton replied out of turn. "Thank You!" the Judge responded, while thinking that any attorney who used her as a witness would have to be suffering from the same malady.

Kaplan alleged that I had refused to call Chadderton as a witness "even though Myers insisted that he be called." Kaplan produced Chadderton during the hearing. Judge Gilmore observed Chadderton's demeanor very carefully when he made a grand entrance into the courtroom at the hearing. The judge stated that "when he entered the room, he took a position of surveying the crowd, straightening his jacket, and walking very erectly over to the witness stand, where he turned and faced the Deputy Sheriff, and in effect, attempted to stare him down. He held this stare for a considerable period of time before he took the oath."

"His distaste for the investigating trooper and the State's Attorney was made quite apparent. If Chadderton had been put on the stand during the trial, numerous damaging conversations and evidence would have been admissible. Hickman demonstrated that during his cross-examination at this hearing." He made Chadderton look foolish and thereby demonstrated why I had been correct not to call him before the jury.

The judge ruled that it wasn't until after all appeals had been exhausted, and as a last resort, Mr. Myers turned against me. In the court's opinion,

"Mr. Keating did an outstanding job in the defense of Mr. Myers," and that my decision "not to put Myers on the stand might very well have saved him from the gas chamber."

Judge Gilmore wrote in his opinion, "Keating was faced with a situation where the circumstantial evidence was now corroborated in every respect through the testimony of Tina Marco Myers."

Judge Gilmore ruled that I had committed no errors during the course of the trial. He said I was in the position of dealing with an extremely difficult case from every aspect: pre-trial publicity, overwhelming circumstantial evidence, and Myers' testimony before the Grand Jury, which was conflicting and extremely damaging.

In reviewing the testimony of some of the witnesses that the State had produced, the Judge found, "Mr. Keating's cross-examination was so extensive, so thorough, and so biting, one had to ask the question: Was this a defense witness or a State's witness? Because he successfully cross-examined the State's witnesses, many of them, to the point that it must have given the jury some considerable hesitation. It was scathing cross-examination."

The judge questioned that if I were going to put Myers on the stand, what would I have gained? "Well, if he gained what Kaplan gained by putting Mr. Myers on the stand in the post conviction proceeding, it would have been very little. In fact, it probably would have been a blood bath." The judge found that I had done an exhaustive piece of defense work in the case, checking out lead after lead, having the Public Defender's staff doing the same, and that I had to evaluate Mr. Myers and still deal with a very difficult decision for a lawyer to make, and that was how to deal with his damaging admissions. Judge Gilmore refused to grant a new trial.

The Appeal of the Denial of Post Conviction Relief was heard by the Appellate Courts but they upheld the lower court ruling that Myers' had a fair trial. Chief Judge Richard P. Gilbert praised the representation I had provided. That was the end of the legal proceedings.

By the time the case was finally over it meant little to me. I never enjoyed the protracted chess game on appeal because gratification came too slowly. I enjoyed the immediacy of the trial court, win and walk away or lose and prepare for sentencing at once. Rather like an affair that had run its course, there were still warm feelings several years later . . . but life moves on and others had my interest. The constant challenge of new trials had soon made Myers a distant memory. I was certain he would not be freed no matter what anybody did.

EPILOGUE

"Never send to know for whom the bell tolls . . . it tolls for thee."
— John Donne

Robert Lee Myers

The other woman in his life, Sandy (the B.W.I. luggage handler) was fiercely loyal up through the trial, and the verdict. She sent me a card of appreciation for my efforts, signed, "Bob and Sandy." She was not heard from again.

During the trial, Myers had exchanged letters with a spectator in the courtroom. Elizabeth "Libby" Sriyapant was a 47-year-old who had been curious about the case. She sat in the packed courtroom, quietly watching. One of Bobby's friends told him to call her. He did, and they began exchanging letters. She chauffeured his 77-year-old post conviction attorney, Morris Kaplan, around while he investigated the case. She announced that she would like to get married while Bobby was still in the Maryland state penitentiary, but he didn't want it that way. "I love him," she said. "He's a kind and gentle man." She also loved the diamond engagement ring that sparkled on her finger. "He's a fun person, with a great sense of humor."

Libby broke down and cried the day the jury convicted Robert Lee Myers. She cried again the day he was sentenced to life in prison, though this time she shed tears of relief; she had been afraid that the jury would send Bobby to the gas chamber. Bobby and Libby were engaged for more than three years. Once his requests for a new trial had finally been denied, she moved on with her life without him.

Tina sent him a Christmas card that first year from Texas. He felt it was more to harass him than out of love. "If she really cared for me, she'd have stayed around Baltimore," he said.

Robert Lee Myers was incarcerated in the Maryland prison system from his arrest on November 25, 1981 until he died from cancer on January 12, 2014. I had last seen him in the Maryland Penitentiary to discuss his appeal in 1983. As we were sitting there in the open visiting area, several correctional officers walked by him and cheerfully greeted him with "Hey Bobby," or "How you doing Bobby?" He smiled and greeted them all, telling me he did their income taxes for them.

Tina Butcher Plessner Botteron Gillen Marco Myers Olenick

Tina had pointed out the irony in her role as the star witness in the case and her childhood dream to be a movie star. "I wanted to be in the public eye, but not this way," she said. "It's not the publicity I had in mind."

"For Bobby, I have regrets. For his sake, I'm sorry. But for me, I'm glad I did it. But I don't want the public to feel I'm getting away scot-free. I don't want them to feel that I am that cold person; that because I'm leaving I feel a hundred times better. This is not something I'll be able to forget. We all have skeletons in our closet. Maybe some are bigger than others. There are a lot of things in my past that I would like to forget, but I can't. You just have to learn to live with it. No one is going to stand in my place before God."

She said she'd received a letter after the trial from the County Commissioners that they wanted her to pay for the costs of her incarceration. She responded that if the county wouldn't pay for her incarceration including medical bills, she intended to make up for the lost funds through the welfare system. "This is to notify you of my intent to fight you bastards all the way to the Supreme Court if need be. I testified in two damn trials, and was promised since March of this year many different dates for my release," she wrote. "You act as if I wanted to stay in this jail, which indeed was not the case. Your county put me here, and your county will (underlined) PAY, not I. And upon release I am hereby advising you now, I will live in Westminster and go on welfare if I should lose this case, I assure you all of that now." She won her case.

As part of her immunity agreement, Tina had to agree to stay in contact with the State's Attorneys' Office of Carroll County for ten years. Several years later, on September 19, 1986, she was married for the sixth time in Galveston,

Texas. She sent Tom Hickman a postcard of the lavish ceremony on a river steamboat. She remained in Houston, Texas for the rest of her life. She had no further contact with Myers, worried that he would seek the return of the property she had acquired.

On January 10, 2014, she died in Texas. Her funeral was held on January 12, 2014—which was the same day Robert Lee Myers died in prison.

Daniel Lee Chadderton

He is currently serving his life sentence at The Maryland Correctional Institution in Hagerstown, MD.

Sherrie Chadderton

Sherrie Chadderton passed away in Maryland in August 2006

James M. Leete, Maryland State Police Detective

As a direct result of the pressures on the participants in the Myers case, several of the participants got divorced. Corporal Leete's marriage fell apart, as did the marriage of Tom Hickman. Twelve years after the cases were concluded, Corporal Leete retired. He is living in Carroll County.

Thomas E. Hickman Esq.

Thomas Hickman served five elected terms as the State's Attorney for Carroll County from January 1975 through January 1995, when he lost his last election. He was subsequently appointed to a national panel of twelve experts to advise the Attorney General of the United States on matters involving federal, state, and county law enforcement relations.

He served in the U.S. military from 1969 to 1999, first as an Army infantry officer in the reserve, and then served for eight years in the Air National Guard as Judge Advocate for 22 years. He retired with the rank of Colonel after serving in England, Italy, Germany, and Bosnia and Herzegovina.

He was a legal advisor to the office of the High Representative in Sarajevo from 1996 to 1998 and assisted in establishing a National Training Center for judges and prosecutors.

For six years he served as a United Nations international prosecutor in Kosovo, trying 32 cases involving war criminals. He tried the first war crimes case in Serbia. He handled the investigation and prosecution of war crimes, corruption, ethnic murders, organized crime, and terrorism. From 2010 to 2011, he was a United Nations advisor to the Afghanistan anti-corruption agency. He tried the longest trial in the history of Kosovo, which lasted for 17 months against 10 defendants, with 22 people examining each witness.

He is presently in the private practice of law in Westminster, Carroll County, Maryland.

Frank D. Coleman, Esq.

Frank Coleman resigned from the prosecutor's office several months after the Myers trial and ran unsuccessfully for The House Of Delegates of Maryland. He entered the private practice of law until he was appointed a Master in Domestic Relations for the Circuit Court of Carroll County. After eight years there he resigned to again practice law privately. He remains in private practice.

The Honorable Donald J. Gilmore Sr.

Judge Gilmore retired from the bench in 1990 after he was diagnosed with cancer, but continued working as a sitting judge for several years. He would often have chemotherapy in the morning and be on the bench in the afternoon. When Baltimore City Comptroller Jacqueline F. McLean was indicted in 1994 on corruption charges, Judge Gilmore was requested to preside over the politically sensitive headline case.

He died in May of 1998, at the age of 66.

The Honorable Fred A Thayer II

Judge Thayer retired from the bench in 1996, after presiding for twenty years. He remained very active in the community developing real estate projects and serving as Director of the First United Bank and Trust from 1996 through 2006. He served as the Pipe Major for The Garrett Highlanders until 2001. He was also Master of the Oakland Lodge and the Royal Order of Jesters.

He died of a heart attack on February 16, 2007 at age 73.

The Honorable Luke K.Burns, Jr.

Judge Burns was an Associate Judge on the Carroll County Circuit Court from September 5, 1979 to January 23, 2004. His wife of 20 years, Sally, died in 1989. His first marriage had ended in divorce. He attended my 50th Birthday Party in August 1993. I felt a lot of affection and respect for him and it was mutual.

In 1997, I was contacted by the State Trooper, James Sherman, who had conducted all the wiretaps and eavesdropping in the case (about 1,200 in all) as the Head of the Maryland State Police Electronics Surveillance Unit. He had been charged with sexually abusing his girlfriend's young daughter over a several year period. The case was to be prosecuted by Tracey Gilmore, the daughter of Judge Gilmore in front of Judge Burns in the same Carroll County courtroom. I was flattered that he had asked me to represent him.

For the only time in my legal career, I exercised none of my twenty pre-emptory challenges on prospective jurors and allowed the first twelve people to sit in the jury box, enabling me to discuss that fact in my opening statement. I told the jurors that the reason O.J. Simpson's lawyers had spent so much time selecting his jury (that case had just been concluded) was that Simpson had been guilty and that my client was not guilty, so I "took the first 12." I also told them that the reason O.J. Simpson had not testified in his case was because he was guilty, but that my client would testify because he was unafraid and could not wait to publicly respond to the prosecutor's charges.

This trooper was a brave man. He had been undercover in the Pagan Motorcycle Gang and had received many citations and honors in his career. His undercover infiltration of the Pagans in the late 70's was so successful that the FBI had to be told to stop an investigation on him. He had infiltrated the group so well he had even fooled the parallel Federal effort.

I asked the alleged victim, who was 14 years old, whether or not she had sexual fantasies. When she said no, I explained to her that it was perfectly normal and healthy to have sexual fantasies, and that the jurors and myself had them from time to time. I looked at Judge Burns and said, "I don't want to speak for the judge." I asked her again if she ever had sexual fantasies, and when she said no, I asked no more questions of her. I was able to call to the stand several police officers, who told of the defendant's honesty and reputation in the law enforcement community.

It was amusing to me that I had interviewed these officers in my room at Lee's Motel where I was staying. Déjà vu all over again, except this time I had a client who was unassailable when he testified, and the State's case had "gross inconsistencies" in it, with their witnesses contradicting each other. In my closing argument, I told the jurors that society had come full circle from ignoring child abuse to questioning the propriety of harmless hugs. The jury acquitted him after deliberating for less than an hour. There was a great celebration in the courtroom. He was re-instated.

Sadly, my friendship with Judge Burns ended after another case of mine that was tried in his courtroom a couple of years later.

In 1999, John Romanoff, a 16-year-old tenth grader from Westminster High School, had traveled to Baltimore's inner city to buy some heroin to take back to school, since some others there had developed a taste for it. He had made the trip once before and was quite smug as he hid the sixteen glassine bags in his locker. That night, he supplied a classmate who had recently joined the group of drug users at school. This 15-year-old had not yet learned discretion, and the next morning he was found by his father—dead from an overdose. He had snorted two bags.

An intensive investigation by the State Police and local State's Attorney led to charges for wrongful death and drug offenses filed in Juvenile court. Once there, the prosecutors convinced the judge to "waive juvenile jurisdiction" and transfer the case to the Circuit Court. In order to do so, the judge is compelled to articulate his reasoning with specific references to five specific established statutory factors. The community was rightfully outraged that one of their kids should have died so needlessly. There were many meetings in local churches, schools, and even in the State's Attorney's Office itself. Committees were established and funds were raised to pay for forty billboards with the logo "HEROIN KILLS" in yellow on a black background. Bumper stickers and refrigerator magnets with that message were distributed to every school for every student, 30,000 in all.

HEROIN KILLS
TURN IN A DEALER
1-800-492-8477 • 410-857-8477
COURTESY OF CARROLL COUNTY STATES ATTORNEY'S OFFICE, M.S.P., M.T.A., W.C.P., R.A.D.

My skinny undersized client and his very decent middle-class working family were genuinely distraught over the death. They knew the prosecutor and most of their neighbors wanted at least a full pound of flesh. The situation was compounded by the fact that my client did not use drugs himself! He was already to be tried as an adult by the time I had been retained. I soon learned that the judge (who was nearing retirement and locally revered) had totally mishandled the juvenile waiver hearing, and I was sure his decision would be reversed by the Maryland Appellate Courts. Not only had he not followed the fairly clear and well established mandatory requirements in order to waive a child into adult court, but the transcript showed the judge to be confused, inarticulate, and generally "out of it."

Five factors must be always be considered in a waiver hearing. It was an embarrassing performance by that judge, and I felt if I could prepare a finished appellant's brief making this judge look as bad as possible, perhaps I could convince the new judge assigned to the matter—my friend, the Honorable Luke Burns—to send the case back to juvenile court. My client could avoid doing time in an adult prison and thereby avoid being potentially brutalized.

In Judge Burns' chambers I distributed copies of the interlocutory appeal which I was ready to file instantly if he refused to send the case back to juvenile court. The two lawyers who had helped me on the case were there, and the Deputy State's Attorney had an assistant prosecutor with him. The crowded chambers also included the judge's law clerk. Everything started well, but even though all present agreed that the waiver hearing had been deficient, "that was in the past, and the youth should accept an 18-month sentence." I reacted angrily when the law clerk spontaneously exclaimed that he should just take the prison time because he deserved it. I cut her down to size, and embarrassed her for being so callous, and a "know it all."

At the very least, I was determined to stall this whole process so that if he had to go to adult prison, he would be in a better position to deal with it if he was a couple of years older. I knew that the local officials were under very close scrutiny and this was a very explosive situation for them. I was disappointed that no one was thinking about my kid client. The more they pressured me to get him to plead and go to an adult prison, the more I resisted and the more I mocked the performance of the hearing judge. I began quoting him, making him look even more like an idiot. I was not bluffing; the reason for getting the briefs ready was to dispel any notion that it would require any more effort or that it was not a slam dunk winner on appeal.

The more my arguments were rejected, the louder I became, and I eventually said, "That judge had to be asleep, incompetent, or drunk." Judge Burns immediately responded, "Don't talk like that about him. He is a friend of mine."

Not heeding his warning, a few minutes later I returned to the same theme—the words had a nice ring to them. "Look come on, he didn't just screw up a little. I have never had a case in front of him—maybe this was a *good* day for him. Maybe I was being generous when I said he was asleep, incompetent or drunk." Judge Burns glared at me: "Get out of my chambers. Get out now!" I started to stammer my apologies but he turned away and I scurried out. I had overplayed my hand.

The local press was following the case very closely and soon contacted me to learn what I had said to enrage the local judiciary. I refused to give details but they printed that I told them that my remarks had been "rude, uncalled for, improper, and unprofessional." They had been.

On the drive back to Baltimore, I started composing my separate apology letters to Judge Burns and the other judge. Time to protect myself and genuinely express my regret for my conduct. I knew I had some well-earned grief coming but I was disappointed that Judge Burns had jumped on me so quickly. I genuinely liked and respected him and the feelings were mutual. We had 'bonded" during Myers. I immediately sent off "my apologia," but the damage had been done.

Burns would never forgive me. He complained about my conduct in a letter to the Attorney Grievance Commission that he had sent to them immediately. The Commission wanted to reprimand me but I refused to accept that sanction, which would have been a public permanent stain on my record. The judge had been incompetent and they knew that fact would be obvious if I made them "prosecute" me and have a publicly contested hearing. The Bar Association and I compromised with a private admonition. They sternly warned me not to repeat the conduct. I readily agreed.

Luke Burns and I never spoke again. That still saddens me, since I was in the wrong and since he was right to stick up for his friend and put me in my place. I had grown to admire him and care about him. He was a kind, considerate person and a great judge.

For my client, I used the appellate process to delay the case for several months by filing my already prepared brief on the last possible day. The appellate court agreed the judge had not properly explained his reasons for sending this 16 year old to adult court. I narrowly missed the chance of looking like a complete fool once again. At the end of the brief I wrote, "For the foregoing reasons the Appellant respectfully requests that the Judgment of the Circuit Court of Carroll County be 'revered.'" I just caught the mistake on the last review. Lucky, since I really wanted the judgment "reversed" rather than "revered."

When the case was returned to Carroll County for a rehearing, all the judges there recused themselves and removed the case to Howard County. Again, I stalled. I feared correctly that another judge would agree that the matter should be tried in adult court. Although I knew that this new judge had complied with the statutory requirements, and that despite my best efforts we would not win on appeal this time, I filed an appeal simply to delay my client's sentencing day. We did lose, and six months later we were back in Carroll County in adult court.

A judge from Baltimore was specially assigned and we entered a guilty plea. The case was no longer fresh. The community was no longer screaming quite so loudly for a pound of flesh. Almost two years after the victim's tragic death, my client entered a guilty plea to the drug distribution charge in return for the State dismissing the negligent homicide and reckless endangerment counts.

At the sentencing hearing, the victim's father testified and before a packed audience, proceeded to lecture and berate all of his son's friends, including my client. It was a gut wrenching courtroom session.

My client had by then finished a lot of college courses and, at my direction, had "found Jesus." I had also "assigned" him a lot of community service at local nursing homes, and so I had a lot to argue in mitigation at his sentencing. He was given a year in the Carroll County Detention Center, rather than in a "Big House" in The Department of Corrections elsewhere. He served his time basically at night since he was allowed to leave for college and work during the day. Four years later he earned a degree from a good university and has stayed trouble free ever since then.

This "victory" was bittersweet since it had cost me a friendship with a good man. Judge Burns remained on the bench until he reached the mandatory retirement age of 70 in 2004, yet still continued to hear cases. In 1996, he had been re-elected to another 15-year term with an astounding 97% of the voters supporting him.

In 1999 Luke Burns married Marcia King, who had served as the forelady of the Myers' jury. He first met her during jury selection, when he made her the forelady. Over the years they had maintained contact and become friends, and ultimately they were married.

He died in 2013 at the age of 79.

Alan H. Murrell, Esq.

In 1929, he married Mildred Deering, who died in 1997. The couple lived from 1929 to 1990 in a house they had built in Ten Hills in Baltimore. He retired from the Public Defender's Office in 1990 at the age of 88. I applied for his position, along with several other people. I was not selected to be the State Public Defender, but I was gratified that The Sun said, "The most intriguing of all the candidates is Mr. Keating. Theatrical and wily in the courtroom, Mr. Keating may be the only candidate who approaches Alan Murrell in abilities as a lawyer."

Alan Murrell died in 1999, at age 97.

Phil M. Sutley, Esq.

After the Myers case, Sutley maintained his private practice. He was never disciplined by the Bar Association and never returned any of the fee or the property he had received.

Several years later Robert Myers sued Phillip M. Sutley in the Circuit Court of Baltimore City. In the complaint, it was asserted "Myers had retained Sutley for services to be rendered concerning Myers' possible complicity relating to the alleged homicide. The suit claimed "Myers suffered because of this dual representation in that he had been deprived of any opportunity to negotiate his own agreement with the prosecutor."

This lawsuit claimed $228,000 in compensatory damages and $1 million in punitive damages. Morris Lee Kaplan, Robert Myers' attorney in the Post Conviction Proceeding, filed this lawsuit but never pursued it properly. He never requested any discovery and never notified me of its existence or requested my assistance in any way. The suit should have been one for breach of contract, but that had not been alleged as a cause of action. Because Myers had been found guilty, and was guilty, there was no basis for punitive damages. After many delays, the suit was dismissed by the Court.

Subsequently, Myers filed a grievance with the Attorney Grievance Commission of Maryland to complain about Sutley's conduct. Myers wrote that Sutley, "who had been further enriched by Tina Myers, attempted to push me into the gas chamber!" Inexplicably, The Commission, without any independent investigation, accepted Sutley's bald denial in response to these allegations.

When the case was finally appealed, the Court of Special Appeals agreed that there was no remedy for Myers. In its reported opinion, however, the court criticized Sutley's conduct. "Generally speaking, joint representation in criminal cases is fraught with potential conflict of interest. Ordinarily, a lawyer should decline to act for more than one of several co-defendants except in unusual situations when, after careful investigation, it is clear that no conflict is likely to develop and when the several defendants have given informed consent to such a multiple representation" (American Bar Association Standards Relating To The Administration of Justice, The Defense Function, 1971). "Sutley does not appear to have displayed the acmic in professional behavior. Nevertheless, absent a showing that the State tainted Myers' defense, reversal is not dictated."

Sutley died from a heart attack on the Clarence Mitchell Courthouse steps in Baltimore in 2007 at age 66.

Orrin C. Brown III, Esq.

After the Chadderton trial, Orrin Brown moved to Michigan and sold cars for a living. In 2012, he returned to Maryland to live on the Eastern Shore. He is now retired.

Rev. Meyer F. M. Tobey

Father Tobey remained the Associate Pastor at the Holy Trinity Church in Washington DC. until 1985. He left to study in Jerusalem from 1985 to 1988, and then returned to live in Baltimore, where he died in 1990 at age 75.

Morris Lee Kaplan Esq.

Morris Kaplan remained in private practice until his death in 1990 at age 83. He had practiced law in Maryland for 62 years.

Anton J.S. Keating, Esq.

I had been with my second wife, Victoria Salner Keating, since 1975. We had been married in 1978. She was an excellent appellate public defender and while we were not best suited for each other, we decided to have a child. Our son Christopher was born on January 17, 1982. Throughout the Myers trial, which started in September, I stayed at Lee's Motel during the week. I rushed back on Friday nights to pick up my daughter, Erin, from my first marriage so I could be with her and my second wife and baby as much as possible on the weekends. I had always wanted children and was determined to be a big part of their lives. Much to my shock, dismay, and anger, my marriage too had fallen apart partly because the stresses of the Myers' case, partly because Chris' mother realized in my absence that life was easier without me. We came to a mutual understanding that she could no longer stand me. We engaged in a protracted custody battle.

In the early 1980s in Maryland, when a couple got divorced if there was a young child involved, invariably the courts favored the mother and awarded her custody and usually assigned the father to the part-time role of a visitor "every other weekend." I decided that I wanted to be a full-time parent and struggled to achieve that goal. Consequently, I joined "Fathers United For Equal Rights" and for several years spent a lot of my energy representing similarly situated males in Circuit Court. The cases, especially my own, were draining and dragged on for a long time. However, it was satisfying to be able to help reform attitudes in this regard and selfishly struggle to improve my own situation. I ended up being a full-time father after years of protracted litigation.

In the meantime, I continued to represent a variety of people charged with crimes and because I was a single parent, I often had my daughter, Erin and son, Chris in court with me during many of these cases. When Erin was four years old I had taken her to the circuit court where a friendly judge allowed her to sit at the trial table with me. He asked me from the bench if I would introduce my co-counsel to the court, which I gladly did. She was quite precocious and well-poised. I beamed with pride when she said "Good morning, Your Honor."

In the middle of the Myers case, Erin came home from summer camp, and I'd missed her very much. On August 23rd, 1982, since she'd just gotten home, I took her to Westminster with me for a scheduled "chambers" meeting in the case. She sat in the corner while the lawyers and Judge Burns discussed the status of each of the motions filed. During the meeting, Erin quietly and patiently passed the time drawing and writing in a notebook. Near the end, after about an hour, I asked her, "Do we have anymore motions, Erin, that you can think of?" She looked up and said, "No, Daddy!" Tom Hickman, Frank Coleman and the judge were very kind to her and I never forgot it.

I took my son, Chris, with me to court many times. When he was 12, I took him to the Central District in Baltimore on a Monday morning. It was packed with the usual confusion, noise and petty criminals. I pushed our way to the second row to give him a good view. A visibly angry judge reacted to the spectators' behavior, and lectured everybody on the need for decorum and dignity. He correctly insisted upon silence from lawyers, police officers, witnesses and all present. We were waiting for my case to be called.

The proceedings came to order. In the first case, solicitation for prostitution, the stocky-looking, unattractive defendant was quickly brought in.

The public defender elected a court trial. An undercover police officer was solemnly sworn, and he testified that he was trolling on Calvert Street a few nights earlier because there had been many citizen complaints about aggressive prostitutes there.

He identified the accused, and said she'd asked him if "he wanted to buy some pussy." After a brief silence, the entire courtroom—except the judge— exploded in raucous laughter. The judge was furious, and he flushed with embarrassment. Chris looked accusingly at me! I shrugged and could not stifle my mirth.

The judge cleared his throat and demanded silence. He stated, "The court takes judicial notice of the fact that (clearing his throat) the street vernacular, 'Do you want to buy some pussy?' (which he enunciated very clearly,) is an of- fer of vaginal intercourse." The well-seasoned public defender, Bert Mazaroff, asked no questions on cross-examination.

The State rested its case and the defense moved for a judgment of acquit- tal: a routine motion, in essence saying that even if you believed everything that the state had offered, the evidence was still defective and could not be the basis for a conviction. Mazaroff made the "impossibility of performance" argument, observing that his client was a man. All eyes then focused on the accused, who on closer observation did have rather large deltoids and a few scraggly hairs on his chin and on his flat chest. His dress had fooled most of us. The judge acquitted the defendant and then gave him a lecture about AIDS and his chosen occupation.

On the way home I explained to Chris that in The Royal Navy, youngsters were disciplined with several birch sticks tied together. This instrument was called a "boy's pussy," and was less brutal than the "cat o' nine tails," used on those over 16. When he was asked a few days later, Chris admitted that his buddies at school had enjoyed hearing about his day in court.

Erin and Chris experienced enough to know that they did not want to spend their lives in the same way, but could use their talents and flair for the dramatic in other "entertainment" venues. They are both successes in their chosen milieus of comedy and music.

*****

A world famous surgical oncologist, who had taught 4,000 medical students, was wrongfully convicted of "fingering" a patient at the University Hospital. He had taken an appeal to the Circuit Court In Baltimore City and had again been wrongfully convicted in a court trial. He then contacted me. He was in his 60s and explained that of the 50,000 patients he had seen in his career, this had been the only complaint ever made against him. It was clearly an attempt by the patient and others to obtain a payday. This most unattractive patient had been the 20th out of the 40 he had helped that day and she did not complain for three months. He passed a polygraph test, however, his legal remedies were limited, so the case presented numerous challenges for me.

At one hearing, I assembled 150 "character witnesses" on his behalf. They were colleagues, patients, nurses, friends, and students. I had an unlimited number of people at my disposal.

One judge who had convicted him had "pretended" to read the textbook on oncology that the doctor had written. It had been offered as an exhibit, to demonstrate the physical examination had been routinely performed. I was able to prove the judge's deception because the courtroom had been one of the first in Baltimore to videotape trials. The recording showed the Judge could not possibly have read the complicated page in seven seconds. Consequently, the judge had failed to properly try the case and he had "rushed to judgment." The doctor's lawyer had also failed to adequately represent him.

I assembled a small group of lawyers and we wrote over twenty versions of our appellate brief. I argued the case before the 7-member Appellate Court in Annapolis, Maryland. A year later, the Court of Appeals agreed that he had been wrongfully convicted, that no crime had been committed, and the doctor was exonerated.

Several years later, I had pains in my chest, and knowing that there was a history of lung cancer in my family and being fearful of the chemotherapy and radiation that might be involved, I decided to let nature take its course. I was then convinced by some friends to call this doctor and get his opinion. He said to bring the x-rays to him and we would have lunch. He remarked, "You were there for me, and I'll be there for you." At lunch, after looking at the film, he said to me, "Now you shut up! I am sending you to the best lung surgeon that I know. You have lung cancer and he might be able to cut it out for you." I followed his advice, and half of my right lung was successfully removed. He consulted on "my case". Thank you, doctors!

*****

For many years in Baltimore jurors remained "on call" for service for a month at a time, and as a consequence, business owners and professional people, who could not take that amount of time away from their enterprises were almost automatically allowed to avoid jury service. This affected the composition of the jury pool. It was much more likely to be composed of those who did not have such a vested stake in the community. There were many unwarranted acquittals.

A jury study conducted in the mid-1970s revealed this fact, and as a consequence the system was changed. Voters were summoned for jury duty every two years. Now they only had to sit for one case. It made a radical difference in the complexion of the juries, no one was excluded—judges and lawyers and everybody else were required to serve.

Defense lawyers rarely want powerful people as jurors but rather they want gullible, uneducated, weak, unsophisticated, dispossessed and pliable people who can perhaps relate to the person on trial and be influenced more easily. For the most part the change in the jury pool necessitated defense counsel using peremptory challenges to eliminate the knowledgeable and aggressive prospects. Over the years on three occasions it came as no surprise when I was challenged as a prospective juror.

In early 2000 I simply ignored my latest jury summons and a few weeks later was informed that if I did so again a bench warrant would be issued for my arrest. The next time, in March when my new notice came I went down to the jury assembly room and waited with the other 250 citizens, in the Clarence Mitchell Courthouse in Baltimore, to do my civic duty. I had chosen over 100 juries there and as a consequence I knew The Jury Commissioner and her staff well, and there were smiles all around at the prospect that I would actually be selected and be allowed to serve.

I waited with everyone else until we were called to the courtroom of Judge John Prevas, who gave me a friendly smile when I entered with all the others for the voir dire process. Prevas had been a hard-nosed prosecutor for many years and I had tried cases against him. He was extremely bright, knowledgeable and dogged. At that point he had been on the bench for over a decade, and looked a little odd because he had serious neck problems and was always hunched over looking as though he was in pain. He was a hard-working judge who drove his staff to work hard. The last time I had seen him was at my Christmas office party a few months before.

My Christmas Party had become a big yearly event, and always included lots of alcohol and music. He was an expert on the history of rock 'n roll and seemed to know all the words to all the songs.

The selection process lasted all day and I sat there working on a brief, only paying attention to respond to relevant questions about knowing the participating lawyers and whether or not any of us had been victims of a crime. I knew both the prosecutor and the defense attorney, and I had been mugged in the alley behind my office, and so I had to go up to the bench to respond in private as to whether these relationships or this experience would affect my ability to fairly try the case. I responded that it wouldn't and returned to my seat in the packed courtroom.

Inexplicably I ended up in the jury box and neither of the lawyers exercised a challenge against me. I was sitting in the first seat and when the selection process was concluded, Judge Prevas, with a twinkle in his eye announced that as a matter of tradition the juror sitting there, was usually proclaimed the foreman of the jury, and asked if I would accept the responsibilities of being "The Foreman of this jury." I responded, "I would."

The Assistant State's Attorney, Mary Jane Schroeder and then Margaret Meade, the defense attorney both made opening statements. The accused was charged with possession with intent to distribute marijuana and possessing a firearm in order to help him do so. In another count he was charged with wearing, carrying and transporting a firearm after having been convicted of a felony. In yet another he was charged with assaulting the mother of his two children.

None of my fellow jurors knew that I was a lawyer and I intended to keep it that way. After lunch, two responding police officers testified that they went to the scene for a domestic complaint and found the victim there crying and complaining that she had been assaulted. The Polaroid photo they had taken was introduced but it showed no real marks on her face. The officers' testimony was inconsistent since one said he saw marks on the left side, and the other insisted it was on the right side of her face. Both recalled that the defendant was seen on the landing. Nearby was a shoebox with loose marijuana in it and a number of small baggies, dime bags, and some empty bags. The defendant had immediately said that it was not his.

The victim consented to a search of the house and the police had found a loaded 9 mm Luger pistol in a closet. Between recesses and other cases, it took three days for the State to put on its case. There was a lot of downtime in the jury room and for a change instead of doing a lot of talking, I watched the dynamic between the others. The panel was comprised of five black females, three black males, one white female and two other white males, and me. One white male alternate juror was eventually excused. The black females started to bond immediately, and after several days, were sharing photos of their families and stories about their lives. Many were laughing and carrying on loudly in what I thought was an inappropriate manner, but I welcomed it, because it was boring sitting for so long. Three people were reading and said nothing. I continued writing my brief and read the newspaper.

Everyone was frustrated, wondering what the delay was, and why we were not in court listening to the case. The clerk, from time to time would come into the room, to placate us. He was quite effeminate and a friend of mine. Every time he left some of the women would mimic and mock his effeminate mannerisms. Some of these women had no respect for the situation they were in at all, or for authority generally, and were not taking the case seriously. Everybody else seemed to feel the pressure.

Each morning we went to the jury assembly room to receive our $15 per diem expense money and I shared a laugh with the employees there who thought it very strange, as I did, that I was the foreman of this jury. We were not adequately kept informed about when each session in the courtroom would start, and everyone started to complain about this complete waste of time.

By the fourth day, it was clear to me that the prosecutor could not locate the victim and a lot of the delay was caused by their attempts to find her. At one point the prosecutor introduced as an exhibit the shoebox containing the loose marijuana and baggies. I felt like grabbing some of it and having a smoke, although I kept thought to myself.

There was clearly a debate going on between the defendant and his lawyer. She of course did not want him to take the witness stand because he could only hurt himself. The State and the Defense had already stipulated to the fact that he had a prior felony conviction, and at that point the state's case was weak and there was a reasonable doubt as to what had happened.

The defendant did take the stand and in my view was an awful witness. He explained that he had not hit the victim but that they had had an argument and that neither the marijuana nor the gun was his, and that the first time he had seen them was when the police showed them to him. I thought the prosecutor's cross examination was quite effective. The defendant directly contradicted the police and in essence was saying that the police had framed him. We were told to come back a couple of days later, because the court had other pressing matters, and that we would hear the closing arguments and deliberate at that time.

There was a lot of grumbling and complaining among the jurors about this additional delay, but we all assembled when we were told to and listened to the presentations. The defense counsel hammered on the inconsistencies and the fact that the defendant was gainfully employed and that we were not to convict him because on a previous occasion he had made mistakes.

In the jury room, since I was the foreman I dictated the procedure. I did not want to have a voice vote because I felt people would get irrevocably committed to what they'd said verbally. I presented everybody with a piece of paper with all the various charges. I asked everyone to complete this small questionnaire marking each count with a G or NG. I then accumulated the pieces of paper and reviewed them. There was no logic or consistency or much agreement.

I then went around the room and asked everyone to express their opinions. Some of them had already changed their minds. Many were vociferous and angrily demanded that the accused be acquitted. I counted nine votes for not guilty and soon it was 10. The only vote other than mine for guilty was a young white male.

I did not feel strongly that I should hang this jury up, so I manipulated the other guilty vote by easily persuading him that if he could not act without hesitation in one of the most important affairs of his own life, then he had a reasonable doubt. I declared that we were unanimous for acquittal. I knocked on the door to get the clerk's attention. A few minutes later we were in open court and I announced when requested by the judge, the "not guilty" verdict as to each charge. We were dismissed with the thanks of the court. The defense attorney smiled over at me and the prosecutor sneered in my direction.

We were all excused, but I delayed a little while. After everybody else had left, I sauntered into the hall and saw the prosecutor standing with the young police officers who had testified. I stopped to chat and told the Assistant State's Attorney that she had done a good job, but that the case went on too long. Because of the delays, several of the jurors had been distracted. She introduced me to one officer who shook my hand. When I went to shake the other one's hand, he just angrily eyeballed me and refused my friendly gesture.

I put my hand out again and he turned away. He was stunned when I said "Well fuck you, you're the one who screwed the case up . . . because of the way you testified the jurors didn't believe you, so don't blame me!" I shook the prosecutor's hand again "You did a nice job . . . It was his fault not yours. Keep up the good work, it was nice seeing you."

I walked down the hall, took the elevator to the ground floor and went out onto Calvert Street. My civic duty was done.

*****

It had always been my goal to be the victim of an un-tragic death, because if you live more than five or six decades, it cannot be a tragedy when you die. Sad perhaps for the survivors but not tragic. I have always wanted my sonofobituary to proclaim that I was not as bad some of the time as I was most of the time, and that I was not as bad as my brother. Also that I tried to obey most of The Ten Commandments. Unlike my father I had no romantic notions about having my ashes taken to Ireland to be deposited there for eternity. I simply wanted to be buried face-down, so that people could pay their respects appropriately. After my father's death at age 80 in 1998, I retained his ashes.

In 2006 after my mother died, we joined my parents' ashes together and took them across the Atlantic to the Seventh Century cemetery in Monasterboice, County Louth, Eire a few miles from where Peg had been born. My adult children and significant others, eight of us in all, conducted a service there which included my parents' favorite music and poems. Half of their remains were buried in my maternal grandmother's grave there, and we then traveled to Newgrange, a prehistoric burial mound complete with an enclosed passageway leading to a large enclosed tomb. It is a National Monument so we had to smuggle the rest of the ashes past the tour guides to be able to deposit them in the stone urns there. This was the burial place for kings and queens, four thousand years ago. It was a suitable resting place for Peg and Chas, they would have approved.

Because my son Chris' band, Yeasayer, has become quite popular, he was invited to share this experience in a radio interview. For his account, Google Yeasayer's Chris Keating Gets Ashy: NPR.

AFTERWORD

Many new statutes had been written to allow executions across the country. By December 2005 in the United States, the 1000th execution had been conducted under these new laws which had been created and had passed "constitutional muster." Faith groups around the nation, including hundreds of churches, marked this milestone by conducting vigils and tolling bells in memory of all the murder victims and execution victims. The Myers case took place in the middle of that 33-year period.

The death squads of prosecutors in their various offices were desperate to kill somebody under the new statutory scheme, but they were frustrated at every turn by the determined defense bar. However, it was inevitable that a small handful of miscreants would be executed in Maryland.

*****

John Frederick Thanos was executed by lethal injection in 1994 but since no Maryland official wanted to take responsibility for the procedure, Lt. Frank Mazzone, retired from the State Police, was requested to become the executioner. He gladly volunteered to establish procedures to be used for lethal injections. He arranged the three separate drugs to be used. The first sodium pentothal makes the condemned unconscious. The second Pavulon stops electrical activity in muscle cells and the third potassium compound plain outright kills. Thanos had fatally shot three Maryland teenagers during a week of crime. He bragged about these killings to television reporters when he was arrested and his execution was considered more of a "Suicide by State" because he had refused to permit any appeals or requests for clemency.

*****

Flint Gregory Lee Hunt, 38 had an extensive criminal record and he admitted shooting a police officer in an alley in East Baltimore, but claimed self-defense. A sentence of death, rendered by a jury in 1986, was reversed and he was resentenced to death in 1988. Hunt fought his execution until he had exhausted all legal maneuvers and he was executed by lethal injection on July 2, 1997.

*****

Tyron X Gilliam, 32 was executed in 1998 for the shotgun killing of a Baltimore accountant during a robbery that netted three dollars.

*****

Stephen Howard Oken, 42 was executed in 2004 for the rape and murder of a newlywed at the beginning of a crime spree in which he also raped and murdered his wife's sister and a motel clerk.

*****

The last federal execution by hanging took place in 1963 when Victor Feguer was hung in the Iowa State penitentiary for a kidnapping. Three federal executions have taken place since then all by lethal injection. They include Timothy McVeigh on June 11, 2001, Juan Raul Garza on June 19, 2001 and Louis Jones, Jr. on March 18, 2003.

*****

In 2005 John Wesley Baker was to be executed in the Maryland Penitentiary just five blocks from my office. Those unlucky few who were still being executed in Maryland were disposed of there, and people who objected to this state-sanctioned killing traditionally gathered across the street from the location of the death gurney to shout their objections. I knew Baker's attorneys. They were excellent and had used all of their experience and energy in an attempt to save him, but to no avail. It had come to this.

   The Baltimore High School for the Performing Arts, with 400 students, is just down the block, and in an attempt to get their interest and energize them, I manufactured several large signs and placed them on a large signboard with the words "The All American Sport—Legalized Lynching." Neither the administration or the student body showed any interest. I approached The Principal to urge the school to take a stand but she could not be made to expand her horizons beyond the traditional curriculum. A great opportunity to sensitize and mobilize the student body was missed.

Governor Ehrlich and his Lieutenant Governor Michael E. Steele allowed the execution to proceed because they perceived it to be in their best political interests. Steele, the hypocrite, announced he was "studying the death penalty" and would have the results in several months. I ghost wrote a letter to them both on John Wesley Baker's behalf, "from the other side" complaining that they had allowed him to die, to further their own agendas.

The only thing that Baker's lawyers could do was ensure that most of the personnel from the Federal Public Defender's Office would be present to shout their protests. These folks understood that for a person and his family to know, almost with certainty, the time and place of his impending death, after he had struggled to avoid it for years in court, is debilitating and terrifying for all concerned.

*****

The Baltimore County State's Attorney's Office was 13 times more likely to pursue death for similar cases than neighboring Baltimore City. In the year 2000, the University of Maryland Paternoster study that examined the 6000 murders that took place, between 1978—when the death penalty was reinstated -through 1999. An eventual death sentence was 23 times more likely in Baltimore County. Local "killer prosecutors" justified the disparities as "minority local rule," thereby rationalizing their conduct and ignoring the reality that there were consequently 24 separate death penalty policies being employed in the state at any one time. Five people had been executed in Maryland since 1978, and four of them originated in Baltimore County. Of the 10 other people sentenced to die, seven of them originated in Baltimore County. Fortunately, these 10 were found to have been sentenced and convicted illegally on appeal. Kirk Bloodsworth was one of these 10. The Baltimore County prosecutors had to finally realize he had been totally innocent of the murder charges all along. When DNA evidence finally exonerated him, the prosecutors—after 14 years—

had to face the fact that they had tried to execute an innocent man.

Much to the outrage of some bloodthirsty prosecutors and others the death penalty was officially abolished in Maryland in 2014.

*****

Over the years I had always stayed physically active, either running, swimming or exercising obsessively. Along with several thousand other people, I ran three 10K races, only throwing up after two of them. I had always amused myself with long-distance swimming, either in a pool or in open water on the Eastern Shore. The 1.7-mile Miles River was fairly easy because I trained to do two miles in a pool over a several-week period. A few years later, during a swim-a-thon I swam 360 lengths of a 25-meter pool—approximately 5.5 miles.

I had over four decades of competition for death and freedom in criminal court. I had still not realized, however, my boyhood ambition to compete in the Olympics. Seizing perhaps a last opportunity, I participated in the Maryland Senior Track and Field Olympics in 2013 in the 70 to 74 age group in the Shot Put and Javelin. I was pleased to place third in the shot but wrecked my arm throwing the spear. I was satisfied that I had given it my best.

*****

Notwithstanding the import of the matters I dealt with throughout my law career, I was mindful of the perspective of an early 20th Century judge, George William Brown. He retired as Chief Judge of the Baltimore Supreme Bench. He had a distinguished career as an advocate. He understood that a lawyer's fame is fleeting, and as he expected, he is almost totally forgotten today—as are most advocates. He wrote, "the reputation of an eminent lawyer does not long survive . . . There are few exceptions to this rule. While he lives he is a conspicuous figure in the community . . . But when he dies he leaves no lasting memorial...His carefully written opinions lose their value when the controversy is ended. His skillfully drawn documents slumber in pigeonholes. His prudent advice is remembered only by those who profited by it. When he leaves the forum, another steps forward to take his place, and his name and fame soon become a dim tradition in the places which knew him so well and delighted to honor him."

CHRONOLOGY

May 1979

Tina Plessner Gillen Botteron Marco was living in Lee's Motel, in Westminster, Carroll County, MD and working as a waitress at Angelo's Restaurant. The Maryland Department of Social Services was threatening to place her two children Tracey (age 8) and Brad (age 10) in foster care.

August 7, 1979

An Emergency Hearing scheduled to remove Tina's two children from her control was postponed.

August 9, 1979

Tina met Robert Lee Myers while waiting on his table at Angelo's. He joked about her old car and she asked him to buy her a better one. He agreed.

August 10, 1979

Myers bought Tina a used Ford for $2,600.

August 14, 1979

Social Services requested a hearing regarding issues of neglect and abandonment of Marco's children.

August 17, 1979

Tina returned to work. The victim, Mary Ruth Myers, Robert's wife, came to Angelo's and Tina talked to her.

August 20, 1979

Tina Marco and Robert Myers were present in court when the judge stated that if Tina changed her marital status, she could keep her children.

August 21, 1979

Robert Myers asked Tina Marco if she knew anyone who would murder Mary

Ruth. Tina contacted Daniel Chadderton, an ex-boyfriend.

August 22, 1979

Marco telephoned Chadderton again to arrange a meeting about the contract. Myers withdrew $36,000 from the receipts at his motel in Ocean City

August 23, 1979

Marco called Chadderton at his job at the Pantry Pride. Marco and Myers drove from Ocean City to meet Chadderton there and give Chadderton a description of the victim, Mary Ruth. Myers called the victim at 1:17 a.m. from the payphone at the Pantry Pride.

August 24, 1979

Tina registered at the Quality Inn, and she and Myers stayed from midnight to 4 a.m.

August 25, 1979

Chadderton requested directions to the Myers' home.

August 26, 1979

Myers and Tina returned to Ocean City from New Jersey, drove to meet Chadderton, and gave him $2,500.

August 27, 1979

Myers and Marco returned to Ocean City. They went to his motel at 12:30 a.m., but the victim was there, so they went to Maria Poulos' apartment to stay.

August 28, 1979

Marco called from Maria's to Pantry Pride at 12:56 a.m. Marco called from the payphone in Ocean City to Pantry Pride at 2:16 a.m. Myers phoned the victim at the motel at 2:30 p.m. Myers hung up. Marco called from Maria's to Chadderton's house at 7:03 p.m. She asked Sherrie, Chadderton's wife, to have him call her. Marco called Jay Gillen, her ex-husband, in Las Vegas at 8:43 p.m.

August 29, 1979

Mary Ruth was shot to death by Chadderton in her home in Carroll County, MD. Chadderton called Myers and Tina at Maria's at 5:20 p.m.

August 30, 1979
Co-workers discovered Mary Ruth's body. Robert Myers was in Ocean City, MD at his Motel. Tina telephoned Chadderton at the Pantry Pride at 2 a.m. Telephone call from Tina to Jay Gillen at 10:18 a.m. for thirty-five minutes. Tina was later questioned by the police.

September 1, 1979
Tina went to Pantry Pride alone with $5,000, but left because Chadderton told her the police were there.

September 3, 1979
Tina moved into the Myers' house in Silver Run Valley.

September 4, 1979
Robert Myers attended the funeral for Mary Ruth.

September 26, 1979
Robert Myers and Tina Plessner Gillen Botteron Marco are married in Bermuda.

January 15, 1980
Phil Sutley wrote to the State's Attorney telling him that he had been retained to represent Robert Myers.

February 8, 1980
Police announced the murder was connected to the murder of "Skip" Botteron, which took placed on April 29, 1979.

February 9, 1980
Tina got Brad and Tracey back permanently. They moved into the new home.

September 1980
The Myers' phones were tapped. The house and Myers' accounting office were bugged with hidden listening devices.

February 17, 1981
Police arrested Chadderton on a gun and traffic charge. He was driving a 1977 Lincoln Continental with an expired registration. The car had previously been registered to Robert Myers. A handgun was also found in his leather jacket.

June 26, 1981
Tina Myers gave birth to a girl, Sabrina.

September 4, 1981
Tina Myers waived her extradition hearing and was turned over to Bermuda authorities on bigamy charges. She was placed in "Casemate's Prison" in Bermuda.

September 9, 1981
Tina was released on bond to live with a family pending trial.

November 20, 1981
Robert Myers testified before the Grand Jury in the morning. Daniel Chadderton testified in the afternoon.

November 23, 1981
Robert Myers flew to Bermuda for Thanksgiving.

November 24, 1981
The Grand Jury returned first-degree murder indictments against Chadderton, Myers and Tina. The State's Attorney's Office announced it will seek death for all three.

November 25, 1981
Robert Myers returned to Westminster under police escort.

November 27, 1981
Robert Myers was ordered held without bail in the Carroll County Detention Center. Daniel Chadderton was arrested.

November 30, 1981
Tina Myers plead guilty to bigamy in Bermuda and was deported to Baltimore, MD.

December 3, 1981
Tina Myers' bail set at $750,000.

December 15, 1981

Robert Myers' civil lawyers announced that his accounting business was on the verge of collapse. His estate valued at more than a million dollars was being liquidated to pay off more than $500,000 in debts.

February 11, 1982

The personal belongings of Robert and Tina Myers were sold at an auction that attracted over a thousand spectators and bidders. The items were sold for a total of $30,000. Phil Sutley, their attorney, was present and received the proceeds.

March 22–23, 1982

Chief Judge Donald J. Gilmore of The Carroll County Circuit Court granted the prosecutor's request to remove the trial to Garrett County, MD.

March 23, 1982

Motions hearing took place in Garrett County. All three defendants were together.

March 24, 1982

Phil Sutley, Esq. negotiated an agreement with prosecutors to give Tina Myers immunity and her freedom in exchange for her testimony.

April 18, 1982

Jury selection began in Chadderton case.

April 23, 1982

The Maryland Court of Appeals in Annapolis agreed to hear Myers' Removal Appeal.

April 27, 1982

Opening statements were made to the Chadderton jury in Garrett County.

May 10, 1982

A sobbing Tina Myers testified against Chadderton.

May 11, 1982

After two hours of deliberation, the jury found Chadderton guilty of first degree murder.

The jury could not unanimously agree to sentence Chadderton to death. He received a term of life in prison.

June 8, 1982

Arguments were heard before the Court of Appeals on the Removal issue. The Myers Case was returned to Westminster, Carroll County.

June 22, 1982

Tina gave birth to a son, her second child by Myers. She cancelled plans to name the child after his father when she learned Myers had a new woman friend whom he "loosely refers to as his fiancée." The stream of cards and letters to Myers ends.

August 18, 1982

Myers' request that Chief Judge Donald J. Gilmore disqualify himself as judge for the Myers trial was granted. Associate Judge Luke K. Burns was assigned.

September 20, 1982

Two-week jury selection began.

October 6, 1982

The Myers trial began. Opening statements.

December 6, 1982

The jury found Myers guilty of first degree murder.

December 9–11, 1982

A sentencing hearing was conducted and Myers was sentenced to Life Imprisonment.

December 12, 1982

Tina Myers was released and sent a Christmas card to Anton Keating, Robert Myers' defense attorney, wishing him and "Bobby" a Happy Healthy Holiday and Great New Year.

September 1984

Robert Myers' conviction was Affirmed on Appeal.

March 1986

Post Conviction Hearing—The Circuit Court of Carroll County conducted a four-day hearing and upheld the verdict. Judge Gilmore found that the way the defense was conducted probably saved Myers from the Gas Chamber.

June 1987

The Maryland Court of Appeals affirmed the Post Conviction Court's ruling.

*****

ACKNOWLEDGEMENTS & WEBSITES

Acknowledgements

The author wishes to thank all those people who expressed their support and encouragement, and to those who contributed their energy and skill to this project over these many years.

In particular, the author is most grateful to Aliza Worthington who helped edit and finalize this book.

WEBSITES

www.imnotreallyguilty.com

This website contains a large collection of relevant materials accumulated during the investigation and trial of this case. It allows interested readers to immerse themselves in materials and details which would otherwise not normally be available to them.

It contains over 200 newspaper articles commencing on the day of the murder, and continuing for five years until the resolution of the case on appeal.

Information about the Audiobook is available through the website as well.

www.jugglingjustice.com contains additional materials relating to the trial and the author's family and background.

BIBLIOGRAPHY

BOOKS

Addison, Paul. *Now the War is Over*. London: British Broadcasting Corporation, 1985.

Batchelor, Denzil. *British Boxing*. London: Collins, 1948.

Beck, E.M. and Stewart E. Tolnay. *A Festival of Violence: An Analysis of Southern Lynchings: 1882–1930*. Chicago: University of Illinois Press, 1995.

Behan, Brendan. *Confessions of an Irish Rebel*. New York: Bernard Geis Associates, 1965.

Behan, Brendan. *The Quare Fellow*. London: Methuen & Co., 1960.

Behan, Brendan. *The Quare Fellow and The Hostage*. New York: Grove Press, 1964.

Briggs, Susan. *Keep Smiling Through: The Home Front, 1939–1945*. Fontana: George Weidenfeld & Nicholson, 1975.

Brown, Edmund and Dick Adler. *Public Justice, Private Mercy: A Governor's Education on Death Row*. New York: Weidenfeld & Nicholson, 1989.

Brown, Robert and Steven P. Olson. *Some Gave All: A History of Baltimore Policy Officers Killed in the Line of Duty: 1808–2007*. Baltimore: Chesapeake Book Company, 2007.

Byrnes, John Carroll. *Histories of the Bench and Bar of Baltimore City*. Baltimore: Baltimore Courthouse and Law Museum Foundation, 1997.

Carey, Tim. *Mountjoy: The Story of a Prison*. Cork: The Collins Press, 2000.

Chestnut, W. Calvin. *A Federal Judge Sums Up*. 1947.

Christianson, Scott. Notorious Prisons: An Inside Look at the World's Most Feared Institutions. London: First Lyons Press, 2004.

Cray, Ed. Chief Justice: *A Biography of Earl Warren*. New York: Simon & Schuster, 1997.

Curtayne, Alice. *The Trial of Oliver Plunkett*. Wicklow: Bray Co., 1975.

Disney, Francis. *Heritage of a Prison*. Somerset: Whitestone Press, 1986.

Dorsey, Hattie. *World Within a City*. Pittsburgh: RoseDog Books, 2004.

Dostoyevsky, Fyodor. *Crime and Punishment*. New York: Random House, 1950.

Duff, Charles. *A Handbook on Hanging*. London: The Journeyman Press, 1981.

Durr, Kenneth. *Behind the Backlash: White Working-Class Politics in Baltimore, 1940–1980*. Chapel Hill: The University of North Carolina Press, 2003.

Epstein, David. *The Sports Gene*. Penguin Books. 2013.

Freud, Anna and Dorothy T. Burlingham. *War and Children*. New York: Ernst Willard, 1943.

Ginzburg, Ralph. 100 Years of Lynchings. Baltimore: Black Classic Press, 1988.

Hammel, Eric. *Air War Europa: America's Air War Against Germany in Europe and North Africa*, 1942-1945. Pacifica: Pacifica Press, 1994.

Ifill, Sherrilyn. *On the Courthouse Lawn: Confronting the Legacy of Lynching in the Twenty-First Century*. Boston: Beacon Press, 2007.

Junkin, Tim. *Bloodsworth: The True Story of the First Death Row Inmate Exonerated by DNA*. Chapel Hill: Algonquin Books, 2004.

Liebling, A.J. *The Sweet Science*. Middlesex: Penguin Books, 1983.

Lifton, Robert Jay and Greg Mitchell. *Who Owns Death?: Capital Punishment, The American Conscience, and the End of Executions*. New York: Harper-Collins, 2000.

Maskell, Henry P. *Recollections of Emanuel School*. London: Phipps and Connor, 1904.

McCabe, Clinton. *History of the Baltimore Police Department*. (Publisher not identified.) 1907 (?).

Moore, Joseph. *Murder on Maryland's Eastern Shore: Race, Politics, and the Case of Orphan Jones*. Charleston: The History Press, 2006.

Morton, James. *Fighters: The Lives and Sad Deaths of Freddie Mills and Randolph Turpin*. London: Time Warner Paperbacks, 2004.

Mosley, Leonard. *The Battle of Britain*. New York: Time-Life Books, 1977.

Pickett, Carroll and Carlton Stowers. *Within These Walls: Memoirs of a Death House Chaplain*. New York: St. Martin's Press, 2002.

Pierrepoint, Albert. Executioner: *Pierrepoint: The Amazing Autobiography of the World's Most Famous Executioner*. Hodder: Coronet Books, 1974.

Prejean, Helen. *The Death of Innocents: An Eyewitness Account of Wrongful Executions*. New York: Random House, 2005.

Radoff, Morris L., ed. *The Old Line State: A History of Maryland*. Baltimore: Twentieth Century Printing Co., 1971.

Scott-Giles, C. Wilfrid. *The History of Emanuel School*. London: Surrey Fine Art Press, 1948.

Semmes, Raphael. *Crime and Punishment in Early Maryland*. Baltimore: The Johns Hopkins University Press, 1996.

Shugg, Wallace. *A Monument to Good Intentions: The Story of the Maryland Penitentiary, 1804–1995*. Baltimore: Maryland Historical Society, 2000.

Solomons, Jack. *Jack Solomons Tells All*. London: Rich & Cowan, 1951.

Sommerville, Donald. *World War II: Day by Day*. Greenwich: Dorset Press, 1989.

Steelwater, Eliza. The Hangman's Knot: Lynching, Legal Execution, and America's Struggle with the Death Penalty. Boulder: Westview Press, 2003.

Turow, Scott. *Ultimate Punishment: A Lawyer's Reflections on Dealing With the Death Penalty*. New York: Farrar, Straus and Giroux, 2003.

Walsh, Liz. *The Final Beat: Gardaí Killed in the Line of Duty*. Dublin: Gill & Macmillan Ltd., 2001.

White, Frank. *The Governors of Maryland, 1777–1970*. Baltimore: Twentieth Century Printing Co., 1970.

Legal Publications

Baltimore City State's Attorney's Office. <u>Report of the State's Attorney's Office of Baltimore City Under the Administration of Charles E. Moylan, Jr., January Term 1967 to January Term 1968</u>. Baltimore: Printing Office, 1968.

   Baltimore City State's Attorney's Office. <u>Report of the State's Attorney's Office of Baltimore City Under the Administration of Charles E. Moylan, Jr., January Term 1968 to January Term 1969</u>. Baltimore: Printing Office, 1969.

Newspapers and Magazines

The author wishes to express his thanks to the many newspapers and other publications which provided information, including articles and obituaries, which have been used in this book. Some of these articles were offered as exhibits during the course of this litigation.

Baltimore Magazine
Carroll County Times
The Evening Sun
Hanover Evening Sun
News American
The Sun
Towson Times
The City Paper, Baltimore

Sketch

Beber, William, Carroll County Courthouse

* 9 7 8 0 6 9 2 6 4 7 6 6 0 *